PENTECOSTAL RATIONALITY

Systematic Pentecostal and Charismatic Theology

Series editors
Wolfgang Vondey
Daniela C. Augustine

PENTECOSTAL RATIONALITY

Epistemology and Theological Hermeneutics in the Foursquare Tradition

Simo Frestadius

LONDON • NEW YORK • OXFORD • NEW DELHI • SYDNEY

T&T CLARK

Bloomsbury Publishing Plc

50 Bedford Square, London, WC1B 3DP, UK

1385 Broadway, New York, NY 10018, USA

29 Earlsfort Terrace, Dublin 2, Ireland

BLOOMSBURY, T&T CLARK and the T&T Clark logo are trademarks of Bloomsbury Publishing Plc

First published in Great Britain 2020
This paperback edition published in 2021

Copyright © Simo Frestadius, 2020

Simo Frestadius has asserted his right under the Copyright, Designs and Patents Act, 1988, to be identified as Author of this work.

For legal purposes the Acknowledgements on p. x constitute an extension of this copyright page.

Cover design by Anna Berzovan
Cover image © naqiewei / GettyImages

All rights reserved. No part of this publication may be reproduced or transmitted in any form or by any means, electronic or mechanical, including photocopying, recording, or any information storage or retrieval system, without prior permission in writing from the publishers.

Bloomsbury Publishing Plc does not have any control over, or responsibility for, any third-party websites referred to or in this book. All internet addresses given in this book were correct at the time of going to press. The author and publisher regret any inconvenience caused if addresses have changed or sites have ceased to exist, but can accept no responsibility for any such changes.

A catalogue record for this book is available from the British Library.

Library of Congress Cataloging-in-Publication Data
Names: Frestadius, Simo, author.
Title: Pentecostal rationality: epistemology and theological hermeneutics in the foursquare tradition / Simo Frestadius.
Description: 1 [edition]. | New York: T&T Clark, 2019. | Series: T&T Clark systematic, Pentecostal, and charismatic theology; 6 | Includes bibliographical references and index.
Identifiers: LCCN 2019009772 | ISBN 9780567689382 (hardback) | ISBN 9780567689405 (epub)
Subjects: LCSH: Pentecostal churches–Doctrines. | Elim Pentecostal Church. | Philosophical theology.
Classification: LCC BX8762.Z5 F74 2019 | DDC 230/.994–dc23
LC record available at https://lccn.loc.gov/2019009772

ISBN: HB: 978-0-5676-8938-2
PB: 978-0-5676-9891-9
ePDF: 978-0-5676-8939-9
eBook: 978-0-5676-8940-5

Typeset by Deanta Global Publishing Services, Chennai, India

To find out more about our authors and books visit www.bloomsbury.com and sign up for our newsletters.

For Caroline, Kaiho and Mailis

CONTENTS

Acknowledgements	x
List of abbreviations	xii

INTRODUCTION 1

Part One
SEARCHING FOR A PENTECOSTAL RATIONALITY 7

Chapter 1
THE 'PENTECOSTAL' RATIONALITIES OF AMOS YONG,
JAMES K. A. SMITH AND L. WILLIAM OLIVERIO JR. 9
   1.1 'Pneumatological imagination': Yong's Pentecostal rationality 9
   1.2 Affective, embodied and narrative knowing: Smith's Pentecostal rationality 20
   1.3 Pentecostal 'hermeneutical realism': Oliverio's Pentecostal rationality 32
   1.4 Conclusion 44

Chapter 2
ON METHOD: MACINTYRE, TRADITION AND RATIONALITY 45
   2.1 MacIntyre's tradition-dependent rationality 45
   2.2 Truth and dialectical justification 52
   2.3 Implications for Pentecostal rationality and epistemology 57

Part Two
NARRATING A TRADITION-SPECIFIC PENTECOSTAL RATIONALITY 61

Chapter 3
PROLOGUES TO THE ELIM TRADITION: THE CONTEXT
AND ROOTS OF THE ELIM ARGUMENT 63
   3.1 The pre-Pentecostal religious context: Modernity, religious pluralism and secularization 64
   3.2 Holiness, revival and Pentecostal roots of Elim 76

Chapter 4
THE BIRTH OF ELIM: THE EARLY OPPONENTS, CONTENT,
RATIONALITY AND EMBODIMENT OF THE ELIM ARGUMENT 92
   4.1   The implied opponents of the Elim argument 92
   4.2   The content of the Elim argument: The Foursquare Gospel 97
   4.3   The rationality of the Elim argument: Pentecostal
         Biblical Pragmatism 103
   4.4   The social embodiment of the Elim argument: The Elim alliance 114
   4.5   Conclusion 119

Chapter 5
THE ELIM ARGUMENT EXTENDED THROUGH TIME (I): THE
RESIGNATION OF JEFFREYS AND ELIM'S FIRST EPISTEMOLOGICAL CRISIS 121
   5.1   The coming King: An overview of Elim's eschatology 123
   5.2   The British Israel controversy 127
   5.3   The 'epistemological crisis' and its resolution 139
   5.4   Conclusion 146

Chapter 6
THE ELIM ARGUMENT EXTENDED THROUGH TIME (II): THE
CHARISMATIC/RESTORATION MOVEMENTS AND ELIM'S SECOND
EPISTEMOLOGICAL CRISIS 147
   6.1   The Charismatic movement: The 'Renewal Charismatics'
         and the 'Restoration Charismatics' 148
   6.2   The Restoration Charismatic movement: Ecclesiologically
         and eschatologically updated Elim argument 151
   6.3   The 'epistemological crisis' and its resolution 154
   6.4   Conclusion 160

Part Three
(RE)CONSTRUCTING PENTECOSTAL BIBLICAL PRAGMATISM 163

Chapter 7
PENTECOSTAL TRUTH: PENTECOSTAL THEOLOGICAL REALISM 165
   7.1   Pentecostal theological realism 166
   7.2   God as ultimate reality 167
   7.3   The possibility for beliefs and talk about reality 169
   7.4   (Under-)realized realism 173
   7.5   Conclusion 174

Chapter 8
BIBLICAL HERMENEUTICS: COMMUNITY DISCERNMENT OF MEANING IN A DIALECTICAL BIBLE — 175
    8.1 Historical reflections on Elim's Pentecostal hermeneutics — 176
    8.2 A proposal for Elim's Pentecostal hermeneutics — 180
    8.3 Conclusion — 187

Chapter 9
PRAGMATIC JUSTIFICATION: EXPERIENTIAL AWARENESS AND PRAGMATIC SIGNS OF THE FOURSQUARE GOSPEL — 189
    9.1 Pentecostal experience and Alston's 'Theory of Appearing' — 190
    9.2 Pentecostal experience as direct and indirect awareness of God — 194
    9.3 (Dis)analogy between sense and mystical perception — 199
    9.4 Pragmatic justification — 201
    9.5 Conclusion — 213

CONCLUSION — 215

Appendix 1: Elim's Chronology — 221
Appendix 2: Front page of *Elim Evangel* 6, No. 1 (January 1925) — 223
Appendix 3: Back page of *Elim Evangel* 6, No. 1 (January 1925) — 224
Index — 225

ACKNOWLEDGEMENTS

This book is a slightly modified version of my PhD thesis titled 'Whose Pentecostalism? Which Rationality? The Foursquare Gospel and Pentecostal Biblical Pragmatism of the Elim Tradition' successfully defended at the University of Birmingham in 2018. I would like to acknowledge my debt to Mark Cartledge and David Cheetham as my supervisors. Mark guided me through the first half of the thesis and instilled in me his passion for Pentecostal theology, and David directed me through the second half while encouraging me to think as a philosophical theologian. At the University of Birmingham, it has been a privilege to be associated with the John Hick Centre for Philosophy of Religion and the Centre for Pentecostal and Charismatic Studies. At the latter, Wolfgang Vondey, Allan Anderson and others have especially facilitated a dynamic learning environment for research students (in fact, I blame Allan's indirect influence for the historical turn in my thesis!). And the friendships formed there with the likes of Dik Allan, Elmer Chen, and Matt Churchouse have been life-giving. I am also particularly grateful to Wolfgang – as one of the SPCT series editors – for his constructive suggestions and constant encouragement throughout the publishing process. His support and guidance has been first class! Thank you also to the wider staff at Bloomsbury for being so helpful.

I would like to express my appreciation to Regents Theological College as my employer and context for carrying out my Christian calling. All of my colleagues and friends at Regents, not least Dave Newton, Gary Gibbs, Geoff Richardson, John Owen, Keith Warrington, Jenny Kimble, Jonathan Black, Liam Hanna, Martin Clay, Mathew Clark, Michael Edwards, Oliver Ward, Paul Folland, Peter Read, Rachel Ager and Richard Hasnip, have spurred me on. A special thanks to Tim Walsh for proofreading a draft of the thesis. Thank you also to various students who have graciously but not uncritically interacted in class with my developing thoughts on Pentecostal epistemology!

As much of the research has focused on Elim's history, there have been many who have given me access to primary material on Elim. Sally Gibbs and Philip Thompsett have enabled me to have unrestricted access to the general Elim Archives, and Sharon Millar has provided me full access to the general superintendent's personal Elim Archives. The Elim historian Maldwyn Jones has not just been an exhorter but a mine of information on Elim. I am also grateful to Chris Cartwright, Elim's general superintendent, for permission to use images from *Elim Evangel* in Appendix 2 and 3.

I want to thank friends and family who have stood with me through the researching and writing. I appreciate that not always having weekends or normal holidays while studying has meant that those closest to me have been affected the most. Thank you to my family (including my English family through marriage) for understanding, praying and providing moments of rest. I particularly want to thank my parents Kyösti and Irma Frestadius for offering their selfless support throughout my studies. And I especially want to thank my wife Caroline, son Kaiho and daughter Mailis. Caroline has been without equal in her steadfast love, patience and encouragement; Kaiho has been my joy, as well as my personal teacher on knights and pirates; and Mailis – born just after the PhD submission but before the viva – has already demonstrated grace beyond her months! Indeed, this book is dedicated to Caroline, Kaiho and Mailis. Finally, I thank God for the gift of life and the privilege of academic study.

ABBREVIATIONS

BI	British Israelism
CH	*Church History*
CPT	Centre for Pentecostal Theology
CSR	*Christian Scholar's Review*
DBSJ	*Detroit Baptist Seminary Journal*
EE	*Elim Evangel*
EIC	Elim International Centre
EJPT	*Eastern Journal of Practical Theology*
HeyJ	*The Heythrop Journal*
IJPR	*International Journal for the Philosophy of Religion*
JAH	*The Journal of American History*
JBPR	*Journal of Biblical and Pneumatological Research*
JEH	*The Journal of Ecclesiastical History*
JEPTA	*Journal of the European Pentecostal Theological Association*
JES	*Journal of Ecumenical Studies*
JPT	*Journal of Pentecostal Theology*
JSRE	*Journal for the Study of Religious Experience*
JUH	*Journal of Urban History*
JVC	*Journal of Victorian Culture*
NB	*New Blackfriars*
NT	New Testament
PC	*Philosophia Christi*
PMU	Pentecostal Missionary Union
PS	*PentecoStudies*
RM	*The Review of Metaphysics*
RS	*Religious Studies*
SC	*The Spirit & Church*
SCM	Student Christian Movement
SJT	*Scottish Journal of Theology*
SPS	Society for Pentecostal Studies
SR	*The Sociological Review*
SRPs	Scientific Research Programmes
US	*Urban Studies*
WTJ	*Westminster Theological Journal*

INTRODUCTION

The quest for a Pentecostal theology shaped by a Pentecostal theological methodology has been the interest of Pentecostal theologians for some time,[1] and the importance of rationality, epistemology and theological hermeneutics is increasingly acknowledged as central in this pursuit.[2] For example, Christopher A. Stephenson in his survey of three Pentecostal systematic theologians, namely Myer Pearlman, E. S. Williams and French Arrington, notes that each one of them 'makes epistemology the starting point' of their theological endeavour, and thus their intellectual framework inevitably ends up influencing, even if not wholly determining, the content and nature of their theologies.[3] It is for this reason that some Pentecostal scholars claim that there cannot be a Pentecostal theology without a distinct Pentecostal epistemology, or at least a rationality that

---

1. The terms 'Pentecostal' and 'Pentecostalism' are used generically as references to classical Pentecostalism, Charismatic Christianity, Christian renewal movements, and indigenous churches in the majority world that embody Pentecostal spirituality (e.g. emphasis on baptism in the Holy Spirit and spiritual gifts). For further discussion on defining 'Pentecostal(ism)', see Wolfgang Vondey, *Beyond Pentecostalism: The Crisis of Global Christianity and the Renewal of the Theological Agenda* (Grand Rapids, MI: Eerdmans, 2010), 8–12; Allan Heaton Anderson, *An Introduction to Pentecostalism*, 2nd edn (Cambridge: Cambridge University Press, 2014), 1–7; James K. A. Smith, 'Pentecostalism', in *The Oxford Handbook of The Epistemology of Theology*, ed. William J. Abraham and Frederick D. Aquino (Oxford: Oxford University Press, 2017), 608.

2. The first paragraph of the introduction is adapted from Simo Frestadius, 'In Search of a "Pentecostal" Epistemology: Comparing the Contributions of Amos Yong and James K. A. Smith', *Pneuma* 38, no. 1–2 (2016): 94.

3. Christopher A. Stephenson, 'Epistemology in Pentecostal Systematic Theology: Myer Pearlman, E. S. Williams, and French L. Arrington', in *The Role of Experience in Christian Life and Thought – Pentecostal Insights: SPS-36 Annual Meeting* (Cleveland, TN: SPS, 2007), 307; cf. Christopher A. Stephenson, 'The Rule of Spirituality and the Rule of Doctrine', *JPT* 15, no. 1 (2006): 84.

is compatible with Pentecostal spirituality, beliefs and practices.[4] Modernistic epistemologies, adopted by much of conservative Evangelical theology, are seen by some as incompatible with Pentecostalism(s),[5] and the so-called postmodern alternatives are not regarded as being without their problems.[6]

In light of this Pentecostal scholarly predicament, the purpose of this study is to contribute to this wider 'search' by offering a distinctive *Pentecostal rationality*. In trying to provide such a rationality, it needs to be clarified that this will *not* be done by following the 'standard strategy' employed by many modern theologians and philosophers – that is, a strategy which seeks to 'develop a general account of rationality or justification and then apply it to theism to see how far belief in God is rational or justified'.[7] The reasons for not adopting this 'modernistic' approach are twofold. First, I believe that that the possibility of a universal, general and timeless rationality devoid of influences from any given tradition is questionable at best.[8] Indeed, the inherent weakness of this 'standard approach' is exemplified in the failure of philosophers of religion to actually agree on what is the so-called 'universal rationality', despite the assumption that this rationality should be universal and thus agreeable to all reasonable people.[9] Second, I assume with Aristotle that the perceived order of things (ontology) should determine how things are known (epistemology).[10] In other words, it is maintained that there

---

4. Steven J. Land, *Pentecostal Spirituality: A Passion for the Kingdom* (Sheffield: Sheffield Academic Press, 1993), 184; Kenneth J. Archer, *The Gospel Revisited: Towards a Pentecostal Theology of Worship and Witness* (Eugene, OR: Pickwick Publishing, 2011), 7; Veli-Matti Kärkkäinen, 'Epistemology, Ethos and Environment: In Search of a Theology of Pentecostal Theological Education', *Pneuma* 34, no. 2 (2012): 248–50.

5. Paul W. Lewis, 'Towards a Pentecostal Epistemology: The Role of Experience in Pentecostal Hermeneutics', *SC* 2, no. 1 (May 2000): 122; Archer, *The Gospel Revisited*, 7.

6. Kärkkäinen, 'Epistemology, Ethos and Environment', 249–50; Robert Menzies, 'Jumping Off the Postmodern Bandwagon', *Pneuma* 16, no. 1 (1994): 116.

7. William J. Abraham, *Crossing the Threshold of Divine Revelation* (Grand Rapids, MI: Eerdmans, 2006), 6.

8. This is a basic assumption of the book and will not be argued for it in detail, although see Chapter 2.

9. Abraham, *Crossing the Threshold of Divine Revelation*, 8–9. For example, two prominent Christian philosophers of religion disagree on the type of religious epistemology one should utilize in philosophizing – that is, Richard Swinburne argues for a form of evidentialism and Alvin Plantinga for a type of reliabilism; Richard Swinburne, *Faith and Reason*, 2nd edn (Oxford: Oxford University Press, 2005); Alvin Plantinga, *Warranted Christian Belief* (Oxford: Oxford University Press, 2000); cf. Richard Swinburne, 'Plantinga on Warrant', *RS* 37, no. 2 (June 2001): 203–14; Alvin Plantinga, 'Rationality and Public Evidence: A Reply to Richard Swinburne', *RS* 37, no. 2 (June 2001): 215–22.

10. Aristotle, *Nicomachean Ethics*, trans. J. A. K. Thompson and Hugh Tredennick (London: Penguin Books, 2004), 1094b, 13–27; cf. Alister E. McGrath, *The Science of God* (London: T&T Clark International, 2004), 107.

should be an appropriate 'epistemic fit' between *what* is studied and *how* the study is carried out.[11] Therefore, a study of a 'Pentecostal God' and his relationship with the world (i.e. Pentecostal theology) is approached in a manner that is informed by these underlying Pentecostal assumptions. This need not result in an unfalsifiable *fideism* (as I hope to show in the book), but it does mean taking the underlying Pentecostal *faith* commitments seriously.

So, rather than following the 'standard strategy' vis-à-vis religious reasoning, the book seeks to construct a Pentecostal epistemology that is grounded in Pentecostal intuitions. It does so by adopting Alasdair MacIntyre's notion that all substantive rationalities are 'tradition-dependent' and 'tradition-constituted', and thus attempts to construct a 'tradition-specific' Pentecostal rationality. This means that the work should be seen primarily as an exercise in philosophical theology, or religious philosophy, rather than in philosophy of religion (unless religion is understood as a subjective genitive).[12] However, since it employs MacIntyre's philosophical methodology, there is also a strong historical element. Consequently, the book aims to make three main contributions to knowledge: (1) provide a MacIntyrian tradition-specific *Pentecostal* rationality, which has not been done before; (2) present the first intellectual history of a major European Pentecostal denomination, namely, the Elim Pentecostal Church; (3) propose a rationality of *Pentecostal Biblical Pragmatism* which emerges from the Elim Foursquare tradition.

Overview of the book

To make these three contributions, the book is divided into three parts. The first part grounds the discussion by exploring the works of Amos Yong, James K. A. Smith and L. William Oliverio Jr. on Pentecostal theological epistemology and rationality (Chapter 1). This first chapter is in essence an analytical literature review of three main Pentecostal academic works on the topic in question. I argue that despite the important contributions of Yong, Smith and Oliverio, they all seem to suffer from an element of *ahistoricism* in their philosophical constructions, which means that it is unclear to what extent their proposals are in fact 'Pentecostal', or at least they

---

11. William J. Abraham and Frederick D. Aquino, 'Introduction: The Epistemology of Theology', in *The Oxford Handbook of The Epistemology of Theology*, 1.

12. For example, David Cheetham contrasts philosophy of religion 'with religious philosophy (or philosophical theology) where *religion* or theology is more the priority and which seeks to critically develop a more tradition-specific line of thinking or refine the articulation of a particular area of a tradition's beliefs'; David Cheetham, 'Comparative Philosophy of Religion', in *Contemporary Practice and Method in the Philosophy of Religion*, ed. David Cheetham and Rolfe King (London: Continuum, 2008), 101. However, Nancey Murphy following MacIntyre's logic calls into question the whole notion and possibility of 'philosophy of religion'; Nancey Murphy, 'MacIntyre, Tradition-Dependent Rationality and the End of Philosophy of Religion', in *Contemporary Practice and Method in the Philosophy of Religion*, 32–44.

appear not to be grounded in any particular Pentecostal tradition. Following from this identified weakness, in Chapter 2, I outline MacIntyre's notion of 'tradition-constituted' and 'tradition-constitutive' rationality, and suggest that MacIntyre's methodological insights are conducive for constructing a truly tradition-specific Pentecostal rationality.

Informed by Chapters 1 and 2, the second part of the book seeks to narrate a Pentecostal tradition with the aim of identifying its tacit rationality. Despite the perceivable family resemblances in worldwide Pentecostalism, my aim is not to construct a global Pentecostal tradition – even if this could be done – but to focus on the Elim Pentecostal Foursquare Gospel Alliance. In doing so I do not claim that Elim's rationality is paradigmatic for all Pentecostals or even Foursquare movements. However, I do maintain that as one of the oldest and largest Pentecostal denominations in Europe, Elim's implicit Foursquare epistemology and theological hermeneutics is representative of wider (classical) Pentecostalism.

Discerning Elim's tacit Pentecostal rationality cannot be adequately done without paying sufficient attention to the Elim tradition as a whole, with particular emphasis on its history. Therefore, in Part Two, I first discuss the 'prologues' to the Elim tradition by looking at its philosophical and theological context, as well as its religious roots, with particular emphasis on British classical Pentecostalism (Chapter 3). I then explore the birth of Elim by focusing on its early opponents, the content of its argument, implied rationality, and initial social embodiment (Chapter 4). A central argument of this chapter is that the theological essence of the Elim tradition is the *Foursquare Gospel* and its rationality is *Pentecostal Biblical Pragmatism*. This is followed by a narration of Elim's two major crises (Chapters 5 and 6), which in MacIntyre's language can also be articulated as 'epistemological crises'. In these chapters I attempt to demonstrate that the foundational theology and rationality identified in the previous chapter was central in helping Elim to overcome its two moments of crises.

The third and last part of the book is more constructive in nature (rather than analytical) by taking Elim's tacit rationality of *Pentecostal Biblical Pragmatism* and developing it in the context of the wider Elim tradition narrated in Chapters 3 to 6. Chapter 7 begins by re-constructing Elim's *Pentecostal* theory of truth and thus provides the metaphysical backdrop for a working rationality. Chapter 8 argues for a recalibrated *biblical* hermeneutic for Elim which is more consistent with its Pentecostal doctrine of the Bible. And Chapter 9 explores Elim's *pragmatic* epistemic justification by developing Pentecostal 'experientialism' and 'experimentalism' in dialogue with William P. Alston.

In relation to the T&T Clark 'Systematic Pentecostal and Charismatic Theology Series' – which this book is part of – my overall argument supports the central claim of Wolfgang Vondey's inaugural volume of the series that the Full Gospel 'captures the theological convictions of the [Pentecostal] movement' and provides a narrative framework for its theologizing,[13] even if my focus is

---

13. See Wolfgang Vondey, *Pentecostal Theology: Living the Full Gospel* (London: T&T Clark, 2017), 5.

on the Fourfold and not the Fivefold Gospel. However, as well as affirming Vondey's central argument, the present work also develops his experiential 'altar hermeneutics' by constructing an explicit Pentecostal epistemology.[14] Indeed, the proposed rationality of *Pentecostal Biblical Pragmatism* in a Foursquare Gospel framework can be seen as an alternative to or development of Vondey's concept of Pentecostal theology as 'play'.[15] To put it differently, it is argued that the experiential logic of Pentecostalism is best articulated not as 'play' but as 'pragmatism', at least if Elim's British Pentecostal rationality is anything to go by.

Methodology

As has already been mentioned, the book should be primarily located within the disciplines of philosophical and historical theology, which naturally contribute to systematic theology. Part One interacts primarily with the work of Pentecostal philosophical theologians (Yong, Smith and Oliverio), as well as an eclectic Catholic philosopher (MacIntyre). The engagements are based on the academic literature written by these four authors and their interlocutors/commentators. Part Two of the book is mainly historical and will deal with a range of primary sources particularly on the Elim movement, such as articles in Elim's official periodical (*Elim Evangel*), books by Elim ministers, Elim Conference minutes and reports, correspondence between Elim leaders, and five semi-structured interviews that I conducted for the purpose of 'oral history' to supplement the limited written material on Elim's history in the 1970s and 1980s (see Chapter 6). These primary sources are also brought into a critical dialogue with key secondary sources on Elim's history. Part Three of the study, like the first part, is primarily theological and philosophical in its focus. That said, since Elim's rationality has a strong biblical component, regular references are made to biblical material in line with Elim's own method of reasoning.

In terms of terminology, throughout the book the terms 'rationality', 'epistemology' and 'philosophical hermeneutics' are used more or less synonymously. In other words, I take all of them to deal with questions relating to the nature of knowledge, sources of knowledge; frameworks of reasoning, and developing and utilizing theories with a view for having justified/warranted beliefs. That said, my personal preference is to use the word 'rationality' because it arguably best captures the embodied and social nature of human reasoning, as well as being MacIntyre's preferred nomenclature. However, since I do not believe that it is possible to have neutral or 'non-traditioned' rationality, I do not use 'epistemology'

---

14. Ibid., 31.
15. Ibid., 12–14.

in this supposedly neutral sense and so distinguish it from the purportedly more linguistically saturated and metaphysically informed 'hermeneutics'.[16]

Finally, on a reflexive note, I am an Elim minister and work at Elim's Regents Theological College. Therefore, I am an insider to both Pentecostalism and Elim. However, I hope that the potential force of my own 'Pentecostal biases' in clouding my academic judgments will be offset by the insights often only available to a 'native' Pentecostal. Furthermore, I trust that the book will be judged on the strength of its argument rather than on the genealogy of my personal convictions.

---

16. For example, Oliverio prefers not to use the word 'epistemology' as for him it still carries the ghost of the Enlightenment with the assumption that there can be a 'first philosophy' that is neutral regarding prior beliefs and metaphysical assumptions; L. William Oliverio Jr., *Theological Hermeneutics in the Classical Pentecostal Tradition: A Typological Account* (Leiden: Brill, 2015), 5.

Part One

SEARCHING FOR A PENTECOSTAL RATIONALITY

An increasing number of Pentecostal scholars have offered theological rationalities that are based on Pentecostal intuitions with the aim of serving Pentecostal theology faithfully.[1] It is not hard to argue that the three central figures in this undertaking have been Amos Yong, James K. A. Smith and L. William Oliverio Jr. who have each developed philosophically mature theories of knowledge stemming from Pentecostal presuppositions, and in doing so have helped pave the way forward for distinctive Pentecostal rationalities. Consequently, the purpose of the first section of the book is to analyse and evaluate the theological epistemologies of Yong, Smith and Oliverio (Chapter 1) in order to appreciate the current landscape of Pentecostal theological rationalities, as well as to identify areas where further contributions could be made.

In Chapter 1 I will argue that Yong's rationality is best identified as *pneumatological correlationism* in that he strives for a public theology and aims to bring the Pentecostal tradition into a mutually transformative dialogue with different sources of theological knowledge exemplified in other traditions/disciplines. However, I will suggest that it is questionable to what extent Yong's Pentecostal rationality actually reflects the Pentecostal tradition he seeks to represent, and that his theory of epistemic justification needs further articulation. With respect to Smith, I will argue that his approach can be seen as a version of Pentecostal postliberalism, since his primary focus is on the internal logic of the Christian tradition which he believes is based on and sustained by the liturgical practices and biblical narrative of the Christian community. I will also suggest

---

1. For example, Land, *Pentecostal Spirituality*; Cheryl Bridges Johns, *Pentecostal Formation: A Pedagogy Among the Oppressed* (Sheffield: Sheffield Academic Press, 1993); Lewis, 'Towards a Pentecostal Epistemology', 95–125; Mark J. Cartledge, *Practical Theology: Charismatic and Empirical Theology* (London: Paternoster, 2003), 41–68; Vondey, *Beyond Pentecostalism*, 16–46; Archer, *The Gospel Revisited*, 1–17; Christopher A. Stephenson, *Types of Pentecostal Theology: Method, System, Spirit* (Oxford: Oxford University Press, 2013), 111–30; Pauli Kuosmanen, 'Towards Pentecostal Epistemology: Being Virtuous in the Spirit' (MA diss., Iso Kirja College, Keuruu, University of Wales, 2016); Daniel Castelo, *Pentecostalism as a Christian Mystical Tradition* (Grand Rapids, MI: Eerdmans, 2017).

that the main weaknesses of Smith's rationality appear to be his one-sided view regarding the relationship between practices/faith and beliefs/theology; the focus on present practices at the expense of the historical, theological and communal narratives that shape these practices; the apparent dilemma in his theory of justification with respect to beliefs/narratives; and his potential anti-realism. When it comes to Oliverio, his Pentecostal rationality is presented to be appropriately captured in his phrase 'hermeneutical realism' with a conviction that all knowing is theory-laden but nevertheless reflects, or at least can reflect, an external reality. Regarding Oliverio, I will seek to point out that, although initially it seems that he provides the needed historical and tradition-focused corrective to the Pentecostal epistemologies of Yong and Smith, his own proposal falls short of providing such a historically informed and tradition-specific Pentecostal rationality.

In light of the above, in the second chapter, I will suggest that despite the important contributions of Yong, Smith and Oliverio, further work towards the development of a truly tradition-specific and historically informed narrative Pentecostal epistemology is still needed. To aid this task I will introduce Alasdair MacIntyre's concepts of practices, tradition and rationality which provide helpful philosophical resources in constructing a truly *narrative Pentecostal rationality*.

The importance of this section is not just to provide the groundwork for the more historical and constructive sections to follow, but it also makes a contribution in its own right by critically evaluating the Pentecostal rationalities of Yong, Smith and Oliverio, as well as introducing the philosophical resources of MacIntyre which will aid the construction of a Pentecostal rationality.

Chapter 1

THE 'PENTECOSTAL' RATIONALITIES OF AMOS YONG, JAMES K. A. SMITH AND L. WILLIAM OLIVERIO JR.[1]

As noted in the introduction to the volume, the aim of this chapter is to analyse and evaluate three major contributions on Pentecostal rationality: (1) Amos Yong's 'pneumatological imagination', (2) James K. A. Smith's 'affective, embodied and narrative knowing' and (3) L. William Oliverio Jr.'s 'hermeneutical realism'. I will engage with each scholar respectively by first describing the main tenets of their Pentecostal rationality; second, by exploring what they consider to be the appropriate sources of theological knowledge or ways of acquiring knowledge; third, by identifying their epistemic criteria regarding justification/warrant with respect to theological beliefs; and fourth, by providing some evaluative comments of their overall approach. Throughout this chapter I will use the words 'rationality', 'epistemology' and 'philosophical hermeneutics' more or less synonymously (see Introduction). That said, for Yong and Smith I will primarily use the word 'epistemology' and for Oliverio 'hermeneutics', as this reflects their preferred terminology.

1.1 'Pneumatological imagination': Yong's Pentecostal rationality

Amos Yong is arguably the most influential Pentecostal theologian today. He is a prolific writer, a creative thinker and a modern polymath who has made significant contributions to a number of topics within contemporary theology. Yong has also been one of the main Pentecostal theologians to provide a theologically and philosophically mature Pentecostal epistemology, hermeneutics and theological methodology.[2] His main works on theological epistemology have been

---

1. This chapter is a fuller elaboration of Frestadius, 'In Search of a "Pentecostal" Epistemology', 93–114.

2. For other interactions with Yong's theological epistemology, see L. William Oliverio Jr., 'An Interpretive Review Essay on Amos Yong's *Spirit-Word-Community: Theological Hermeneutics in Trinitarian Perspective*', *JPT* 18, no. 2 (2009): 301–11; Peter D. Neumann, *Pentecostal Experience: An Ecumenical Encounter* (Eugene, OR: Pickwick Publications, 2012), 274–309; Stephenson, *Types of Pentecostal Theology*, 89–91; L. William Oliverio Jr.,

Spirit-Word-Community: Theological Hermeneutics in Trinitarian Perspective (2002)[3] and a collection of articles published in *The Dialogical Spirit: Christian Reason and Theological Method in the Third Millennium* (2014),[4] which Yong refers to as the practical exemplification and outworking of the method presented in the *Spirit-Word-Community*.[5]

1.1.1 'Pneumatological imagination'

Yong's theological rationality is captured in his concept of *pneumatological imagination*. It is *pneumatological* because Yong argues for a 'foundational pneumatology', which means that ontology and metaphysics are best understood pneumatologically.[6] His foundational pneumatology is grounded on three theological principles. First, following Augustine, Yong understands the role of the Spirit as the bond of love between the Father and the Son, and hence in the Trinity the Spirit is the divine mediator *in* and *into* the life of God.[7] Second, for Yong the Spirit is the 'Spirit of power of life in creation' as in Gen. 1.2 the Spirit hovers over 'the deep void and darkness' in a preparatory fashion so that 'the Word of God that creates is carried by the *ruach*'.[8] In this sense the Spirit provides the connection between the creation and the Creator, and so is central in sustaining the creation

---

'The One and the Many: Amos Yong and the Pluralism and Dissolution of Later Modernity', in *The Theology of Amos Yong and the New Face of Pentecostal Scholarship: Passion for the Spirit*, ed. Wolfgang Vondey and Martin William Mittelstadt (Leiden: Brill, 2013), 51–4; Christopher A. Stephenson, 'Reality, Knowledge, and Life in Community: Metaphysics, Epistemology, and Hermeneutics in the Work of Amos Yong', in *The Theology of Amos Yong*, 63–81; Oliverio Jr., *Theological Hermeneutics in the Classical Pentecostal Tradition*, 232–47; Stian Eriksen, 'The Epistemology of Imagination and Religious Experience', *Studia Theologica – Nordic Journal of Theology* 69, no. 1 (2015): 53–4.

3. Amos Yong, *Spirit-Word-Community: Theological Hermeneutics in Trinitarian Perspective* (Eugene, OR: Wipf & Stock, 2002).

4. Amos Yong, *The Dialogical Spirit: Christian Reason and Theological Method in the Third Millennium* (Eugene, OR: Cascade Books, 2014). Amos Yong, *The Hermeneutical Spirit: Theological Interpretation and Scriptural Imagination for the 21st Century* (Eugene, OR: Cascade Books, 2017) focuses predominantly on 'theological interpretation of scripture' rather than on theological hermeneutics.

5. Yong, *The Dialogical Spirit*, 1.

6. Yong's pneumatology should be understood in a Trinitarian context; see Yong, *Spirit-Word-Community*, 215.

7. Ibid., 59–72. Yong builds the Augustinian model of the Spirit on the Irenaean concept of the 'two hands of God'; Ibid., 50–9.

8. Ibid., 43; Yong also emphasizes that in the creation of humanity the *imago Dei* 'derives in part from our having received the divine breath of life'; Amos Yong, *Beyond the Impasse: Toward a Pneumatological Theology of Religions* (Grand Rapids, MI: Baker Academic, 2003), 131.

within the life of the Triune God. Third, the Spirit is not just the Spirit of Creation, but in the dispensation of the Pentecost event the Spirit is redemptively 'poured out on all flesh' (Acts 2.17) inaugurating a new era of God's presence among people.[9]

Since Yong follows the common epistemic principle of allowing the order of things (ontology) to determine how things are known (epistemology),[10] it naturally follows that for him God can only be known truly in the Spirit, and hence Yong's epistemology is logically pneumatically orientated.[11] Moreover, in Yong's foundational pneumatology it is evident that the Spirit is the mediator par excellence and thus utterly relational, whether that is within the Godhead, creation or at Pentecost. Therefore, if ontology is pneumatological then 'whatever else reality might be, it is relational',[12] and thus epistemology should also be relational.

The *imagination*, within Yong's pneumatological imagination, is the human belief-forming faculty in relation to God and the world. Yong uses the term 'imagination' not as a reference to fanciful ideas, or to *a priori* concepts, but as images formed in the mind through experiencing the world.[13] In this sense all knowledge is experientially based and Yong's rationality can be perceived as a form of empiricism.[14] Following Charles Sanders Peirce (an important influence on Yong's epistemology), Yong identifies two aspects within this experiential image forming.

First, images are formed in the mind through passive perceiving, where images are automatically reproduced based on observed sense data.[15] In Peircean language this first aspect of image forming is 'perceptual judgments' being 'the uncontrollable operation of grasping, assenting and acting on sensation'.[16]

The second aspect of the imagination moves beyond simply reproducing images from experience to a negotiation of meaning by actively producing and constructing images of the world and thus can be seen as a type of 'worldmaking'.[17] Peirce referred to this second aspect as 'perceptual facts' which are 'the controlled cognitions or ideas that follow upon perceptual judgments'.[18] Yong also calls perceptual facts 'knowledge', that is, our articulated beliefs.[19]

---

9. Yong, *Spirit-Word-Community*, 30; Yong, *Beyond the Impasse*, 131.
10. See Aristotle, *Nicomachean Ethics*; McGrath, *The Science of God*, 107.
11. Yong, *Spirit-Word-Community*, 83–118; Amos Yong, *The Spirit Poured Out on All Flesh: Pentecostalism and the Possibility of Global Theology* (Grand Rapids, MI: Baker Academic, 2005), 301–2.
12. Yong, *Spirit-Word-Community*, 87.
13. Ibid., 151.
14. Ibid., 133.
15. Ibid., 128.
16. Amos Yong, 'The Demise of Foundationalism and the Retention of Truth: What Evangelicals Can Learn from C. S. Peirce', *CSR* 29, no. 3 (Spring 2000): 570.
17. Yong, *Spirit-Word-Community*, 144.
18. Yong, 'The Demise of Foundationalism', 571.
19. Yong, *Spirit-Word-Community*, 177.

Regarding these two aspects of the imagination, knowledge (perceptual facts) is dependent on and preceded by primary experience of perceptual judgments. This means that knowledge 'is one step removed from basic, inarticulate beliefs (perceptual judgments) and two steps removed from the richness of the world and of our experience of the world',[20] which lays the foundation for Yong's epistemic fallibilism discussed below ('justification/warrant').

However, it is worth noting that these two aspects of the imagination should not be seen as simply objective processes, but 'the imagination is selective, dividing what is trivial from what is important among experiential inputs in order for humans to engage the world evaluatively'.[21] That is, the axiological nature of the imagination seeks to form images that most accurately reflect the world and 'shape habits' that enable the best 'practical human life' in the world.[22] These value judgments of the imagination are not simply the result of the objective competence of the imaginative faculty in forming accurate images of the world, but of the 'heart' (i.e. affections, will and the spirit) of the observer,[23] because it is the heart that is central in informing what a good practical human life looks like. Therefore, the imagination is also affective in nature and the disposition of the heart matters in forming accurate images of the world.

To summarize thus far, for Yong knowledge is gained through the faculty of imagination which through experience forms images of the world both passively and actively, shaped by the disposition of the knower's heart; and the world in which humans find themselves in is a pneumatically charged relational reality. Hence, Yong's theological epistemology and rationality is best captured in his root metaphor of pneumatological imagination.

1.1.2 Sources of knowledge/acquiring knowledge

Following on from the concept of pneumatological imagination, Yong does not restrict his sources of theological knowledge to the biblical foundationalism of conservative Evangelicalism or to a spiritual experience as understood within one specific 'cultural-linguistic' tradition. Since Yong maintains that reality as a whole is pneumatologically charged, divine encounters are not restricted to certain holy books or experiences within specific traditions but the divine can be encountered in other people, cultures, religions, history, nature and science.[24] In other words, Yong interprets the whole world semiotically/symbolically as pointing to a deeper reality – namely, God, that can be experienced.[25] Consequently, it is unsurprising

---

20. Ibid.
21. Ibid., 132.
22. Ibid.
23. Ibid., 129.
24. Ibid., 212–14, 300–1, 298–9.
25. Ibid., 200; see also Yong, *Beyond the Impasse*, 61.

that Yong has actively engaged with other religions,[26] politics,[27] and the natural sciences,[28] because for him the pneumatological world in its fullness is the source for theological knowledge.

Yong is not, however, naïve about the direct nature of these divine encounters in the world, because he does not believe that there can be a direct unmediated spiritual experience. In fact, he argues that 'the cultural-linguistic argument has got the better of the experiential-expressivist argument – to use Lindbeck's terminology', and that 'all knowledge is semiotically mediated and therefore at least one step (or sign) removed from the richness of experience'.[29] Nevertheless, this does not lead him into Lindbeck's postliberal position because he still maintains that there are no truly homogenous 'forms of life' or 'grammars' but there always exists 'a complex togetherness of multiple histories, traditions, sources and experiences'.[30] Moreover, Yong's foundational pneumatology creates a further point of contact between different communities since the Spirit is the divine mediator among people. Therefore, despite acknowledging the mediated nature of all knowledge, Yong strongly argues for a public theology and sees it as a necessity if a theology seeks to claim universal applicability.[31] Thus, theological knowledge should be acquired from all possible sources in the world because 'all truth is God's truth, wherever it may be found'.[32]

It is this emphasis on public theology and the multiple sources of theological knowledge that makes Yong's epistemology effectively correlationist with similarities to the mutually critical correlationism of David Tracy.[33] Yong himself

---

26. For example, Amos Yong, *Discerning the Spirit(s): A Pentecostal-Charismatic Contribution to Christian Theology of Religions* (Sheffield: Sheffield Academic Press, 2000); Yong, *Beyond the Impasse*; Amos Yong, *Hospitality and the Other: Pentecost, Christian Practice, and the Neighbor* (New York, NY: Orbis Books, 2008).

27. For example, Amos Yong, *In the Days of Caesar: Pentecostalism and Political Theology* (Grand Rapids, MI: Eerdmans, 2009).

28. For example, Amos Yong, 'How Does God Do What God Does? Pentecostal–Charismatic Perspective on Divine Action in Dialogue with Modern Science', in *Science and the Spirit: A Pentecostal Engagement with the Sciences*, ed. James K. A. Smith and Amos Yong (Bloomington, IN: Indiana University Press, 2010), 50–71; Amos Yong, *The Spirit of Creation: Modern Science and Divine Action in the Pentecostal-Charismatic Imagination* (Grand Rapids, MI: Eerdmans, 2011).

29. Yong, *Spirit-Word-Community*, 208.

30. Ibid., 302. For Lindbeck's classic text, see George A. Lindbeck, *The Nature of Doctrine: Religion and Theology in a Postliberal Age*. 25th Anniversary Edition (Louisville, KY: Westminster John Knox Press, 2009).

31. Yong, *Spirit-Word-Community*, 304; Yong, *The Hermeneutical Spirit*, 31.

32. Yong, *Spirit-Word-Community*, 305.

33. Tracy advocates 'mutually critical correlations between the interpretations of tradition and situation or church and world'; David Tracy, *The Analogical Imagination: Christian Theology and the Culture of Pluralism* (London: SCM, 1981), 80.

has noted that his pneumatological imagination 'charts a path forward from the crossroad where Gelpi's pneumatology and Tracy's fundamental theology meet'.[34] In other words, Yong's pneumatological imagination utilizes Donald Gelpi's understanding of pneumatological experience and applies it to all of humanity, enabling a truly public theology à la Tracy. Therefore, it is reasonable to suggest that Yong's theological epistemology could be seen as a development of Tracy's fundamental theology and is perhaps best captured in the phrase *pneumatological correlationism*.

It is here that my reading of Yong also differs from that of Mark Mann, who argues that Yong's epistemology, with respect to Tracy's correlationism and Lindbeck's postliberalism, has 'much stronger affinity to postliberalism'. Mann notes that Yong's 'sympathy' for postliberalism 'has become especially clear in his more recent work', particularly Yong's *Hospitality and the Other*.[35] However, although Mann acknowledges Yong's critique of postliberalism, he seems to overlook the extent to which Yong finds postliberalism wanting. For example, even in *Hospitality and the Other*, which, according to Mann, is Yong's more sympathetic work on postliberalism, Yong supplements Lindbeck's proposal with his foundational pneumatology and its concomitant 'universalist' epistemological implications.[36]

1.1.3 Justification/warrant

However, although Yong believes in the universal presence of the Spirit in the world and thus in the possibility of divine encounters in all spheres of life, he is careful to qualify that not all experiences in the world are, in fact, divine encounters, but rather one must 'test the Spirit(s)' (1 Jn 4.1). In terms of identifying the truthfulness of one's images/beliefs about the world, Yong offers two theories of justification. The first, and his main theory of justification, is a *pragmatic* one. According to this, 'true beliefs are those reached when the effects predicted are borne out in experience'.[37] To test the truthfulness of an image or belief is to see whether it obtains 'desirable results, not in the sense of that which human beings simply wish or want, but in the sense of harmonizing or comporting with the way reality is'.[38]

From this Yong argues that the truthfulness of our images/beliefs is dependent on how in practice they are congruent with the world; and that our practices,

---

34. Yong, *Beyond the Impasse*, 63.

35. Mark Mann, 'Traditionalist or Reformist: Amos Yong, Pentecostalism and the Future of Evangelical Theology', in *The Theology of Amos Yong*, 207 n. 22.

36. Yong, *Hospitality and the Other*, 57, 128. For a further critique of postliberalism and narrative theology by Yong, see Amos Yong, 'Radically Orthodox, Reformed, and Pentecostal: Rethinking the Intersections of Post/Modernity and the Religions in Conversation with James K.A. Smith', *JPT* 15, no. 2 (2007): 241–2, 246–7.

37. Yong, 'The Demise of Foundationalism', 572.

38. Yong, *Spirit-Word-Community*, 165.

behaviour and habits should be transformed to reflect this reality.[39] The latter assertion implies that truthful engagement in the world is 'such that our activities and habits are transformed as a result of engaging the world', which means that truth is not just cognitive but also ethical.[40] That is, our beliefs/images are justified pragmatically in as much they reflect both the ontological/metaphysical reality and the ethical/soteriological reality.[41] Therefore, Yong's pragmatic justification means that we test the truthfulness of our images/beliefs in practice and that we allow the truth to shape our habits to enable further truthful engagement in the pneumatic world.

Yong's second test is that of *coherence*. That is, beliefs are justified if they are coherent with a person's/community's other beliefs.[42] In Yong's more recent work he has especially emphasized that a pneumatological criteria of discernment in a Christian context needs to be 'christological, Trinitarian, and canonical'.[43] In other words, (Pentecostal) beliefs formed in a pneumatically charged world should effectively cohere with knowledge about the divine Christ, the Triune God and the biblical narrative.

It is worth noting, however, that although Yong uses pragmatism and coherence as theories of justification, he does not accept them as appropriate theories of truth.[44] In fact, he favours a 'correspondence theory of truth' in which correspondence is seen as 'correlation', rather than 'congruence', implying that true propositions need not be identical with their referents but should, nevertheless, resemble them sufficiently. He favours 'correspondence as correlation' because, following Peirce, he maintains that 'all human experience is mediated semiotically'.[45] Therefore, Yong is effectively a critical realist who sees pragmatism and coherence as appropriate theories of warrant.[46] Yong summarizes his approach to epistemic justification by stating that 'theological truth works and coheres because it corresponds – to put it crassly – with reality (nature) which is its measure'.[47]

Yong's critical realism, as well as his pragmatic and coherence theories of epistemic justification, is also very much shaped here by Peirce's 'triadic'. Peirce, as interpreted by Yong, believed that all entities exist in triadic relationships consisting of *Firstness* which is the 'thing itself', *Secondness* which is 'that by which a thing is related to others', and *Thirdness* which 'is what mediates between Firstness

39. Ibid.
40. Ibid., 166.
41. Ibid.
42. Ibid., 169–74.
43. Yong, *The Hermeneutical Spirit*, 261.
44. Yong, *Spirit-Word-Community*, 174.
45. Ibid., 167–8, 185.
46. Yong refers to himself as a 'committed metaphysical realist'; Yong, *Beyond the Impasse*, 71.
47. Yong, *Spirit-Word-Community*, 298.

and Secondness' (e.g. universals, laws and generalities).[48] Yong states: 'All things are what they are only as Firsts, Seconds, and Thirds – viz. having self-identity independent of anything else, having relational identity in reaction to other things, and having a meditative aspect of through which they are brought into relation with other things.'[49] This means that the 'realism' aspect of Yong's epistemology is maintained by things having independent self-identity (Firstness), the 'critical' element is characterized by all-knowing being semiotic (Secondness), and the possibility of 'critical realism' to correlate with reality is enabled by the consistent universals and laws in the world (Thirdness). Peirce's triadic also underscores the relational element of Yong's pneumatological imagination; that is, all knowing and being known takes place within this triadic relationship, facilitated by the Spirit of God.

Yong's critical realism and the concept of triadically mediated knowledge naturally leads to his notion of epistemic fallibilism. He asserts three reasons for the fallibilistic nature of human knowledge. First, all knowledge is *partial*.[50] It is partial not only because the knower is working with images, signs and symbols but also because what is known is either partial or incomplete (i.e. the world),[51] or inexhaustible (i.e. God).[52] Second, knowledge is *perspectival* in character as 'all thinking is conditioned by the biological, cultural-linguistic, and purposive contexts of inquiry. These contexts determine, in some ways, what is considered to be valuable or important'.[53] The third reason is the '*finitude* of knowledge'. To be human is to be finite and limited, an aspect reflected in our knowing.[54] The significance of Yong's epistemic fallibilism is that the process of justification of beliefs through pragmatic and coherence theories must be perennial because of the fallible nature of all human knowing. In Yong's own words, spiritual discernment 'is a never-ending process'.[55]

1.1.4 Evaluative comments

To summarize the discussion so far, the key concept in Yong's theological epistemology is the *pneumatological imagination*. The pneumatological aspect stems from Yong's foundational pneumatology, and the imagination from his Peircean understanding that all human knowing is based on experience in which

---

48. Yong, *The Dialogical Spirit*, 66.
49. Ibid.
50. Yong, *Spirit-Word-Community*, 176.
51. Yong's thinking about the nature of the world is not very different from process theology. He states that 'the world is not static but evolving or becoming. Things are incomplete in this sense'; ibid., 178.
52. Ibid., 210.
53. Ibid., 180.
54. Ibid., 182.
55. Yong, *Beyond the Impasse*, 164.

images of the world, and of God in the world, are formed both passively ('perceptual judgments') and actively ('perceptual facts') in the human mind. Furthermore, this image forming process is not an objective activity in the mind, but an activity orientated by the observer's 'heart'. When it comes to acquiring knowledge since God is present in all of creation by the Spirit, the world in its fullness is the source of theological knowledge and thus knowledge of God is not simply limited to certain spheres of life, traditions or disciplines of enquiry. Nevertheless, not all experiences in the world are divine encounters, and therefore justification for appropriate images/beliefs of God must be discerned through *pragmatic* and *coherence* criteria. The need for seeking warrant for beliefs is further highlighted by the triadic and fallibility of all human knowing.

Yong's Pentecostal (read: pneumatological) rationality has a number of strengths. At the forefront, it is developed on the doctrine of the Spirit, which is one of the central aspects of Pentecostalism(s). A great emphasis is also placed on pneumatological experience, and, as Keith Warrington puts it, 'a personal, experiential encounter of the Spirit' is central to Pentecostals.[56] This experience is not understood, however, in a naïve realist fashion because Yong acknowledges that all experience is semiotically mediated, but at the same time, he does not restrict the experience simply to a cultural-linguistic tradition but allows the experience of God to also transform that tradition.[57] Yong's epistemology can also be seen as moving beyond Cartesian rationalism and classical foundationalism,[58] which has been common in Evangelical epistemologies and thus an influence on Pentecostal theology. It acknowledges the holistic nature of knowledge and the value of the heart in the formation of images/beliefs.[59] Nevertheless, Yong's concept of the faculty of pneumatological imagination is not a retreat into subjectivism, relativism or fideistic confessionalism, due to his empiricism and the pragmatic justification of beliefs/images. Yong's pragmatism not only is philosophically robust but also reflects the strong pragmatic disposition already present within

---

56. Keith Warrington, *Pentecostal Theology: A Theology of Encounter* (London: T&T Clark, 2008), 20.

57. For the importance of a transcendent Pentecostal experience beyond a semiotic framework, see Lewis, 'Towards a Pentecostal Epistemology', 100; Frank D. Macchia, 'Christian Experience and Authority in the World: A Pentecostal Viewpoint', in *The Authority of the Church in the World: National Council of Churches USA Faith and Order Commission*, accessed 10 September 2013, http://www.ncccusa.org/faithandorder/authority.macchia.htm.

58. Although Yong does seem to suggest that his foundational pneumatology provides a weak form of foundationalism; Yong, *Beyond the Impasse*, 80; cf. Neumann, *Pentecostal Experience*, 286. For a critical overview of classical foundationalism, see Plantinga, *Warranted Christian Belief*, 67–107.

59. Clear similarities can be seen here with Land's 'orthopathy' and Johns concept of *yada*; see Land, *Pentecostal Spirituality*, 134–6; Johns, *Pentecostal Formation*, 39.

the Pentecostal movement, which Yong seeks to represent.[60] Therefore, Yong's pneumatic epistemology with its pneumatological correlationism can be seen as an alternative to classical foundationalist and postliberal theological epistemologies, and thus as a plausible option for Pentecostal theologians and philosophers to utilize.[61]

Having identified these strengths, there are at least two aspects of Yong's theological epistemology that merit further discussion: (1) the general adequacy of his public theology and correlationism from a Pentecostal perspective, and (2) the effectiveness of his theory of justification/warrant.

Regarding the first issue, it seems that Yong's theological project is effectively that of a (supra) 'natural theologian' since he emphasizes the possibility of a universal pneumatic experience that finds its basis in his foundational pneumatology. Now the question is whether Yong's pneumatology in the context of Pentecostal theology and pneumatology is sufficiently robust to justify this position. For example, Smith has argued that Yong pushes the metaphor of 'Spirit poured out on all flesh' too far by not acknowledging its particular connection to Christians, rather than all people, in Acts.[62] This criticism is further articulated by the Pentecostal theologian Roger Stronstad who strongly opposes Yong's reading of Acts 2.17 by claiming that 'the interpretation espoused by Amos Yong is factually incorrect. Contrary to Yong's meaning, the Spirit is NOT poured out on all flesh.'[63] Thus, the potential danger is that Yong's pneumatology emphasizes the universal Spirit of Creation at the expense of the particular Spirit of Christ; that is, epistemologically, not soteriologically, speaking.[64] Or to pose the question differently, is (Yong's) natural theology a 'natural' bedfellow for Pentecostal theology, even when it is pneumatically based?

Interestingly, L. William Oliverio Jr. has pointed out, after explicating Yong's theological methodology, that 'the question remains how Yong's theological forays relate to the Pentecostal traditions that Yong seeks to represent and to those particularities he attends'.[65] This is a crucial question because if Yong's epistemology does not relate to the Pentecostal traditions appropriately, this not only undermines his global/public theology by excluding Pentecostals but also

---

60. See Lewis, 'Towards a Pentecostal Epistemology', 106; Grant Wacker, *Heaven Below: Early Pentecostals and American Culture* (Cambridge, MA: Harvard University Press, 2003), 13; Macchia, 'Christian Experience and Authority in the World'; Neumann, *Pentecostal Experience*, 152.

61. See Yong, 'The Demise of Foundationalism', 579–87.

62. James K. A. Smith, 'The Spirit, Religions, and the World as Sacrament: A Response to Amos Yong's Pneumatological Assist', *JPT* 15, no. 2 (2007): 254 n. 9.

63. Roger Stronstad, 'A Review Essay on Amos Yong, *Who is the Holy Spirit? A Walk with the Apostles*', *JPT* 22, no. 2 (2013): 297.

64. Yong rejects soteriological universalism due to human freedom enabled by the Spirit; Yong, 'Radically Orthodox, Reformed and Pentecostal', 247.

65. Oliverio, 'The One and the Many', 60.

potentially destroys the foundations upon which he hopes to build his public theology, namely Pentecostal presuppositions. I am not necessarily suggesting that Yong's epistemology does not accurately reflect Pentecostalism, but that this issue simply needs further assessment if Yong's Pentecostal epistemology is to be adopted and adapted by Pentecostal scholars going forward.

Second, when it comes to Yong's theory of justification/warrant, Yong has himself stated that he is 'convinced that the Achilles' heel of any pneumatological approach to theology of religions will be its failure to develop a criteriology of discernment adequate for the dynamic complexity of lived human religious experience'.[66] At the same time, however, in his most philosophical and theoretical work Yong acknowledges that 'the possibility, conditions, and justification of knowledge' are not comprehensively discussed,[67] and, as one might expect, this does cause some ambiguity in Yong's epistemology and also leaves the Achilles' heel of his epistemology very exposed.

For example, Yong maintains that, in the light of his pragmatic justification, beliefs are justified in practice in how they correspond to reality and this informs right habits in a person, enabling them to more truthfully interact with reality. However, Yong also asserts that truth, that is, reality is fundamentally eschatological.[68] If this is the case, then simply testing our beliefs in the world, even if the world is pneumatic, will not help us reach the truth of the matter or necessarily develop right epistemic habits unless one maintains a fully realized eschatology. The reason being, that if the eschaton has not yet been fully realized, the current reality experienced in the world and the habits formed by it do not necessarily correspond to the age to come, which will reflect a different reality at least to some extent. Perhaps this is why Paul, among other NT writers, encourages his readers through his example to 'walk by faith, not by sight' (2 Cor. 5.7). However, Paul's exhortation begs the question: 'how does one know that one is genuinely walking by faith and that one's faith is warranted, if experience and practice cannot fully confirm this?' The answer from a Christian perspective seems to point towards God's special revelation in Christ mediated by the Bible and the Christian community.

In fairness to Yong, his more recent articulation of theological epistemology has focused increasingly on Christ as the revelation of God and he has also argued for a closer relationship between Christology, pneumatology, ecclesiology, practice and eschatology.[69] Nevertheless, the relationships between Spirit and Word, experience and the Bible, practice and tradition, eschatology and history, could be

---

66. Yong, *Beyond the Impasse*, 166.

67. Yong, *Spirit-Word-Community*, 120. To be fair to Yong, he has tried to remedy this lack to some extent in his later work.

68. Yong, 'The Demise of Foundationalism', 580.

69. Amos Yong with Jonathan A. Anderson, *Renewing Christian Theology: Systematics for a Global Christianity* (Waco, TX: Baylor University Press, 2014), chapter 12; Yong, *The Dialogical Spirit*, 285; Yong, *The Hermeneutical Spirit*, 261–3.

still further developed with a more direct focus on epistemic justification. It is here that Yong's pragmatic warrant and habit formation might also be strengthened by Smith's notion of habits being formed through the liturgy of the community of faith, which is the eschatological community (see 1.2).

In conclusion, Yong's theological epistemology captured in his phrase 'pneumatological imagination' characterized by pneumatological correlationism is pneumatically orientated, pragmatically based and universal in its aspiration. It is rich both philosophically and theologically, and thus offers potential for further Pentecostal epistemic engagement. Nevertheless, two questions remain: (1) To what extent does it reflect the Pentecostal traditions? and (2) Is Yong's theory of justification/warrant sufficiently strong within and in dialogue with those outside the Pentecostal community?

1.2 Affective, embodied and narrative knowing: Smith's Pentecostal rationality

James K. A. Smith, like Yong, has been one of the pioneers of Pentecostal philosophical theology in the twenty-first century. His main work focusing explicitly on Pentecostal philosophy and epistemology is *Thinking in Tongues: Pentecostal Contributions to Christian Philosophy* (2010);[70] although many of the ideas presented here are expressed, as well as developed, in his other works. In his own words, Smith's philosophical and theological journey has been from Christian 'fundamentalism' to 'postliberalism'.[71] Some of his main philosophical and theological influences and dialogue partners along this intellectual journey have been reformed and Pentecostal theologians/philosophers, the Radical Orthodoxy movement, continental philosophy and, more recently, American Pragmatism.[72]

---

70. James K. A. Smith, *Thinking in Tongues: Pentecostal Contributions to Christian Philosophy* (Grand Rapids, MI: Eerdmans, 2010). For a more recent articulation see Smith, 'Pentecostalism', 606–18.

71. James K. A. Smith, *The Fall of Interpretation: Philosophical Foundations for a Creational Hermeneutic*, 2nd edn (Grand Rapids, MI: Baker Academic, 2012), 5–9.

72. For example, Smith, *The Fall of Interpretation*; James K. A. Smith, *Speech and Theology: Language and the Logic of Incarnation* (Abingdon: Routledge, 2002); James K. A. Smith, *Introducing Radical Orthodoxy: Mapping a Post-secular Theology* (Grand Rapids, MI: Baker Academic, 2004); James K. A. Smith, *Who's Afraid of Postmodernism? Taking Derrida, Lyotard, and Foucault to Church* (Grand Rapids, MI: Baker Academic, 2006); James K. A. Smith, *Desiring the Kingdom: Worship, Worldview and Cultural Formation* (Grand Rapids, MI: Baker Academic, 2009); James K. A. Smith, *Imagining the Kingdom: How Worship Works* (Grand Rapids, MI: Baker Academic, 2013); James K. A. Smith, *Who's Afraid of Relativism? Community, Contingency and Creaturehood* (Grand Rapids, MI: Baker Academic, 2014); James K. A. Smith, *How (Not) to be Secular: Reading Charles Taylor* (Grand Rapids, MI: Eerdmans, 2014).

My discussion on Smith's Pentecostal epistemology shares the structure of the previous section; that is, I will (1) describe the main tenets of Smith's Pentecostal epistemology, (2) discuss his identified sources of theological knowledge, (3) explore the epistemic criteria regarding justification/warrant, and (4) provide some evaluative comments on Smith's theological epistemology.

1.2.1 Affective, embodied and narrative knowing

Smith hopes to develop a Pentecostal epistemology that is based on the tacit epistemic principles present within Pentecostal faith and spirituality.[73] His emphasis on constructing a theological epistemology of faith/spirituality follows his distinction between 'faith/spirituality' and 'theology'.[74] Faith, according to Smith, is a 'pre-theoretical experience',[75] whereas theology is 'associated with the more narrow, propositional aspect of faith – doctrines, dogma, and theoretical reflection',[76] and in this sense theology is a 'second-order' discipline 'one step back' from the reality of faith.[77] Moreover, for Smith, it is the practices of faith/spirituality 'that give rise to (articulated) beliefs' of theology, *not the other way around*.[78] Consequently, it seems that for Smith a Pentecostal epistemology stemming from a Pentecostal theology would be a construction from a secondary source, rather than the primary source of practiced faith and spirituality. Therefore, to avoid dealing with lesser sources (read: theology), Smith seeks to build his theological epistemology on the primary source of Pentecostal spirituality, or at least his direct reflection on it.

In reflecting on Pentecostal spirituality, Smith effectively identifies three key aspects for a Pentecostal theory of knowledge: knowing is (1) *affective*, (2) *embodied* and (3) *narrative*. He pitches these three principles against the Cartesian anthropology that reduces humans to 'thinking things' which, he argues, has resulted in the idolization of reason and the failure of modernistic epistemologies.[79] Smith in fact suggests that 'the epistemology implicit in Pentecostal spirituality ... call[s] into question ... [the] embrace of rationalist models of knowledge' which 'reduces Christian faith to a set of logical propositions'.[80] In this sense he sees Pentecostalism as a type of *proto-postmodernism* or *countermodernism*, having

---

73. Smith, *Thinking in Tongues*, 52.
74. Ibid., 25–6.
75. James K. A. Smith, 'Dialogue: Scandalizing Theology: A Pentecostal Response to Noll's *Scandal*', *Pneuma* 19, no. 2 (1997): 235.
76. Smith, *Thinking in Tongues*, 25–6.
77. Smith, 'Dialogue', 235.
78. Smith, *Thinking in Tongues*, 31 n. 35.
79. Ibid., 53. Unlike Yong's epistemology that starts from ontology, Smith bases his epistemology on anthropology; Smith, *Desiring the Kingdom*, 37; cf. Smith, *Thinking in Tongues*, 54.
80. Smith, *Thinking in Tongues*, 55 n. 17.

great affinity with postmodern epistemologies,[81] which is not necessarily surprising with respect to Smith's own interest in postmodern theology and philosophy.[82]

So how does Smith interpret these three Pentecostal epistemic intuitions? First, he argues that for Pentecostals the *affections* and the 'heart', not the 'head', are at the centre of theological knowledge (and knowledge in general).[83] Smith insists that this should not be seen as a Pentecostal rejection of reason per se or a return to naïve anti-intellectualism, but 'the point is to affirm the *primacy* of the heart and affections as the *basis* for a rational, intellectual engagement with and interpretation of the world'.[84] Building on the philosophies of Martin Heidegger and Charles Taylor, Smith argues that we can 'know' (*Wissen*) only what we 'understand' (*Verstehen*) and we can understand only what we 'love/desire'.[85] To put it differently, what we love shapes who we are;[86] who we are is significant in shaping our worldview, that is, the way we 'see', 'inhabit' and 'engage' the world;[87] and, our worldview then sets the boundaries for our reasoning, intellectual engagement and beliefs about the world. Therefore, Smith infers that 'we love before we know', and in a sense we can only know what we love because it is love that forms our plausibility structures of what could be.[88] This is why, for Smith, Pentecostal knowledge is fundamentally affective.

The second element of Smith's Pentecostal epistemology is *imaginative embodiment* which follows from his notion of affective knowledge. As seen above, for Smith the heart is the 'heart' of theological knowing, and he goes on to claim that 'the way to the heart is through the body', as well as through the imagination.[89] Smith closely links embodiment and imagination, and like Yong, he does not see imagination as 'the stuff of make-believe creativity ... or merely an act of pretense', rather he sees

> it more as a quasi-faculty whereby we construe the world on a precognitive level, on a register that is fundamentally aesthetic precisely because it is so closely tied to the body ... the imagination is a kind of midlevel organizing or synthesizing faculty that constitutes the world for us in a primarily affective mode ... There is a kind of precognitive perception that is to be distinguished from perception proper – that is, from perception as being cognizant of and attentive to an 'object' in front of me.[90]

---

81. Ibid., 52.
82. See Smith, *Introducing Radical Orthodoxy*; Smith, *Who's Afraid of Postmodernism?*; Smith, *Who's Afraid of Relativism?*
83. Smith, *Thinking in Tongues*, 58. In many ways Smith follows Land in building his epistemology on the notion of 'orthopathy'; Land, *Pentecostal Spirituality*, 134.
84. Smith, *Thinking in Tongues*, 59.
85. Smith, *Desiring the Kingdom*, 70.
86. Ibid., 40.
87. Smith, *Thinking in Tongues*, 27.
88. Smith, *Desiring the Kingdom*, 70; Smith, *Imagining the Kingdom*, 14 n. 26.
89. Smith, *Imagining the Kingdom*, 14; 162.
90. Ibid., 16–18.

The 'precognitive perception', as distinct from 'perception proper', is also referred to by Smith as 'primary perception'.[91] It is this primary perception which is our embodied 'way of being-in-the world as being-*with*-the-world', attuning our imagination to reflect our embodied experience of the world around us.[92] Smith's primary perception is similar to Yong's first aspect of the imagination (Peirce's 'perceptual judgments') in which images are formed passively in the mind, although Smith places greater emphasis on the embodied nature of this passive image forming. Furthermore, like Yong's second aspect of the imagination, or Peirce's 'perceptual facts', the rationality, intellection and 'objective knowledge', according to Smith, is only made possible through this primary perception.[93] In fact, 'objective knowledge' seems to be a reflection on the 'primary perception'. Hence, Smith argues that as embodied creatures we firstly '*feel* our way around the world more than we *think* about it, *before* we think about it'.[94] And it is this embodied being in, and feeling our way around, the world that informs our imagination.

Smith points out that this principle of understanding humans as embodied and imaginative beings who imbibe images through their bodies is acted out in Pentecostal worship. He states that 'there could be no Pentecostal spirituality without the matter of bodies; in other words, for Pentecostalism, *bodies matter*'.[95] He supports his claim by noting how the importance of divine healing and expressive worship (e.g. lifting up of hands, laying on of hands, dancing and shaking) highlights the centrality of embodied encounters for Pentecostals with the divine and opposes the reduction of humans to mere rational beings.[96]

Third, from the affective and embodied/imaginative aspects of knowing God, Smith proposes that *narrative* knowledge naturally ensues;[97] he reasons that the form of knowing needs to be narrative/testimonial in order to carry the affective and embodied aspects. That is, 'if the testimony is translated into mere' facts, codified into propositions, distilled into ideas, then we are dealing with a different animal: I would both "know" something different and "know" it differently'.[98] In other words, only narrative knowledge, not propositional knowledge, can do justice to the affective and embodied nature of knowing and is therefore irreducible to rational propositions. The role of the narrative within Smith's epistemic triad is to provide a framework to help make 'sense of our world, our experience, and events'.[99] To use N. T. Wright's terminology,

---

91. Ibid., 70.
92. Ibid.
93. Ibid.
94. Smith, *Thinking in Tongues*, 72.
95. Ibid., 82.
96. Ibid., 61.
97. Ibid., 64.
98. Ibid.
99. Ibid., 70.

the narrative functions as a 'controlling story',[100] helping to interpret the images formed through embodiment in the world. Or, in the words of Smith, 'narrative is the scaffolding of our experience'.[101]

1.2.2 Sources of knowledge/acquiring knowledge

In the light of Smith's affective, embodied and narrative Pentecostal epistemology, I will now seek to further explore how in Smith's terms we come to 'know' and what are the main 'sources' of knowledge. At the forefront, similarly to Yong, Smith sees experience as the central source of theological knowledge.[102] In fact, Smith acknowledges that his view of embodied knowing 'by the images of the world that are absorbed by our bodies' is a form of empiricism.[103] So in simple terms, for Smith, as for Yong, we come to acquire knowledge through our *experience* of the world.

Smith, more so than Yong,[104] however, emphasizes that the affective, embodied and narrative theological knowing is shaped by *practices*, which can be seen as 'rituals' and 'liturgies' in which we participate,[105] and these practices end up causing *habits* in our lives. Habit, as understood by Smith, is the 'embodied know-how (the 'practical sense')' that 'orients my perception of the world without me realizing it'.[106] The 'know-how' or 'practical sense' is also referred to by Maurice Merleau-Ponty as the *praktognosia* 'by which I "understand" the world without recourse to discursive, propositional processing'.[107] In other words, habits transform our imagination and thus our primary perception of the world. Hence, Smith concludes that 'rituals make the man who makes the world'[108] because practices (read: rituals) shape our habits, and habits in turn inform our 'know-how'/'practical sense'/*praktognosia*/imagination.

Smith argues that our culture is full of these 'identity-forming practices' (i.e. liturgy) which influences our understanding and knowledge of the world and God, and in this sense liturgical practice, whether Christian or non-Christian, precedes our worldviews.[109] To corroborate this claim, Smith notes that people in 'the church were worshipping long before they got all their doctrines in order

---

100. N. T. Wright, *The New Testament and the People of God* (London: SPCK, 1992), 42.
101. Smith, *Imagining the Kingdom*, 108.
102. Smith, *Thinking in Tongues*, 81.
103. Smith, *Imagining the Kingdom*, 17 n. 38.
104. Although see Amos Yong, 'Ignorance, Knowledge and Omniscience: At and Beyond the Limits of Faith and Reason after Shinran', *Buddhist-Christian Studies* 31 (2011): 205.
105. Smith, *Desiring the Kingdom*, 86.
106. Smith, *Imagining the Kingdom*, 80, 88.
107. Ibid., 56.
108. Ibid., 107.
109. Smith, *Desiring the Kingdom*, 89–90.

or articulated the elements of a Christian worldview; and they were engaged in and developing worship practices long before what we now call our *Bible* emerged and was solidified, so to speak'.[110] Hence, it seems that for Smith a good source of theological knowledge is a context which enables us to participate in a form of liturgy which will shape our affective, embodied/imaginative and narrative knowing in a way that will increase true knowledge of God, because to shape a worldview and to form knowledge is to practise a specific liturgy.[111] It is not hard to argue that, at least ideally, participation in the life of the church provides this context and thus the church as a liturgical community is an ideal, even if not the only, source of theological knowledge.[112]

1.2.3 Justification/warrant

It appears from Smith's epistemological triad and the emphasis on knowing through liturgical participation that we should engage in those practices that help align our affections, imagination and personal narratives increasingly with the reality of God and His Kingdom.[113] So how does one know that they have participated in the right liturgy and that their narrative knowledge of God is justified? For a person to discern the validity of their knowledge, Smith suggests placing their 'micronarratives' of the kingdom within the 'macronarrative of Scripture' which portrays the true picture of God's Kingdom.[114] In other words, a person needs a sanctified perception which means 're-*story*-ing' their 'being-in-the-world'.[115] Smith elaborates this by noting that 'we need to be regularly immersed in the "true story of the whole world" – that is, our imaginations need to be restored, recalibrated, and realigned by an affective immersion in the story of God in Christ reconciling the world to himself'.[116] The 're-*story*-ing' happens best within the worshipping community which participates in liturgies that accurately reflect the biblical metanarrative – that is, the 'true story of the whole world'. Thus, it seems that for Smith the justification for the Pentecostal community's narrative is determined by the extent to which it accurately corresponds to and coheres with the Bible.

---

110. Ibid., 135. It is here that Smith's views are very similar to the Wittgensteinian notion of systems of beliefs within 'forms of life'; see Ludwig Wittgenstein, *Philosophical Investigations*, trans. G. E. M. Anscombe, P. M. S. Hacker and Joachim Shulte, 4th edn (Malden, MA: Blackwell Publishing, 2009).
111. Smith, *Desiring the Kingdom*, 155–214.
112. Smith states that 'the church is the language-game in which we learn to read the world aright'; Smith, *Who's Afraid of Relativism?*, 72.
113. Smith, *Desiring the Kingdom*, 48.
114. Smith, *Thinking in Tongues*, 63.
115. Smith, *Imagining the Kingdom*, 161.
116. Ibid., 163.

This, however, raises the question of how, in a pluralist world, does the community know that their macro-narrative, namely Scripture, is in fact the true macro-narrative? Smith suggests two theories of justification for the biblical macro-narrative in relation to the contending stories. First, there is the performative effectiveness of the narrative in lived experience vis-à-vis alternative and competing narratives 'in the marketplace of ideas',[117] which lends itself to a type of *pragmatic justification*.[118] It is important to highlight here that Smith is adamant that there is no public rationality or neutral ground between different traditions.[119] This means that it is not possible to justify one's narrative from some form of common criteria, and hence Smith strongly opposes any type of 'correlated Christian theology'.[120] In the absence of common ground between traditions, Smith argues that the biblical narrative is justified pragmatically with respect to competing narratives. The process of pragmatic justification has two steps. The first is to show that there is, in fact, no neutral point of view, and consequently to try to cling on to objective modernistic theories of warrant is disingenuous. For example, the secular ontology is also a '*mythos* and thus equal in epistemic status to the Christian *mythos*'.[121] The next step is then to 'out-narrate' the competing *myths* not by arguments but by the language of life, through a lived witness.[122] In the words of Smith, 'the church does not *have* an apologetic; it is an apologetic.'[123] As well as pragmatically justifying beliefs/narratives through this two-step process, Smith secondly argues that the beliefs/narratives can be also tested regarding their inner coherence, resulting in a coherence theory of justification.[124] In other words, if the biblical narrative is internally coherent and consistent then one is not irrational in believing it.

In summary, the justification/warrant for Pentecostal narrative knowing is provided by three factors: (1) the way it fits with the biblical macro-narrative; the biblical macro-narrative, on the other hand, is justified by (2) a *pragmatic* criteria in its ability to 'out-narrate' competing narratives, as well as (3) the biblical macro-narrative's own inner *coherence*.

1.2.4 Evaluative comments

It has been suggested that Smith aspires to build his Pentecostal epistemology on the tacit epistemic principles present within Pentecostal practice and spirituality,

---

117. Smith, *Introducing Radical Orthodoxy*, 181.
118. See Smith, 'Pentecostalism', 613.
119. Smith, *Introducing Radical Orthodoxy*, 181.
120. Smith, *Who's Afraid of Postmodernism?*, 123–7; cf. Smith, *Introducing Radical Orthodoxy*, 31–42.
121. Smith, *Introducing Radical Orthodoxy*, 181.
122. Ibid; Smith, *Who's Afraid of Relativism?*, 174–5.
123. Smith, *Introducing Radical Orthodoxy*, 181.
124. Ibid., 181–2.

rather than on Pentecostal theology. Within Pentecostal practice/spirituality he identifies three main aspects of Pentecostal theory of knowledge, namely that epistemology is (1) affective, (2) embodied and (3) narrative. Knowledge of the world and God is gained through habit-forming practices, that is, rituals and liturgies, which shape this epistemic triad and one's 'know-how' of the world. To discern whether one is participating in the appropriate practices, one needs to continually 're-story' themselves within the biblical macro-narrative in the context of a Christian community to ensure that one's narrative *corresponds* with the biblical macro-narrative, and the warrant with respect to the biblical macro-narrative is determined by *pragmatic* and *coherence* criteria.

The Pentecostal scholarly community has been significantly enriched by Smith's philosophical vigour, insights and creativity in articulating a Pentecostal epistemology. Smith's impressive work on Pentecostal philosophy as a whole, and epistemology, in particular, has proved to be a significant contribution and catalyst for Pentecostal philosophical theology. Klaas Bom has gone so far as to claim that Smith's epistemological 'contribution provides a first step toward developing … a [Pentecostal epistemological] framework'.[125] Bom's assertion seems somewhat bold, not least in the light of Yong's prior epistemological work but, nevertheless, rightly highlights the importance of Smith's contribution for Pentecostal epistemology. Particularly, Smith's emphasis on spirituality, liturgical practice and (biblical) narrative as a source for Pentecostal epistemology is very valuable. It is also this aspect of Smith's epistemology that makes it postliberal, a label with which Smith is happy to identify.[126]

That said, there seem to be four weaknesses within Smith's epistemology that merit further discussion: (1) his one-sided view regarding the relationship between practices/faith and beliefs/theology; (2) the focus on present practices at the expense of the historical, theological and communal narratives that shape these practices; (3) the apparent dilemma in his theory of justification with respect to beliefs/narratives; (4) Smith's concept of '"realism" without correspondence'.[127]

1.2.4.1 One-sided relationship between faith and theology As discussed above, Smith makes a distinction between practised 'faith/spirituality' and articulated 'theology'. He believes that the practised faith informs theology, and not vice versa, and therefore to deal with the primary material of Pentecostalism he develops

---

125. Klaas Bom, 'Heart and Reason: Using Pascal to Clarify Smith's Ambiguity', *Pneuma* 34, no. 3 (2012): 347.

126. Smith, *Who's Afraid of Relativism?*, 152–3.

127. Bom has also noted Smith's silence on 'the specific role of reason' and the ambiguity between 'heart' and 'reason'; Bom, 'Heart and Reason', 349. However, Smith seems to have responded to Bom's enquiry, at least indirectly, in *Who's Afraid of Relativism*, 115–49. For a criticism of Smith's narrative epistemology with respect to relativism, see Richard B. Davis and W. Paul Franks, 'Against a Postmodern Pentecostal Epistemology', *PC* 15, no. 2 (2013): 399.

his Pentecostal epistemology from the implicit epistemic assumptions within Pentecostal faith/spirituality rather than from Pentecostal theology or historical tradition. However, this approach is not without its difficulties.

First, Smith's insistence that it is practice that informs theology and not theology that informs practice seems to be overly simplistic,[128] not least in the light of the two authors that Smith utilizes in developing his idea of giving primacy to faith/spirituality over articulated beliefs (read: theology). Smith refers to Stephen Land's definition of spirituality as 'the integration of beliefs and practices in the affections which are themselves evoked and expressed by those beliefs and practices'.[129] What is evident here is not the superiority of practice over beliefs, but the value of both in informing spirituality. In fact, Land explicitly states that for Pentecostals there is a '*mutually conditioning interplay* between knowledge and lived experience' (my emphasis).[130] Moreover, Charles Taylor's notion of 'social imaginary', which Smith also employs in developing a Pentecostal imaginary,[131] does not support the pre-eminence of practice informing spirituality and beliefs. In fact, Taylor argues that the social imaginary is created by the mutual interplay of beliefs and practices, and that it is 'absurd to believe that the practices always come first, or to adopt the opposite view, that ideas somehow drive history'.[132] So, although Smith rightly emphasizes the importance of practices informing beliefs and theology, he seems to overlook the role theology plays in influencing religious practices. The implications of this omission are that Smith's Pentecostal epistemology does not make the most of Pentecostal theology, which has shaped and is currently shaping Pentecostal spirituality, and therefore Smith's interpretation of Pentecostal spirituality, which is the foundation of his epistemology, is arguably not fully informed.[133]

Second, even if Smith is right in maintaining that the relationship between practised faith and articulated beliefs works one way only, he is still unable to avoid theology in developing his Pentecostal epistemology. The reason is that to construct an epistemology from Pentecostal faith/spirituality, Smith first needs to interpret the nature of Pentecostal faith/spirituality, which means that he inevitably ends up articulating a theoretical and theological framework upon which his epistemology is then based. For example, when constructing his Pentecostal epistemology Smith begins by providing a narrative description of a Pentecostal worshipping community, followed by a (theological) interpretation and articulation of this

---

128. See Smith, *Thinking in Tongues*, 31 n. 35.
129. Land, *Pentecostal Spirituality*, 13 quoted in Smith, *Thinking in Tongues*, 26.
130. Land, *Pentecostal Spirituality*, 75.
131. Smith, *Thinking in Tongues*, 29.
132. Charles Taylor, *Modern Social Imaginaries* (London: Duke University Press, 2004), 63; cf. Charles Taylor, *A Secular Age* (London: Harvard University Press, 2007), 172.
133. In fairness to Smith, his most recent article on Pentecostal epistemology engages more with Pentecostal history and theology; Smith, 'Pentecostalism', 606–18.

worshipping community, before developing a Pentecostal epistemology.¹³⁴ Consequently, it seems that what Smith ends up building his epistemology on is not the unmediated spirituality of the faith community but rather his interpretation and articulation of this community's faith; that is, Smith's own *Pentecostal theology*. Since Smith is not able to bypass theology, Smith's epistemology would benefit from a greater interaction with other Pentecostal theologians, who, like Smith, commonly see themselves as 'witnesses' of the Pentecostal community. In a true Pentecostal fashion, acknowledging the community's many witnesses would provide a more informed theology (read: articulated beliefs from practiced faith), reflecting the richness of the experienced Pentecostal faith and spirituality, and thus providing better foundations for a distinctive epistemology.¹³⁵

1.2.4.2 Non-narrative, ahistorical and 'experiential-expressive' Pentecostal epistemology Smith's Pentecostal epistemology, however, would benefit not only from Pentecostal theology but also from greater appreciation of the history of Pentecostal communities. In fact, Smith's ahistorical approach means that his purported narrative Pentecostal epistemology is in fact non-narrative. The reason being that Smith focuses mainly on *present* Pentecostal practices at the expense of the historical developments of a theology which gives meaning to these practices. This means that his epistemology seems to focus on the contemporary Pentecostal scene without reflecting on the historical scenes (read: theology and historical narrative) that help put the present scene in its right context. The problem with a 'one scene narrative' is that it effectively becomes non-narrative altogether because you cannot have a story with a single scene.¹³⁶ Therefore, to construct a truly narrative Pentecostal epistemology, Smith, and those who seek to build on his epistemology, need to pay closer attention to the historical and theological developments of the Pentecostal narrative, as well as its contemporary expressions.

Not giving sufficient attention to Pentecostal history/tradition also weakens Smith's attempt in providing a truly communal and 'postliberal' Pentecostal epistemology. As has already been noted, Smith identifies himself as a postliberal and, therefore, like Lindbeck, aims to provide an alternative to the so-called cognitive-propositional and experiential-expressive approaches to religion.¹³⁷ 'Experiential-expressivism' is seen as the model of liberal Christianity, and for Lindbeck, whom Smith quotes, a main difference between 'liberals' and 'postliberals' is that 'Liberals start with experience, with an account of the present,

---

134. Smith, *Thinking in Tongues*, 48–85.

135. Bom also highlights the need for Pentecostal (systematic) theology to influence Pentecostal epistemology; Bom, 'Heart and Reason', 363–4.

136. To be fair to Smith his purpose in *Thinking in Tongues* is to provide a sketch of a Pentecostal epistemology, not a full thesis. Nevertheless, without paying due respect to theology-shaping practices, as well as practices-shaping theology, it is difficult to see how Smith could provide such a narrative Pentecostal epistemology.

137. Smith, *Who's Afraid of Relativism?*, 151–78.

and then adjust their vision of the kingdom of God accordingly, while postliberals are in principle committed to doing the reverse'.[138] In other words, liberals start with experience and postliberals with tradition. Interestingly, when constructing his Pentecostal epistemology Smith seems to adopt more of a liberal rather than the postliberal approach since he starts his description of epistemology from the experience of a Pentecostal believer, even if they are part of a community, and then from this experience draws his epistemic principles for a Pentecostal epistemology.[139]

Now to be fair to Smith, his articulation of an epistemology from a Pentecostal worship service tries to capture a communal rather than just an individual religious experience, and thus Smith's attempt in making 'explicit' what is 'implicit' in Pentecostal worship can be seen as *'communal* expressivism'.[140] Moreover, his description of the Pentecostal service does not just focus on experience but also on practices within the worship service. Nevertheless, without locating his 'communal expressivism' or practices within the wider Pentecostal tradition and its historical narrative, Smith's epistemology seems to resemble too closely the 'experiential-expressive' Liberalism, which he seeks to distance himself from, rather than his preferred 'cultural-linguistic' postliberalism.

1.2.4.3 Epistemic priority: communal practices or creeds/canons? Smith also seems to have a possible problem in his theory of justification/warrant; that is, Smith claims that practice precedes belief, not vice versa, and the church was worshipping long before it canonized its Scriptures or articulated its doctrines.[141] For Smith, it was this worshipping community that gave us the canon and the creeds. Nevertheless, Smith also maintains that the worshipping community needs to regularly 'recalibrate' and 're-story' its narrative in the light of the biblical metanarrative in order for its narrative knowing to be justified and warranted,[142] and the doctrines of the church provide the rules and 'grammar' for authentic practices within the community of faith.[143]

This causes an apparent dilemma for Smith because (1) either the practices of the worshipping community are authoritative, and not the Scriptures or doctrines which simply reflect the community's practices or (2) the Scriptures and doctrines are authoritative and are the norm that should shape the practices of the worshipping community. It appears inconsistent for Smith to hold both assertions. If Smith adopts the first proposition, his theory of warrant needs reshaping and he needs to develop some sort of experiential, or further refine his pragmatic,

---

138. George Lindbeck, *The Nature of Doctrine: Religion and Theology in a Postliberal Age* (Philadelphia: Westminster, 1984), 126 quoted in *Who's Afraid of Relativism?*, 156.
139. Smith, *Thinking in Tongues*, 48–50.
140. Smith, *Who's Afraid of Relativism?*, 163.
141. Smith, *Desiring the Kingdom*, 135; Smith, *Thinking in Tongues*, 31 n. 35.
142. See Smith, *Imagining the Kingdom*, 161–3.
143. Smith, *Who's Afraid of Relativism?*, 162–4.

criterion for justified beliefs. If, on the other hand, he decides to give primacy to the second proposition, a more robust theory of warrant with respect to the biblical narrative, or special revelation, needs to be constructed. Either way, Smith's theory of justification needs further clarification and articulation.

1.2.4.4 Pentecostal (anti-)realism without correspondence Smith identifies his contextual and pragmatic approach to epistemology as '"realism" without correspondence'.[144] In other words, from a theological perspective he sees the need to affirm a 'sacramental ontology, with its Christian "realism," [which maintains]: (1) the reality and *independence* of the transcendent God on whom creation depends for its existence; and (2) the participatory relation of created reality "in" God (per Acts 17; Col. 2)'.[145] However, from a philosophical perspective rather than seeing 'reality' as something that is actually 'outside' of the knower's language game or conceptual framework as it is traditionally understood, Smith argues 'that representation and correspondence and even "realism" are games that we learn to play from a community of social practice … [thus] our realisms (and attendant claims to correspondence) are dependent upon communities of practice. In short, our claims about "reality" are relative to a community of social practice and the "environment" we inhabit'.[146]

Thus, it seems that for Smith 'representation', 'correspondence' and 'realism' are terms within an intratextual language game without necessarily referring to or reflecting an outside reality. However, such a definition of 'realism' seems at odds with how the term is commonly understood. For example, in philosophy of science, Smith's view is more similar to anti-realist 'instrumentalism' than what is generally understood as scientific realism.[147] Moreover, and more importantly for Smith's Pentecostal epistemology, his definition of 'realism' does not seem to fit how a typical Pentecostal believer understands the term (see Chapters 3–6), and therefore Smith is in danger of not just making the implicit practiced Pentecostal epistemology explicit, but actually revising and transforming it into something else. Indeed, both Yong and Oliverio see 'realism' as an important feature of a Pentecostal epistemology, and therefore Smith's unconventional '(anti-)realism' may not sit comfortably with Pentecostal convictions or intuitions.

In summary, despite the various strengths of Smith's affective, embodied and narrative theological epistemology, his *narrative postliberal* approach is in danger of being *liberal* (read: 'experiential-expressivist') by not paying sufficient attention to the Pentecostal community's theology, and *non-narrative* by effectively being ahistorical. The fact that it also seems to lean towards anti-realism would probably

---

144. Ibid., 101.
145. Ibid., 106.
146. Ibid., 107.
147. Kent W. Staley, *An Introduction to Philosophy of Science* (Cambridge: Cambridge University Press, 2014), 171.

raise concerns for most classical Pentecostals, which again suggests that Smith's rationality may not be so Pentecostal after all.

1.3 Pentecostal 'hermeneutical realism': Oliverio's Pentecostal rationality

L. William Oliverio Jr. is the third major contributor to Pentecostal epistemology and rationality, although Oliverio prefers the term 'theological hermeneutics', rather than theological epistemology, to characterize his methodological constructions.[148] His preference for philosophical hermeneutics stems from his rejection of the common modernistic assumption that sees epistemology as *'the* first philosophy' providing neutral and rational epistemic criteria for one's philosophical quest for knowledge. In contrast to this modernistic ideal, and in accordance with the so-called linguistic turn within Western philosophy, Oliverio maintains that epistemological systems cannot be constructed prior to or independently of existing metaphysical or philosophical paradigms. Consequently, he prefers to frame his own project within the language of theological hermeneutics rather than within theological epistemology, even when the primary focus of his work is set around traditional epistemological questions, such as, 'what are the sources of the knowledge of God? And how are these sources approached and utilized for developing Pentecostal theology?'[149]

As discussed in the introduction of the book, I share Oliverio's criticisms of the Enlightenment approach to epistemology, but unlike Oliverio I do not believe that the term epistemology should be abandoned, as long as it is appropriately qualified and defined. Nevertheless, in this last section of the chapter I will mainly use Oliverio's preferred term of 'philosophical/theological hermeneutics'. Moreover, the fourfold structure employed above for engaging with Yong and Smith will also be utilized for interacting with Oliverio's *Pentecostal theological hermeneutics*.

1.3.1 Pentecostal theological hermeneutics

Oliverio's discussion on Pentecostal hermeneutics is more accurately a discussion on classical Pentecostal hermeneutics. By classical Pentecostalism, Oliverio means the first wave of Pentecostalism which emerged in the early-twentieth-century America (Bethel Bible College in Topeka, Kansas [1901] and Azusa Street in Los Angeles [1906]), which 'has gone well beyond a movement within Christianity to the point that it has formed a significant Christian tradition'.[150] Oliverio believes that the Pentecostal tradition is part of the wider Christian tradition, but it is also

---

148. Oliverio's main work on theological hermeneutics/epistemology is Oliverio, *Theological Hermeneutics*.
149. Ibid., 5.
150. Ibid., 10.

a tradition in its own right with an emphasis on 'Spirit baptized living' informed by the narrative of Acts 'as a normative model'.[151]

Oliverio's work on theological hermeneutics makes at least two valuable contributions. First, it provides a historical account of four *types* of Pentecostal theological hermeneutics. Second, Oliverio makes his own contribution to the future of Pentecostal hermeneutics. I will begin by outlining Oliverio's four types of Pentecostal hermeneutics, before looking at his own version.

1.3.1.1 Four types of Pentecostal theological hermeneutics After noting the theological roots of early Pentecostalism,[152] Oliverio argues that over the hundred-year history of classical Pentecostalism four types of hermeneutics can be identified: (1) the Original Classical Pentecostal Hermeneutic, (2) the Evangelical-Pentecostal Hermeneutic, (3) the Contextual-Pentecostal Hermeneutic and (4) the Ecumenical-Pentecostal Hermeneutic.

When exploring the first type, Original Classical Pentecostal Hermeneutic, Oliverio engages with the works of early American Pentecostal pioneers, Charles Fox Parham (1873–1929), William Joseph Seymour (1870–1922), Charles Harrison Mason (1866–1961) and Garfield Thomas Haywood (1880–1931). He argues that despite some of the differences between these first-generation Pentecostal leaders, the theological hermeneutic at work in their writings comprise four core characteristics. First, for these early Pentecostals, 'the Scriptures were the sole ultimate authority for belief and living, but they functioned dialogically with religious and general experience in producing Pentecostal beliefs'.[153] Second, the restorationist and Latter Rain motif provided the historical narrative and eschatological posture for their understanding of God and the world. Third, the four/fivefold gospel set the grounding beliefs and the underlying doctrinal framework, and in doing so functioned as hypotheses in helping to make sense of the Bible and religious experiences. Fourth, the Pentecostal rationality was characterized by pragmatic and naïve realism which combined 'a folksy version of common sense realism … with a strong affirmation of the supernatural'.[154] In this sense, according to Oliverio, the early Pentecostal rationality served as 'an alternative to a more complex and naturalistic modern scientific rationality'.[155]

In discussing the Original Classical Pentecostal Hermeneutic, Oliverio provides some insightful observations on the role of doctrine, Scripture and experience within early Pentecostalism. For example, he argues that the first Pentecostals seemed to use doctrines as 'organizing ideas'; that is, what 'theories are to facts

---

151. Ibid., 11.
152. Oliverio, *Theological Hermeneutics*, 19–30. Oliverio is very much influenced by Donald W. Dayton, *Theological Roots of Pentecostalism* (Grand Rapids, MI: Baker Academic, 1987).
153. Oliverio, *Theological Hermeneutics*, 78.
154. Ibid., 81.
155. Ibid., 82.

in Baconian science, so were doctrines and theological discourse to Scripture and experience in the original Classical Pentecostal hermeneutics'.[156] Oliverio continues by pointing out that on this matter early Pentecostals were significantly influenced by modern rationality, and in line with Baconian common sense science, 'doctrines acted as explanatory hypotheses which were supported by the facts, biblical texts, which were thus cited as proofs for the doctrines'.[157]

The second type of theological hermeneutics identified by Oliverio is the Evangelical-Pentecostal Hermeneutic. The scriptural emphasis and the common-sense rationality of early Pentecostals made it relatively easy for them to align themselves with an Evangelical-type hermeneutic. In fact, Oliverio notes that by the mid-1910s Pentecostals began increasingly to justify their beliefs and experiences biblically. He states: 'While in the original Classical Pentecostal hermeneutic new doctrines explained Scripture and life anew, in the Evangelical-Pentecostal hermeneutic demonstrating that Pentecostal doctrines were the result of the proper readings of the Bible came to the fore. Doing theology became a matter of discovering what the Bible taught – biblical doctrines – and systematically or topically integrating them'.[158] One of the implications of the shift from the Original Classical Pentecostal Hermeneutic to the Evangelical-Pentecostal Hermeneutic was that the openness to theological innovation present in early Pentecostalism was curtailed.

Oliverio argues that this Evangelical-Pentecostal Hermeneutic quickly became the dominant hermeneutical approach among American classical Pentecostals, particularly among Pentecostal scholars and not least after Pentecostals joined the National Association of Evangelicals in the early-1940s. However, he also highlights some of the internal differences and developments within this hermeneutic. For example, the early advocates of the Evangelical-Pentecostal Hermeneutic 'began to account for the internal context and history in the biblical texts' (e.g. William Kerr and Myer Pearlman), whereas the later and more contemporary hermeneuts have also emphasized 'the external context behind the text' (e.g. Gordon Fee and William Menzies).[159]

The third type noted by Oliverio is the Contextual-Pentecostal Hermeneutic which is 'informed by the theoretical and existential concerns in the human experience of interpretation raised by contemporary philosophical or general hermeneutics. For a number of its proponents, this hermeneutic has developed through criticisms of the Evangelical-Pentecostal hermeneutic'.[160]

Oliverio believes that the Contextual-Pentecostal Hermeneutic has four main emphases. First, there 'is an emphasis on the situation and context of the interpreter, going beyond the affirmation of the historicity and context of the biblical texts

---

156. Ibid., 79.
157. Ibid., 80.
158. Ibid., 84.
159. Ibid., 131.
160. Ibid., 185.

already present in the contemporary Evangelical-Pentecostal hermeneutic'.[161] Second, since the context of the hermeneut is not negligible, the way Scripture is understood and interpreted changes. Following from the hermeneutics of Hans-Georg Gadamer, who Oliverio notes as 'the most critical' philosopher 'to the background of the contextual-Pentecostal hermeneutic',[162] according to this type the meaning of the text can only be discerned when the horizon of the reader and the horizon of the text come together in a 'fusion of horizons'.[163] Thus, to speak of meaning outside of this fusion is believed to be misleading. Third, the understanding of hermeneutics changes in that the biblical text is no longer seen as the (only) text, but the whole world and human life within it are seen semiotically as a 'text'.[164] Based on this conviction, fourthly, the advocates of this approach have increasingly engaged with broader questions in contemporary philosophy and philosophical theology.[165]

The fourth type is the Ecumenical-Pentecostal Hermeneutic. Like the Contextual-Pentecostal Hermeneutic, the Ecumenical-Pentecostal Hermeneutic places a strong emphasis on one's context and/or tradition. This hermeneutical approach gives tradition a twofold significance. First, the Pentecostal hermeneut should be aware of their tradition, including its history, narrative and doctrines. Second, other (Christian) traditions should be respected and viewed as worthy interlocutors for the Pentecostal tradition in the hermeneut's quest for theological knowledge. This twofold emphasis on tradition means that the Ecumenical-Pentecostal Hermeneutic is effectively a 'dialogical hermeneutic' where truth is discerned in the dialectical process between the Pentecostal tradition and other traditions.[166] Scripture remains central in this process of discernment, but the Spirit's revealing work and the ability to interpret Scripture is appreciated beyond the Pentecostal tradition.[167]

1.3.1.2 Hermeneutical Realism Informed by these four types of Pentecostal hermeneutics, and particularly influenced by the Contextual-Pentecostal Hermeneutics of Yong and Smith, Oliverio offers his own Pentecostal theological

---

161. Ibid.
162. Ibid., 187. For Gadamer's classic text, see Hans-Georg Gadamer, *Truth and Method*, trans. William Glen-Doepel (London: Sheed & Ward, 1975).
163. Oliverio, *Theological Hermeneutics*, 188.
164. Ibid., 186.
165. Ibid. Oliverio identifies Timothy Cargal, James K. A. Smith, John Christopher Thomas, Kenneth Archer and Amos Yong as the main champions of this type of Pentecostal hermeneutics. He is very sympathetic towards this approach and locates his own work within it, even if he argues for the need to maintain 'hermeneutical realism'; Ibid., 247–52.
166. Ibid., 255.
167. Oliverio states that the key theologians of the Ecumenical-Pentecostal Hermeneutic include Ernest Swing Williams, Cecil M. Robeck Jr., Frank Macchia, Veli-Matti Kärkkäinen, Simon Chan, and Koo Dong Yun; ibid., Chapter 6.

hermeneutics, which he calls 'hermeneutical realism'. It is *hermeneutical* because Oliverio maintains that a '"text" ... is any*thing* that is interpreted theologically'.[168] This means that all (theological) understanding and knowledge is effectively 'textual' and thus must be approached hermeneutically. The implications of all knowledge being textual and semiotic are that one's hermeneutical approach cannot be divorced from the linguistic framework and worldview within which it has been constructed or within which it functions. In Oliverio's own words: 'My thesis is that theological hermeneutics is best understood in terms of holistic paradigms, our best theological accounts of the reality of our world which intertwine the ontologies implicit in our hermeneutics, the specific discernments made concerning the truths of historical existence, and what has come to be the structures of the hermeneutics themselves.'[169]

Nevertheless, despite the hermeneutical nature of all-knowing and the impossibility to transcend one's linguistic framework, Oliverio also argues for hermeneutical *realism*. The realism he advocates, however, is not a version of naïve-realism assuming the possibility of 'universally available reason, autonomous from culture, tradition or special revelation that corresponds to reality as it actually and statistically is'.[170] But it is grounded on the belief that there is a reality beyond one's cultural-linguistic framework and it is possible for individuals and/or communities to have better or worse interpretations of this 'reality'.[171]

In developing both the *hermeneutical* and *realist* aspects of his theological epistemology, Oliverio draws from the works of the philosophers of science Thomas Kuhn and Imre Lakatos, the scientific theologian Nancey Murphy, and the Catholic philosopher Charles Taylor. With respect to Kuhn, Oliverio states that his hermeneutical approach shares similarities with Kuhn's notion of *paradigms*, which Kuhn believed to consist of 'a set beliefs, methods and values'.[172] Moreover, like Kuhn, Oliverio believes that epistemological enquiry and progress cannot be carried outside but always within existing paradigms.[173]

However, to further develop Kuhn's concept of paradigm, and particularly the possibility of choosing rationally between various paradigms, Oliverio builds on Lakatos's concept of *Scientific Research Programmes* (SRPs).[174] Lakatos is significant because he argued that in a post-Kuhnian era his notion of SRPs was the best way to differentiate science from pseudoscience, which both moved beyond the potential

---

168. Ibid., 319.
169. Ibid., 320.
170. Ibid., 323.
171. Ibid., 324.
172. Ibid., 327.
173. See Thomas S. Kuhn, *The Structure of Scientific Revolutions*, 4th edn (London: The University of Chicago Press, 2012).
174. See Imre Lakatos, *The Methodology of Scientific Research Programmes: Philosophical Papers Volume 1*, ed. John Worrall and Gregory Currie (Cambridge: Cambridge University Press, 1980).

irrationality and anti-realism of Kuhn's paradigm theory, but at the same time did not return to a new version of naïve justificationism or falsificationism critiqued by Kuhn.[175] Moreover, unlike some philosophers of science influenced by logical positivism, he was not against metaphysical beliefs per se. In fact, he claimed that SRPs are commonly stimulated by metaphysical beliefs and assumptions.[176] Thus, Lakatos is a natural dialogue partner for Oliverio, as Oliverio seeks to develop a theological (read: metaphysical) epistemology with both hermeneutical and realist dimensions.

Lakatos argued that an SRP does not consist of an 'isolated hypothesis but rather a research programme' comprises a set of hypotheses and theories.[177] These hypotheses/theories within an SRP can be categorized into two types. First, there are theories that make the *hard core* of the SRP which 'includes the methods, theories, and core beliefs of that program that are non-negotiable'.[178] The hard inner core sets the agenda for the SRP and also serves as the *positive heuristic* of the programme. This hard core is the central part of the SRP and thus to abandon it equates to abandoning the SRP as a whole. Second, there are *auxiliary hypotheses* that in relation to the hard inner core help explain observed data, and also provide a *protective belt* around the hard core. The auxiliary hypotheses function as the *negative heuristic*, directing possible criticisms away from the hard inner core.[179] There is greater flexibility within the auxiliary hypotheses as they can be adapted, or even replaced, in an attempt to relate observed data to the hard inner core in a more consistent way.

Among Christian theologians/philosophers, Murphy is perhaps best known for utilizing Lakatos's notion of SRPs in developing a theological methodology.[180] Oliverio acknowledges this and affirms many aspects of Murphy's adaptation of Lakatos's work. Oliverio writes: 'I find that much of Murphy's appropriation of Lakatos is helpful … if entire traditions and types of theological hermeneutics are understood similarly to SRPs. They are ways of understanding reality, as programs for accounting for it, given certain core affirmations and attendant agendas.'[181]

Oliverio agrees with Murphy that theology is not merely 'the internal discourse of the Church', but like the natural sciences has an external reality to which it relates, and therefore there is a public element to theology which transcends any given context. However, due to the contextual, linguistic and theory-laden nature of all knowing, there is no direct or unmediated access to this external reality. Rather, the data about God for the theological research programme is provided by (religious)

---

175. Lakatos, *The Methodology of Scientific Research Programmes*, 1–7.
176. Nancey Murphy, *Theology in the Age of Scientific Reasoning* (Ithaca, NY: Cornell University Press, 1993), 59, 199.
177. Lakatos, *The Methodology of Scientific Research Programmes*, 4.
178. Oliverio, *Theological Hermeneutics*, 329.
179. Staley, *An Introduction to the Philosophy of Science*, 74.
180. See Murphy, *Theology in the Age of Scientific Reasoning*.
181. Oliverio, *Theological Hermeneutics*, 330–1.

communities.[182] This is where Oliverio builds on the work of Smith where a distinction is made between 'faith' and 'theology'. In other words, faith is the lived experience of a religious community, whereas theology is a theoretical reflection on the experience of this community; and therefore, in Anselmian terms, theology is understood as 'faith seeking understanding'.[183] This means that for Oliverio, like for Murphy, theology is both a contextual and a public discourse; that is, the data for theology arises from within religious (or non-religious) communities, but the data referred to is seen to refer to this 'reality' either accurately or inaccurately.

Nevertheless, despite the similarities between Oliverio's and Murphy's approaches, there are also some differences. The main difference seems to be that Murphy's work sees theology more through the lens of the natural sciences, whereas Oliverio approaches 'theological hermeneutics in terms of qualitative and linguistic categories rather than the scientific and quantitative ones found in the language of "probable reasoning"'.[184] Oliverio's motivation for this appears to be a desire to guard theology against becoming 'something akin to a social science'.[185] As part of this move, he distinguishes his 'hermeneutical realism' from the more commonly known 'critical realism'. Oliverio claims that while the latter focuses on a 'single, proper critical method', his hermeneutical realism affirms 'a historically contingent hermeneutic ... [and] the ubiquity of interpretation'.[186]

It is questionable whether Oliverio's distinction between 'hermeneutical realism' and 'critical realism' is justifiable;[187] nevertheless, it is in this context that Oliverio also draws from the work of Taylor who sees epistemological traditions closely connected with 'the most important moral and spiritual ideas' of communities, traditions or civilizations.[188] In agreement with Taylor, Oliverio states that epistemology 'functions in order to form our best account of reality, and this best account is what it means to best "make sense" of our lives'.[189] Therefore, hermeneutical realism is an all-encompassing endeavour as a hermeneutic of life, and so cannot be reduced to one particular field or scientific discipline.

In sum, Oliverio's hermeneutical realism follows the trajectory of the so-called Contextual-Pentecostal Hermeneutic with a strong emphasis on the contextual, linguistic and theory-laden nature of all-knowing, but at the same time, it maintains a 'reality' beyond any given paradigm. Oliverio's contextual and realist epistemology is influenced by Kuhn's concept of paradigms; Lakatos' notion of

---

182. Ibid., 332.
183. Ibid., 343–4.
184. Ibid., 331.
185. Ibid., 332.
186. Ibid., 320.
187. For example, N. T. Wright's critical realism seems very similar to Oliverio's 'hermeneutical realism'; see Wright, *The New Testament and the People of God*, 32–7.
188. Charles Taylor, 'Overcoming Epistemology', in *Philosophical Arguments*, ed. Charles Taylor (Cambridge, MA: Harvard University Press, 1997), 8.
189. Oliverio, *Theological Hermeneutics*, 339.

SRPs, as well as its employment by Murphy within theological methodology; and Taylor's holistic approach to epistemology as hermeneutics of life.

1.3.2 Sources of knowledge/acquiring knowledge

As has already been noted, for Oliverio, it appears to be the experience of religious and non-religious communities that provides the data for theology. Consequently, the underlying source for knowledge in Oliverio's hermeneutical realism is experience; that is, general human experience but also more specifically human religious experiences of 'the other'. Oliverio claims that for Pentecostals it is particularly 'the experience of the presence of the Spirit [which] functions as the guide ... in theological interpretation'.[190] While reflecting historically on the Pentecostal movement, he notes that 'the Azusa Street Revival provides reason for considering the experience of the Spirit as central to the founding of Classical Pentecostal tradition, and thus at the core of its theological hermeneutic'.[191] Therefore, like Yong's and Smith's theological epistemologies, Oliverio's epistemology also seems to be fundamentally experiential and empiricist in nature.

In light of this, Oliverio goes onto identify three specific sources for the pneumatic experience of the Pentecostal community. The first and 'primary revelatory source for theological understanding' is the Son of God who is also the Word of God.[192] The Word of God is fundamentally revealed in the incarnation of Jesus of Nazareth, and it is the Scriptures that bear witness to the living Word of God. However, Oliverio also seems to want to move beyond the Barthian idea of the Bible simply being a witness to Christ and hence he adopts Nicholas Wolterstorff's claim that the written words of the Bible are human words appropriated by God and thus are both human and divine discourse.[193]

The second source of theological knowledge is 'creation and culture', with Oliverio's emphasis being on culture; that is, human cultivation of creation (e.g. human languages, traditions, actions and beliefs).[194] Oliverio writes that 'the hermeneutical task is not only to recognize that culture provides the context for interpretation but also that it provides both the venue for God's revelation and the place of constructive interpretive action to better cultivate the world'.[195] Although not developed in detail, it seems that Oliverio advocates some form of (general) revelation being present in various human cultures, and particularly in those cultures that have been influenced by the Gospel.[196] He believes that despite an individual's inability to experience and think outside of any given paradigm,

---

190. Ibid., 354–5.
191. Ibid., 356.
192. Ibid., 357.
193. Ibid.
194. Ibid., 359.
195. Ibid.
196. Ibid., 359–60.

commensurability with other paradigms is possible through 'our common humanity and common world to which we relate'.[197] Hence, Pentecostal theology should learn from other disciplines, even if Oliverio rejects what he calls the 'correlationist strategy' in recent theology.[198]

The third source of theological knowledge is the Christian tradition. Oliverio suggests that Pentecostal theological hermeneutics needs to draw on the richness of the wider Christian tradition as a whole, and also on the distinctiveness of the Pentecostal traditions. However, apart from referring to the importance of understanding a tradition's historical past, present context and current actions which help create its future, Oliverio provides very little explanation of what in fact constitutes the Christian or the Pentecostal traditions.[199]

1.3.3 Justification/warrant

If, as suggested by Oliverio, one's beliefs about God are based on general and religious experiences, the Bible, creation and culture, and the wider Christian and Pentecostal tradition, how does one discern whether their interpretations of these sources do in fact reflect reality? To put it differently, how can a person or a community be justified in believing their particular interpretations of the data from these identified sources of knowledge?

In developing a theory of justification, Oliverio utilizes the criteria provided by Lakatos and Taylor for choosing between competing SRPs and paradigms. As has already been mentioned, Lakatos sought to develop a scientific method that moved beyond the perceived arbitrariness and irrationality of Kuhn's paradigm theory vis-à-vis choosing between alternative paradigms. To guard against any potential epistemological anarchism, Lakatos argued that the validity of an SRP is based on whether it is considered to be either a *progressive* or *degenerating* programme. A progressive programme is characterized by its internal coherence/consistency, explanatory power regarding the observed data, and also its ability to predict *novel facts*; that is, ability to predict previously unknown facts rather than 'merely explain what is already known'.[200] A degenerating programme, on the other hand, finds its hard core increasingly challenged and is only able to protect it by making 'ad hoc modifications' to its auxiliary hypotheses, which is seen to indicate inconsistencies within its hard core.[201] A degenerating programme has also lost its ability, if it ever possessed such ability, to predict novel facts.

Scientific progress is achieved through the ongoing competition between various SRPs, with the *progressive programmes* eventually gaining prominence over the *degenerating programmes*. However, it is worth reinforcing that for Lakatos, like for Oliverio, the preference of one SRP over another is not determined by a

---

197. Ibid., 326.
198. Ibid., 327.
199. Ibid., 360–1.
200. Staley, *An Introduction to the Philosophy of Science*, 80.
201. Murphy, *Theology in the Age of Scientific Reasoning*, 59.

set of neutral facts mediating between the two competing SRPs, as all facts are considered to be theory-laden, and therefore independent and neutral criteria is assumed to be practically impossible. This, nonetheless, according to Lakatos, need not lead to relativism (a common objection to Kuhn's paradigm theory), since the progressive SRPs are superior to the degenerating ones in explaining data and in generating predictions of novel facts which can be empirically corroborated.

In relation to choosing between two paradigms or SRPs, Oliverio also refers to Taylor who has argued against both epistemological foundationalism and relativism.[202] Taylor has pointed out that deciding between paradigms A and B does not require a third and neutral criteria C. One can reasonably choose B over A without the need for C to mediate because (1) choosing B over A can be seen to overcome some 'error-inducing factor, such as confusion, an elision, a too-simple palette of possibilities, and the like';[203] (2) there is *asymmetry* between A and B, because there is gain by moving from A to B but not from B to A.[204]

In summary, paradigms, according to Oliverio, seem to be justified or unjustified primarily in light of coherence and pragmatic criteria. In other words, a paradigm is judged based on the coherence/consistency of its various beliefs, and pragmatically in its ability to predict and corroborate 'novel facts'. It appears that those paradigms that are able to outdo their competitors in the above in an 'asymmetrical' manner are most likely to correspond with 'reality'.[205] Like Yong, Oliverio also believes that the truth of any paradigm can only be 'eschatologically verified', and thus his epistemology is also characterized by fallibilism and the task of justification/corroboration is ongoing.[206]

1.3.4 Evaluative comments

To recapitulate, Oliverio begins his exploration of Pentecostal theological hermeneutics by offering four types of hermeneutics based on the history of classical Pentecostalism, namely, (1) the Original Classical Pentecostal Hermeneutic, (2) the Evangelical-Pentecostal Hermeneutic, (3) the Contextual-Pentecostal Hermeneutic, and (4) the Ecumenical-Pentecostal Hermeneutic. He follows this by making his own contribution to Pentecostal hermeneutics by developing his 'hermeneutical realism'. This hermeneutical realism falls within the Contextual-Pentecostal Hermeneutic type, assuming that all theological knowing takes place within linguistic paradigms and thus there is no escape from interpretation (i.e. all knowing is hermeneutical). Nevertheless, what is potentially known and

---

202. Oliverio, *Theological Hermeneutics*, 338.

203. Charles Taylor, 'A Philosopher's Postscript: Engaging the Citadel of Secular Reason', in *Reason and the Reasons of Faith*, ed. Paul J. Griffiths and Reinhard Hütter (London: T&T Clark, 2005), 340 quoted in Oliverio, *Theological Hermeneutics*, 338.

204. Oliverio, *Theological Hermeneutics*, 338.

205. Oliverio does not distinguish between theories of justification and theories of truth; ibid., 325.

206. Ibid., 342.

interpreted transcends one's cultural-linguistic context, reflecting a reality beyond one's paradigm. The main source of theological knowledge is the experience of the (Pentecostal) community, with particular emphasis on its experience of the Word of God, creation and culture, and tradition(s). The justification or corroboration of paradigms is determined by which beliefs systems are most 'progressive' (see Lakatos) or provide the best account of lived experience (see Taylor) with respect to other paradigms of religious beliefs.

Oliverio's contribution to Pentecostal hermeneutics/epistemology is manifold. To note some of them, Oliverio seems to provide the first systematic and historical analysis of Pentecostal hermeneutics, and he therefore supplements the more ahistorical Pentecostal epistemologies provided by Yong and Smith. In his historical work, he astutely demonstrates how Pentecostalism is a unique Christian tradition which has evolved theologically and philosophically over its hundred-year history, perhaps best reflected in the four types of Pentecostal hermeneutics. Oliverio also deals with both academic and nonacademic Pentecostal theologians and hence appreciates that Pentecostal theology and philosophy is not just the privilege of academically educated theologians but also the practice of the wider Pentecostal community. Moreover, Oliverio's own contribution to the future of Pentecostal epistemology is insightful and his interaction with Kuhn, Lakatos, Murphy and Taylor is informative.

However, despite these valuable insights, the main weakness/limitation of Oliverio's work is that his own Pentecostal 'hermeneutical realism' remains somewhat undeveloped.[207] This has at least two implications.

First, although Oliverio's hermeneutical realism assumes that all hermeneutical activity can only take place within an existing paradigm because all interpreting and knowing is contextually conditioned, Oliverio does not provide any real articulation of what constitutes the Pentecostal SRP and/or paradigm. To put this in Lakatosian terms, there is no real description of what the *hard core* and *auxiliary protective belt* of the Pentecostal paradigm might be. The closest Oliverio seems to come to identifying the hard core of Pentecostal hermeneutics is when he states that 'the Azusa Street Revival provides reason for considering the experience of the Spirit as central to the founding of classical Pentecostal tradition, and thus at the core of its theological hermeneutic'.[208] However, the 'experience of the Spirit', unless developed theologically, is a very vague hard core for Pentecostal hermeneutics. For example, within the Pentecostal experience of the Spirit what positive heuristic does it provide for the Pentecostal research programme or what novel facts does this hard core predict? Oliverio provides few clues here. Moreover, there is no explication regarding what the main Pentecostal auxiliary hypotheses might be surrounding the hard core of pneumatic experience.

---

207. I will not focus on the accuracy of the historical analysis or the four types of Pentecostal hermeneutics identified by Oliverio.
208. Ibid., 356.

Of course, it is impossible for Oliverio to do everything in a relatively short work on Pentecostal hermeneutics. Nevertheless, it is somewhat surprising that he does not articulate what he sees as the central tenets of the Pentecostal theological paradigm, not least as Murphy, who Oliverio engages with in detail, makes it clear that to develop a genuine 'Lakatosian Theology' one needs to combine both method *and* content.[209] Furthermore, in light of Oliverio's astute historical analysis of classical Pentecostalism, he interacts with plenty of Pentecostal material which could have been utilized in providing the content for a Pentecostal paradigm. In fact, it seems ironic that despite most of Oliverio's project being historical in nature with respect to the four types of Pentecostal hermeneutics, his own Pentecostal hermeneutical realism is not more explicitly shaped by Pentecostal traditions and their histories. For example, could the Original Classical Pentecostal Hermeneutic provide the hard inner core for his advocated Pentecostal hermeneutical realism? The lack of articulation on this matter means that the potential of Oliverio's Pentecostal hermeneutics in its current form remains largely unrealized.

Now of course it is possible that even if Oliverio would have had the space and time to develop a Pentecostal paradigm along Lakatosian lines, he may have decided not to do so due to his desire to distinguish Pentecostal theology from the natural/social sciences, and develop a Pentecostal hermeneutic more reflective of Taylor's phenomenological approach. However, if this is the case, the same critique would still apply as Oliverio's work would then have to identify the Pentecostal 'moral frameworks' and the 'hypergoods' that are central to a Pentecostal 'social imaginary', according to Taylor.[210] So whether one follows the approach of Lakatos or Taylor, there seems to be no escape from developing the core content of a Pentecostal paradigm in order to be able to truly engage in Contextual-Pentecostal hermeneutics.[211]

Second, because Oliverio has not (yet) articulated what constitutes a Pentecostal paradigm, SRP or 'social imaginary', it is not possible to actually evaluate whether Oliverio's Pentecostal hermeneutical realism is epistemologically speaking fit for purpose. In other words, is it coherent within itself as a hermeneutical paradigm in light of its own Pentecostal tradition (however that may be conceived)? And is it progressive or degenerative vis-à-vis competing theological and anti-theological hermeneutical paradigms?[212] These questions cannot be answered without identification of what makes the Pentecostal paradigm.

---

209. Murphy, *Theology in the Age of Scientific Reasoning*, 183.

210. See Deane-Peter Baker, *Tayloring Reformed Epistemology: Charles Taylor, Alvin Plantinga and the de jure challenge to Christian belief* (London: SCM, 2007), 105–24.

211. Articulating a Pentecostal worldview is seen as an important precursor for Smith and Kuosmanen as they develop their contextual Pentecostal epistemologies; Smith, *Thinking in Tongues*, 17–47; Kuosmanen, 'Towards Pentecostal Epistemology', 20–46.

212. For example, Herman Philipse has criticized theistic paradigms for lack of predictive power; Herman Philipse, *God in the Age of Science? A Critique of Religious Reason* (Oxford: Oxford University Press, 2014), 140–60.

In conclusion, there is much to commend in Oliverio's Pentecostal hermeneutics, not least the historical explication of Pentecostal hermeneutics through four main ideal types. However, although at first it seems that Oliverio follows his historical typologies by providing a historically informed and tradition specific Pentecostal hermeneutics, he does not actually achieve this, or at best does so only in a sketch form. Therefore, a truly historical and tradition-specific Pentecostal philosophical hermeneutics is still to be articulated.

1.4 Conclusion

In this chapter I have outlined three major Pentecostal theological rationalities, epistemologies and/or hermeneutics. At the outset, it needs to be acknowledged that the contributions of Yong, Smith and Oliverio in the search for a Pentecostal rationality have been seminal for Pentecostal studies. To use Oliverio's categories, all three theological methodologies can be, broadly speaking, located within the camp of 'Contextual-Pentecostal Hermeneutics'. That said, Yong and Smith seem to represent the two sides within this category and Oliverio can be seen to hold a mediating position between the two. In other words, Yong is effectively a *pneumatological correlationist* in his epistemological approach with a firm grounding in the Pentecostal tradition and pneumatological theology; Smith is a type of *Pentecostal postliberal* with an affinity to Pentecostal spirituality and practices; and Oliverio is a *hermeneutical realist* informed by classical Pentecostal history.

In my evaluation of these three positions, I have noted that Yong's rationality would merit further exploration regarding the extent to which it accurately reflects any given Pentecostal tradition. Smith's approach seems to suffer from not fully appreciating Pentecostal theology, as well as being ahistorical, which appears to undermine the 'Pentecostal' aspects of his Pentecostal epistemology. In terms of tradition-specific and historically informed Pentecostal rationality, Oliverio's approach is the most promising. But unfortunately he does not fully develop his own Pentecostal theological hermeneutics along the lines of his proposed methodology.

In light of the analysis above, my aim is to develop a historical and tradition-specific Pentecostal rationality (see Part Two). However, although many of the building blocks for doing so are already provided by Oliverio – particularly those gleaned from Kuhn, Lakatos, Taylor and Murphy – it appears that Alasdair MacIntyre provides further methodological insights about how to do this in a philosophically mature way.

Chapter 2

ON METHOD: MACINTYRE, TRADITION AND RATIONALITY

Despite the important epistemological contributions of Amos Yong, James K. A. Smith and L. William Oliverio Jr., the main weakness of these three proposals seems to be their ahistoricism (Oliverio more in practice than in theory), which means that they are in danger of not fully representing any particular Pentecostal tradition and its implicit epistemology. It is in the light of this that the philosophical work of Alasdair MacIntyre appears to provide important resources for constructing and developing a truly historically informed, tradition-specific and narrative Pentecostal epistemology. Consequently, the purpose of this chapter is to explore the philosophical methodology of MacIntyre which will then be employed in the next section for constructing a Pentecostal rationality.

The chapter will first explore MacIntyre's concept of tradition-dependent rationality. Second, it will seek to demonstrate that contrary to some common objections, MacIntyre's methodology does not lead to relativism or fideism, but through his notions of truth and dialectical justification a progressive quest for genuine knowledge is possible. Finally, it will conclude by discussing the potential benefits and implications of adopting MacIntyre's methodology in constructing a Pentecostal rationality.

2.1 MacIntyre's tradition-dependent rationality

According to Stanley Hauerwas, 'few dispute that Alasdair MacIntyre is one of the most important philosophers of our time.'[1] MacIntyre's academic oeuvre is indeed impressive as it covers a multitude of topics in an interdisciplinary manner over a number of decades.[2] Despite MacIntyre's many interests, his primary work has

---

1. Stanley Hauerwas, 'The Virtues of Alasdair MacIntyre', *First Things*, October 2007, accessed 20 January 2017, https://www.firstthings.com/article/2007/10/the-virtues-of-alasdair-macintyre

2. For summaries of MacIntyre and his work, see Kelvin Knight, 'Introduction', in *The MacIntyre Reader*, ed. Kelvin Knight (Cambridge: Polity Press, 1998), 1–27; Hauerwas, 'The Virtues of Alasdair MacIntyre'; Christopher Stephen Lutz, *Tradition in the Ethics of Alasdair MacIntyre: Relativism, Thomism, and Philosophy* (Plymouth: Lexington Books, 2009), 7–32;

been on moral and political philosophy. He has been an ardent critic of modernity and his concepts of tradition and rationality have been widely debated. For the purposes of this chapter, I will simply focus on MacIntyre's notion of tradition-dependent rationality, since this provides the methodological tools for my later construction of a Pentecostal rationality.

2.1.1 Formal and substantive rationality

Ironically, MacIntyre's concept of rationality has been criticized on the basis that it leads to relativism because of its inherent historicism[3] and on the basis that it is not '*sufficiently* relativistic or historicist' due to its dialectical nature.[4] These seemingly conflicting criticisms highlight two important aspects within MacIntyre's concept of rationality, or what David Trenery refers to as his 'hybrid position' regarding Enlightenment rationality.[5]

Generally speaking, MacIntyre views rationality as the criterion used for judging 'truth and falsity'.[6] However, within this basic view he understands there to be two kinds of rationality or first principles. First, there is *formal rationality* which includes the basic laws of logic (e.g. the law of non-contradiction),[7] and in his own words these first principles 'are evident to all rational persons [and] do indeed provide standards and direction from the outset'.[8] These aspects of rationality are seen to be universal and accessible to all (rational) people due to our 'common humanity'.[9] It is this universal aspect of rationality that MacIntyre shares with the so-called Enlightenment thinkers, as well as many modernistic epistemologies.[10]

Nevertheless, although MacIntyre believes that formal rationality and the laws of logic are 'necessary' conditions of rationality, he does not believe that they are 'sufficient' conditions.[11] In other words, formal rationality provides the

---

David Trenery, *Alasdair MacIntyre, George Lindbeck, and the Nature of Tradition* (Eugene, OR: Pickwick Publications, 2014), 4–139.

3. Neil Ormerod, 'Faith and Reason: Perspectives from MacIntyre and Lonergan', *HeyJ* 46 (2005): 11.

4. John Milbank, *Theology and Social Theory: Beyond Secular Reason*, 2nd edn (Oxford: Blackwell Publishing, 2006), 328–9.

5. Trenery, *Alasdair MacIntyre*, 129.

6. Lutz, *Tradition in the Ethics of Alasdair MacIntyre*, 9.

7. Ibid.

8. Alasdair MacIntyre, 'First Principles, Final Ends, and Contemporary Philosophical Issues', in *The Tasks of Philosophy: Selected Essays, Volume 1*, ed. Alasdair MacIntyre (Cambridge: Cambridge University Press, 2007), 160.

9. Alasdair MacIntyre, 'Philosophy Recalled to Its Task: A Thomistic Reading of *Fides et Ratio*', in *The Tasks of Philosophy*, 194.

10. Trenery, *Alasdair MacIntyre*, 129.

11. Alasdair MacIntyre, *Whose Justice? Which Rationality?* (London: Gerald Duckworth, 1988), 4.

grounding for human reasoning, but on its own, it does not enable us to make any meaningful judgments about truth and falsity. What is needed for making genuine epistemic judgments is not just formal rationality but *'substantive rationality',* which 'includes all those determinations and judgments about good reasons and acceptable evidence, that arise through tradition and convention'.[12] A major difference between this second kind of rationality, vis-à-vis the first kind, is that it is 'self-evident only to those educated to understand its principles';[13] that is, it only makes sense to those who have been appropriately 'traditioned' within this particular form of reasoning. Moreover, MacIntyre notes that 'argument to [these second kind of] first principles cannot be demonstrative, for demonstration is *from* [these] first principles'.[14] It is this second aspect of rationality that distances MacIntyre from the Enlightenment ideals of universal justification and common rational criteria, and also what makes his concept of rationality tradition-dependent and tradition-constituted.

In fact, much of MacIntyre's work has been an argument for substantive rationality and an attempt to recover 'a conception of rational enquiry as embodied in a tradition'.[15] In his so-called mature philosophical work, he has tried to (re)establish that substantive rationalities are tradition-dependent, implying that rational enquiry is 'inseparable from the intellectual and social tradition in which it is embodied'.[16] He states that 'there is no standing ground, no place of enquiry, no way to engage in the practices of advancing, evaluating, accepting, and rejecting reasoned argument apart from that which is provided by some particular tradition or other'.[17] Thus, argues MacIntyre, there are no 'traditionless' arguments or (substantive) rationalities, and those that claim such neutral status can be shown to be rooted in a specific tradition within a certain historical context.[18] Following from this, MacIntyre maintains that the Enlightenment project in its current form is bound to fail since it is based on the 'fiction' that there can be a neutral, traditionless and universal substantive rationality.[19]

---

12. Lutz, *Tradition in the Ethics of Alasdair MacIntyre*, 9.
13. Ibid., 129.
14. MacIntyre, 'First Principles', 161.
15. MacIntyre, *Whose Justice?*, 7.
16. Ibid., 8.
17. Ibid., 350.
18. For example, see MacIntyre's analysis of liberal rationality within the liberal tradition; ibid., 326–48.
19. Alasdair MacIntyre, *Three Rival Versions of Moral Enquiry: Encyclopaedia, Genealogy, and Tradition* (London: Gerald Duckworth, 1990), 117; see also John Horton and Susan Mendus, 'Alasdair MacIntyre: *After Virtue and After*', in *After MacIntyre: Critical Perspectives on the Work of Alasdair MacIntyre*, ed. John Horton and Susan Mendus (Cambridge: Polity Press, 1994), 3; Murphy, 'MacIntyre, Tradition-Dependent Rationality and the End of Philosophy of Religion', 35. For an 'Enlightenment' critique of MacIntyre's diagnosis, see Robert Wokler, 'Projecting the Enlightenment', in *After MacIntyre*, 108–26.

2.1.2 Tradition-constitutive and tradition-constituted rationality

If then substantive rationality is tradition-dependent, what does MacIntyre mean by tradition and how is rationality tradition-constituted? According to MacIntyre, a tradition is a 'historically extended, socially embodied argument, and an argument precisely in part about the goods which constitute that tradition'.[20] Or as he puts it elsewhere,

> A tradition is an argument extended through time in which certain fundamental agreements are defined and redefined in terms of two kinds of conflict: those with critics and enemies external to the tradition who reject all or at least key parts of those fundamental agreements, and those internal, interpretive debates through which the meaning and rationale of the fundamental agreements come to be expressed and by whose progress a tradition is constituted.[21]

In light of these two definitions by MacIntyre, a tradition can be seen to have at least four significant features. First, a tradition is an argument, and as an argument it is by its very nature *about something*; that is, it has an object of enquiry which it makes claims about. A tradition is, therefore, a quest and an argument towards a certain *telos*, and the 'goods which constitute that tradition' are geared towards reaching this goal.[22]

Second, a tradition is not just an argument about something, but also an argument *by someone*. For MacIntyre, however, it is not just an argument by individuals, but by a community of people interested in and committed to the common object of enquiry. And since the argument is carried out by a group of people over time, it inevitably becomes 'socially embodied' and 'historically extended'. Moreover, for the argument to be successful and sustained, it needs to be supported by appropriate institutions created by the community.[23] Consequently, a tradition cannot be understood apart from the community of 'arguers', including their history, social embodiment and institutions.

Third, the argument is *with someone*. This could be either those external to the tradition, who nevertheless make claims about the same goal of inquiry or it could be with those internal to the tradition. Either way, to truly appreciate the nature of the argument one should be aware of the interlocutors and the tradition's response to them.[24]

---

20. Alasdair MacIntyre, *After Virtue*, 3rd edn (Notre Dame, IN: University of Notre Dame Press, 2012), 222.
21. MacIntyre, *Whose Justice?*, 12.
22. MacIntyre, *After Virtue*, 219.
23. Ibid., 194.
24. In the context constructing an appropriate philosophical curriculum for universities, MacIntyre writes: 'we have to give due recognition to the conflicts of the past within and between cultures ... Texts have to be read *against* one another if we are not to misread them'; MacIntyre, *Three Rival Versions*, 229.

Fourth, the argument of the past and present community is shaped not just by its subject matter and its dialogue partners but also by *how* it is being carried out. Indeed the 'how' is the community's method of argumentation and therefore effectively its rationality. However, as has already been noted, for MacIntyre the rationality of the tradition is not some universal or general rationality applicable to all traditions throughout all ages. Rather, the rationality of the community is tradition-specific. So, what exactly then makes the rationality tradition-specific and tradition-constituted?

According to MacIntyre, rationality is fundamentally a *practice* of the community.[25] As a practice, it is characterized by its 'intentions',[26] which if they are 'internally good' are oriented to achieve the *telos* of the tradition's inquiry.[27] So in an Aristotelian manner the order of things (ontology) is allowed to determine how things are known (epistemology),[28] and therefore the rationality of the tradition will be significantly influenced by how the community perceives the nature of its *telos*. Furthermore, rationality as a practice is also informed by its 'setting'[29] – that is, by the history and context of the community of practitioners, as well as by their interaction with the interlocutors, which means that the rationality will always be socially and historically conditioned. And finally, rationality as a practice is shaped by a 'narrative', which is the community's attempt to make its practice of reasoning intelligible by locating it in its historical context with an understanding of the origins (*protos*) and the goal (*telos*) of the argument. The practice of reasoning will only make sense within a narrative framework in which the community identifies how the argument has gone thus far, including telling stories of the successes and failures of the argument to date.[30] In sum, rationality is 'a practice emerging from a history, or rather as an enacted form of a narrative interpretation of the events of a history';[31] therefore, rationality is tradition-constituted.

However, although rationality in MacIntyrian lines is 'tradition-constituted', it is also 'tradition-constitutive'.[32] In other words, the practice of reasoning is not only shaped by the tradition but also itself shapes the tradition by clarifying the nature and goal of the enquiry, helping to construct appropriate institutions to uphold

---

25. Lutz, *Tradition in the Ethics of Alasdair MacIntyre*, 46.
26. MacIntyre, *After Virtue*, 206.
27. MacIntyre distinguishes between 'internal goods' and 'external goods'. The first are goods internal to a particular practice, whereas the latter are good external to it. For example, in the practice of playing football, one's intentions may be driven by the internal goods of a game of football, such as helping one's team to win through skill, fitness and determination; or one's intentions may be driven by external goods, such as becoming famous or rich through football; ibid., 188.
28. Aristotle, *Nicomachean Ethics*; MacIntyre, *Three Rival Versions*, 69.
29. MacIntyre, *After Virtue*, 206.
30. Ibid., 208–16.
31. Lutz, *Tradition in the Ethics of Alasdair MacIntyre*, 46.
32. MacIntyre, *Whose Justice?*, 10.

the argument of the community, and to modify and sharpen the community's argument in relation to internal and external critics.

2.1.3 The development of traditions

Thus far I have suggested that MacIntyre sees traditions as 'arguments extended through time' which are teleologically driven, socially embodied and contextually located, with a particular form of rationality specific to the tradition. In light of the above, I will now try to show through examples from MacIntyre's own work how traditions as arguments may be formed, developed and even possibly defeated.

In *Three Rival Versions of Moral Enquiry: Encyclopaedia, Genealogy and Tradition* (1990), MacIntyre identifies what he sees as three dominant, and to some extent archetypal, intellectual traditions emerging in the late-nineteenth-century Western philosophical and moral discourse.[33] The first one is the Enlightenment tradition (read: *Encyclopaedia*), which MacIntyre equates with Adam Gifford's supposedly neutral, unitary and ahistorical approach to rationality embodied in the ninth edition of the *Encyclopaedia Britannica*.[34] The second is Nietzsche's genealogist approach (read: *Genealogy*), which sees both rationality and truth as relative to a particular context, and in doing so maintains that 'there are no rules of rationality as such to be appealed to, there are rather strategies of insight and strategies of subversion.'[35] The third, and MacIntyre's preferred approach is traditionalism seen in the Thomism of Pope Leo XIII (read: *Tradition*), which, on the one hand, agrees with the genealogist in rejecting the ahistorical rationality of the encyclopaedist but, on the other hand, attempts to transcend the relativism of the genealogist.[36] I will now use these three 'traditions' as examples of how traditions may emerge and evolve over time.

MacIntyre sees intellectual traditions developing in three stages.[37] During the first stage, a community is formed around a common object of enquiry, and authority is bestowed by this community on specific people, texts and/or doctrines with respect to the object of enquiry. For example, the three rival moral traditions identified above roughly speaking share the same object of enquiry (i.e. morality), but they differ because of their alternative authority figures, foundational beliefs and grounding texts, which influence the nature of their quest for morality. So it could be said that the 'Encyclopaedist Tradition' affirms people like Gifford as its intellectual champions; it adopts the Enlightenment concepts of universal reason, autonomy and progress as its foundational 'doctrines'; and it sees the ninth edition of the *Encyclopaedia Britannica* as its canonical text. Within the 'Genealogist

---

33. In *After Virtue* and *Whose Justice? Which Rationality?* MacIntyre also explores various moral traditions from antiquity to the present day.
34. MacIntyre, *Three Rival Versions*, 18.
35. Ibid., 42.
36. Ibid., 59–60.
37. MacIntyre, *Whose Justice?*, 354–5.

Tradition', on the other hand, Nietzsche emerges as the enlightened ethicist; the close coupling of social conditioning and human beliefs becomes the controlling maxim; and Nietzsche's *Genealogy of Morals* is identified as the grounding work. For the 'Thomists Tradition' then, Aquinas is viewed as the *Doctor Angelicus*; Thomism as the appropriate philosophical framework; and *Summa* and *Aeterni Patris* as the foundational documents.[38]

At the second stage, inadequacies and incoherencies are identified within the authoritative sources of the community, which can be fuelled by internal debates within, or external critique from outside the community. This second stage can also be seen as an 'epistemological crisis' within the emerging tradition.[39] Thus, for the encyclopaedist the epistemological crisis might be caused by the seeming failure to actually establish the nature of universal rationality, exposing a weakness in a central belief of the tradition. The genealogist might find it difficult to explain and evaluate his or her own project without falling into a 'nongenealogical, academic mode';[40] and the Thomist might find their Aristotelian metaphysics challenged by current scientific discoveries.

The third stage provides a potential remedy for the epistemological crisis encountered during the second stage, resulting in reformulations and reinterpretations of the tradition's authoritative sources and central beliefs. This means that when it comes to the intellectual challenges faced by the encyclopaedist, genealogist or the Thomist, the central question is to what extent they can reinterpret the foundational sources and grounding beliefs of their particular tradition in order to overcome their current incongruities. According to MacIntyre, the degree to which the inadequacies can be resolved depends on the resources available within the community's tradition and upon the community's inventiveness. For the tradition to continue after the reformulation, 'some core of shared belief, constitutive of allegiance to the tradition, has to survive',[41] because without some continuity the tradition bears no resemblance to its authoritative origins and thus has been transformed altogether into something else. As living traditions evolve and develop stages two and three are regularly revisited, and it is this continual process that makes an intellectual tradition effectively 'an argument extended through time'.[42]

MacIntyre's concept of rationality embodied within a tradition and tradition being formed over a narrative history means that any 'tradition-constituted and tradition constitutive rational enquiry cannot be elucidated apart from its

---

38. For MacIntyre's reflection on the importance of the foundational documents for the three traditions, see MacIntyre, *Three Rival Versions*, 19, 25.
39. See Alasdair MacIntyre, 'Epistemological Crises, Dramatic Narrative, and the Philosophy of Science', 3–23.
40. MacIntyre, *Three Rival Versions*, 53.
41. MacIntyre, *Whose Justice?*, 356.
42. Ibid., 12.

exemplifications.'[43] This means that to identify rationality, and rational justification, within a tradition cannot be done apart from a narrative enquiry into the tradition's history, which is characterized by its origins (stage one), internal/external debates (stage two) and remedies (stage three).[44] In fact, MacIntyre's so-called trilogy of *After Virtue, Whose Justice? Which Rationality?* and *Three Rival Versions of Moral Enquiry* has tried to provide this historical exemplification with the aim of demonstrating the superiority of Aristotelian and Thomist moral philosophy.[45]

It must be noted that this kind of 'historicism' leads to a fine tension in MacIntyre's work, as pointed out by Terry Pinkhard, which MacIntyre shares with both Hegel and Wittgenstein – that is, 'the double awareness of the historical and social *contingency* of all our points of view and the necessity to provide *justifications* of those points of view'.[46] Indeed some, like Robert George, have suggested that MacIntyre fails to adequately balance this tension and his emphasis on historical particularism results in a form of philosophical relativism.[47] However, as will be argued below this conclusion is unwarranted as MacIntyre seems to escape relativism, despite his particularism.

2.2 Truth and dialectical justification

It has been described thus far that all rationalities are seen by MacIntyre as tradition-dependent and historically specific. However, as will be argued below this particularism should not be seen as relativism because of MacIntyre's concepts of truth and dialectical justification.

2.2.1 Truth

MacIntyre is clear that truth should not be equated 'with what is rationally justified in terms of the scheme of each particular standpoint',[48] and thus he cannot be seen as merely advocating pragmatic or coherence theories of truth. Rather, truth is

---

43. Ibid., 10.

44. Gordon Graham rightly notes that 'the belief that philosophical questions require historical illumination runs through all of MacIntyre's writings'; Gordon Graham, 'MacIntyre's Fusion of History and Philosophy', in *After MacIntyre*, 163.

45. Whether MacIntyre has been successful in demonstrating this is not the focus of the chapter.

46. Terry Pinkard, 'MacIntyre's Critique of Modernity', in *Alasdair MacIntyre*, ed. Mark Murphy (Cambridge: Cambridge University Press, 2003), 196.

47. For example Robert P. George, 'Moral Particularism, Thomism, and Traditions', *RM* 42, no. 3 (March 1989): 599; cf. John Haldane, 'MacIntyre's Thomist Revival: What Next?', in *After MacIntyre*, 97; Ormerod, 'Faith and Reason', 11.

48. Alasdair MacIntyre, 'Moral Relativism, Truth and Justification', in *The Task of Philosophy*, 56.

understood by him as being closely connected to the object of inquiry within a specific tradition. In other words, since traditions are by nature about something, their adequacy is defined by their accuracy vis-à-vis their object of enquiry.[49] This means that a tradition, and its concomitant rationality, may, in fact, be flawed because they inaccurately reflect their object of enquiry, or to put it more starkly, do not appropriately 'correspondent' with 'truth'. MacIntyre notes that 'the most primitive conception of truth is of the manifestness of the objects which present themselves to mind; and it is when mind fails to re-present that manifestness that falsity, the inadequacy of mind to its objects, appears'.[50]

This does not imply that MacIntyre is favouring a simplistic correspondence theory of truth, or what he calls 'truth as correspondence-to-fact',[51] but truth and truthful enquiry, nevertheless, are seen as the mind adequately corresponding to its object (*adaequatio intellectus ad rem*).[52] Following from this, like Aristotle and Aquinas, MacIntyre believes 'truth to be the *telos* of rational enquiry; and rational enquiry so conceived must involve progress toward that *telos* through the replacement of less adequate by more adequate forms of rational justification'.[53]

MacIntyre's position regarding truth can thus be seen as a form of critical realism;[54] that is, his concept of tradition-dependent rationality commits him to believe that our conceptualization and categorization of the world and objects of enquiry are inevitably shaped by our traditions, but these conceptualization and categorizations are only truthful to the extent to which they reflect the reality of the world and the objects of enquiry. In light of this, MacIntyre rejects the common anti-realist criticism of realist positions which assume that to claim 'that there are realities that exist independently of and prior to any apprehension of them … [is tantamount to] claiming to be able to conceive of things as they are apart from our conceiving of them'.[55] MacIntyre's response to such anti-realist objection is to argue that although the objects of enquiry cannot be conceived 'apart from our conceiving of them', this does not mean that there is no mind-independent reality. The reason being that our conceptual schemes can still reflect appropriately

---

49. Jean Porter, 'Tradition in the Recent Work of Alasdair MacIntyre', in *Alasdair MacIntyre*, 52; Lutz, *Tradition in the Ethics of Alasdair MacIntyre*, 9.

50. MacIntyre, *Whose Justice?*, 357; cf. MacIntyre, 'First Principles', 165.

51. MacIntyre argues that discrediting 'truth as correspondence-to-fact should not be allowed to discredit any conception of truth as correspondence.' He goes on to state that 'it is individuals and their properties and relations, not facts or states of affairs, that make asserted sentences true or false'; Alasdair MacIntyre, 'Truth as a good: a reflection on *Fides et Ratio*', in *The Task of Philosophy*, 200, 203.

52. MacIntyre, *Whose Justice?*, 356; cf. P. Mark Achtemeier, 'The Truth of Tradition: Critical Realism in the Thought of Alasdair MacIntyre and T. F. Torrance', *SJT* 47, no. 3 (August 1994): 364.

53. MacIntyre, 'Moral Relativism', 68–9.

54. See Trenery, *Alasdair MacIntyre*, 175.

55. MacIntyre, 'Philosophy Recalled to Its Tasks', 189.

or inappropriately the objects of enquiry, and it is possible to move from a less adequate to a more adequate concept of this object. Indeed,

> it is precisely in moving from less adequate to more adequate categorical and conceptual schemes and judgments that we recognize that the realities which we formerly categorized and conceptualized in one way, and now recategorize and reconceptualize in another are the same realities, and that they exist and have the characteristics that warrant or fail to warrant our categories and our conceptualizations independently of those categories and conceptualizations. We need therefore to be able and we do have the ability to identify and to reidentify objects independently of those categorizations and conceptualizations, whether mistaken or accurate.[56]

All of this suggests that not all conceptual schemes, traditions and rationalities are equally valid with respect to truth (read: the objects and *telos* of rational enquiry), and some can even cease to be living options altogether for simply not reflecting truth sufficiently.[57] This, however, does raise the question of how traditions in practice can then progress towards 'truth', or indeed be found wanting and even defeated in the process?

2.2.2 Dialectical justification

As has been described above, traditions develop over time through encountering incoherencies (stage two) and by providing remedies to them (stage three). This second stage can also be seen as an 'epistemological crisis' within a tradition,[58] and it is a constant threat to all progressive traditions because they are dealing with 'reality', which may or may not be adequately reflected by the tradition. When a tradition does find itself in an 'epistemological crisis', the solution (stage three) requires, according to MacIntyre, 'the invention or discovery of new concepts and the framing of some new types of theory' that have three characteristics.[59] First, the new reformulation 'must furnish a solution to the problems which had previously proved intractable in a systematic and coherent way'.[60] Second, it must be able to explain what had made the tradition before this modification susceptible to the epistemological crisis. Third, 'these first two tasks must be carried out in

---

56. Ibid., 190.

57. MacIntyre advocates fallibilism regarding traditions; see MacIntyre, 'Epistemological Crises', 22.

58. Ibid., 3–23.

59. MacIntyre, *Whose Justice?*, 362. Christian Early makes a stark contrast between the resolution for an 'epistemological crisis' and 'stage three' of tradition development. This distinction, however, does not seem to be found in MacIntyre; Christian Early, 'MacIntyre, Narrative Rationality and Faith', *NB* 82, no. 959 (January 2001): 39–40.

60. MacIntyre, *Whose Justice?*, 362.

a way which exhibits some fundamental continuity of the new conceptual and theoretical structures with the shared beliefs in terms of which the tradition of enquiry has been defined up to this point.'[61]

However, it is not guaranteed that a tradition will survive its 'epistemological crisis'. In fact, there seem to be two ways by which it can be defeated. First, 'the lack of resolution itself defeats the tradition,' as the inconsistency by its own standards makes the tradition incoherent and non-progressive.[62] It is worth underscoring here that, although MacIntyre believes that all rationalities are tradition-dependent, he maintains that the 'laws of logic' are universal (i.e. formal rationality) and hence should be followed by all sufficient rationalities.[63] It is this commitment to logic that grounds MacIntyre's rejection of incoherent traditions, and which opens the possibility for a tradition to be defeated by its own inconsistency.

The second way in which a tradition can be defeated is that during the 'epistemological crisis' a competing tradition is discovered that is able to meet, unlike one's own tradition, the first two requirements of the solution to the crisis, namely resolve the crisis and show why the crisis emerged (see above). In this kind of a scenario, those inhabiting the tradition in crisis should acknowledge 'that the alien tradition is superior in rationality and in respect of its claims to truth to their own'.[64] As highlighted by MacIntyre, the relationship between the two competing traditions in a situation like this is asymmetrical in that the superior tradition is able to do something that the defeated tradition fails to do, namely, resolve the crisis and explain why it arose in the first place.[65] Therefore, in a situation like this, a reasonable enquirer of truth ought to, at least in theory, align themselves with the more progressive tradition.

Now, of course, for one to be able to perceive how an 'alien tradition' is able to solve the epistemological crisis, this alien tradition needs to be understood by the adherents of the tradition in crisis, and consequently there needs to be an element of commensurability between the competing traditions. Aware of the need for commensurability, MacIntyre believes that competing traditions do in fact share some common features, that is, logic and similar, if not the same, object of enquiry. Indeed, apart from some similarities and shared aspects between traditions, there would be no possibility for disagreement in the first place.[66] Moreover, MacIntyre maintains that people can embody more than one tradition, just like they can

---

61. Ibid.
62. Ibid., 365. MacIntyre appears to follow a coherence/pragmatic theory of epistemic justification here.
63. Ibid., 4.
64. Ibid., 364–5.
65. MacIntyre, 'Moral Relativism', 73; Charles Taylor has also underscored this asymmetrical relationship between superior and inferior traditions; Charles Taylor, 'Explanation and Practical Reason', in *Philosophical Arguments*, ed. Charles Taylor (Cambridge, MA: Harvard University Press, 1997), 34–60.
66. MacIntyre, *Whose Justice?*, 351.

speak more than one language fluently, and therefore they can be bilingual or multilingual with respect to traditions.[67] That said, for anyone to move beyond their dominant tradition and embrace the resources of an alien tradition in a meaningful way, albeit a 'second first language', does require 'a rare gift of empathy' and 'intellectual insight'.[68]

In summary, MacIntyre's tradition-dependent rationality should not be seen as an escape into relativism or fideism as any tradition and rationality engages with 'truth' and is thus faced with the possibility of falling 'into a state of epistemological crisis'.[69] In fact, the test for truth in the present, according to MacIntyre, 'is always to summon up as many questions and as many objections of the greatest strength possible; what can be justifiably claimed as truth is what has sufficiently withstood such dialectical questioning and framing of objections'.[70] Hence, justification for one's tradition is essentially the 'best account so far' regarding the object of enquiry. This 'best account' is dialectical in nature and takes the form of 'intelligible narrative history'.[71]

The influences of the philosophers of science such as Karl Popper, Thomas Kuhn and Imre Lakatos are evident in MacIntyre's concept of dialectical justification.[72] MacIntyre's notion of 'epistemological crises and dramatic narrative' is particularly informed by Imre Lakatos's notion of SRPs.[73] Nevertheless, despite engaging with Lakatos's idea of SRPs, MacIntyre does not fully utilize Lakatos's insights regarding the 'hard core' and 'auxiliary hypotheses' of SRPs, and this causes some ambiguity in his methodology with respect to the essential and more peripheral beliefs of a tradition. Indeed, David Trenery has argued that this is a notable weakness in MacIntyre's methodology and has sought to ameliorate this with George Lindbeck's postliberalism.[74] Although I share Trenery's criticism of MacIntyre here, rather than borrowing from Lindbeck's cultural-linguistic framework, in Part Two of the book I will employ Lakatos's concepts of 'hard core' and 'auxiliary hypotheses' of an SRP to help clarify the real essence of an intellectual tradition from its surrounding tenets. In doing this I will effectively follow in the methodological footsteps of Nancey Murphy and L. William Oliverio Jr., who have both referred to Lakatos in identifying the essential and peripheral beliefs of a theological tradition as discussed in Chapter 1 (see Section 1.3). In summary, although I maintain that MacIntyre's notions of tradition and rationality are conducive for constructing a Pentecostal rationality, I also believe that Lakatos's reflections on the essence

---

67. Ibid., 364.
68. Ibid., 167.
69. Ibid., 364.
70. Ibid., 358.
71. MacIntyre, 'Epistemological Crises', 22; cf. MacIntyre, *Whose Justice?*, 360.
72. See MacIntyre, 'Epistemological Crises', 15–23.
73. See Lakatos, *The Methodology of Scientific Research Programmes*. See also section 1.3.
74. Trenery, *Alasdair MacIntyre*, 181–9.

and periphery of SRPs provide further resources for articulating more precisely a Pentecostal intellectual tradition.

2.3 Implications for Pentecostal rationality and epistemology

So what are the benefits of utilizing MacIntyre's ideas of tradition-dependent rationality, truth and dialectical justification for constructing a Pentecostal rationality and epistemology? At least five helpful aspects can be identified.

First, Pentecostal theologians in search of a Pentecostal epistemology have been quick to point out the incompatibility of modernistic epistemologies, adopted by much of conservative Evangelical theology, with Pentecostalism (e.g. see Yong, Smith and Oliverio in Chapter 1).[75] However, the postmodern alternatives are themselves not without problematic features (although see Smith in Section 1.2).[76] It is here that MacIntyre offers a way forward by providing a clear alternative to modernistic epistemologies, without falling into what many Pentecostals fear about postmodern (de)constructions, namely relativism. For example, Richard Davis and Paul Franks have argued against narrative Pentecostal epistemologies due to a fear of what they call '*story*-ism: favouring one's own story over others without legitimate reason or justification'.[77] However, as I have tried to demonstrate above, although MacIntyre's approach is narrative in nature, his concept of dialectical justification means that his '*story*-ism' does not suffer from 'favouring one's own story' without having adequate reasons. Hence, it seems that MacIntyre's approach has great potential for articulating a rationality of a movement which has been identified as 'paramodern';[78] that is, neither positivistically modern nor postmodern.[79]

Second, following from MacIntyre's 'hybrid position' regarding modernity and postmodernity, his (critical) realist concept of truth makes him compatible with the basic Pentecostal intuition regarding truth and realism (e.g. see my critique of Smith in Section 1.2.4 and see Chapter 7). Moreover, MacIntyre's Aristotelian and Thomistic idea of truth is teleologically driven, which again seems to fit well with the eschatological emphasis of Pentecostals; that is, the assumption that ultimate reality will be fully revealed in the eschaton to come.

---

75. Lewis, 'Towards a Pentecostal Epistemology', 122; Archer, *The Gospel Revisited*, 7.

76. Kärkkäinen, 'Epistemology, Ethos and Environment', 249–50; Menzies, 'Jumping Off the Postmodern Bandwagon', 116.

77. Davis and Franks, 'Against a Postmodern Pentecostal Epistemology', 395.

78. Kenneth J. Archer, *A Pentecostal Hermeneutic for the Twenty-First Century* (London: T&T Clark, 2004), 33.

79. MacIntyre's distinction of formal and substantive rationality has similarities to Yong's pneumatological correlationism by displaying universal and contextual dimensions vis-à-vis reasoning.

Third, Walter J. Hollenweger has pointed out that one of the central characteristics of Pentecostalism is its narrative form,[80] and therefore it is reasonable to suggest that a genuine Pentecostal epistemology should also be narrative in nature. As seen in Chapter 1, Smith has argued that the Pentecostal focus on 'testimony points to the irreducibility (and perhaps primacy) of "narrative knowledge."'[81] However, although Smith's emphasis on narrative knowing and epistemology is apposite for Pentecostalism, his own attempt to construct a Pentecostal epistemology seems to fail at delivering a truly narrative epistemology (see Section 1.2.4). It is here that MacIntyre's emphasis on historical narrative and tradition formation will provide a way forward towards the development of a truly narrative Pentecostal rationality.

Fourth, following from this narrative approach, MacIntyre's methodology shares the contextual elements of Yong's, Smith's and Oliverio's epistemologies, but his concept of tradition increasingly invites a Pentecostal community's many witnesses (past and present) to testify to the formation of the Pentecostal narrative, tradition and rationality. This seems to be a genuine 'testimony in the Spirit'[82] since it takes into consideration the many witnesses of any given Pentecostal tradition and allows for the development of a Pentecostal epistemology and rationality that is particular to that tradition.

Fifth, as a cursory reading of the main Pentecostal journals suggests, Pentecostalism in the twenty-first century is increasingly trying to articulate its identity and its key characteristics.[83] It seems that MacIntyre's approach can provide fresh methodological insights into analysing Pentecostal traditions. In fact, MacIntyre astutely points out that 'There characteristically comes a time in the history of tradition-constituted enquiries when those engaged in them may find occasion or need to frame a theory of their own activities of enquiry. What kind of theory is then developed will of course vary from one tradition to another.'[84]

Arguably, this has not yet been sufficiently done for (classical) Pentecostalism and not done at all for British Pentecostalism. The purpose of this volume is not to construct a unified and global Pentecostal tradition, even if that could be done,

---

80. Walter J. Hollenweger, *Pentecostalism: Origins and Developments Worldwide* (Peabody, MA: Hendrickson, 1997), 18–19; cf. Land, *Pentecostal Spirituality*, 74–5.

81. Smith, *Thinking in Tongues*, 64; cf. Archer, *The Gospel Revisited*, 13.

82. See Mark J. Cartledge, *Testimony in the Spirit: Rescripting Ordinary Theology* (Farnham: Ashgate, 2010).

83. For example, see Cheryl Bridges Johns, 'The Adolescence of Pentecostalism: In Search of a Legitimate Sectarian Identity', *Pneuma* 17, no. 1–2 (1995): 3–17; Gary B. McGee, '"More Than Evangelical": The Challenge of Evolving Theological Identity of the Assemblies of God', *Pneuma* 25, no. 2 (2003): 289–300; Allan Anderson, 'When is a Pentecostal Not a Pentecostal? When She's a Charismatic! Responding to Irvin, Lopez Rodriquez and Waldrop', *JPT* 16, no. 1 (2008): 58–63; Kimberly Ervin Alexander, 'Standing at the Crossroad: The Battle for the Heart and Soul of Pentecostalism', *Pneuma* 33, no. 3 (2011): 331–49.

84. MacIntyre, *Whose Justice?*, 359.

but to focus on a particular British Pentecostal movement, namely on the Elim Pentecostal Church. The benefits of focusing on a particular tradition is that it pays due respect to the 'glocal' nature of Pentecostalism[85] and thus to the uniqueness of different Pentecostal traditions, despite their common family resemblances. That said, since Elim is one of the oldest and largest Pentecostal denominations in Europe, it can be seen as a representative example of European Pentecostalism generally, and therefore narrating its tradition and rationality can also be seen as making a broader contribution to understanding global Pentecostalism.

As a final methodological reflection, it should be noted that MacIntyre's approach is similar to the historical methodologies employed by Pentecostal scholars such as L. William Oliverio Jr. and Kenneth J. Archer in their constructions of Pentecostal theological and biblical hermeneutics respectively.[86] Indeed my criticism of Oliverio (see Section 1.3.4) was not directed primarily at his methodology – although I do believe that MacIntyre's approach provides further tools for understanding the exact nature of a Pentecostal tradition – but rather for not seeing it being put to use. In a MacIntyrian fashion I believe that 'the concept of tradition-constituted and tradition-constitutive rational enquiry cannot be elucidated apart from its exemplifications.'[87] Therefore, to truly test either MacIntyre's or Oliverio's methodology in relation to constructing a Pentecostal rationality, one needs to do this through an 'exemplification' and narration of an existing Pentecostal tradition. My reason for favouring MacIntyre's approach over Archer's is that MacIntyre's developed concept of tradition with an emphasis on how traditions emerge and evolve through epistemological crises offers new insights on the nature of Pentecostal traditions. My basic point is that utilizing MacIntyre's methodology should not be seen as relying on 'strange fire' for developing a historically informed Pentecostal rationality. Rather, MacIntyre offers important philosophical resources that are both compatible with Pentecostal intuitions and help make sense of their inner logic.[88]

---

85. Following Roland Robertson, Wolfgang Vondey states, 'Instead of proposing the globalization *of* local Pentecostalism and thereby effectively juxtaposing the global *against* the local, the understanding of Pentecostalism as a glocal phenomenon embraces the relationship between the local and the global because Pentecostalism as a whole depends on both realities'; Wolfgang Vondey, *Pentecostalism: A Guide for the Perplexed* (London: Bloomsbury T&T Clark, 2013), 25.

86. Oliverio Jr., *Theological Hermeneutics in the Classical Pentecostal Tradition*; Archer, *A Pentecostal Hermeneutic*.

87. MacIntyre, *Whose Justice?*, 10.

88. A MacIntyrian historical and narrative approach also supports and/or complement those Pentecostal theological/philosophical works that are clearly historically informed but do not recount this history in detail; e.g. see Vondey, *Pentecostal Theology*; Neumann, *Pentecostal Experience*.

Part Two

NARRATING A TRADITION-SPECIFIC PENTECOSTAL RATIONALITY[1]

In the first part of the book I explored the 'Pentecostal' rationalities of Amos Yong, James K. A. Smith and L. William Oliverio Jr. (chapter 1). I concluded that the merits of their epistemological constructions are many, but they all seem to suffer from an element of ahistoricism when it comes to the construction of their theological hermeneutics (Yong and Smith more so than Oliverio). Consequently, I have proposed that Alasdair MacIntyre's concept of tradition-constituted rationality provides the necessary methodological insights for developing a truly historical, narrative and tradition-specific Pentecostal rationality (Chapter 2). However, this cannot be done apart from providing a historical narrative and exemplification of a particular Pentecostal tradition. Therefore, Part Two of the work seeks to present a MacIntyrian narrative account of a particular Pentecostal tradition, namely, the Elim Pentecostal Church.

I will do so by first providing 'prologues' to the Elim tradition by exploring its early context and roots (Chapter 3). This is important for understanding *how* the Elim movement emerged, *why* it emerged in the way it did, and *what* theological and philosophical resources it inherited from its intellectual ancestors.[2] This exploration is followed by an analysis of the emergence of the Elim 'argument' with particular emphasis on its early opponents, content, rationality and social embodiment (Chapter 4). In many ways this chapter is foundational for understanding what constitutes the Elim tradition, since in MacIntyrian lines the early makeup of any given tradition establishes its central ethos and, in doing so, sets its future prospects regarding what it can and cannot become (without effectively

---

1. Chapters 4–6 of this section have been presented in a shortened form in Simo Frestadius, 'The Elim Tradition: "An Argument Extended through Time" (Alasdair MacIntyre)', *JEPTA* 36, no. 1 (2016): 57–68.

2. In articulating the 'Catholic Philosophical Tradition', MacIntyre has a section on 'Prologues to the Catholic Philosophical Tradition'; Alasdair MacIntyre, *God, Philosophy and Universities: A Selective History of the Catholic Philosophical Tradition* (Lanham, MD: Rowman & Littlefield Publishers, 2011), 19.

morphing into another tradition).³ Indeed, the central argument of this chapter is that the essence of the Elim tradition is the *Foursquare Gospel* and its rationality is *Pentecostal Biblical Pragmatism*. The following two chapters (Chapters 5 and 6) continue the narration of the Elim 'argument extended through time' by focusing on two of its main 'epistemological crises' to date; that is, the resignation of its founder George Jeffreys (Chapter 5) and the challenge posed by the Charismatic and Restoration movements (Chapter 6). In my evaluation of these two crises, I will seek to further substantiate that the hard core of Elim is the Foursquare Gospel and its rationality is Pentecostal Biblical Pragmatism. Moreover, in Chapters 5 and 6, it should also become clear that Elim has demonstrated significant flexibility in restructuring itself – in accordance with its pragmatism – to facilitate the future flourishing of its argument.

Finally, it needs to be underscored that this part of the book is predominantly historical, and I have sought to engage with a number of primary sources on Elim, as should become evident in the references. I believe the historical detail I have attempted to provide is important in establishing correct foundations for the more constructive theological and philosophical contributions offered in the last section of the book, not least as I have critiqued Yong, Smith and Oliverio on aspects of their ahistoricism. That said, this part also offers the first comprehensive intellectual history of the Elim Pentecostal Church, and thus in its own right contributes to the history of ideas and Pentecostal historical theology.⁴

---

3. This parallels the view of those scholars who identify the roots and early expression of Pentecostalism as its *essence* rather than mere *infancy*; Harvey Cox, *Fire From Heaven: The Rise of Pentecostal Spirituality and the Reshaping of Religion in the Twenty-First Century* (London: Cassell, 1996), 262; Hollenweger, *Pentecostalism*, 397; Allan Anderson, *An Introduction to Pentecostalism* (Cambridge: Cambridge University Press, 2004), 45.

4. For a timeline of Elim's general history, see 'Appendix 1: Elim's Chronology'.

Chapter 3

PROLOGUES TO THE ELIM TRADITION: THE CONTEXT AND ROOTS OF THE ELIM ARGUMENT

Pentecostals have often self-identified their movement as originating directly from 'heaven' without having 'earthly' roots.[1] According to this view, the birth of the Pentecostal movement was a providential act of God at the beginning of the twentieth century, which catapulted the church back to experiencing the reality of Pentecost. This act not only restored the fullness of Apostolic and NT Christianity but in doing so also allowed the emerging Pentecostal movement to sidestep two thousand years of church history.

Despite the attractiveness of this view for 'primitivist' Pentecostal intuitions, such a reading of Pentecostal origins is not supported by the historical data. The likes of Vinson Synan, Walter J. Hollenweger and Donald W. Dayton have all persuasively argued that Pentecostalism should not be seen as a movement emerging *ex nihilo*, but rather as having deep historical, theological and social roots in other Christian traditions.[2] This does not mean that early Pentecostalism did not have its own distinctives, but it does mean that these distinctives were part of a broader theological framework much of which had been inherited from, and was shared with, other Christian streams.

---

1. This historiographical approach is identified by Cerillo and Wacker as 'the providential approach'; A. Cerillo Jr. and G. Wacker, 'Bibliography and Historiography of Pentecostalism in the United States', in *The New International Dictionary of Pentecostal and Charismatic Movement*, ed. Stanley M. Burgess and Eduard M. van der Maas (Grand Rapids, MI: Zondervan, 2002), 397–9. See also Cornelis van der Laan, 'Historical Approaches', in *Studying Global Pentecostalism: Theories and Methods*, ed. Allan Anderson et al. (Berkeley, CA: University of California Press, 2010), 202–19; Cecil M. Robeck Jr., 'The Origins of Modern Pentecostalism: Some Historiographical Issues', in *The Cambridge Companion to Pentecostalism*, ed. Cecil M. Robeck Jr. and Amos Yong (New York, NY: Cambridge University Press, 2014), 13–30.

2. Vinson Synan, *The Holiness Pentecostal Tradition: Charismatic Movements in the Twentieth Century* (Grand Rapids, MI: Eerdmans, 1997); Hollenweger, *Pentecostalism*; Dayton, *Theological Roots of Pentecostalism*.

This appears to be true for classical Pentecostalism as a whole, and it also seems to be the case for Elim. Consequently, to appropriately narrate the Elim tradition as 'an argument extended through time', it is necessary to start by identifying the 'prologues' to Elim; that is, to articulate its theological and intellectual roots. I aim to do this by first outlining the philosophical and theological context of the late-nineteenth- and early-twentieth-century Britain to help understand these roots within their surrounding habitat. Second, I will explore how Elim's direct roots can be located in the Anglo-American Holiness movements of the nineteenth century, the Welsh Revival (1904–05), and fundamentally in early British Pentecostalism (1907–14). These two aspects of 'context' and 'roots' are important in shedding light on why the Elim argument emerged in the first place, whose argument(s) did Elim adopt and adapt, against whom was the Elim argument directed, and what rational resources were available for Elim within the existing religious climate.

3.1 The pre-Pentecostal religious context: Modernity, religious pluralism and secularization

The Victorian era was a period of significant religious change in Britain, as an increasingly *modernizing* Britain moved from a dominant form of Christian faith to religious *pluralism* and *secularization*.[3] In other words, the long held hegemony of the Church of England in society was now being challenged and different religious, as well as non-religious, alternatives were becoming real 'live options'. As noted by Hugh McLeod, there does not appear to have been one 'master-factor' to explain these unprecedented religious changes, but a number of factors played their part.[4] Therefore, to set the general context for the arrival of British Pentecostalism in 1907 and Elim in 1915, I will briefly note some of the

---

3. *Modernity* is defined with Peter Berger 'as the changes brought about by the science and the technology created in the last few centuries'; Peter L. Berger, *The Many Altars of Modernity: Towards a Paradigm for Religion in a Pluralist Age* (Boston, MA: De Gruyter, 2014), 5. Religious *pluralism* is understood in David Martin's terms as 'voluntaristic pluralism'; that is, 'open competition of life-worlds and styles, each with a stall – more or less centrally placed – in the supermarket of beliefs'; David Martin, *On Secularization: Towards A Revised General Theory* (Farnham: Ashgate: 2005), 157. *Secularization*, on the other hand, is seen as (1) the decline of religious influence in the common institutions of society and (2) the decline of religious beliefs and practices among individuals. This definition of secularization reflects Charles Taylor's first two definitions of secular. Taylor's third and preferred definition of secular in many ways amounts to (religious) pluralism; Taylor, *A Secular Age*, 1–3.

4. Hugh McLeod, *Secularisation in Western Europe, 1848–1914* (London: MacMillan, 2000), 184.

philosophical and theological factors that contributed to the transformation of the religious landscape in Britain during the nineteenth and early twentieth centuries.⁵ This *intellectual* history cannot be adequately understood without appreciation of the wider *social* history, since throughout history there seems to have been a mutual interplay between intellectual and social history.⁶ Thus – even if my discussion does not focus on the wider social context – it is acknowledged that changes in society caused by urbanization, rail network, proliferation of newspapers and liberalization in politics and education contributed to the philosophical and religious developments explored below.⁷

3.1.1 Philosophical context: Change in the conditions of knowledge

The seventeenth- and eighteenth-century Enlightenment with its emphasis on reason, empiricism and science changed the 'intellectual conditions' of knowledge in Britain.⁸ The influence of the Enlightenment during these centuries, however, was mainly contained among the social elite, whereas the nineteenth century saw a proliferation and development of the Enlightenment principles among the wider population. As noted by Owen Chadwick, this seemed to cultivate religious doubt within society. Chadwick has proposed that the 1840s can be characterized as 'the time of doubts' vis-à-vis traditional religious beliefs and theological methodologies, but as the nineteenth century progressed this mood gathered momentum, meaning that by the 1860s Britain had entered 'the age of Doubt'.⁹ Although Chadwick's identification of the Victorian society first facing 'doubts' and then moving to a singular and capitalized form of 'Doubt' somewhat exaggerates the prominence of religious doubt in the late Victorian era,¹⁰ it does, nevertheless, correctly highlight

---

5. Cf. William K. Kay, 'Modernity and the Arrival of Pentecostalism in Britain', *PS* 10, no. 1 (2011): 50–71.

6. MacIntyre, *Whose Justice?*, 8. Cf. Owen Chadwick, *The Secularization of the European Mind in the 19th Century* (Cambridge: Cambridge University Press, 1975), 14; Taylor, *Modern Social Imaginaries*, 63.

7. See Simo Frestadius, 'Whose Pentecostalism? Which Rationality? The Foursquare Gospel and Pentecostal Biblical Pragmatism of the Elim Tradition' (PhD diss., University of Birmingham, Birmingham, 2018), 95–101.

8. Chadwick, *The Secularization of the European Mind*, 144. For works paying particular attention to the British Enlightenment, see Roy Porter, *Enlightenment: Britain and the Creation of the Modern World* (London: The Penguin Press, 2000); Gertrude Himmelfarb, *The Roads to Modernity: The British, French and American Enlightenments* (London: Vintage Books, 2008).

9. Chadwick, *The Secularization of the European Mind*, 184.

10. See Timothy Larsen, *Crisis of Doubt: Honest Faith in Nineteenth-Century England* (Oxford: Oxford University Press, 2008).

the change in the expected epistemic conditions of belief, as well as the rise in religious doubt, towards the end of the nineteenth century.[11]

3.1.1.1 Developments in science and history: From common-sense realism to scientific empiricism Scientific and historical developments both seemed to contribute to this epistemic change. Unlike much of the French Enlightenment, the British Enlightenment was not intrinsically hostile to organized religion or Christian beliefs.[12] In fact, up to the mid-nineteenth century majority of (Evangelical) Christians claimed perfect harmony between scientific knowledge and Christian truth. In the words of Bebbington, for them there 'was no possibility of divorce between faith and reason'.[13] However, the first clear test for this harmony seemed to come from geology, which now propounded that the earth was millions of years old and thus appeared to oppose a 'literal' and 'common-sense' reading of Genesis.[14] Charles Darwin's influential works *Origin of Species* (1859) and *Descent of Man* (1871) further undermined this common (Evangelical) reading of Genesis. Moreover, Darwin's theory provided an explanation for biological life without appealing to teleology and so challenged what had previously been seen as a strong argument for the existence of God, and also raised serious questions about the uniqueness of humanity being specially created in the image of God.[15]

However, it was not just the new scientific discoveries that influenced people's understanding of and approach to religion, but the scientific method itself was modified in the nineteenth century. In the early nineteenth century the Common Sense Realism of Thomas Reid combined with the inductive scientific methodology of Francis Bacon was the predominant intellectual paradigm, particularly among Evangelicals in Britain.[16] In other words, along Reidian lines, it was believed that the world could be experienced and understood directly through the innate faculty

---

11. McLeod, *Secularisation in Western Europe*, 147; James C. Livingston, *Religious Thought in the Victorian Age: Challenges and Reconceptions* (London: Continuum, 2006), 31; David Hempton, *Evangelical Disenchantment: Nine Portraits of Faith and Doubt* (New Haven, CT: Yale University Press, 2008), 2.

12. Himmelfarb, *The Roads to Modernity*, 50; Porter, *Enlightenment*, 128–9.

13. David W. Bebbington, *The Dominance of Evangelicalism: The Age of Spurgeon and Moody* (Leicester: Intervarsity Press, 2005), 111.

14. Bernard M. G. Reardon, *Religious Thought in the Victorian Age: A Survey from Coleridge to Gore*, 2nd edn (Abingdon: Routledge, 1995), 212.

15. Reardon, *Religious Thought in the Victorian Age*, 215–16; Alister E. McGrath, *Science and Religion: A New Introduction*, 2nd edn (Oxford: Wiley-Blackwell, 2010), 38. Copleston notes that 'it is difficult for us now to appreciate the ferment which was caused in the last century by the hypothesis of organic evolution, particularly in its application to man'; Frederick Copleston, *A History of Philosophy: Volume 8. Bentham to Russell* (London: Search Press, 1977), 103.

16. See Harriet A. Harris, *Fundamentalism and Evangelicals* (Oxford: Oxford University Press, 2009), 100; David Bebbington, *Evangelicalism in Modern Britain: A History from the*

of 'common sense' present in all humans; along with Bacon's inductive method this understanding was believed to be achieved by (1) examining the evidence in question, (2) gathering facts from this examination, and (3) then classifying these facts according to a coordinating law/maxim.[17] The challenge to the common-sense approach is well captured in John Stuart Mill's *System of Logic* (1843), which became 'the definitive account of the philosophy of science and social science' for the remainder of the century.[18] Mill's positivist empiricism undermined both the intuitionist common sense advocated by Reid and Baconianism,[19] as Mill believed that a scientific method should be characterized by (1) starting with a range of hypothesis, (2) then examining data that eliminates 'all hypothesis but one' and (3) finally concluding that the 'uneliminated hypothesis is true'.[20] In other words, Mill thought that hypotheses were fundamental to scientific progress,[21] and that it was possible for induction to exceed the simple data of experience.[22] Thus, the modified approach to science and knowledge exemplified by Mill subjected previously assumed common-sense beliefs to rigorous empiricism and increasingly introduced the concept of hypothesis to scientific inquiry, undermining aspects of the naïve realism of Baconianism.

In fact, it seemed that Darwin's theory of evolution was developed by utilizing Mill's method of hypothesis/induction. For example, the Victorian intellectual T. H. Huxley defended Darwin's scientific methodology against its critics – who claimed that it was 'not inductive enough, not Baconian enough' – by arguing that Darwin's method was in line with that of Mill and was 'the only adequate method'.[23] This debate is significant because it highlights that the opponents of Darwin's theory were opposing not just his conclusions but also his methodology; that is, the modified scientific method. Among Darwin's critics were particularly conservative

1730s to the 1980s (Grand Rapids, MI: Baker Book House, 1992), 59; Copleston, *A History of Philosophy: Volume 8*, 1.

17. Harris, *Fundamentalism and Evangelicals*, 96–116; Bradford McCall, 'The Pentecostal Reappropriation of Common Sense Realism', *JPT* 19, no. 1 (2010): 61–4.

18. Fred Wilson, 'John Stuart Mill', in *The Stanford Encyclopedia of Philosophy*, ed. Edward N. Zalta (Spring 2016 Edition), accessed 24 May 2016, http://plato.stanford.edu/archives/spr2016/entries/mill/.

19. Steve Wilkens and Alan G. Padgett, *Christianity and Western Thought: Volume 2. Faith and Reason in the 19th Century* (Downers Grove, IL: InterVarsity Press, 2000), 198.

20. Fred Wilson, 'John Stuart Mill'. For 'Mill's Method' in more detail see John Stuart Mill, *A System of Logic: Ratiocinative and Inductive*. Vol. 1, 7th edn (London: Longmans, 1868), Book III, Chapter 8.

21. Copleston, *A History of Philosophy: Volume 8*, 74.

22. 'Induction, then, is that operation of the mind, by which we infer that what we know to be true in a particular case or cases, will be true in all cases which resemble the former in certain assignable respects'; Mill, *A System of Logic*, Book III, Chapter 2:1.

23. T. H. Huxley, *Lay Sermons, Addresses, and Reviews* (New York: D Appleton, 1880), 293, accessed 12 February 2017, https://archive.org/details/laysermonsaddre08huxlgoog.

Evangelicals who on the whole still followed the 'common-sense' approach. All of this suggests that the scientific debate in the nineteenth century was as much about appropriate *rationalities*, as it was about the actual *content* of the debates. Indeed, the twentieth-century disputes between the so-called Liberal and Fundamentalist Christians were characterized by these opposing rationalities carried over from the nineteenth century.[24] This is important not only for appropriately understanding the religious disputes of the late nineteenth and early twentieth centuries but also for locating and making sense of the emerging Pentecostal and Elim rationality.

What makes this 'clash' of rationalities even more significant is that the 'new' scientific method was not only utilized in the domain of natural science but also applied to other spheres of knowledge in a positivistic manner. The Utilitarian movement – first articulated by Jeremy Bentham and then further developed by Mill – is a good example of the new empirical principles being put to use for understanding and grounding morality within society. Mill is known for praising Bentham 'for employing a scientific method in morals and politics'.[25] Moreover, T. H. Huxley noted that his own agnosticism regarding religion was composed of applying what he saw as the new scientific method to all of human experience, and in doing so he rejected metaphysical speculations and Christian doctrines as either unproven or unprovable.[26] W. K. Clifford took his positivism even a step further by arguing that those who failed to apply scientific reasoning to their beliefs were not just mistaken but morally culpable. His well-known positivist and evidentialist maxim was: 'It is wrong always, everywhere, and for anyone, to believe anything upon insufficient evidence'.[27]

The scientific method was also utilized in the study of history and historical texts, including the Bible. Like the natural scientist, the ideal historian and religious scholar was seen as an objective scientific enquirer. Scripture was now to be analysed like any other document, which seemed to undermine its authority and divine origins. Moreover, the refusal of historical criticism to look beyond natural explanations challenged concepts like providence and miracles. This meant that a divide was created between sacred history (the sphere of faith) and secular history (the sphere of science), with the latter having epistemic primacy.[28] The apparent *locus classicus* of this new secular and positivist historical approach was David Strauss's *The Life of Jesus* (1835) translated from German into English by the

---

24. See Nancey Murphy, *Beyond Liberalism and Fundamentalism: How Modern and Postmodern Philosophy Set the Theological Agenda* (Harrisburg, PA: Trinity Press International, 1996), 5; Harris, *Fundamentalism and Evangelicals*, 95.

25. Copleston, *A History of Philosophy: Volume 8*, 16.

26. Livingston, *Religious Thought in the Victorian Age*, 27.

27. W. K. Clifford, 'The Ethics of Belief', in *Contemporary Review*, 1877, accessed 1 January 2016, http://people.brandeis.edu/~teuber/Clifford_ethics.pdf.

28. Reardon, *Religious Thought in the Victorian Age*, 6. Chadwick identifies the nineteenth century as the period when the 'secularization of history' took place; Chadwick, *The Secularisation of the European Mind*, 193.

ex-Evangelical George Elliot (Mary Ann Evans) in 1846. Strauss's work exemplifies the demythologizing effects of the new historical criticism on both biblical studies and traditional Christian beliefs.

3.1.1.2 Alternatives to Empiricism: Romanticism and Idealism However, not all were satisfied with the Enlightenment and empiricist legacy being applied to religious and historical knowledge in a positivist manner. The nineteenth century saw the emergence of a new cultural and intellectual mood: Romanticism. Although Romanticism was a diverse phenomenon, its essential aspects can be articulated in its reaction against the Enlightenment.[29] Its emphasis was not on argument but experience, not on reason but on 'will, spirit and emotion'.[30] One of its most influential voices, Samuel Taylor Coleridge, captures the Romantic sentiment well with respect to religion: 'I more than fear the prevailing taste for books on Natural Theology, Physico-Theology, Demonstrations of God from Nature, Evidences of Christianity, and the like. *Evidences* of Christianity! I am weary of the word. Make a man feel the *want* of it; rouse him, if you can, to the self-knowledge of his *need*.'[31]

For Coleridge, Christian belief is based on inner experience and feeling rather than on arguments or external evidences. This Romantic emphasis on intuition and experience was carried on later in the century by the Oxford movement,[32] and especially by its champion John Henry Newman who strongly opposed scientific positivism. In his seminal work *An Essay in Aid of Grammar of Assent* (1870), Newman argued that the positivist epistemic standards were too narrow for general human beliefs and religious beliefs in particular. British Idealism of the late nineteenth century, although different from Coleridge's Romanticism and Newman's Traditionalism, also shared this critique of 'a positivist empirical account of human knowledge'.[33]

29. Although one must be careful not to strictly demarcate between the Enlightenment and Romanticism, or between Empiricism and Idealism. For example, after a nervous breakdown in 1826 John Stuart Mill began appreciating the Romantic poets, despite his scientific empiricism, and the phenomenalism of the empiricists influenced the idealists; Copleston, *A History of Philosophy: Volume 8*, 26, 146.

30. Bebbington, *The Dominance of Evangelicalism*, 139. Bebbington notes that although Romanticism is often identified as a movement from late eighteenth century to 1830s, 'it is important to insist that what was novel at that time gathered increasing popularity throughout the Victorian era'; Bebbington, *The Dominance of Evangelicalism*, 140.

31. Samuel Taylor Coleridge, *Aids to Reflection and the Confessions of An Inquiring Spirit* (n.p.: Anboco, 2016), Kindle.

32. David Bebbington, *Holiness in Nineteenth-Century England* (Carlisle: Paternoster Press, 2000), 13.

33. Sandra M. Den Otter, *British Idealism and Social Explanation: A Study in Late Victorian Thought* (Oxford: Clarendon Press, 1996), 2. Wilkens and Padgett note that when 'ideas common to Romanticism are systematized, the movement is in the direction of Idealism'; Wilkens and Padgett, *Christianity and Western Thought*, 66.

However, despite the force of the Romantic mood in the late-nineteenth-century British philosophy, these sentiments, particularly in the form of British Idealism, were challenged in the early twentieth century by realists such as G. E. Moore and Bertrand Russell.[34] In fact, it was Russell who emerged as the most influential British philosopher of the twentieth century and thus the dominance of Idealism in British universities was short-lived.[35]

It is worth pointing out at this point that unlike in America where Pragmatism became the dominant philosophical movement in replacing Idealism,[36] in Britain, despite the effort of F. C. S. Schiller, this philosophical movement never gained prominence (at least not in the academy).[37] This is noteworthy, as I will argue below that in relation to the main Anglo-American philosophical 'schools' of the late nineteenth and early twentieth centuries Pentecostalism and Elim share many similarities with Pragmatism.

In summary, the intellectual context of the nineteenth century can be seen as continuing the Enlightenment and British Empiricist legacy, albeit with an increased emphasis on hypothesis and positivistic scientific method which began permeating society's epistemic standards regarding all spheres of knowledge, including that of religious knowledge. The 'new' methods of induction and hypothesis exemplified in the work of J. S. Mill provided a direct challenge to Common Sense Realism as the dominant philosophical position. Applying this more positivistic methodology to religious beliefs, coupled with Darwinian evolution, also raised doubts for many regarding the traditional Christian doctrines. Romanticism in its various forms sought to counter scientific positivism and offer an experiential epistemic alternative, but its philosophical influence, as least in the form of Idealism, was diminishing as the new century dawned. The general significance of the nineteenth-century intellectual context for religious belief was that whether one was a positivist or romanticist (or indeed neither!), it was increasingly difficult to take Christian beliefs for granted because the conditions for knowledge had been challenged and changed. As a result, the Victorian intellectuals had become 'religious/philosophical *seekers*' in search of justified beliefs.[38] This change had implications for individual believers, as well as their religious institutions.

---

34. See particularly G. E. Moore, 'The Refutation of Idealism', *Mind* 12 (1903), accessed 17 February 2017, http://www.ditext.com/moore/refute.html.

35. See Copleston, *A History of Philosophy: Volume 8*, Part IV.

36. On American Pragmatism see Cheryl Misak, *The American Pragmatists* (Oxford: Oxford University Press, 2015); Robert B. Talisse and Scott F. Aikin, eds. *The Pragmatism Reader: Form Peirce through the Present* (Princeton, NJ: Princeton University Press, 2011).

37. On Schiller see Misak, *The American Pragmatists*, 91–6; Copleston, *A History of Philosophy: Volume 8*, 346–51.

38. David Nash, 'Reassessing the "Crisis of Faith" in the Victorian Age: Eclecticism and the Spirit of Moral Inquiry', *JVC* 16, no. 1 (2011): 70.

3.1.2 Theological context: Evangelical conversionism and diversity of religious options

It was not, however, simply changes in the philosophical environment of the Victorian era that facilitated secularization, plurality of beliefs, and the need for individuals to justify their beliefs and make religious choices accordingly. The Evangelical emphasis on genuine Christianity and true conversion also made its contribution.

3.1.2.1 Evangelical conversionism In the nineteenth century Evangelicalism was a dominant religious force in Britain and its theological influence was significant.[39] In the previous century, John Wesley, a founding father of British Evangelicalism, had argued that it is possible for an individual to have the outward appearance of being a Christian without actually truly being one.[40] The nineteenth-century Evangelical tradition shared Wesley's conviction and reinforced the idea that a genuine Christian should not just participate in religious rituals but have a conversion experience, which was understood as consisting of a personal decision for Christ, as well as having a deeply held conviction of the gospel's truth.[41]

These two aspects (i.e. decision and conviction) of the Evangelical conversion paradigm were important in shaping people's religious psyche. First, there was a strong emphasis on individual choice. This marked an important shift from the church tradition of the so-called *ancien régime* where one was born into the church rather than choosing to belong to it. Callum Brown states that it was in fact this aspect of choosing that 'broke the mental chains of the *ancien régime* in Britain', enabling people to see the previously dominant church tradition as simply one religious option among many.[42]

Second, there was an expectation that a real Christian would have a firm conviction of the truth of Christianity.[43] Timothy Larsen points out that a 'person who had internalized such a way of thinking learned that continuing with a life of worship while quietly doubting the claims on which it is based was not only of no spiritual benefit but was also a craven thing to do'.[44] In other words, whereas individuals before could quite comfortably remain in the church despite their religious doubts, this was less of an option for the Evangelical doubter. Thus, Evangelical conversionism seemed to either push Victorians *towards* a more

---

39. See Bebbington, *The Dominance of Evangelicalism*, 249; Larsen, *Crisis of Doubt*, 11; Callum Brown, *The Death of Christian Britain: Understanding Secularisation 1800–2000*, 2nd edn (London: Routledge, 2009), 37.
40. Larsen, *Crisis of Doubt*, 12.
41. Ibid., 13.
42. Brown, *Death of Christian Britain*, 36–8.
43. For the connection between the Evangelical doctrine of assurance and the Enlightenment quest for certainty, see Bebbington, *Evangelicalism in Modern Britain*, 50.
44. Larsen, *Crisis of Doubt*, 13.

committed form of (Evangelical) Christianity or push them *out* of Christianity altogether.

Charles Taylor has identified *Reform* as the main cause of Western secularization. He refers to it as the 'Reform Master Narrative' of secularization and summarizes it in the following way:

> Reform demanded that everyone be *real, 100 percent* Christian. Reform not only disenchants, but disciplines and re-orders life and society. Along with civility, this makes for a notion of moral order which gives a new sense to Christianity, and the demands of the faith. This collapses the distances of faith from Christendom. It induces an anthropocentric shift, and hence a break-out from the monopoly of Christian faith.[45]

Although Taylor's historical scope is broader than the nineteenth century, the Evangelical emphasis to reform Victorian Christianity through the conversion paradigm seems to have had the exact effects identified by Taylor. To put it differently, the Evangelicals articulated new 'demands of the faith', distancing what was perceived to be true Christian faith from nominal Christianity of Christendom, and in doing so, induced an anthropocentric shift by prioritizing individual choice. It also polarized these two groups, namely, what it saw as true Christians and non-Christians, and thus undermined the monopoly status of the so-called Christian faith of Britain.

Whether Evangelicals of the nineteenth century pursuing religious reform were aware of or even intended the secularizing effects of their conversionist agenda is difficult to know for certain.[46] Nevertheless, it is telling that John Wesley in the eighteenth century predicted that something like this would happen when he wrote 'that in a century or two the people of England will be fairly divided into real Deists and real Christians'.[47] Wesley himself did not only predict this but also welcomed it, and was personally happy to use sceptical arguments to wake 'nominal Christians from their dogmatic slumbers'.[48]

3.1.2.2 Diversity of religious options That said, the Victorians of the late nineteenth century should not be simply divided into two homogenous religious groups; that is, (Evangelical) Christians and non-Christians, or what Wesley saw as Christians

---

45. Taylor, *A Secular Age*, 774.

46. Gregory has argued that secularization was the unintended cause of the sixteenth-century Reformation; Brad S. Gregory, *The Unintended Reformation: How a Religious Revolution Secularized Society* (Cambridge, MA: The Belknapp Press of Harvard University Press, 2012), 2.

47. John Wesley, 'A Letter to the Reverend' quoted in William J. Abraham, *Aldersgate and Athens: John Wesley and the Foundations of Christian Belief* (Waco, TX: Baylor University Press, 2010), 51.

48. Abraham, *Aldersgate and Athens*, 51.

and Deists. There were, in fact, several 'religious' options for both Christians and non-Christians.

Regarding the latter, McLeod has noted that 'in the second half of the nineteenth century non-religious views of the world became a possibility for the mass of the people, rather than only for small elite groups'.[49] Like Christianity, these various views offered their own paths to 'salvation' and human fulfilment. McLeod has identified four common non-Christian views and/or paths. First, there was 'salvation by politics alone' which followed the legacy of the French Revolution and was promulgated by 'republicans', 'radicals', 'nationalists' and 'socialists'. Second, there was 'salvation by science' which saw scientific discoveries and technological advances as the harbinger of the golden age of humanity. The third way to salvation was through 'aesthetics' which advocated art, music and literature as the path for true human flourishing. Fourth, there was 'spiritualism' which rejected both materialism and Christianity, offering a new way between the two.[50] All of these were seen as viable options, and it was not uncommon for people to pick and mix from the above to construct their own paths to fulfilment.

In terms of Christian options, Evangelicalism, with its various denominational incarnations, was also one option among others. The two most prominent Christian alternatives to Evangelicalism were Broad Church Liberalism and Anglo-Catholicism. Both movements, like Evangelicalism, were influenced by the contemporaneous general trends identified above, and were particularly aware of biblical criticism, the questioning of the plausibility of miracles and scepticism towards orthodox Christian beliefs.

The 1860 publication of *Essays and Reviews* proved to be a seminal work for articulating the theology of Broad Church Liberalism.[51] The seven articles in the work, among other things, urged the Bible to be treated like any other book (Benjamin Jowett), seemed to deny the possibility of miracles (Baden Bowell), and questioned the nature of Christian doctrines such as that of hell (Henry Bristow Wilson). The aim of *Essays and Reviews* was to modernize Christian theology. The work was received with great hostility by many, but as stated by Reardon, '*Essays and Reviews* gave liberalism a place in English theology from which it could not in future be dislodged and might extend a continuously widening influence'.[52] Thirty years later the publication of *Lux Mundi* (1889) continued this legacy. Its editor Charles Gore referred to the *Lux Mundi* as a reconciliation between 'new knowledge' and the Christian religion.[53]

Indeed, the prevailing theological trend during late nineteenth century was towards a liberal stance,[54] at least from an Evangelical perspective. *Essays and*

---

49. McLeod, *Secularisation in Western Europe*, 150.
50. Ibid., 150–1.
51. Reardon, *Religious Thought in the Victorian Age*, 237.
52. Ibid., 251.
53. Ibid., 321.
54. Bebbington, *The Dominance of Evangelicalism*, 171.

Reviews and *Lux Mundi* argued that Christian theology had to reconcile itself with modernity. This had implications for traditional Christian views on creation, providence, the Fall, sin, evil and theodicy, miracles, free-will and theology of religions.[55]

However, like Evangelicalism, Anglo-Catholicism, especially those aligning themselves with the Oxford movement (i.e. Tractarianism), was critical of the liberal trends in theology. Influenced by Romanticism, the Oxford movement from 1830s onwards attacked liberalism, but unlike Evangelicalism, it did not do so by seeking to reassert the Reformation doctrines (e.g. authority and primacy of Scripture), but by seeking to revive 'a high doctrine of the church and its ministry'.[56] From 1840s onwards the movement inclined towards Roman Catholicism and at the end of 1845 its charismatic leader John Henry Newman joined the Roman Catholic Church.[57] Although the dominance of the Oxford movement declined after Newman's departure, its influence was lasting in emphasizing the authority of the church, holiness and ritualism in worship. The Oxford movement's legacy was its ability to reinstate Catholic spirituality and theology into British Christianity.

3.1.3 Elim's context: An argument within modernity

In discussing some of the philosophical and theological trends of the Victorian era, I have tried to show that the nineteenth and early twentieth centuries were a period of increasing modernization, secularization and pluralization of beliefs within Britain. This trajectory was fuelled by Enlightenment rationality, scientific positivism, Romanticism, Evangelical conversionism and the emergence of viable Christian and non-Christian options with respect to 'salvation' and human flourishing. Religious plurality in society meant that it was difficult to take any religion or worldview for granted. In the words of Charles Taylor, the 'conditions of belief' had changed,[58] implying that adhering to any religion increasingly became a choice and for this choice to be justified one had to have reasons, not least when many of the religions and worldviews were in direct competition. However, as the Victorian era reached its twilight, having reasons for one's beliefs was not a straightforward task because there was not just one form of rationality available to ground one's beliefs. Rather, versions of Common Sense Realism, Mill's Scientific Empiricism, Romanticism, Idealism, and the New Realism of Moore and Russell were all on offer.

This is the wider intellectual and theological context for the emergence of British Pentecostalism in 1907 and Elim in 1915. Indeed, it seems difficult to fully

---

55. For a detailed exploration of these doctrines, see Livingston, *Religious Thought in the Victorian Age*.

56. Noel S. Pollard, 'The Oxford Movement', in *The New International Dictionary of the Christian Church*, ed. J. D. Douglas (Grand Rapids, MI: Zondervan, 1978), 739.

57. Ibid.

58. Taylor, *A Secular Age*, 539.

understand the Elim argument without locating it in this context. Three aspects are particularly noteworthy from the discussion above in locating and better appreciating the emerging Pentecostal and Elim tradition in Britain. First, in line with the early-twentieth-century *sitz im leben*, the Pentecostal faith from its inception was a religion of *radical choice*. That is, Pentecostalism was not seen as an inherited faith, but one would actively choose to become a Pentecostal. This choice would typically mean having a conversion experience, deciding to get baptized in water, and then seeking baptism in the Holy Spirit. As a religion of choice, Pentecostalism was very much in line with the spirit of the era.

Second, the decision for Pentecostalism/Elim meant that one would *choose what was claimed as 'apostolic faith' or the 'Full Gospel'*. As has been argued above, this was not the only option in the marketplace of religions, and therefore in choosing Pentecostalism one would also explicitly, or at least implicitly, reject the non-religious alternatives, Roman Catholicism, Liberal Christianity and cessationist forms of Evangelicalism. Consequently, the choice *for* Pentecostal Christianity was shaped also by the decision *against* its alternatives. Indeed, the very concepts of apostolic faith and the Full Gospel were understood in relation to what it stood against in the contemporaneous religious discourse. I will argue in Chapter 4 that the Elim argument spearheaded by George Jeffreys was particularly shaped by its antagonism against the so-called theological Liberals, Christian ritualism and cessationist Evangelicals. However, it should be added that the Pentecostal and Elim argument against some religious traditions of the late nineteenth and early twentieth centuries was not an argument per se against modernity, even if Pentecostals often saw themselves as opposing aspects of modernistic (read: Liberal) theologies.

Third, in the context of competing religious and non-religious options, some *reasons were needed for choosing Pentecostalism* over its alternatives. This task was not without complexity, as the nineteenth- and early-twentieth-century intellectual environment did not simply have one form of rationality but embodied various rationalities. Now the average religious seeker was probably not fully cognizant of these various epistemological options, but, nevertheless, they were expected to make rational choices in an environment of competing rationalities. Thus, the question of justification for religious belief was not merely about having 'good reasons' but also about having a 'good rationality'. Interestingly, Pentecostalism and Elim would not simply adopt any existing rationality, but developed its own rationality and ways of reasoning for accepting and promulgating the Pentecostal faith. This Pentecostal/Elim rationality was certainly influenced by the smorgasbord of existing rationalities but, as I hope to demonstrate below, it cannot simply be equated with a single rationality on offer. Therefore, what made British Pentecostalism and Elim unique traditions was not just *what* they believed, but *how* they justified these beliefs. And their approach to justification of beliefs was very much influenced by contemporary ways of reasoning, and thus could be seen as another modern rationality.

In conclusion, the foundations for British Pentecostalism and Elim were provided by the nineteenth- and early-twentieth-century philosophical and theological environment. This was a context of modernity, plurality of beliefs and increasing secularization. Although British Pentecostalism would react against some aspects of this context, it would be misleading to call Pentecostalism in Britain simply a 'protest against modernity' and its consequences.[59] To put it simply, the context had changed too drastically for early British Pentecostals to return to pre-modernity, and more importantly, British Pentecostals were themselves children of modernity (e.g. emphasis on choice and ways of reasoning) to be able to fully protest against modernity. Perhaps early British Pentecostalism could be called a 'paramodern' movement à la Kenneth J. Archer; that is, a movement emerging within modernity and sharing some aspects with it, but simultaneously not able to 'accept Modernity's worldview completely'.[60] However, although Archer's concept of 'paramodern' is insightful, it can also give the wrong impression that 'modernity' is somehow a uniform concept, which Pentecostalism opposes. To avoid this possible misconception, it is better to speak with Berger of 'multiple modernities',[61] and to view the emerging British Pentecostalism and Elim as modern religious movements with some unique emphases. Therefore, in light of Elim's first prologue, namely its intellectual and theological context, the emerging Elim movement discussed in Chapter 4 is best seen as a modern religious tradition.

3.2 Holiness, revival and Pentecostal roots of Elim

I have suggested above that in late nineteenth- and early-twentieth-century Britain there were effectively three main Christian 'streams': Evangelicalism, Anglo-Catholicism and Broad Church Liberalism. Pentecostalism in Britain is best located within the Evangelical stream and seen as 'part of the larger quest for evangelical spirituality'.[62] Early Pentecostals would share many of the theological beliefs, ways of reasoning and religious practices of other Evangelicals, even if they were to develop their own distinctives. However, within this broader Evangelical framework, it was the radical Evangelicalism of the Holiness movements and the Welsh Revival that were particularly significant in laying the foundations for British Pentecostalism.

---

59. Margaret Poloma sees the growth of American Assemblies of God as an 'anthropological protest against modernity'; Margaret Poloma, *The Assemblies of God at the Crossroads: Charisma and Institutional Dilemmas* (Knoxville, TN: The University of Tennessee Press, 1989), 19.

60. Archer, *A Pentecostal Hermeneutic*, 33.

61. Berger, *The Many Altars of Modernity*, 68. Berger attributes the concept of 'multiple modernities' to Shmuel Eisenstadt.

62. Ian M. Randall, 'Old Time Power: Relationships between Pentecostalism and Evangelical Spirituality in England', *Pneuma* 19, no. 1 (1997): 54.

3.2.1 *The Holiness movements*

Like their American counterparts, early British Pentecostal leaders had deep roots in the Holiness movements of the nineteenth century.[63] For example, the so-called Father of British Pentecostalism, Alexander Boddy, regularly attended the Keswick Conventions and was also a member of the Pentecostal League of Prayer founded by Richard Reader Harris.[64] George Jeffreys, the founder of Elim, also seemed to have visited the Keswick Conventions,[65] and other Elim pioneers, such as E. J. Phillips,[66] R. E. Darragh[67] and Ernest C. W. Boulton,[68] all had strong links with the Holiness traditions.

David Bebbington has identified four main Holiness traditions in nineteenth-century England; that is, the High Church tradition, the Calvinist tradition, the Wesleyan tradition and the Keswick tradition.[69] The High Church tradition, incorporating the Oxford movement, seems to have had little direct influence on British Pentecostalism or Elim, not least due to its Anglo-Catholic spirituality and opposition to Evangelicalism.[70] The Calvinist, Wesleyan and Keswick traditions, on the other hand, did have a significant influence on early British Pentecostalism. Keswick is particularly important as it can be seen as a 'synthesis' of the Wesleyan and Calvinist Holiness streams.[71]

The Keswick tradition emerged in the summer of 1875 when its first convention was held in Keswick at the Lake District.[72] From inception its focus was on 'the higher

---

63. Donald Gee, *The Pentecostal Movement: A Short History and an Interpretation for British Readers* (Milton Keynes: Lightning Source, n.d.), 4; Timothy B. Walsh, *To Meet and Satisfy a Very Hungry People: The Origins and Fortunes of English Pentecostalism, 1907–1925* (Milton Keynes: Paternoster, 2012), 3.

64. Boddy seems to have been converted at Keswick in 1876; Gavin Wakefield, *Alexander Boddy: Pentecostal Anglican Pioneer* (Milton Keynes: Authentic Media, 2007), 19–20.

65. Randall, 'Old Time Power', 58; cf. George Jeffreys, 'Jesus Christ *the* Baptiser', *EE* 7, no. 23–4 (6 December 1926): 297–8.

66. Maldwyn Jones, 'An Assessment of the Leadership of E. J. Phillips' (MA diss., Regents Theological College, Malvern, 2011), 9.

67. James Robinson, *Pentecostal Origins: Early Pentecostalism in Ireland in the Context of the British Isles* (Milton Keynes: Paternoster, 2005), 22.

68. W. G. Hathaway, 'Home-Call of a Pentecostal Pioneer', *EE* 41, no. 2 (9 January 1960): 20.

69. Bebbington, *Holiness in Nineteenth-Century England*, 6.

70. Ibid., 10–12.

71. Ibid., 73. Andrew David Naselli, 'Keswick Theology: A Survey and Analysis of the Doctrine of Sanctification in the Early Keswick Movement', *DBSJ* 13 (2008): 19. Dieter identifies Keswick as more Calvinist than Wesleyan; Melvin E. Dieter, *The Holiness Revival of the Nineteenth Century*, 2nd edn (London: The Scarecrow Press, 1996), 249.

72. See J. C. Pollock, *The Keswick Story: The Authorized History of the Keswick Convention* (London: Hodder and Stoughton, 1964), 11–37; David D. Bundy, 'Keswick

Christian life' and 'sanctification by faith'.[73] It was the emphasis on sanctification that it held in common with the Wesleyan Holiness tradition. However, the Keswick Holiness views were also informed by the Reformed Holiness teachings of the Americans Charles Finney, Asa Mahan and William E. Boardman, making it more acceptable to Calvinists.[74] Regarding sanctification, the Keswick tradition taught that 'sin was not eradicated' but 'repressed' by the working of the Holy Spirit.[75] In other words, the experience and process of sanctification for the Keswick movement did not imply sin being completely removed from the believer but counteracted by the presence of the Holy Spirit. To experience the fullness God's empowering presence, one was encouraged to *surrender* fully to God ('let go') and to place one's *faith* completely in Him ('let God').[76] For some Wesleyans, like Reader Harris, the emphasis on 'repression' of sin, rather than its 'eradication', was seen as unbiblical,[77] but the Keswick emphasis on 'higher Christian life', sanctification, and the role of the Spirit seemed to be broad enough to attract adherents from both Wesleyan and Calvinist Holiness camps.[78]

3.2.1.1 Theology and rationality of Keswick The Keswick movement, as well as the broader Wesleyan and Calvinist Holiness traditions, was significant in providing theological and rational roots for early British Pentecostalism and Elim. In terms of *theology*, it effectively provided the framework for the Fourfold Gospel (Jesus as Saviour, Healer, Baptiser in the Holy Spirit, and coming King), which was to become a central tenet for early Pentecostals and, as I will argue in Chapter 4, the doctrinal 'hard core' for Elim.

In terms of the Fourfold Gospel, the Keswick movement first shared the Evangelical emphasis on conversion. Second, its focus on sanctification and the need for a deeper Christian experience of the Holy Spirit suggested the need for a crisis moment that was subsequent to conversion. In fact, Donald Gee notes that thanks to the Holiness movements the 'phrase "Baptism of the Holy Ghost"

Higher Life Movement', in *The New International Dictionary of Pentecostal and Charismatic Movements*. Revised and expanded edition, ed. Stanley M. Burgess and Eduard M. van der Maas (Grand Rapids, MI: Zondervan, 2003), 820.

73. Bebbington, *Holiness in Nineteenth-Century England*, 73.

74. Ibid., 76. Boardman's *The Higher Christian Life* (1858) is considered to be influential for the Keswick Movement; see Pollock, *The Keswick Story*, 13; Dieter, *The Holiness Revival of the Nineteenth Century*, 49–50.

75. Bebbington, *Holiness in Nineteenth-Century England*, 83; Dayton, *Theological Roots of Pentecostalism*, 105.

76. Pollock, *The Keswick Story*, 74–6.

77. Bebbington, *Holiness in Nineteenth-Century England*, 87.

78. Alexander Boddy is a good example as he attended Keswick Conventions and was a member of Reader Harris's Pentecostal League of Prayer; see Mark J. Cartledge, 'The Early Pentecostal Theology of *Confidence* Magazine (1908–1926): A Version of the Five-Fold Gospel?', *JEPTA* 28, no. 2 (2008): 122.

began to appear and become familiar in the sense of a real spiritual crisis for the Christian subsequent to regeneration'.[79] This notion of having a spiritual experience subsequent to conversion, coupled with the 'higher life' teaching that the Spirit baptism was not just for personal sanctification but for the purpose of empowerment[80] paved the way for the Pentecostal doctrine of Spirit baptism.

Third, the doctrine of sanctification was also seen by many Keswick and Holiness teachers as connected to the divine healing of the body.[81] This emphasis would be carried into the Pentecostal movement, for example, Mary Boddy – the wife of Alexander Boddy and a British Pentecostal pioneer in her own right – taught a close 'relation of "full sanctification to Divine Life and Healing"'.[82] Finally, the Keswick tradition advocated premillennialism over postmillennialism,[83] which would become the eschatological position of most classical Pentecostals, including Elim.

In terms of *rationality* the 'Higher Life' and 'Holiness' advocates were biblical primitivists searching for a deeper spiritual experience. This meant that they saw great value in what they believed to be true biblical religious experiences. For example, the influential American Holiness preacher A. J. Gordon stated that 'experience is the surest touchstone of truth. It is not always infallible [but] this is a kind of testimony which is not easily ruled out of court.'[84] And the regular Keswick speaker F. B. Meyer encouraged Christians to move from 'the realm of shadows into that of realities'.[85] It is thus not surprising that space was given for spiritual encounters to take place at the Keswick Conventions and 'testimonies' of people who had had these types of experiences were an important part of the meetings.[86]

Thus, in many ways the rationality of Keswick was 'Romantic' in nature; that is, it preferred personal experience over argument.[87] For example, the view of

79. Gee, *The Pentecostal Movement*, 4.
80. Grant Wacker, 'The Holy Spirit and the Spirit of the Age in American Protestantism, 1880–1910', *JAH* 72, no. 1 (June 1985): 48; Dieter, *The Holiness Revival of the Nineteenth Century*, 251–2.
81. Dayton, *Theological Roots of Pentecostalism*, 136; Vinson Synan, *The Holiness Pentecostal Tradition*, 192; William K. Kay, *Pentecostalism: SCM Core Text* (London: SCM Press, 2009), 33.
82. T. M. Jeffreys, 'Sunderland International Pentecostal Congress – Teaching', *Confidence* 2, no. 6 (June 1909): 135.
83. Bebbington, *Holiness in Nineteenth-Century England*, 83.
84. A. J. Gordon, *The Ministry of Healing; or, Miracles of Cure in All Ages* (Brooklyn, 1882), 175 quoted in Wacker, 'The Holy Spirit and Spirit of the Age', 56–7.
85. F. B. Meyer, *The Way into the Holiest: Expositions of the Epistle to the Hebrews* (London, n.d.), 221–2 quoted in Wacker, 'The Holy Spirit and Spirit of the Age', 61.
86. Steven Barabas, *So Great Salvation: The History and Message of the Keswick Convention* (London: Marshall, Morgan and Scott, 1952), 34; Dieter, *The Holiness Revival of the Nineteenth Century*, 157–8.
87. See Bebbington, *Holiness in Nineteenth-Century England*, 79.

the Romantic 'Lake Poet' Samuel Taylor Coleridge regarding the importance of experience and feeling in grounding true Christianity over 'evidences' and 'arguments' (see Section 3.1.1.2)[88] seemed to have been shared by the Keswick movement.

These spiritual experiences at Keswick were primarily seen as individual and inner experiences for Christians. In other words, the Keswick Conventions focused on inner religious experience, and discouraged 'emotionalism' and physical manifestations;[89] there was a dislike for mass meetings and using 'devices for attracting large crowds';[90] and the purpose of the experience was to renew the Christian, not to convert the unbeliever, even if Christians were encouraged to fulfil the Great Commission.[91]

This kind of Keswick rationality characterized by experientialism and testimony would be shared by the Welsh Revival as well as by the early Pentecostals. However, both the Welsh Revival and Pentecostalism would move beyond the Keswick concept of experience by focusing also on external manifestations, facilitating collective spiritual experiences and not limiting religious encounters just to Christians (this will be developed below).

In sum, the influence of the Holiness ethos, particularly in its Keswick expression, was significant for the emergence of early British Pentecostalism and Elim, and it is central for understanding their roots. In the words of Malcolm Hathaway: 'The Keswick movement played a seminal role in the origins of the Welsh Revival and the Pentecostal movement. It raised the level of spiritual life and commitment in the churches, against the wider background of decline caused by higher criticism, theological liberalism and the religion-science conflict.'[92] The 'higher life' and Holiness traditions fitted well into the Victorian *sitz im leben*. They sought true and authentic Christian spirituality, were Romantic in their intellectual mood by emphasizing spiritual experience over 'arguments' and opposed the so-called Liberal theology by holding strongly to key Evangelical beliefs.[93]

---

88. Coleridge, *Aids to Reflection*. Kindle.
89. Barabas, *So Great Salvation*, 31; Pollock, *The Keswick Story*, 129.
90. Barabas, *So Great Salvation*, 37; Pollock, *The Keswick Story*, 126.
91. Barabas, *So Great Salvation*, 31; Pollock, *The Keswick Story*, 88.
92. Malcolm R. Hathaway, 'The Elim Pentecostal Church: Origins, Developments and Distinctives', in *Pentecostal Perspectives*, ed. Keith Warrington (Carlisle: Paternoster, 1998), 3.
93. The Holiness movement as a reaction against liberal tendencies in later nineteenth-century Christianity has been noted by Vinson Synan, *The Holiness Pentecostal Tradition*, 46. However, Wacker makes the valid point that the so-called new theology (read: Liberals) and higher life theology (read: Holiness movements) also had a number of similarities and were both children of the nineteenth-century 'religious womb'; Wacker, 'The Holy Spirit and the Spirit of the Age', 49.

3.2.2 The Welsh Revival

The Welsh Revival of 1904–05 was influenced by 'the Keswick movement and its Holiness teaching'.[94] Like Keswick, the revival at Wales had a significant impact on British and worldwide Pentecostalism.[95] The early American participant-historian of Pentecostalism, Frank Bartleman, wrote in 1925 that the Pentecostal movement was 'rocked in the cradle of little Wales';[96] a view shared by his British contemporaries Alexander Boddy, Ernest C. W. Boulton and Donald Gee, who all acknowledged the Welsh Revival as one of the main precursors for the birth of Pentecostalism.[97]

Indeed many British Pentecostal pioneers had been personally impacted by the revival. The 'father of British Pentecostalism', Alexander Boddy, made contact with the Welsh revivalist Evan Roberts and visited Tonypandy in South Wales to see the revival. Thomas Ball Barratt, who is often acknowledged as bringing Pentecostalism to Europe, was also in contact with Roberts and began midday prayer meetings for revival in Norway.[98] Moreover, some key early British Pentecostal leaders were converted through the revival. Daniel P. Williams, the founder of the Apostolic Church, claimed that he was 'saved' through the ministry of Roberts;[99] and Donald Gee, the future Assemblies of God statesman, in his own words, 'personally accepted Christ as his Saviour' in a London meeting held by the Welsh revivalist Seth Joshua.[100] Of particular significance to Elim is that George Jeffreys and his older brother Stephen were both converted during the revival in Wales.[101] With respect to George Jeffreys, Andrew Walker and Neil Hudson have

---

94. Robert Pope, 'Demythologising the Evan Roberts Revival, 1904–1905', *JEH*, no. 3 (2006): 520. See also David D. Bundy, 'Welsh Revival', in *The New International Dictionary of Pentecostal and Charismatic Movements*, 1187.

95. Bundy, 'Welsh Revival', 1187; Edward J. Gitre, 'The 1904–05 Welsh Revival: Modernization, Technologies, and Techniques of the Self', *CH* 73, no. 4 (December 2004): 826; Pope, 'Demythologising the Evan Roberts Revival', 520–1; Kyuhyung Cho, 'The Importance of the Welsh Religious Revival in the Formation of British Pentecostalism', *JEPTA* 30, no. 1 (2010): 22–5.

96. Frank Bartleman, *Azusa Street: The Roots of Modern-day Pentecost* (Plainfield, NJ: Logos International, 1980), 19.

97. Alexander A. Boddy, 'The Pentecostal Movement. The Story of Its Beginning at Sunderland and Its Present Position in Great Britain', *Confidence* 3, no. 8 (August 1910): 194; Ernest C. W. Boulton, *George Jeffreys: A Ministry of the Miraculous* (London: Elim Publishing, 1928), 2–3; Gee, *The Pentecostal Movement*, 5–7.

98. Cho, 'The Importance of the Welsh Religious Revival', 23–4.

99. Ibid., 24.

100. Gee, *The Pentecostal Movement*, 37.

101. Desmond Cartwright, *The Great Evangelists: The Remarkable Lives of George and Stephen Jeffreys* (Basingstoke: Marshall Morgan and Scott, 1986), 18–19; William Kay, *George Jeffreys: Pentecostal Apostle and Revivalist* (Cleveland, TN: CPT Press, 2017), 28.

persuasively argued that the Welsh Revival was the place of his conversion and also became the benchmark for what Pentecostalism should achieve,[102] a position further supported by Noel Brooks who was an associate of Jeffreys.[103] In this sense George Jeffreys and other Pentecostal pioneers were truly 'children of the Welsh Revival'.

The Welsh Revival can be seen to have lasted from the autumn of 1904 to the summer of 1905, although there were reports of spiritual awakening in Wales from 1903 onwards.[104] The revival was facilitated by a band of revivalists, including Seth Joshua, Joseph Jenkins and most notably Evan Roberts.[105] During the revival there were 32,000 to 100,000 converts and many more attended meetings claiming spiritual renewal.[106] It began in South Wales but ended up impacting North Wales, the wider British Isles and various overseas nations.[107]

One key aspect of the Welsh Revival, as stated by Edward J. Gitre, is that it was arguably 'the first distinctly modern religious revival'.[108] Its local and global effect was partly enabled by modern developments of 'mass communication and mass public transportation'.[109] In other words, the press spread the news of the revival like 'wildfire' and the British rail network enabled ordinary people to come and experience the 'revival fire' for themselves. These tools of modernity would also be utilized by British Pentecostals later on to further their cause.

3.2.2.1 Theology and rationality of the Welsh Revival The main significance of the Welsh Revival for Pentecostals was not its theology as such – although on the whole it reaffirmed the Evangelical theology of Keswick – but (1) its ethos and rationality and (2) its non-institutional nature. Regarding the first, the Welsh Revival shared the underlying Romantic rationality of the Keswick movement which emphasized religious experience over arguments. However, the Welsh Revival also developed and modified the Keswick concept of religious experience

---

102. Andrew Walker and Neil Hudson, 'George Jeffreys, Revivalist and Reformer: A Revaluation', in *On Revival: A Critical Examination*, ed. Andrew Walker and Kristin Aune (Cumbria: Paternoster Press, 2003), 140; Neil Hudson, 'The Development of British Pentecostalism', in *European Pentecostalism*, ed. William K. Kay and Anne E. Dyer (Leiden: Brill, 2011), 45.

103. Noel Brooks, *Fight for the Faith and Freedom* (London: The Pattern Bookroom, 1948), 22.

104. Pope, 'Demythologising the Evan Roberts Revival', 516–19; Kay, *Pentecostalism*, 61.

105. Bundy, 'Welsh Revival', 1187. For other significant figures, see Pope, 'Demythologising the Evan Roberts Revival', 516–18.

106. Bundy, 'Welsh Revival', 1187; Gitre, 'The 1904–05 Welsh Revival', 794; Anderson, *An Introduction to Pentecostalism*, 36.

107. Gitre, 'The 1904–05 Welsh Revival', 794.

108. Ibid.

109. Ibid., 824.

from an internal and individualistic encounter of God for Christians *to* an emotional, spontaneous and collective divine encounter accompanied by external manifestations to be experienced by both believers and sceptics alike.

To put it differently, the Welsh Revival meetings were characterized by emotionalism and informality, commonly channelled through spontaneous music and corporate prayer.[110] Roberts himself was an exemplar of spontaneity as he sought direct guidance of the Holy Spirit in the meetings and did not necessarily prepare beforehand what he would say or do.[111] The meetings also tended to be democratic in nature where members of the congregations, who had previously often been marginalized (e.g. women and young people), were given freedom to contribute in their own way and contrary to the traditional patterns of the Welsh Nonconformist churches.[112] There is also some evidence of charismata, like glossolalia, healing and 'words of knowledge' in the revival meetings.[113]

Moreover, the spiritual experience was not just to renew existing Christians but also to convert the sceptics. S. B. Shaw's reporting in 1905 of the revival highlights stories of agnostics and atheists converting to Christianity.[114] The story of Tom Hughes is his primary example where a sceptic who was a member of the 'Ethical Society' was not converted to Christianity through arguments but by both witnessing and experiencing something in the revival meetings. These encounters caused Hughes to not only convert but also burn his books, which supposedly advocated non-Christian sentiments. The moral of Shaw's story about the conversion of Hughes seems to be that no arguments were needed to win the sceptic, only a deep spiritual experience. This experience was sufficient to refute and win over the cynic to the Christian faith.[115] Indeed, this was seen as the answer for re-converting what was seen as 'backsliding' Britain.[116]

These characteristics – particularly emotionalism, informality, spiritual manifestations, and evangelistic emphasis – made the Welsh Revival different from Keswick, which was significantly more reserved in its ethos and spirituality.[117] This revivalist ethos would be later emulated by Pentecostals, even if some of the

---

110. Cho, 'The Importance of the Welsh Religious Revival', 25–6. The Welsh Revival was referred to as 'Quakerism with a song' due to not only its openness to the leading of the Holy Spirit but also its emphasis on spontaneous singing; S. B. Shaw, *The Great Revival in Wales*, ed. Larry Martin (Pensacola, Florida: Christian Life Books, 2002), 220.

111. Pope, 'Demythologising the Evan Roberts Revival', 522.

112. Gitre, 'The 1904–05 Welsh Revival', 796; Pope, 'Demythologising the Evan Roberts Revival', 522; Cho, 'The Importance of the Welsh Religious Revival', 26–7.

113. Kay, *Pentecostalism*, 63; Pope, 'Demythologising the Evan Roberts Revival', 524.

114. Shaw, *The Great Revival in Wales*, 188–93.

115. For a similar story see David Matthews, *I Saw the Welsh Revival: 1904 – Centenary Edition - 2004* (Belfast: Ambassador Publications, 2004), 35–40.

116. See Shaw, *The Great Revival in Wales*, 213.

117. Pollock, *The Keswick Story*, 129.

excesses of the Welsh Revival witnessed by many early Pentecostal pioneers would be guarded against.[118]

Second, despite the immediate 'successes' of the Welsh Revival, its long-term potential did not seem to be fully realized. Roberts did not appear to have a clear ecclesiology and the leaders of revival did not make an effort to strategically organize its results.[119] The new converts were welcomed into the existing Nonconformist churches, but these churches did not seek to reform their liturgical practices to accommodate the revivalist spirituality of their new converts and simply continued with their traditional approaches to Christian worship. Robert Pope sees this failure to reform as the great mistake of the Welsh Nonconformist churches and the possible cause of its twentieth-century decline.[120] It is not hard to argue that the Pentecostal denominational leaders, many of who themselves were 'children of the revival', did not want to find their revival in a similar predicament where either due to a lack of ecclesial structure people would fall away or due to existing rigid ecclesial structures the momentum of Pentecostalism would be lost. Consequently, many Pentecostal leaders sought to create new church structures with the aim of avoiding both of these pitfalls and to provide institutions for the Pentecostal experience to flourish.[121] In this sense, the Welsh Revival was not just an influence for British Pentecostalism in what it achieved but also in what it failed to achieve.

In sum, the Welsh Revival set a model of spiritual renewal for the early Pentecostals. Like the Keswick movement, its emphasis on spiritual experience and Holiness motifs would be shared by the early Pentecostals. However, more so than Keswick, it was its ability to facilitate spiritual encounters for the masses with spiritual manifestations that left a lasting impression on the Pentecostal pioneers, particularly George Jeffreys. It was this aspect of spiritual experiences with external signs on a large scale that provided the spiritual, theological and rational resources for the emerging British Pentecostals. And it was the seeming failure of the Welsh Nonconformist churches to reap the full benefits of the revival that may have motivated some early Pentecostal pioneers to form new Pentecostal denominations.

3.2.3 British Pentecostalism

By 1907 Britain seemed to be ready for the emergence of Pentecostalism. The underlying context of increasing religious pluralism and secularization of society,

---

118. Walsh, *To Meet and Satisfy a Very Hungry People*, 111.
119. Bundy, 'Welsh Revival', 1188.
120. Pope, 'Demythologising the Evan Roberts Revival', 534.
121. For the justification for new denominational structures from both Elim and Assemblies of God perspectives, see Ernest C. W. Boulton, *George Jeffreys: A Ministry of the Miraculous*, ed. Chris Cartwright (Tonbridge: Sovereign World, 1999), 20–3. Gee, *The Pentecostal Movement*, 140–6.

the theology and spiritualty of the Holiness movements, and the revivalist experientialism and hunger generated by the Welsh Revival, provided a fertile ground for the emergence and spreading of Pentecostalism in Britain. Donald Dayton, writing about the birth of Pentecostalism in United States, notes that the 'higher Christian life' and Holiness movements with their emphasis on salvation, baptism in the Spirit, divine healing and the second coming functioned as 'a sort of pre-Pentecostal tinderbox awaiting the spark that would set it off'.[122] He goes on to point out that when Pentecostalism did finally emerge, the leaders within the Holiness movement 'recognized that it was only the gift of tongues that set it apart from their own teachings'.[123] A similar comment can be said of British Pentecostalism – that is, the Holiness movement(s) and the Welsh Revival provided the theological framework, spiritual expectation and rational resources for the Pentecostal renewal, and like in America it seemed to be glossolalia that was mainly condemned by the British Pentecostals' Holiness counterparts.[124] However, I will argue that it was not just the theology of glossolalia that was the difference between the early Pentecostals and their Holiness predecessors but also the rationality that accompanied this doctrine.

3.2.3.1 Los Angeles, Barratt and Boddy The question of Pentecostal origins has been widely debated. For example, was there a single origin (monogenesis) or multiple origins (polygenesis) for the global movement?[125] Moreover, if there was a single origin, was it Topeka with Charles Fox Parham or Los Angeles with William Seymour?[126] My aim is not to discuss the global origins of Pentecostalism as such, but rather to focus on the origins of British Pentecostalism in as much as it is relevant for understanding Elim. As has already been argued, the emergence of British Pentecostalism can only be understood in the context of the broader British religious context, the Holiness movements and the Welsh Revival. However, the American Pentecostal influence on British Pentecostalism cannot be ignored. Cornelis van der Laan has demonstrated from early British Pentecostal periodicals that in self-identifying the origins of British Pentecostalism 'Azusa Street plays a very important role as the place where the fire first fell and from where it spread

---

122. Dayton, *Theological Roots of Pentecostalism*, 174.

123. Ibid., 175; see also D. William Faupel, *The Everlasting Gospel: The Significance of Eschatology in the Development of Pentecostal Thought* (Sheffield: Sheffield Academic Press, 1996), 14.

124. Some of the major British Holiness critics of the Pentecostal notions of 'tongues' were Reader Harris, Oswald Chambers and Jessie Penn-Lewis; Walsh, *To Meet and Satisfy a Very Hungry People*, 44–6.

125. See Michael McClymond, '"I will Pour Out of My Spirit Upon All Flesh": An Historical and Theological Meditation on Pentecostal Origins', *Pneuma* 37, no. 3 (2015): 356–74.

126. See Hollenweger, *Pentecostalism*, 20–4.

over the world', whereas 'the Topeka event and Parham are completely absent'.[127] For example, in early *Elim Evangels*, Thomas E. Hackett refers to April 1906 and Los Angeles as the place where the Pentecostal 'movement commenced',[128] and Elizabeth Sisson refers to Los Angeles and Azusa Street as the birthplace of the global Pentecostal revival.[129]

This link with Los Angeles for British Pentecostalism was largely created by three influential British Pentecostal pioneers: Thomas Ball Barratt, Alexander Boddy and Cecil Polhill. While visiting America and residing in New York at A. B. Simpson's 'Missionary Home', Barratt heard of the Azusa Street revival taking place in Los Angeles. Inspired by the Azusa events, in October 1906 Barratt had a profound religious experience which was then followed by 'speaking in tongues' in November 1906.[130] When Barratt returned to Norway, he began preaching the Pentecostal message and holding revival meetings in Oslo.

Boddy received news of the events taking place at Azusa Street and also of the Oslo meetings under Barratt's leadership. Encouraged by what he heard, he visited Barratt in Oslo in March 1907 for four days.[131] According to Boddy's own reflection of his time in Christiania (Oslo), 'the presence and power of God were even beyond that of the meetings in Wales ... [and] in one meeting ... [I] received a blessed and wonderful 'Baptism' of the Holy Ghost'.[132] He was clearly impressed with what he witnessed and experienced in Oslo, and when he returned to England, he began advocating the Pentecostal message, including speaking in tongues. Boddy also invited Barratt to visit Sunderland and it was at the end of August 1907 that Barratt finally arrived at Sunderland. At Sunderland, Barratt held a number of revival meetings with the result of many receiving baptism in the Spirit accompanied with speaking in tongues.[133] Although these were not the first instances of individuals experiencing baptism in the Spirit understood through a Pentecostal lens in Britain,[134] they seemed to be the first occasion where collective

127. Cornelis van der Laan, 'What Good Can Come from Los Angeles? Changing Perceptions of the North American Pentecostal Origins in Early Western European Pentecostal Periodicals', in *The Azusa Street Revival and Its Legacy*, ed. Harold D. Hunter and Cecil M. Robeck (Cleveland, TN: Pathway Press, 2006), 159.

128. Thomas E. Hackett, 'The Nearing Advent of Our Lord', *EE* 2, no. 3 (June 1921): 43.

129. Elizabeth Sisson, 'Reminiscences', *EE* 10, no. 16 (16 August 1929): 245–6.

130. David Bundy, 'Thomas Ball Barratt: From Methodist to Pentecostal', *EPTA Bulletin: JEPTA* 13, no. 1 (1994): 37.

131. Wakefield, *Alexander Boddy*, 81.

132. Boddy, 'The Pentecostal Movement', 194.

133. Wakefield, *Alexander Boddy*, 84–9.

134. Catherine Price of Brixton (London) spoke in tongues in January 1907 and is credited as the first person in Britain to speak in tongues in the twentieth century; Neil Hudson, 'The Earliest Days of British Pentecostalism', *JEPTA* 21, no. 1 (2001): 52.

speaking in tongues took place.[135] In fact, Donald Gee referred to Barratt's meetings as the moment when the 'Pentecostal Revival had commenced in the British Isles'.[136]

That said, Boddy's influence on British Pentecostalism and Sunderland's significance as *the* early centre of the emerging movement was not just down to Barratt's visit.[137] From 1908 to 1914 annual Pentecostal conferences were conducted by Boddy at Sunderland and from 1908 to 1926 Boddy also edited the *Confidence* magazine. Both of these proved to be formative for British Pentecostal practice and theology.[138] In fact, when it comes to Elim it was at the Sunderland convention in 1913 where George Jeffreys was first introduced to William Gillespie, who subsequently invited Jeffreys to Ireland leading to the birth of Elim in 1915.[139] Moreover, the Pentecostal Missionary Union (PMU) was founded in 1909 with Boddy's close associate Cecil Polhill as its president (who himself had received the Pentecostal experience at Azusa in February 1908),[140] and Boddy as the editorial secretary.[141] The PMU was pivotal in training many early British Pentecostal pioneers, such as Elim's George Jeffreys and E. J. Phillips.[142] The formation of the PMU also meant that British Pentecostalism under the leadership of Boddy and Polhill would travel overseas with the organization's missionaries.

3.2.3.2 Theology and rationality of early British Pentecostalism As has already been suggested, the early British Pentecostals shared the fourfold/fivefold doctrinal emphasis common in the Holiness movement. Indeed, Mark Cartledge has argued that the early Pentecostal theology of the *Confidence* magazine was very much characterized by the fourfold/fivefold framework, despite the actual absence of the phrases 'Fourfold-Gospel' or 'Fivefold-Gospel'.[143] Cartledge's conclusion is supported by the early issues of *Confidence*, where the themes of Jesus as saviour, sanctifier, healer, baptiser in the Spirit and coming King are common topics of

---

135. William K. Kay, 'Sunderland's Legacy in New Denominations', *JEPTA* 28, no. 2 (2008): 193.

136. Gee, *The Pentecostal Movement*, 24.

137. For analysis of other important 'centres' of British Pentecostalism, see Walsh, *To Meet and Satisfy a Very Hungry People*.

138. Kay, 'Sunderland's Legacy in New Denominations', 193–6. Hudson, 'The Earliest Days of British Pentecostalism', 66–7.

139. Cartwright, *The Great Evangelists*, 39.

140. See John Usher, 'Cecil Henry Polhill: The Patron of the Pentecostals', *Pneuma* 34, no. 1 (2012): 48.

141. Wakefield, *Alexander Boddy*, 136.

142. Boulton, *George Jeffreys* (1928), 13.

143. Cartledge, 'The Early Pentecostal Theology of *Confidence* Magazine (1908–1926)', 118–32.

discussion.[144] Furthermore, the programme of the first 'Whitsuntide Conference' held at Sunderland in June 1908 highlights the centrality of the Fourfold Gospel for the emerging British Pentecostalism. In other words, there are three themed sessions for the conference which cover three of the four aspects of the Fourfold Gospel; that is, there is a session on (1) '"Tongues" as a Sign of 'Pentecost', (2) 'The Coming of the Lord', and (3) 'Divine Life – Health and Healing in Christ'.[145] Boddy's own reflective conclusion on the Sunderland Conference further affirms the importance of the Christocentric Fourfold/Fivefold Gospel. He writes:

> Glory to God! Souls are being *saved* and *sanctified, bodies healed,* demons cast out, and the *Holy Ghost poured out 'as at the beginning',* but far above all '*we see Jesus*', and His Love is flooding our own souls, and in our gathering of 1908 we felt that we were knit together by a love that burst all bonds of Church organization and social position, and made us truly 'one in Christ Jesus' – '*Till He comes*'. (My italics)[146]

The distinctive feature of the British Pentecostal movement vis-à-vis the wider British Holiness fraternity, is the emphasis on receiving 'Pentecost' or 'Baptism in the Holy Spirit' with tongues as the evidence. Boddy notes in his first editorial of *Confidence* that the magazine could have legitimately been called 'Pentecost with signs',[147] and interestingly, those coming to the first Sunderland Conference were expected to sign a declaration stating: 'I declare that I am in full sympathy with those who are seeking "Pentecost" with the Sign of the Tongues. I also undertake to accept the ruling of the chairman'.[148] This declaration underscores both the centrality of glossolalia as the sign and also the seeming opposition from some (presumably from the Holiness traditions), who may have wanted to attend the first British Pentecostal Conference. This same sentiment is reflected in one of the first British Pentecostal theological statements, namely, the 'London Declaration' on 'The Baptism in the Holy Ghost' – signed in November 1909 by prominent Pentecostal leaders – which starts by stating that 'THE "PROMISE OF THE FATHER" (Acts i., 4) was, and is, *evidenced* by the Speaking in *"Tongues"*' (my italics).[149]

---

144. E.g. Alexander A. Boddy, '"Confidence" – Our First Number', *Confidence* 1 (April 1908): 3; Alexander A. Boddy (ed.), 'The Gift of Tongues', *Confidence* 2 (May 1908): 4–5; Mary Boddy, 'Health and Healing in Jesus', *Confidence* 2 (May 1908): 16–17; Alexander A. Boddy, 'Pleading the Blood', *Confidence* 5 (August 1908): 3–6.

145. Alexander A. Boddy (ed.), 'Conference Programme', *Confidence* 1 (April 1908): 2.

146. Alexander A. Boddy, 'The Sunderland Conference, June 1908', *Confidence* 3 (June 1908): 13.

147. Boddy, '"Confidence" – Our First Number', 3.

148. Alexander A. Boddy (ed.), 'Whitsuntide Conference at Sunderland', *Confidence* 1 (April 1908): 2.

149. Alexander A. Boddy (ed.), 'A London Declaration (November 1909): The Baptism in the Holy Ghost. What we teach concerning the Evidence and the Results', *Confidence* 2, no. 12 (December 1909): 287.

The significance of the 'Sign of the Tongues', however, is not just in emphasizing the importance of 'tongues' within early Pentecostal theology, but in the actual need to have a *sign*. In other words, there appears to be an 'experiential' and 'evidentialist' dimension in the rationality of the emerging Pentecostals. To put it differently, Pentecostals needed to have evidence for their encounter with God, and a genuine spiritual experience for them needed to be supported by external evidence, namely, 'tongues'. In fact, the common synonym for the word 'sign' on the pages of *Confidence* is 'scriptural evidence(s)'.[150] Consequently, it seems that the rationality of early Pentecostalism could be categorized as a form of *biblical and experiential Evidentialism*.

Indeed, Kenneth J. Archer, L. William Oliverio Jr. and Bradford McCall have noted that early American Pentecostalism affirmed the authority of both 'Scripture' and 'experience'.[151] In the words of Oliverio, 'the Protestant Christian Scriptures were the sole ultimate authority for Christian belief and living which functioned dialogically with the religious and general experiences of early Pentecostals to form a theological understanding of their world.'[152] This dual emphasis on the 'Bible' and 'experience' was also strongly present in the British Pentecostal psyche, and it is what makes them different from the early-twentieth-century Protestant Liberals, who primarily emphasized (inner) experience, and Protestant Fundamentalist, who primarily emphasized the Scriptures. Pentecostals focused on *both* experience and scripture and, thus in the words of Nancey Murphy, would hold a 'middle position between fundamentalism and liberalism.'[153]

Nevertheless, Pentecostals in both America and Britain did not simply understand experience as an inner spiritual matter of the heart but as an external spiritual manifestation with visible evidences along biblical lines. This kind of biblical and experiential Evidentialism is interesting in the light of the late-nineteenth- and early-twentieth-century intellectual context discussed above. The Pentecostal logic seems to be, perhaps somewhat ironically, a combination of Coleridge's Romanticism of 'experience over arguments' and Clifford's Evidentialism of 'it is wrong always, everywhere, and for anyone, to believe anything upon insufficient evidence.'[154] In combining Romanticism and Evidentialism Pentecostalism shows developments from the Keswick and Welsh Revival understandings of what is deemed as an authoritative spiritual experience. At the risk of oversimplification,

---

150. For example, Alexander A. Boddy (ed.), 'India – A Message from Mukti', *Confidence* 6 (September 1908): 14; Alexander A. Boddy, 'Speaking in Tongues. Is this of God?', *Confidence* 8 (November 1908): 9.

151. Archer, *A Pentecostal Hermeneutic*, 63; Bradford McCall, 'A Contemporary Reappropriation of Baconian Common Sense Realism in Renewal Hermeneutics', *Pneuma* 32, no. 2 (2010): 228.

152. Oliverio Jr., *Theological Hermeneutics in the Classical Pentecostal Tradition*, 31.

153. Murphy, *Beyond Liberalism and Fundamentalism*, n. 8 on 6; cf. Archer, *A Pentecostal Hermeneutic*, 63.

154. Clifford, 'The Ethics of Belief'.

the Keswick emphasis appears to have been on personal inner spiritual experience in line with the Romantic mood. The Welsh Revival develops this inner Keswickian experience by intensifying it in the context of revival meetings, and starts to show some 'signs' of external spiritual manifestations. The Pentecostal movement then further moves from the 'inner' to the 'outer' aspects of experience by now articulating the need for there to be specific and verifiable evidence for one's encounter with God. Boddy himself suggests that there is a difference between the Keswick and the Pentecostal movement possibly along the lines I have suggested. In his words: 'Many of us thank God for Keswick in the past … [but we] feel that the Lord is calling to His people to "go forward." He is calling His people to an *experimental Pentecost*' (my italics).[155]

Therefore, the Pentecostal distinctive with respect to the Holiness movements and the Welsh Revival is not only the theology of 'tongues', but the Pentecostal movement also demonstrates a unique element within its rationality. It takes on the Romantic experientialism of Keswick and adds an element of external verification to it. To put it simply, *Pentecostalism is Keswick Romanticism 'baptised' with Evidentialism*.[156] This Evidentialism, however, is not simply aligned to Mill's new scientific method or simply a retreat to Baconian Common Sense philosophy. It does carry elements of both, particularly the latter,[157] but it also offers its own nascent rationality of *biblical pragmatism* which Elim would adopt and develop, as will be argued in Chapter 4.

3.2.4 Elim's roots: From Keswick 'Romanticism' to Pentecostal 'Evidentialism'

The purpose of this chapter has been to outline the 'prologues' to the Elim tradition. In doing so, the first part has explored the philosophical and theological *context* within which British Pentecostalism and Elim emerged, and this second section has identified the *roots* which nourished British Pentecostalism and Elim to life. Regarding the roots, I have argued that British Pentecostalism is best seen within the tradition of British Evangelicalism with more direct theological and rational links to the nineteenth-century Holiness traditions (particularly Keswick) and the early-twentieth-century Welsh Revival. The theology of early Pentecostals in Britain was on the whole Evangelical with an emphasis on the Fourfold/Fivefold Gospel that had been largely inherited from Keswick and the Welsh Revival. The main theological difference between early British Pentecostals and their Holiness ancestors was the Pentecostal emphasis on Spirit Baptism with the 'sign of tongues'.

155. Alexander A. Boddy, 'Brief Items', *Confidence* 5 (August 1908): 14.

156. For a similar conclusion regarding the Pentecostal doctrine of 'tongues as initial evidence', albeit from an American perspective, see Kenneth Richard Walters Jr., *Why Tongues? The Initial Evidence Doctrine in North American Pentecostal Churches* (Dorset: Deo Publishing, 2016).

157. Cf. Archer, *A Pentecostal Hermeneutic*, 63; McCall, 'A Contemporary Reappropriation', 227–32.

However, as I have tried to demonstrate, an important distinction between early Pentecostals and the Holiness fraternity was not just on the 'theology of tongues' but on the underlying rationality at work within this doctrine. In other words, Pentecostals took the Romantic experientialism of Keswick, which had been externalized in the Welsh Revival, and 'baptized it in Evidentialism' by demanding 'evidences' and 'signs' for the validity of one's Spirit baptism. It was this move that gave Pentecostals their distinct theological emphasis and unique rationality. Elim, as a British Pentecostal tradition, would go on to embody and develop this innovation.

Chapter 4 will move from Elim's *context* and *roots* to focusing explicitly on Elim. However, as noted by MacIntyre, we are all 'born with a past',[158] and thus we can only make sense of the emerging Elim argument if we understand its pre-history. In sum, Elim was birthed in the context of modernity and its early nourishment was from Keswick, Welsh Revival and nascent British Pentecostalism as it went on to argue its own case.

---

158. MacIntyre, *After Virtue*, 221.

Chapter 4

THE BIRTH OF ELIM: THE EARLY OPPONENTS, CONTENT, RATIONALITY AND EMBODIMENT OF THE ELIM ARGUMENT

In Chapter 3 I identified the 'prologues' to the Elim tradition by first outlining its broader philosophical and theological *context*, and then narrating its theological and intellectual *roots* within Keswick, the Welsh Revival and British Pentecostalism. Shaped by this wider context and firmly rooted in the British Pentecostal heritage, Elim emerged as a movement on 7 January 1915. Elim's initial eighteen years (1915-33) can be seen along MacIntyrian lines as the first stage in the formation of the Elim tradition and thus foundational in the development of the 'Elim argument'.[1]

To identify the essence of the emerging Elim argument, I will utilize the methodology presented in Chapter 2 by first discussing Elim's implied opponents. Second, I will seek to discern exactly what the Elim movement was arguing for, with particular emphasis on its early theological *hard core* and *auxiliary hypotheses*. Third, I will explore how Elim in its early days sought to proceed with this argument; that is, what was the movement's tacit rationality? And finally I will explore the social embodiment of the argument.

The primary sources used in this chapter are *Elim Evangel* (the authorized Elim periodical depicting the views of the movement to its own adherents and other interested parties), Elim books and pamphlets (particularly those written by George Jeffreys), letter correspondence, and Elim's early constitutional and doctrinal documents.

4.1 The implied opponents of the Elim argument

When the Elim argument entered the British religious scene it quickly articulated both what it stood *for* and also what it stood *against*. In Elim's first official statement

---

1. The formational stage of Elim seems to end in 1934 when the Deed Poll effectively cements Elim's constitution. Moreover, around the same time Jeffreys increasingly shifted his emphasis away from evangelistic campaigns to revisiting established Elim churches, which also implies an end to Elim's formational period. In fact, Walker and Hudson refer to 1915 to 1934 as Jeffreys' 'golden years'; Walker and Hudson, 'George Jeffreys, Revivalist and Reformer', 141.

of beliefs, the movement is presented as 'earnestly contending for the Faith which once was delivered to the saints' (Jude 3) in a 'Laodicean age of apostasy' that was making the church 'powerless to cope with the sin and unbelief which is overwhelming in the world in the present age'.[2] For Elim this purported 'apostasy' seems to have been caused by three trends within early-twentieth-century Western Christianity, namely, (1) *Liberalism* (often equated with 'Modernism') with its 'higher criticism' and 'New Theology'; (2) *cessationism* regarding the supernatural gifts of the Holy Spirit in the current dispensation; and (3) *ritualism* which was seen as a distraction from the true essence of Christianity. It was against these three opponents that Elim directed its argument.

4.1.1 Contending against Liberalism

As discussed in Chapter 3 (see particularly Sections 3.1.2 and 3.1.3), in the late-nineteenth- and early-twentieth-century religious scepticism and theological Liberalism was on the rise in Britain. Russell Spittler has noted that classical Pentecostalism as a whole, just like Fundamentalism and Neo-Orthodoxy, can be seen as reacting against this liberal trend within European and American Christianity.[3] This seems to be true also for Elim, as from its inception it opposed theological Liberalism,[4] and from May 1931 onwards the *Elim Evangel* explicitly identified on its first page that Elim 'stands uncompromisingly for the whole Bible as the inspired word of God and contends for THE FAITH *against modern thought, Higher Criticism, and New Theology*' (my italics).[5]

Elim seemed to have three major concerns with so-called modern thought. First, along with higher criticism, it appeared to challenge the divine authority of the Bible. George Jeffreys lamented that 'it was considered a terrible thing a few years ago for a person to openly condemn the Scriptures', but today the 'Bible as the inspired word of God is disputed'.[6] This 'disputing' of the Bible's divine

---

2. George Jeffreys, *Elim Christ Church: What We Believe* (Belfast: Wm. Brown and Sons, 1916), 1. To be precise this document is a statement of faith for Elim's first local church in Belfast. Nevertheless, it is reasonable to assume that it reflects the ethos of the emerging movement and functioned as the benchmark for Elim's subsequent statements.

3. Russell P. Spittler, 'Are Pentecostals and Charismatics Fundamentalists? A Review of American Uses of These Categories', in *Charismatic Christianity as a Global Culture*, ed. Karla Poewe (Columbia, South Carolina: University of South Carolina Press, 1994), 107.

4. For example, Jeffreys, *Elim Christ Church*, 1–2.

5. No author, 'The Elim Evangel and Foursquare Gospel Revivalist', *EE* 12, no. 18 (1 May 1931): 273. Reflecting on the Elim movement and its founder, Boulton declares in 1928 how 'George Jeffreys with the rod of the inspired Word fearlessly smote the water of an incredulous and invasive modernism, opening up a passage by which many others might pass'; Boulton, *George Jeffreys* (1999), 8.

6. George Jeffreys, *The Miraculous Foursquare Gospel – Doctrinal* (London: Elim Publishing, 1929), 51.

authority was seemingly carried out by the higher critics in undermining Moses' authorship of the Pentateuch, questioning the historicity of Noah's Flood, and attempting to reconcile Darwinian evolution with Genesis 1–2.[7] Secondly, the Modernists rejected the miraculous nature of the Christian faith as understood by Elim. Indeed, the anti-supernaturalism of the higher critics was believed to be a major reason for them not accepting the (full) divine inspiration of Scripture.[8] Thirdly, in denying the supernatural aspects of Christianity the New Theologians were believed to be inappropriately rewriting orthodox doctrines by rejecting Christ's divine incarnation, atonement, resurrection and second coming.[9]

Elim was resolute in its attack against these liberal trends, not least as the Modernist approach to the Bible and Christian beliefs was argued to originate from the 'devil … the Father of lies' who was believed to be the 'first higher critic' in questioning the truthfulness of God's words.[10] Writing in 1923 George Jeffreys went as far as to suggest that 'if Germany, with the other nations, had rejected the poison of New Theology and Higher Criticism, they would have escaped the awful judgments that were now falling upon them'.[11] Consequently, Elim's opposition to theological Liberalism was based not just on the latter disputing the authority of the Bible, rejecting supernaturalism and undermining orthodox Christian doctrines, but on the conviction that these beliefs emanated from 'the devil' and thus in due course would receive divine punishment.

So does this opposition to 'Modernism' make Elim effectively a Fundamentalist movement? Elim certainly rejected Liberal theology with the vehemence of the Fundamentalists.[12] Moreover, Elim shared many of the same religious roots with the Fundamentalists in the Holiness traditions, and also held a number of similar theological convictions, with particular emphasis on the authority of the Bible and the second coming of Christ.[13] Indeed, the Elim movement was quite happy

---

7. D. J. Davies, 'The Bible and Modernism', *EE* 6, no. 23 (1 December 1925): 273–4.

8. George Jeffreys, *Healing Rays*, 4th edn (Kent: Henry E. Walter LTD, 1985), 7.

9. Jeffreys, *The Miraculous Foursquare Gospel – Doctrinal*, 51–2; A. M. H., 'Modernism: Self-confessed & Self-exposed', *EE* 12, no. 5 (30 January 1931): 66; J. N. Hoover, 'The Tragedy of Modern Theology', *EE* 14, no. 35 (1 September 1933): 549.

10. Davies, 'The Bible and Modernism', 129.

11. George Jeffreys, 'Pentecost in Scandinavia', *EE* 4, No. 11 (November 1923): 231.

12. For studies on Fundamentalism, see Ernest R. Sandeen, *The Roots of Fundamentalism: British and American Millenarianism 1800–1930* (Chicago: The University of Chicago Press, 1970); George M. Marsden, *Fundamentalism and American Culture*, 2nd edn (New York: Oxford University Press, 2006); Harris, *Fundamentalism and Evangelicals*.

13. Gerald King identifies the premillennial commitment of Pentecostals and Fundamentalists as the factor that 'most closely found the two movements'; Gerald W. King, *Disfellowshiped: Pentecostal Responses to Fundamentalism in the United States, 1906–1943* (Eugene, OR: Pickwick Publications, 2011), Loc 2164.

to be associated with Fundamentalism,[14] and George Jeffreys together with the Fundamentalist Professor J. Robertson were even visualized by *Elim Evangel* as 'the two champions of Fundamentalism'.[15]

Nevertheless, there were also significant differences between Elim and Fundamentalism with respect to their *rationality* and *theology*. Regarding rationality, the Fundamentalists effectively followed Baconian common-sense approach,[16] whereas Elim would adopt a Pentecostal type experiential/pragmatic rationality (this will be developed in Section 4.3). In terms of theology, the Fundamentalists embraced a more *cessationist* view regarding the gifts of the Spirit, whereas Elim promulgated what it saw as the 'Full Gospel' (this will be developed in Section 4.2). It was these types of theological differences (grounded in differing rationalities) that appeared to lead to the 1928 condemnation of Pentecostals by the World's Christian Fundamentals Association,[17] and also what made many of the Fundamentalists Elim's second implied opponents.

4.1.2 Contending against Fundamentalist cessationism

George Jeffreys claimed that by contending for the miraculous Gospel, Elim was not just against the 'higher critic', but also what he called the 'lower critic'. According to Jeffreys,

> The lower critic is the one who unreservedly accepts the Bible as the inspired Word of God, but who endeavours to shew from its pages that we are not living in the days of miracles. If he cannot succeed in proving that the miraculous was withdrawn at the end of the apostolic days, he attempts to postpone the supernatural element to a future millennium ... the lower critic is the most inconsistent with his own standpoint, and indeed presents a pitiable sight. He starts off by declaring his absolute faith in a present-day miraculous Bible with all its commands and promises, and then argues that miracles are not for the present age ... While professing to believe in a supernatural religion, he is all the time undermining its foundations.[18]

Elim's criticism of the 'lower critic' was partly a reaction to the lower critics' opposition to Elim's belief in present-day miracles. Indeed, ever since the

---

14. Earle V. Pierce, D.D. 'Why I am a Fundamentalist?', *EE* 14, no. 8 (24 February 1933): 116–18.

15. Percy Le Tissier, 'A Champion of Fundamentalism: Rev. Professor J. Robertson, D.D. at the City Temple, Glasgow', *EE* 13, no. 27 (1 July 1932): 427.

16. For the philosophical roots of Fundamentalism, see Harris, *Fundamentalism and Evangelicals*, 94–130.

17. For the statement of the World's Christian Fundamentals Association on Pentecostals, see Spittler, 'Are Pentecostals and Charismatics Fundamentalists', 109.

18. Jeffreys, *Healing Rays*, 8–9.

Pentecostal movement emerged in Britain, it was heavily criticized, particularly by the Holiness fraternity.[19] Desmond Cartwright insightfully points out that in 1907–13 the opposition towards Pentecostalism was mainly with respect to 'speaking in tongues', but by the 1920s the criticism had shifted to the Pentecostal practice and theology of 'divine healing'.[20] George Jeffreys was a healing evangelist reaching increasing influence in the 1920s and thus it was this rejection of 'divine healing' (read: miracles) by certain Evangelical groups that was a major concern for Jeffreys and Elim.

That said, Elim did accept some criticism against the 'experiential excesses' of certain Pentecostals. To this effect Elim identified itself as a movement that 'condemns extravagances and fanaticism in every shape and form'.[21] Nevertheless, Elim saw itself as promulgating 'the old time Gospel in old time power'.[22] Therefore, it was the assumption of the cessationists that the gifts of the Holy Spirit had been withdrawn, not their criticism of experiential fanaticism, that Elim contended against.[23]

4.1.3 Contending against ritualism

As well as directing its argument against the 'higher critics' and the 'lower critics', Elim was also opposed to 'ritualism'. George Jeffreys maintained that 'in some quarters, even if they claim to believe the old truths [the orthodox Christian beliefs, including miracles], they are lost to sight behind the rituals of crucifixes, vestments, masses, confessionals'.[24] The main perceived problem with the Roman Catholic Church, as well as Anglo-Catholicism, was its ritualism, which was seen as a barrier for experiencing the Full Gospel.[25] For example, when George and Stephen Jeffreys visited Rome in 1922, they said that they 'saw great Church buildings which were like prison houses, altars, statutes, vestments and everything

---

19. Reflecting on the early years of British Pentecostalism, Alexander Boddy notes how the Pentecostal message was 'rejected by many'; Boddy, 'The Pentecostal Movement', 195.

20. Desmond Cartwright, 'Everywhere Spoken Against: Opposition to Pentecostalism 1907–1930', accessed 20 April 2017, http://smithwigglesworth.com/index.php/smith-wigglesworth-pensketches/miscellaneous/everywhere-spoken-against. Cf. Jessie Penn-Lewis, *War on the Saints: A Text Book for Believers on the Work of Deceiving Spirits among the Children of God* (Leicester: The 'Overcomer' Office, 1912).

21. 'The Elim Evangel and Foursquare Gospel Revivalist', 273.

22. Ibid.

23. See Jeffreys, *Elim Christ Church*, 2; Ernest C. W. Boulton, 'Christian Liberty', *EE* 3, no. 6 (June 1922): 93.

24. Jeffreys, *The Miraculous Foursquare Gospel – Doctrinal*, 52.

25. There are also some suggestions within early Elim literature that the Papacy would become the Church of the anti-Christ; Charles Kingston, 'The Coming of Christ – and After. The Tribulation Period – The Antichrist', *EE* 6, no. 18 (15 September 1925): 205–6; E. J. Phillips, 'The Editor's Page', *EE* 10, no. 3 (March 1929): 41.

the carnal mind could devise to in order to obscure the light of the Gospel'.[26] And when the Elim Bible College was opened in 1925, Boulton contrasts how a building that had previously been a Roman Catholic Convent characterized by 'bitterness' and 'medieval monasticism' was now turned into a place of 'joyous praise issuing from lives immersed in the fullness Divine'.[27]

4.2 The content of the Elim argument: The Foursquare Gospel

The response of Elim to Liberalism, cessationism and ritualism was the promulgation of the 'Full Gospel'. Hence, when the Elim Evangelistic Band was formed by George Jeffreys and six others in Monaghan, Ireland, on 7 January 1915, the minutes of the instituting meeting indicate that the purpose of the new movement was to reach 'Ireland with the Full Gospel on Pentecostal lines'.[28] So what exactly was this Pentecostal Full Gospel? Or to put it differently, what was the content of the Elim argument?

4.2.1 What We Believe (1916)

The first official articulation of the Full Gospel was published in January 1916 under the title *Elim Christ Church: What We Believe*,[29] although Jeffreys seems to have been working on the booklet since August 1915. This doctrinal document is not so much a statement of faith as a statement of distinctives.[30] In other words, there is no real discussion on general doctrines found in traditional Christian creeds with which Elim concurred, but the focus is primarily on the differences from other Christian traditions, not least cessationist Evangelicalism and modernist Liberalism. Nevertheless, it does provide an early explanation of the Full Gospel as perceived by Elim.

The document begins by underscoring that Elim is advocating the 'faith which was once delivered to the saints' (Jude 3), with particular emphasis on the faith's supernatural and spiritual elements.[31] Thus, the Full Gospel was not seen by Elim as a new invention, unlike the New Theology of Liberalism, but it was understood as the orthodox truth proclaimed by the NT Church, and thus the new movement identified itself with what it saw as the faith of the Apostles.

---

26. Boulton, *George Jeffreys*, 118.
27. Ibid., 142–3.
28. Minutes of the 'First informal meeting of Christian brethren at Monaghan, Thursday Jan. 7th 1915', in *Elim Evangelistic Band Minute Book*, Archives of the General Superintendent, EIC, Malvern.
29. Jeffreys, *Elim Christ Church*.
30. Hathaway, 'The Elim Pentecostal Church', 34.
31. Jeffreys, *Elim Christ Church*, 1–2.

The doctrines identified in this early articulation include (1) the sinfulness of all humanity, (2) salvation by faith and through the atoning sacrifice of Christ, (3) baptism in the Holy Spirit, (4) restoration of the gifts of the Holy Spirit, (5) 'eternal conscious punishment of all Christ rejectors', (6) the 'personal and pre-Millennial' return of Christ, (7) healing in the atonement and promised healing according to Jas 5.14, and (8) whole body ministry of the church, with particular emphasis on the offices of Eph. 4.11.[32] This is followed by two ordinances, namely, (1) believers' water baptism, and (2) holy communion open for all regenerate Christians.[33]

To help interpret Elim's first statement of beliefs, I will compare it with 'The Doctrinal Basis of Faith of the World's Evangelical Alliance (1846)', which to a great extent served as the baseline for Evangelical theology of the period;[34] and Thomas B. Barratt's proposed 'Standards of Truth' for European Pentecostalism (1911), which was an early attempt to provide a Pentecostal equivalent to the doctrinal statement of the Evangelical Alliance.[35] In relation to these two statements, the obvious omission in Elim's *What We Believe* is that there is no article on the Bible or the Godhead/Trinity (an 'oversight' that was corrected in Elim's next doctrinal statement). With Evangelical Alliance, Elim effectively shares the doctrines on human sinfulness, Christ's incarnation and atonement, justification by faith, eternal state of both the righteous and the wicked, and the ordinances. However, unlike the Evangelical Alliance, Elim has included articles on Baptism in the Holy Spirit, restoration of the spiritual gifts, premillennial return of Christ and divine healing in the atonement. Unsurprisingly, Barratt also has statements on Baptism in the Spirit, gifts of the Spirit and the second coming of Christ. But what is surprising is that unlike Barratt, the Elim statement does not explicitly mention 'speaking in tongues' either in relation to Spirit Baptism or spiritual gifts, but instead has a distinct article on divine healing. Perhaps one should not to read too much into this, but it does seem to highlight how the gift of tongues was not considered as *the* unique 'gift/sign' of Baptism in the Spirit within Elim, whereas divine healing was of particular importance for the movement from its inception. In sum, Elim adopted the basic Evangelical beliefs; with fellow Pentecostals it emphasized Baptism in the Spirit, spiritual gifts and second coming of Christ, but it also developed its own Pentecostal distinctive in appearing to emphasize divine healing over the gift of tongues. Indeed, for Elim this was the Full Gospel.

The Full Gospel would later be expressed in 1920s as the Foursquare Gospel. This later articulation, however, should not be seen as a novel development, because the fourfold pattern is already strongly present in *What We Believe* with

---

32. Ibid., 3–5.

33. The fourth and final section is on 'Church Discipline'; ibid., 6–8.

34. Ian Randall and David Hilborn, *One Body in Christ: The History and Significance of the Evangelical Alliance* (Carlisle: Paternoster Press, 2001), Appendix 2, 358–9.

35. Thomas B. Barratt, 'An Urgent Plea for Charity and Unity', *Confidence* 4, no. 3 (March 1911): 63–4.

statements covering the role of Jesus as (1) Saviour, (2) Healer, (3) Baptiser in the Holy Spirit and (4) coming King. In other words, in *What We Believe* Jesus is already identified as the saviour of fallen individuals who can become 'new creations' by receiving the gift of eternal life, and freedom from 'the penalty and power of sin' through his atoning work. The 'saved' must also produce the fruit of the Spirit, which highlights that sanctification is seen as part of salvation.[36] The article on divine healing emphasizes healing in the atonement and the promise of healing, according to Jas 5.14-15, which notes church elders anointing the person suffering with oil, praying in faith and seeing him/her restored to health.[37] Baptism in the Holy Spirit is seen as something that 'every regenerate person should seek' for empowerment and hence is understood as a subsequent experience to conversion, but, as has already been noted, unlike for many early British Pentecostals, tongues is *not* seen, or at least not mentioned, as the initial evidence of Spirit baptism.[38] Finally, 'the personal and premillennial' return of Jesus is affirmed.[39] Therefore, it seems that the explicit references to and centrality of the Foursquare Gospel from the mid-1920s onwards should not be seen as an unexpected development from the earlier Full Gospel of 1915-16, but rather as Elim's theological articulation of the implicit beliefs already present in Elim's Full Gospel.[40]

4.2.2 'Statement of Fundamental Truths' (1922)

The 1916 doctrinal document was followed by Elim's 'Statement of Fundamental Truths' in 1922, with some revisions from the original *What We Believe*.[41] The new additions in the 1922 statement are articles on the Bible, the Trinity, and ordination of ministers.[42] As mentioned above, it is interesting that the centrality of the Bible is not explicitly stated in the 1916 document, although it is assumed

---

36. Jeffreys, *Elim Christ Church*, 3. Barratt's 'Standards of Truth …' emphasize sanctification in more Wesleyan Holiness terms; Barratt, 'An Urgent Please for Charity and Unity', 64.

37. Jeffreys, *Elim Christ Church*, 5.

38. Ibid., 3. The 'London Declaration' on 'The Baptism in the Holy Ghost' signed by the early British Pentecostal pioneers clearly identifies speaking in tongues as the evidence of Spirit Baptism; 'A London Declaration (November 1909)', 287–8.

39. Jeffreys, *Elim Christ Church*, 4.

40. This inference is further supported by surveying the articles of *Elim Evangel* from 1919 to 1924, which demonstrate a strong Christological emphasis and a clear focus on the themes of the Fourfold Gospel. The 'Special Pentecostal Number' of December 1922 is a good example of the Foursquare Gospel fully at play within Elim from an early stage; see *EE* 3, no. 12 (December 1922).

41. George Jeffreys, *The Constitution of the Elim Pentecostal Alliance* (London: Battley Bros., 1922), 6–7.

42. Ibid.

throughout.⁴³ The doctrine of the Trinity may have been introduced due to the increasing influence of Oneness Pentecostals in North America in the early 1920s.⁴⁴ The addition of ordination of ministers as the third 'ordinance', with water baptism and Holy Communion, is possibly caused by the expanding movement's need to formulate a doctrine regarding its own accredited and approved ministers.

However, like in 1916 the Foursquare Gospel motif is central in the 1922 statement. The articles on Jesus as saviour are more or less identical to those of 1916. Healing is also still seen to be in the atonement and therefore available to 'all who believe', although there is no more mention of Jas 5.14. The personal and premillennial return of Jesus is also reaffirmed.⁴⁵ However, the doctrine of Baptism in the Holy Spirit is revised to include speaking in tongues as the initial evidence,⁴⁶ bringing Elim in line with the majority view of early British Pentecostals,⁴⁷ even if George Jeffreys himself never held tightly to this view.⁴⁸

4.2.3 'Fundamental Truths of the Foursquare Gospel Churches' (1928/1934)

In the late 1920s Elim articulated its core doctrines for the third time.⁴⁹ In these statements there is a new article on the church, and assertions on the 'fruit of the Spirit' and 'anointing with oil' which had been present in 1916 but omitted in 1922. It appears that as Elim was coming of age as a denomination there was an intensified need to identify what constitutes the church catholic. To put it differently, as a new denomination Elim needed to increasingly clarify how it perceived and related to other Christian traditions.

For the first time the Foursquare Gospel received an explicit articulation; that is, there were four articles with the titles 'The Saviour', 'The Healer', 'The Baptiser' and 'The Coming King'.⁵⁰ This clear fourfold categorization seems to have been

---

43. For example, all the doctrines are provided with proof texts; Jeffreys, *Elim Christ Church*.
44. See Gee, *The Pentecostal Movement*, 138–9.
45. Jeffreys, *Constitution* (1922), 6–7.
46. Ibid., 6.
47. 'A London Declaration (November 1909)', 287.
48. Hathaway, 'The Elim Pentecostal Church', 36.
49. The Fundamental Truths of 1928 and 1934 are almost identical and thus treated as part of the same doctrinal articulation; George Jeffreys, *Constitution of the Foursquare Gospel Churches of the British Isles* (no city: no publisher, 1928), 6–7; George Jeffreys, *Elim Foursquare Gospel Alliance: Deed Poll* (London: Electrical Law Press, 1934), 3–4. It should also be noted that the 'Statement of Fundamental Truth' in the 1925 Constitution differs from the 1922 Constitution by not having an article on ordination of ministers. However, apart from this the 1925 doctrinal statements are the same as those in the 1922 Constitution and thus are not discussed further; George Jeffreys, *The Constitution of the Elim Pentecostal Alliance* (London: Elim Publishing, 1925), 4–5.
50. Jeffreys et al., *Constitution* (1928), 6.

influenced by the North American tour of Jeffreys and other Elim leaders in 1924. During this visit, the group was exposed to the work of the Christian and Missionary Alliance (CMA) founded by Albert Benjamin Simpson, who had first coined the term 'Fourfold Gospel' in 1890; they also visited Aimee Semple McPherson's International Church of the Foursquare Gospel.[51] From North America, Jeffreys wrote to E. J. Phillips that he wanted Elim 'to be in Great Britain what the CMA is in America, with the difference that we retain the whole truth of Pentecost with signs'.[52] Consequently, like McPherson, Jeffreys substituted 'baptism in the Holy Spirit' for 'sanctification', and on his return to England began explicitly promulgating the Foursquare Gospel. In 1929 the name of the Elim Pentecostal Alliance, which in 1918 had subsumed the Elim Evangelistic Band, was changed to the Elim Foursquare Gospel Alliance, and Jeffreys also went on to further define these four core beliefs in his two-volume *The Miraculous Foursquare Gospel* (1929–30).[53]

When comparing the 1928 document with that of 1922, Jesus as Saviour and coming King effectively remain unchanged. However, baptism in the Spirit is yet again changed in that tongues as the initial evidence is replaced with the phrase 'with signs following'.[54] This restores the 1916 emphasis on general 'signs' rather than elevating tongues as *the* 'sign'.[55] Moreover, the doctrine of healing is altered by deleting the explicit mention of healing being in the atonement, and there is also an added phrase that 'those who will walk in obedience to His [Christ's] will can claim Divine Healing for their bodies'.[56]

4.2.4 The Foursquare Gospel and doctrinal statements: Elim's hard core *and* auxiliary hypotheses

In light of the first three doctrinal statements, I will now try to articulate what appears to have been the essence of the early Elim argument. Nancey Murphy has noted that the *hard core* of a 'philosophical and/or theological tradition' (to use MacIntyre's language) is its 'central organizing idea ... while theories regarding the various doctrines would constitute *auxiliary hypotheses* elaborating that central

---

51. Hathaway, 'The Elim Pentecostal Church', 6.
52. George Jeffreys, letter to E. J. Phillips (5 August 1924), Elim Archives, Malvern.
53. Jeffreys, *The Miraculous Foursquare Gospel – Doctrinal*; George Jeffreys, *The Miraculous Foursquare Gospel – Supernatural* (London: Elim Publishing, 1930).
54. Jeffreys, *Deed Poll* (1934), 3.
55. The role of tongues as initial evidence was not uniformly held by other European Pentecostals (e.g. see Jonathan Paul (Germany) and Gerrit R. Polman (Holland)); Alexander Boddy, ed., 'The Place of Tongues in the Pentecostal Movement: Address at a Friendly Conference of Leaders and Workers at Sunderland Wednesday, June 7th, 1911', *Confidence* 4, no. 8 (August 1911): 176–9, 182.
56. Jeffreys, *Deed Poll* (1934), 3.

idea and relating it to the data' (my italics).⁵⁷ For Elim this 'central organizing idea' (read: hard core) seems to be the Foursquare Gospel for at least three reasons.

First, as I have tried to demonstrate above, the first references to the 'Full Gospel along Pentecostal lines' already implies the Foursquare Gospel. Second, it is the fourfold theological emphasis of Jesus as (1) Saviour, (2) Healer, (3) Baptiser in the Holy Spirit and (4) coming King that makes Elim different from mainstream British Evangelicalism, and thus in Lakatosian terms makes Elim, like other classical Pentecostal denominations who share this fourfold focus, a distinct *research programme*. Third, and perhaps most importantly, Elim itself during its formational period identifies the Foursquare Gospel as its 'central organizing idea'. This is reflected in Elim changing its name from 'Elim Pentecostal Alliance' to 'Elim Foursquare Gospel Alliance' in 1929. Moreover, from 1925 onwards the Foursquare Gospel is also presented as the guiding principle in providing the four sides that hold together Elim's other beliefs (see Appendix 3).⁵⁸ And these four aspects are also depicted symbolically as the corners of the *Elim Evangel* and the core ideas for which it stands (see Appendix 2).⁵⁹

If the Foursquare Gospel is Elim's hard core, as I suggest, then the doctrines articulated in Elim's theological statements of 1916, 1922 and 1928/1934 can be identified as the *auxiliary hypotheses* unpacking this controlling fourfold Christological conviction. As such the doctrinal statements have two important functions. First, they provide further descriptions of the hard core's *positive heuristic*. For example, the governing idea of 'Jesus is Healer' is further expressed in the doctrinal statement that Jesus provides healing in the atonement. In other words, the doctrine of 'healing in the atonement' provides a more elaborate model of what it means to believe that 'Jesus is Healer', and thus positively explains a central aspect of Elim's hard core.

Second, as auxiliary hypotheses, these doctrinal statements also provide the *negative heuristic* for the Elim tradition in protecting 'the hard core from falsification by making additions or changes in the belt of auxiliary hypotheses'.⁶⁰ For example, the concept of Jesus as Baptiser in the Holy Spirit was first presented as something that all Christians should seek (1916); later this doctrine was developed by stating that Spirit baptism is evidenced by speaking in tongues (1922); the doctrine was modified further by replacing tongues as the unique sign with the more general concept of baptism in the Spirit being accompanied 'with signs following' (1928).

---

57. Murphy, *Theology in the Age of Scientific Reasoning*, 176. As noted in Section 2.2.2, I will supplement MacIntyre's methodology here regarding the 'content of the Elim argument' with the Lakatosian concepts of 'hard core' and 'auxiliary hypotheses'.

58. No author, 'What We Believe', *EE* 6, no. 1 (1 January 1925): last page [no page number].

59. No author, 'The Elim Evangel', *EE* 6, no. 1 (1 January 1925): front cover [no page number]. Kay also refers to the Foursquare Gospel as Jeffreys' 'organising principle'; Kay, *George Jeffreys*, 221.

60. Murphy, *Theology in the Age of Scientific Reasoning*, 184.

These changes may well reflect the 'data' of the Pentecostal experience shaping Elim's interpretation of Jesus as Spirit Baptiser. To put it differently, throughout these three doctrinal statements the hard core of Jesus as Baptiser in the Spirit is maintained, but the auxiliary hypotheses/doctrines change as they seek to relate the data with the hard core. Indeed, seeing Elim's doctrinal statements as the auxiliary hypotheses provide reasons why the statements changed during the first fifteen years.

In sum, it is not hard to argue that the Foursquare Gospel is the hard core of Elim,[61] and the doctrinal statements are the protective belt that are subject to change as it connects the theological data to Elim's hard core. This argument will be further developed and substantiated when looking at Elim's two epistemological crises (Chapters 5 and 6).

4.3 The rationality of the Elim argument: Pentecostal Biblical Pragmatism

To summarize the discussion thus far, the early Elim argument seems to have been primarily directed at the so-called higher critics (read: modernist Liberal Christians), lower critics (read: cessationist Evangelical Christians) and ritualists (read: Roman Catholics and Anglo-Catholics). The content of the argument can be captured in the phrase Full Gospel, which was later explicitly articulated as the Foursquare Gospel. This Foursquare Gospel can be seen as Elim's hard core and the various doctrinal statements as Elim's auxiliary hypotheses. Indeed, the content of the Elim argument appears to have directly challenged the modernist attempts to demythologize Christianity by seeking to re-establish the purported scriptural and orthodox Christocentric doctrines of old, counter cessationism by highlighting the miraculous aspects of the Gospel for the current age and oppose ritualism in presenting the raw potency of the Full Gospel.

So how then did Elim justify its argument? To put it differently, what was Elim's underlying rationality and epistemology, and what did the movement consider as appropriate sources for its theological 'data'? In exploring these questions, I will propose that Elim affirmed three main sources for theological knowledge, namely, (1) its (pre-)Pentecostal tradition, (2) the Bible and (3) experience. These three sources not only provided Elim with theological data for formulating beliefs but also functioned as its epistemic core in helping to formulate its theory of justification and warrant. In short, I will argue in this section that in light of these three aspects Elim's tacit rationality is best identified as *Pentecostal Biblical Pragmatism*.

---

61. Elim as a British classical Pentecostal movement shares this fourfold/fivefold Gospel emphasis with American classical Pentecostalism; Dayton, *Theological Roots of Pentecostalism*; John Christopher Thomas, 'Pentecostal Theology in the Twenty-First Century', *Pneuma* 20, no. 1 (Spring 1998): 17.

4.3.1 Pentecostal *Biblical Pragmatism: The role of tradition*

The Evangelical and Pentecostal heritage of Elim provided the movement's background theological beliefs. As has already been pointed out, Elim's first doctrinal statements share a number of similarities with the 'The Doctrinal Basis of Faith of the World's Evangelical Alliance (1846)' and Thomas B. Barratt's 'Standards of Truth' for European Pentecostalism (1911). This is not surprising as many Elim pioneers had received their early religious nurturing within British Evangelicalism (see Section 3.2.1), and later spiritual nourishment from British Pentecostalism before joining Elim (see Section 3.2.3).

The early Elim literature underscores the importance of the wider Evangelical and Pentecostal traditions for Elim's theological identity. For example, Ernest C. W. Boulton writes how the Elim story 'flows out of what was designated the Pentecostal Movement in the British Isles as it emerged in 1907'.[62] And R. E. McAlister explains how Pentecostalism, among other things, is an 'Evangelical' movement.[63]

Consequently, it is reasonable to suggest that the wider Evangelical and Pentecostal traditions gave Elim its basic beliefs and frameworks of thinking. This does not mean that Elim did not go on to develop its own distinctives with respect to theology and ways of reasoning, but it does mean that these distinctives were not developed *ex nihilo* but in the context of British Evangelicalism and emerging Pentecostalism. Indeed, Elim's *biblicism* and *pragmatism* 'flowed out of' this (pre-)*Pentecostal* heritage.

4.3.2 Pentecostal *Biblical Pragmatism: The role of the Bible*

In line with Elim's inherited Evangelicalism and Pentecostalism, the Bible was the grounding document and primary theological source for the early Elim argument.[64] In fact, from the mid-1920s onwards the phrase 'Foursquare on the Word of God' became the movement's motto (see Appendix 2 and 3).[65] Moreover, as already noted, although there is no article on the Bible in the 1916 *What We Believe*, its centrality is assumed throughout the document, and this assumption is formalized in the 1922 Statement of Fundamental Truths with the first article stating: 'we believe that the Bible is the inspired Word of God, and that none may add or take away therefrom, except at their peril.'[66] In the 1928 Fundamental Truths this same article is repeated verbatim.[67]

---

62. Boulton, *George Jeffreys* (1999), 17.
63. R. E. McAlister, 'The Pentecostal Movement', *EE* 4, no. 1 (January 1923): 16.
64. Ibid.; Boulton, *George Jeffreys* (1999), 186; Jeffreys, *Healing Rays*, 109.
65. See also *EE* cover pages from Vol. 6, no. 1 (1 January 1925) until Vol. 18, no. 1 (1 January 1937).
66. Jeffreys, *Constitution* (1922), 6.
67. Jeffreys et al., *Constitution* (1928), 6.

Elim appeared to give epistemic primacy to the Bible for two reasons. First, although Elim did not have a developed theory of truth, consistent with its Evangelical worldview Elim seemed to assume that 'truth' and true knowledge was effectively theocentric.[68] This view is reflected in R. E. McAlister *Elim Evangel* article on 'What is Truth?' when he writes that 'if I have God's viewpoint regarding any subject, I have the truth respecting that subject'.[69] In other words, as the ultimate reality, God is the source and justifier of all truth, and therefore true beliefs about any given subject equals to having God's beliefs on that particular subject. This kind of theory of truth is very similar to the one advocated by Jonathan Edwards when he writes that 'the only adequate definition of Truth is, the agreement of our ideas with existence', and since God is the only necessarily existing being, truth is the 'consistence and agreement of our ideas, with the ideas of God'.[70]

Following from this theocentric concept of truth, secondly, it was further believed by Elim, again with many Evangelicals, that the 'Bible gives us the mind of God [read: truth] on every subject pertaining unto life and godliness'[71] because the Bible is divinely inspired by God. This 'divine inspiration' was not assumed to apply to some parts of the Bible, but was believed to be *verbal* and *plenary*. For example, Percy Parker in discussing the issue quotes Clarence Larkin that inspiration 'extends to *every sentence, word, mark, point, jot and title* in the original parchments'.[72] Parker also agrees with the 1893 General Assembly of the Presbyterian Church of America that the Bible 'is the very Word of God, and consequently wholly without error',[73] and concludes with James Martin Gray of the Moody Institute, against any Neo-Orthodox sentiments, that 'the Bible does not merely contain the Word of God; it is the Word of God'.[74] To summarize, the Bible's primacy as a theological source for Elim stems from the notion that (1) 'truth' fundamentally corresponds with God and his ideas, and (2) God's nature and his ideas are revealed in the Bible due to its divine inspiration.

---

68. Peter Hicks points out that Jonathan Edwards and John Wesley, the two eighteenth-century 'fathers' of Evangelicalism, believed that truth is theocentric; Peter Hicks, *Evangelicals and Truth: A Creative Proposal for a Postmodern Age* (Leicester: Apollos, 1998), 55–6.

69. R. E. McAlister, 'What is Truth?' *EE* 13, no. 2 (8 January 1932): 25.

70. Jonathan Edwards, *Remarks in Mental Philosophy – The Mind*, 10, in *Works*, vol. 1, p. ccxxv, quoted in Hicks, *Evangelicals and Truth*, 50, 210.

71. McAlister, 'What is Truth?', 25.

72. Percy Parker, 'To What Extent *is the* Bible Inspired?', *EE* 9, no. 2 (16 January 1928): 26.

73. Ibid.

74. Percy Parker, 'In What Way *is* the Bible *the* Word of God?', *EE* 9, no. 3 (1 February 1928): 46. 'Verbal inspiration' is also argued for in J. Robinson, 'Why I Believe in Verbal Inspiration', *EE* 12, no. 30 (24 July 1931): 473; F. A. Conners, 'Verbal Inspiration of the Scriptures', *EE* 13, no. 45 (4 November 1932): 707–9.

Since the Bible as a whole was believed to be verbally inspired by God, it seemed logical for Elim to also maintain that the Bible was infallible in what it affirmed or taught since God was assumed to be infallible.[75] Elim's similarities here with the 'Old Princeton' theology regarding inspiration, infallibility and inerrancy of the Bible à la Charles Hodge, Archibald Alexander Hodge and Benjamin Warfield are noteworthy.[76] In fact, Archibald Alexander Hodge is affirmingly quoted in *Elim Evangel* on divine inspiration and the infallibility of the Bible.[77] This means that Elim's concept of biblical inspiration would have also been shared by the cessationist Fundamentalists, and thus Elim's view on the Bible's divine authority is more or less identical with that of the Fundamentalist movement of the early twentieth century.

So what justification did Elim then provide for believing that the Bible was in fact divinely inspired and therefore accurately conveyed the mind of God? In the Elim literature three common arguments are provided for believing that the Bible is inspired by God. First, and probably the most common argument is the *argument from transformed lives*.[78] It is suggested that when it comes to the divine authority and inspiration of the Bible, 'one of the greatest, if not the greatest proofs, is its miraculous regenerative power in the lives of men'.[79] F. A. Conners echoes this notion when he writes that 'the greatest proof of the inspiration of the Bible is its transforming power in the lives of men'.[80] Second, the divine inspiration of the Bible is supported by the *argument from the uniqueness of the Bible*.[81] This argument seeks to demonstrate how the Bible is supreme in its message, unity and ability to transcend cultures and languages. Furthermore, it is suggested that the Bible's fulfilled prophecies, preservation throughout the ages and phenomenal publication history points towards its supernatural origins. Third, there is the *argument from its own testimony*.[82] In other words, the words of Jesus as recorded in the Gospels, as well as the accounts in 2 Tim. 3.16 and 2 Pet. 1.21, are seen as evidence that the Bible is the verbally inspired Word of God.

---

75. So argued by Robinson, 'Why I Believe in Verbal Inspiration', 474.

76. See Harris, *Fundamentalism and Evangelicals*, 135–42.

77. Conners, 'Verbal Inspiration of the Scriptures', 708.

78. D. W. G. H., *The 'Elim' Foursquare Gospel Churches of the British Isles (Incorporated 1927). For what do they stand? And why?* (Eastbourne: C. A. Holmes, n.d.), no page numbers; Franck Peckham, 'The Bible is the Word of God', *EE* 11, no. 46 (14 November 1930): 723; Robinson, 'Why I Believe in Verbal Inspiration', 473; Conners, 'Verbal Inspiration of the Scriptures', 707.

79. D. W. G. H., *The 'Elim' Foursquare Gospel Churches of the British Isles*.

80. Conners, 'Verbal Inspiration of the Scriptures', 707.

81. Peckham, 'The Bible is the Word of God', 721–2; Robinson, 'Why I Believe in Verbal Inspiration', 473; Conners, 'Verbal Inspiration of the Scriptures', 707; P. H. Shaayman, 'The Bible', *EE* 13, no. 45 (4 November 1932): 714.

82. D. W. G. H., *The 'Elim' Foursquare Gospel Churches of the British Isles*; Peckham, 'The Bible is the Word of God', 721.

It seems that the first two types of arguments for divine inspiration, namely, argument from transformed lives and argument from the Bible's uniqueness, indicate a *pragmatic rationality* at work within Elim. In other words, these arguments to a great extent assume that *results*, such as changed lives, fulfilled prophecies, relevance in different cultures, preservation against the odds and publishing success, point towards the Bible's divine origins. In fact, it seems that the first two arguments provide the underlying rationale for the Bible's divine authority, and the third argument is then used to explain the nature of this authority; that is, the Bible carries divine authority because it is divinely inspired along the lines of 2 Tim. 3.16 and 2 Pet. 1.21. Furthermore, the third argument also provides some justification why inspiration should be applied to the whole Bible and not just some passages.

When it came to Elim's early biblical hermeneutics, this 'verbally inspired and infallible Word of God' appears to have been interpreted in a common-sense fashion, or what Kenneth Archer has referred to as 'the Bible Reading Method', where Scriptures are read in a pre-critical and canonical proof-text manner through a devotional lens.[83] Elim's 'Bible Reading Method' is well demonstrated in the *Elim Evangel* article on 'How to Study the Word'.[84] In studying the Bible the reader is encouraged to (1) '*seek the Literal Meaning*' of the text in a pre-critical manner; (2) '*use the best Possible Translation*' in terms of its accuracy and English expression; (3) '*use the Marginal References*' and thus read the text canonically; (4) '*trust Christ for ... Openings*', that is, rely on Christ to reveal the Scriptures; and (5) '*study for Your Own Life*', that is, read the Bible devotionally.

In sum, the Bible was seen by Elim as a grounding document for theological knowledge because God was seen as the ultimate truth and the Bible was believed to be His fully inspired and infallible word. Elim had primarily pragmatic reasons for believing in the divine inspiration of the Bible, and it encouraged its members to adopt a form of 'Bible Reading Method' to gather theological data from Scripture.

4.3.3 Pentecostal Biblical Pragmatism: *The role of experience*

However, the Bible and the Evangelical/Pentecostal tradition were not Elim's only sources of theological knowledge. The pragmatic rationality, already evident in Elim's justification for the divine inspiration of the Bible, meant that 'experience' played an important role as a source of knowledge and particularly in providing justification for theological beliefs.

Elim's basic understanding of 'religious experience' was inherited from early British Pentecostalism (see Section 3.2.3). As suggested in Chapter 3, (British)

---

83. Archer, *A Pentecostal Hermeneutic*, 74–5. Although Archer's work focuses on American Pentecostal hermeneutics, the similarities with Elim's British Pentecostal hermeneutics are noteworthy.

84. No author, 'How to Study the Word', *EE* 12, no. 45 (6 November 1931): 713–15; cf. J. T. Bradley et al., *Elim Lay Preachers' Handbook* (London: Elim Publishing, 1946), chapter 1.

Pentecostalism is best seen as *Keswick Romanticism 'baptized' with Evidentialism*. In other words, like the Welsh Revival, early British Pentecostals externalized the inner religious experience of Keswick, but they also moved beyond the Welsh Revival by expecting specific biblical *signs* and *evidences* to accompany genuine spiritual encounters. In early British Pentecostal thinking the distinctive religious experience was 'baptism in the Spirit' and the biblical sign was 'speaking in tongues'. As has been noted, for Elim the notions of baptism in the Spirit accompanied by biblical evidences remained central, but the idea of tongues as 'the initial evidence' was not maintained (despite its inclusion in the 1922 doctrinal statement). Instead the general manifestation of spiritual gifts, with particular emphasis on divine healing, was seen as the evidence of the outworking of Spirit baptism.

In light of the above, the role of 'experience' was central for Elim to justify its early argument. Moreover, this experience-based rationality seems to have been characterized by what I will call *experientialism* and *experimentalism*, which together constituted Elim's *pragmatic rationality*.

First, by *experientialism* I simply mean the foundational role that experience played in shaping Elim's rationality. George Jeffreys fondly referred to a quote from his Bible College days asserting that '*He that hath an experience is not at the mercy of him that hath an argument*.'[85] Jeffreys particularly saw this to be the case when one's experience was Scriptural, and thus in his mind there was a close relationship between the Bible and personal experience, each mutually confirming the other. This same line of thinking was shared by Donald Gee's *Elim Evangel* article written in 1922 where he argued that 'No man possessed of a Scriptural experience need be afraid of an argument, he is beyond its reach. Any man rejoicing in a living experience of God in his life has a power independent of, and mighty beyond, all external training in logic or theology.'[86]

Jeffreys' and Gee's reasoning reflects the nineteenth-century Romantic preference for 'experience over argument' (see Section 3.1.1). To put it differently, within Elim's rationality *the experience becomes the 'argument'*. In some ways this approach is epistemologically similar to the so-called Reformed epistemology which claims that belief in God is a 'basic belief' rising from a 'spiritual intuition/*sensus divinitatis*' (Alvin Plantinga) or 'religious experience' (William P. Alston), and therefore supposedly needs no further evidence to be warranted.[87]

Nevertheless, Elim's second aspect of *experimentalism* moves beyond subjective experientialism as it tries to provide 'evidences' or 'signs' to authenticate the religious experience. This is the *Evidentialist* addition to the *Romantic* experientialism. Interestingly, in contemporary philosophy of religion the idea of 'confirming empirical evidence' is often expected by those critiquing the Reformed

---

85. Jeffreys, *Healing Rays*, 56.
86. Donald Gee, 'A Plea for Experience', *EE* 3, no. 5 (May 1922): 76.
87. See William P. Alston, *Perceiving God: The Epistemology of Religious Experience* (Ithaca, NY: Cornell University Press, 1991); Plantinga, *Warranted Christian Belief*.

epistemologists more subjective accounts of spiritual experience.[88] Moreover, this is the type of empirical evidence demanded by John Locke – regarded by some as the father of modern 'Evidentialism'[89] – when discussing religious 'enthusiasm' of his day, characterized by spiritual experientialism and intuitive revelation. Locke proposed that if the 'enthusiasts' are to be justified in their beliefs based on their personal experience and revelations, they need to be like

> the holy men of old, who had *revelations* from GOD, [but also] had something else beside that internal light of assurance in their own minds, to testify to them, that it was from GOD. They were not left to their own persuasions alone, that those persuasions were from GOD; but had outward signs to convince them of the author of those revelations. And when they were to convince others, they had a power given them to justify the truth of their commission from heaven; and by visible signs to assert the divine authority of the message they were sent with.[90]

It appears that the 'outward signs' and 'visible signs' demanded by Locke are exactly what Elim sought to provide when justifying its experientialism and the content of its Full Gospel. To give some examples of its evidentialist *experimentalism* in action, in 1928 Ernest C. W. Boulton wrote a history of the early Elim movement in which he referred to George Jeffreys as 'a minister whose weapon is the Word, and who relies wholly upon the Spirit of God to produce the *desired results*' (my emphasis).[91] Much of Boulton's description of the ministry of Jeffreys and the initial developments of Elim emphasize how Scriptural truths (i.e. the Foursquare Gospel) were substantiated through experiential and empirical evidence. For example, after reporting the testimony of a woman who had been healed of a tubercular knee, he boldly states: 'And then the modern biblical exegete would persuade us that the miraculous is impossible. In the face of such positive proofs we cannot but accept the statements of Scripture, confirmed as they are by the evidences of our eyes.'[92]

It was this type of experimental justification that seemed to provide Elim with the epistemic grounds for both its belief in the authority of the Bible and its Foursquare Gospel reading of it. R. E. Darragh follows a very similar logic when

---

88. Jerome I. Gellman, 'Mysticism and Religious Experience', in *The Oxford Handbook of Philosophy of Religion*, ed. William J. Wainwright (Oxford: Oxford University Press, 2005), 155–6.
89. Plantinga refers to Locke as 'both paradigm evidentialist and the proximate source of the entire evidentialist tradition'; Plantinga, *Warranted Christian Belief*, 82.
90. John Locke, *An Essay Concerning Human Understanding*, ed. Roger Woolhouse (London: Penguin Books, 2004), 621–2 [XIX.15].
91. Boulton, *George Jeffreys* (1999), 178.
92. Ibid., 137.

he reflects on the first seventeen years of Elim's history in his book *In Defence of His Word* by stating that if

> all those who have proved Jesus Christ to be the same to-day in the twentieth century [would say] Hallelujah ... Hallelujahs would come from thousands of voices, and thousands of hands would be raised as testimony that they have proved this to be true, for some have had their ears opened, others have received their sight, and many lame have discarded their crutches and stepped out of wheeled carriages, never to get into them again. Some have had cancers and growths removed in answer to prayer, and many with weak bodies have been made strong.[93]

The rest of Darragh's book is a collection of short testimonies of purported healings from Jeffreys' ministry, which seek to demonstrate that Elim's argument is supported by its results; that is, *experientialism* is backed up by *experimentalism*.

David Middlemiss has argued that the twentieth-century Pentecostal/Charismatic movement has simply followed the epistemology of the seventeenth- to nineteenth-century religious 'enthusiasm', and that 'within the charismatic movement, there is little evidence of a concern for philosophical epistemology'.[94] Although this claim may apply to some Pentecostals and Charismatics, it does not accurately reflect early British Pentecostalism or Elim. In other words, Elim's rationality, which reflected the early British Pentecostal rationality, was effectively *evidentialist enthusiasm* and thus fulfilled John Locke's epistemic requirements for Christian 'enthusiasm'. And although Elim may not have had the academic resources in constructing a 'philosophical epistemology' to be studied and critiqued in universities, Elim nevertheless was 'concerned' in providing an epistemology to justify its beliefs, as sketched above.

Elim's *experientialist experimentalism* or *enthusiast Evidentialism* as a rationality has a number of similarities to American Pragmatism of the late nineteenth and early twentieth centuries. First, in line with the views of William James, Elim seems to believe that the essence of 'religion' is identified as a spiritual experience (read: *experientialism*), rather than merely a form of 'theology' or 'ecclesiasticism', albeit for Elim this experience was understood in a canonical context and interpreted through a Pentecostal lens. To put it differently, James's conviction that 'knowledge about a thing is not the thing itself' is reflected well in Elim's experientialism.[95] For example, this sentiment is well captured by Elim's Henry Proctor when he writes that a 'real, vital Christian experience is a progression from faith to knowledge'[96] – that

---

93. R. E. Darragh, *In Defence of His Word* (London: Elim Publishing House, 1932), 9.
94. David Middlemiss, *Interpreting Charismatic Experience* (London: SCM, 1996), 45.
95. William James, *The Varieties of Religious Experience* (London: The Fontana Library, 1960), 49, 467.
96. Henry Proctor, 'Faith and Knowledge', *EE* 6, no. 3 (1 February 1925): 36.

is, an experience confirms the truth of one's faith, or in Jamesian language moves one from the 'knowledge about a thing' to 'the thing itself'.

Second, like American Pragmatism, Elim's *experientialism* is effectively empiricist. In other words, knowledge of God and the world is gained primarily through the senses. Experience is king.

However, third, like the American pragmatists William James and Charles Sanders Peirce, Elim also moves beyond the empiricists paradigm with its *experimentalism* that focuses on 'results' and 'effects' vis-à-vis beliefs and concepts. To put it simply, 'empiricism' focuses primarily on *what produces the belief*, whereas 'pragmatism' focuses on *what the belief produces*. This is well captured in Peirce's famous pragmatic maxim, also adopted and elaborated by James,[97] which states that when it comes to beliefs about objects, 'consider what effects, that might conceivably have practical bearing, we conceive the object of our conception to have. Then, our conception of these effects is the whole of our conception of the object.'[98] Based on this pragmatic principle, Peirce developed his inferential method of 'abduction', 'deduction' and 'induction'. In other words (1) the 'inferential knowing' starts abductively by formulating a hypothesis based on the raw data of experience (e.g. 'the earth is round, not flat'); (2) this is followed by a deductive inference predicting 'operational consequences of the hypothesis' (e.g. if one sails across the Atlantic Ocean one will eventually reach the Orient, rather than fall off the face of the earth); and (3) finally after testing the deductive inference (e.g. sailing across the Atlantic), through inductive reasoning a general rule/law can then be established (e.g. 'the laws of nature had in fact made the earth round rather than flat').[99]

While it would be misguided to assume that Elim's early rationality came even close to the philosophical sophistication of Peirce's inferential logic, it does seem that Elim's underlying rationality shares central aspects of Peirce's pragmatism (or pragmaticism as Peirce preferred to call it). For example, it is not difficult to imagine that Elim's central belief of Jesus as Healer was tacitly formulated along the lines of Peircean logic; that is, (1) experience and testimony suggests that Jesus heals people today (abduction); (2) in an evangelistic meeting people will be healed after being prayed for (deduction); (3) after praying for people in an evangelistic meeting and witnessing their purported healings, a general 'rule' of Jesus as healer can be established (induction).

---

97. William James, *Pragmatism and Other Writings*, ed. Giles Gunn (New York, NY: Penguin Books, 2000), 25. The direction of James's development of Peirce's pragmatic maxim was not always appreciated by Peirce, and thus Peirce later coined his more scientific pragmatism as 'pragmaticism' to distinguish it from James's more therapeutic pragmatism.

98. Charles Sanders Peirce, 'How to Make Our Ideas Clear', in *The Pragmatism Reader*, 57; cf. Charles Sanders Peirce, 'The Fixation of Belief', in *The Pragmatism Reader*, 37–49.

99. Donald L. Gelpi, *Varieties of Transcendental Experience: A Study in Constructive Postmodernism* (Eugene, OR: Wipf and Stock, 2000), 235–7; cf. Misak, *The American Pragmatists*, 47–50.

Indeed, as has been discussed above, Elim's understanding about the nature of Jesus as healer and Jesus as baptiser in the Holy Spirit were modified in 1922 and 1928/1934 from the original 1916 statement. It is not hard to argue that the adaption of these doctrinal statements demonstrates Elim's Peircean-type pragmatic rationality at work. In other words, with respect to divine healing, in the earlier doctrinal statements healing is believed to be in the atonement. However, in the 1928/1934 statement it is no longer assumed to be in the atonement but that 'those who will walk in obedience to His [Christ's] will can claim Divine Healing for their bodies'. This change can easily be explained in the light of Elim's pragmatic rationality (even if it does not fully follow Peirce's abductive, deductive and inductive logic) – that is, (1) based on scripture and experience Elim believed that Jesus heals; (2) initially this was believed to be because healing was in the atonement; (3) however, not everyone who was prayed for received healing in the same way as they seemed to receive forgiveness of sins; (4) therefore, healing may not be in the atonement but those can claim healing who walk in obedience because Jesus is still the Healer. Interestingly, the doctrine of healing was further modified in 1993 by deleting the notion that those who walk in obedience can claim healing, and again this modification seems to have been largely caused by 'results' and 'effects' not supporting a doctrine of perfect health for perfectly obedient Christians.

When it comes to baptism in the Holy Spirit, the same pragmatic logic seems to explain the changing understanding of the doctrine – that is, (1) in the 1916 statement Jesus is identified as the Baptiser in the Holy Spirit; (2) in 1922 speaking in tongues is identified as the initial evidence of one's Spirit baptism; (3) however, experience did not seem to support the idea that only those who spoke in tongues had been filled with the Holy Spirit; (4) thus in 1928/1934 tongues as initial evidence is replaced by the more generic idea of signs following, which better reflects the experience of Elim.

Consequently, Elim's pragmatic experiential experimentalism appears to have strong family resemblances to Peirce's 'critical common sensism', which like other common-sense rationalities of the time appreciates sense experiences, but with Peirce is also critical of common sense and seeks to test these intuitions in practice.[100] This means that Elim's pragmatism is also fallibilistic, acknowledging that one's beliefs can be wrong (e.g. healing in the atonement and tongues as initial evidence), which is another important feature of Peirce's and James's Pragmatism.

In 1907 William James argued that pragmatic philosophy provided the alternative to the cold religious scholastic rationalism and the atheistic positivist empiricism. In fact, he believed that pragmatism would be an appropriate religious philosophical method for the modern era (although he believed that both the religious and non-religious could utilize the pragmatic method).[101] Interestingly, despite F. C. S. Schiller's efforts to advocate pragmatism under

---

100. Gelpi, *Varieties of Transcendental Experience*, 249.
101. James, *Pragmatism and Other Writings*, 12, 20.

the name 'humanism' in Britain, philosophical pragmatism never gained prominence in British universities. Nevertheless, even if James's vision of a religious pragmatic philosophy may have not infiltrated the academic halls of Oxford or Cambridge, it seems that a version of it was developed and embodied by the British Pentecostal movement which was birthed the very same year James published his *Pragmatism* (1907). Elim went on to modify and develop this Pentecostal pragmatic method as its own religious rationality, or what I have called *Pentecostal Biblical Pragmatism*. Therefore, if my analysis is correct, Elim and British Pentecostalism represent a genuine British philosophical and religious pragmatism, and something future histories of British philosophical pragmatism should not ignore. Although Elim pioneers may have lacked philosophical erudition in articulating their rationality, they did not lack the practical energy in living out their pragmatism, and thus were in some sense *true pragmatic pragmatists*.

4.3.4 Pentecostal Biblical Pragmatism: 'Tradition-constituted and tradition-constitutive rationality' (MacIntyre)

In this section I argue that Elim's rationality should be seen as *Pentecostal Biblical Pragmatism*. It is *Pentecostal* because Elim inherited many of the underlying theological and epistemological assumptions of early British Pentecostals. It is *biblical* because for Elim the Bible was the grounding document and a primary source of theological knowledge. It is *pragmatic* because Elim believed that its argument was justified by religious experience (*experientialism*) and evidenced by life transforming 'signs', 'effects' and 'results' (*experimentalism*).

Following Alasdair MacIntyre's methodology (see Section 2.1), Elim's rationality seems to naturally emerge from within the Elim tradition, namely, it is 'tradition-constituted'. To put it differently, Elim's Pentecostal Biblical Pragmatism stems from the content of its argument (the experiential Foursquare Gospel), it is shaped by its social, religious and intellectual context (late-nineteenth- and early-twentieth-century Britain), it is informed by its implied opponents (Liberals, cessationists and ritualists) and characterized by its institutions (discussed below). In short, it is truly a tradition-specific rationality.

However, as noted by MacIntyre, rationalities are not only 'tradition-constituted' but also 'tradition-constitutive'.[102] This 'tradition-constitutive' element is also true of Elim's rationality as its pragmatism is not only informed by the experiential Foursquare Gospel but also ends up shaping the nature of the Foursquare Gospel by modifying doctrines about baptism in the Holy Spirit and divine healing. Therefore, Elim's Pentecostal Biblical Pragmatism fits well within MacIntyre's concept of 'tradition-constituted and tradition-constitutive rationality'.

---

102. MacIntyre, *Whose Justice?*, 10.

4.4 The social embodiment of the Elim argument: The Elim alliance

In MacIntyrian terms the Elim argument was not just against someone (opponents), about something (content) or justified in a particular way (rationality), but it was also carried out by a community that socially embodied the argument (see Section 2.1.2). This 'Elim community' created social systems and shared methods that helped to sustain, develop and propagate the Elim argument in its historical context. Alvin Goldman points out that such 'social systems' can be seen as 'epistemic systems' which 'house social practices, procedures, institutions, and/or patterns of interpersonal influence that affect the epistemic outcomes of its members'.[103] Elim seemed to have at least three types of prominent epistemic systems for, and social expressions of, its argument, namely (1) revivalistic meetings; (2) alliance of local churches, ministers and ministries; and (3) publishing and training institutions.

4.4.1 Revivalistic meetings: The primary platform of the Elim argument

Elim's founder George Jeffreys was first and foremost an evangelistic revivalist. Jeffreys was converted during the Welsh Revival (see Section 3.2.2), and in the words of Andrew Walker and Neil Hudson, 'his whole life and ministry would reflect the fact that he was a child of the Welsh Revival.'[104] In fact, some of the first references to George and his brother Stephen Jeffreys in British Pentecostal periodicals identify the brothers as the Pentecostal 'Welsh Revivalists'.[105] George Jeffreys describes some of these first revivalistic meetings held with his brother in 1913 in Wales:

> The work here is deepening, and numerous conversions are taking place daily, and many have received the Baptism of the Holy Ghost with the Signs following. Praise the Lord! Some miraculous cases of healing have also taken place, and it is a real Apostolic Revival ... The dear Lord is once again drawing multitudes after Him. We think of commencing at Llandrindod next week.[106]

This concept of holding a series of revival meetings in one town after another, characterized by preaching the Full Gospel with an expectation of 'signs' following (e.g. dramatic conversions, Spirit baptisms and divine healings), was to be George Jeffreys' focus and modus operandi for Elim between 1915–33. Indeed,

---

103. Alvin I. Goldman, 'A Guide to Social Epistemology', in *Social Epistemology: Essential Readings*, ed. Alvin I. Goldman and Dennis Whitcomb (Oxford: Oxford University Press, 2011), 18.

104. Walker and Hudson, 'George Jeffreys, Revivalist and Reformer', 140.

105. Alexander A. Boddy, 'The Welsh Revivalists Visited', *Confidence* 6, no. 3 (March 1913): 47–9.

106. George Jeffreys quoted by Alexander A. Boddy, 'An Apostolic Welsh Revival', *Confidence* 6, no. 2 (February 1913): 28.

it seems that the primary purpose of the Elim Evangelistic Band (the first social embodiment of Elim) and Elim's later Revival Party was to carry out this type of ministry.

With George Jeffreys at the helm, these two revivalistic organizations held meetings with significant pulling power, filling some of the largest venues in the British Isles for a number of years. For example, it is recorded that in 1930 Jeffreys filled the Bingley Hall in Birmingham (seating 15,000 people) 26 times with the final service commencing half an hour early due to the venue already being full. Moreover, it is claimed that during these meetings 10,000 people were converted, 1,100 were baptized in water and 3,000 attended the first service of Elim's newly established Graham Street Church.[107]

It is difficult to verify or falsify these early accounts (although there is no prima facie reason to suspect their accuracy). Nevertheless, at least in Elim's own understanding these revivalistic meetings facilitated by George Jeffreys and his evangelistic team provided an important social embodiment for the Elim argument. In other words, they became a primary platform for the full force of the Elim argument to be experienced as Elim proclaimed what it saw as the biblically grounded Foursquare Gospel and as it sought to demonstrate this truth through experiential and empirical means.

4.4.2 Alliance of congregations, ministers and ministries: The faithful advocates of the Elim argument

However, to sustain the ministry of the revivalist meetings and to disciple its new converts, Elim saw it as necessary to also establish local congregations, churches and/or Pentecostal centres. In fact, the instituting minutes of the Elim Evangelistic Band state that George Jeffreys was appointed as an evangelist and 'that a centre be chosen by him for the purpose of establishing a church out of which evangelists would be sent'.[108] The first local church was founded in Belfast in the summer of 1915.[109] At this stage Jeffreys and other Elim leaders had no intention of starting a new denomination.[110] Nevertheless, as the movement grew during its early years – not least due to the success of the revivalist meetings – a number of new assemblies were established and new workers recruited,[111] which meant that the formation of a denomination was becoming inevitable. Indeed, on 7 June 1918 the Elim Pentecostal Alliance was formed – subsuming the Elim Evangelistic Band, Elim

---

107. Chris Cartwright, *Defining Moments: 100 Years of the Elim Pentecostal Church. Elim 100 Centenary* (Malvern: Elim Pentecostal Church, 2014), 48.

108. 'First informal meeting of Christian brethren at Monaghan. Thursday Jan. 7th 1915.'

109. Cartwright, *The Great Evangelists*, 44.

110. Ibid.; Hathaway, 'The Elim Pentecostal Church', 13.

111. Chris Cartwright mentions that by 1920 there were fifteen churches in Ireland; Cartwright, *Defining Moments*, 26; cf. Kay, *George Jeffreys*, 82.

assemblies and Elim missions – and effectively constituted Elim as a denomination (although at this stage members of the alliance could also be members of their existing churches and Elim was not 'encouraging members to leave their own denominations').[112] George Jeffreys was made the superintendent of this new denomination with the power to nominate its council who would function as the denomination's governing body, making Elim a centrally governed movement.[113]

In the 1920s Elim expanded from Ireland to Wales, England and Scotland, and further structures and increasing central control were introduced in the 1922 constitution.[114] George Jeffreys remained as the unchallenged founder and leader of the movement with an ability to choose a team of overseers 'for the purpose of consultation and decision on any matter affecting the Elim Pentecostal Alliance as the need arises'.[115] The constitution also highlighted a specific role for the general secretary as Jeffreys' right-hand person, as well as for the district superintendents to look after workers and assemblies within their area.[116] The increasing structure and control was believed to make the movement and its congregations more effective in 'the proclamation of the full Gospel'.[117]

As suggested in Chapter 3 (see Section 3.2.2), one of the perceived failures of the Welsh Revival was its inability to provide sufficient social structures and institutions to maintain its revivalistic success. And it seems that Elim was wary of finding British Pentecostalism and its own revivalism in the same predicament. This fear is reflected in Ernest C. W. Boulton's analysis of the development of British Pentecostalism and Elim. He writes:

> Within six years of its introduction into Great Britain, the Pentecostal revival had assumed such proportions as to necessitate the creation of some form of scriptural organisation. To observant minds it was evidence that unless some stable, scriptural government was established, the whole thing would become unwieldy and unmanageable, and much of the rich results reaped during those early years would fail to be conserved.[118]

Boulton continues by arguing that it was at this stage that Jeffreys and Elim entered the religious scene with its 'scriptural organisation'. However, constructing such an organization was not a simple task. In fact, the 1922 constitution was revised a number of times in the 1920s – partly to attract existing British Pentecostal congregations into the Elim ranks by giving them greater autonomy in an

---

112. Minutes of 'Elim Evangelistic Band Meeting, June 7, 1918,' in *Elim Evangelistic Band Minute Book*, Archives of the General Superintendent, EIC, Malvern.
113. Kay, *George Jeffreys*, 78–9.
114. Effective organisation was seen as a necessity for Elim's work to flourish; Jeffreys, *Constitution* (1922), 3.
115. Ibid., 7.
116. Ibid., 9–10, 12.
117. Ibid., 2–3.
118. Boulton, *George Jeffreys* (1999), 20–3.

otherwise centrally governed alliance – before it was finally cemented in the 1934 Deed Poll.[119] For understanding the social embodiment of the Elim argument as a new denomination, there are at least three important factors to note from the Deed Poll.

First, the Deed Poll firmly articulates the purpose of the Elim movement. That is, Elim's name as 'Elim Foursquare Gospel Alliance' is confirmed and the 'objects of the Alliance are to spread and propagate the full Gospel of our Lord Jesus Christ and the Fundamental Truths'.[120] These statements affirm that the content of the Elim argument is to be the Foursquare Gospel with its supporting doctrines.

Second, the objectives of Elim are to be carried out through 'the training and sending of Ministers and Evangelists, the establishment of Churches, the formation of Sunday Schools and the issue of religious publications throughout Great Britain and elsewhere' (commas added).[121] In other words, the Elim argument is to be embodied by ministers, evangelists, local congregations, children/youth ministries, training and publications.

Third, the governance of Elim is transferred from George Jeffreys to the executive council consisting of nine members.[122] As the founder of the movement, Jeffreys was still an ex-officio member of the executive and was also able to personally nominate three of its nine members. The other ex-officio member of the executive was the general secretary (E. J. Phillips). Nevertheless, the remaining four members were to be chosen by the ministerial conference, consisting of Elim's increasing number of ministers. Thus, Jeffreys could no longer govern without the support of the executive approved by its ministers. For Elim, this began the process of sharing power within the wider Elim community, which would increasingly become the case through the movement's first and second epistemological crises (see Chapters 5 and 6).

Thus, the Deed Poll can be seen as ending the first stage of Elim's tradition formation. That is, the Deed Poll seeks to articulate the purpose, nature and structure of Elim, and deliberately makes it difficult to change these going forward.[123] Elim had now 'come of age'; it had developed from the Elim Evangelistic Band to a denomination comprising of assemblies, ministers and ministries.

4.4.3 Publishing and training: The supporting systems of the Elim argument

As well as having an Evangelistic Band, assemblies, ministers and other ministries, Elim also developed additional systems to further sustain its argument, namely, publishing and training. In terms of publishing, the *Elim Evangel* was launched in December 1919. The *Evangel* was Elim's official organ of communication with

---

119. Jeffreys, *Deed Poll* (1934).
120. Ibid., 2.
121. Ibid., 3.
122. Ibid., 4–6.
123. Jones, 'An Assessment of the Leadership of E. J. Phillips', 26.

the aim of promulgating the movement's theology, reflecting on and advertising Elim's various ministries (particularly the revivalistic meetings), and encouraging the Elim community to increasingly live out the Full Gospel. For the interested 'outsiders' the periodical also functioned as a window into Elim. Elim was also the first Pentecostal movement 'to move into independent publishing' when, in April 1924, it opened its purpose-built printing press.[124] The press was used effectively to publish pamphlets/books and by 1936 it had published over fifty books.[125] Like the *Evangel*, these publications helped to consolidate Elim's Pentecostal message in the minds of its adherents and to introduce the movement's message to new audiences.

These early Elim books, pamphlets and articles were generally characterized by their biblicism and testimonial nature. This is not surprising vis-à-vis Elim's rationality. The reason being that Elim's epistemic *biblicism* demanded that the movement's argument be consistently supported, explained and developed in light of the Christian Scriptures. Its *pragmatism*, on the other hand, meant that experience accompanied with visible effects should also be central stage in its rhetoric, and the next best thing to personal experience is a second person account of such phenomena (i.e. testimony).

When it came to training, Elim opened its Bible College in 1925. As Elim expanded in England, there was an increasing need for new ministers to lead the recently established churches. Most of these ministers, however, had received little or no theological training, and thus it was deemed necessary for Elim to open its own Bible College.[126] The purpose of the college is made clear in an *Elim Evangel* notice titled 'Elim Bible College: Four Square on the Word of God'.[127] The notice states that 'studies in all things essential to the four square ministry of the Word will be given, as well as practical training in the ever increasing Elim centres in London and elsewhere'.[128]

Malcolm Hathaway observes that the early theological curriculum of the Elim Bible College 'was very basic, majoring on Pentecostal doctrines and practices, and evangelism'.[129] The early courses tended to be short (some students staying only for a few months), and the first tutors were not academically qualified theologians or biblical scholars.[130] Nevertheless, it was believed that there was a need to instruct future ministers in the Bible as well as in Pentecostal doctrines. The fact that the lecturers were not academically trained did not seem to be an issue, as long as they were considered to be well versed in the Bible, possessed a good understanding

---

124. Hathaway, 'The Elim Pentecostal Church', 18. The *EE* celebrated the opening of the publishing house; E. J. Phillips and Ernest C. W. Boulton, 'The New Publishing Office', *EE* 5, no. 5 (May 1924): 102.

125. Hathaway, 'The Elim Pentecostal Church', 18.

126. Ibid., 19.

127. E. J. Phillips, 'Elim Bible College', *EE* 6, no. 9 (1 May 1925): 102.

128. Ibid.

129. Hathaway, 'The Elim Pentecostal Church', 20.

130. Ibid.

of the Full Gospel and were perceived to be practically effective. Indeed, Elim's rationality of Pentecostal Biblical Pragmatism and its message of the Foursquare Gospel did not require academic credentials of the college tutors, as long as they effectively exemplified the Elim ethos and were able to instruct others accordingly.

In summary, the Elim argument was socially embodied first in its revivalistic meetings facilitated by the Elim Evangelistic Band and then by the Revival Party. This provided the space for Elim to demonstrate the strength of its arguments by drawing people to experience what it deemed as the biblical Full Gospel. Second, the assemblies, ministers and various ministries, which in the end constituted the Elim denomination, provided the structures for maintaining and discipling the faithful advocates of the Elim argument. Elim's various constitutions from 1922 to 1934 sought to clarify and formalize these structures. Third, publishing and training institutions functioned as supporting systems to inspire and educate people in the ways of the Full Gospel.

4.5 Conclusion

In this chapter, I have argued that the Elim argument was directed at and offered as an alternative to Liberal Christianity, cessationist Fundamentalism and ritualistic religion. The content of the argument was essentially the Foursquare Gospel ('hard core') surrounded by Elim's doctrinal statements ('auxiliary hypotheses'). The rationality of the argument was Pentecostal Biblical Pragmatism – that is, Elim's epistemology was shaped by the wider Pentecostal tradition; Elim saw the Bible as the grounding document with respect to truth and its theories of justification were effectively pragmatic with an emphasis on experience and 'results'/'effects'. The content and rationality of the Elim argument was socially embodied in revivalistic meetings, in the emerging Elim denomination consisting of local churches, ministers and various ministries and in its publishing and training institutions.

The Pentecostal rationality articulated in this chapter is 'contextual' and thus follows in the methodological footsteps of Amos Yong, James K. A. Smith and L. William Oliverio Jr. However, in identifying a tradition-specific rationality along MacIntyrian lines the chapter also makes its own contribution to the search for a Pentecostal rationality in four ways.

First, it acknowledges that Pentecostal rationalities need to be understood in their historical contexts and in relation to their dialogue partners and implied opponents. Consequently, Smith's point that early-twentieth-century Pentecostalism can be seen as a reaction to and within modernism is supported by the description of the emerging Elim argument.

Second, the theological guiding principle for Pentecostal rationality has been identified as the Christological Foursquare Gospel. This Full Gospel motif of early British Pentecostalism and Elim is shared with American classical Pentecostals.[131]

---

131. Dayton, *Theological Roots of Pentecostalism*; Thomas, 'Pentecostal Theology in the Twenty-First Century', 17; Archer, *The Gospel Revisited*, 14.

Therefore, even if I do not claim that it should apply to all Pentecostals at all times, with Wolfgang Vondey I maintain that it is at least close to capturing 'the theological convictions of the [Pentecostal] movement'.[132] It thus offers a genuine alternative to those Pentecostal rationalities that start with pneumatology (e.g. Yong's 'pneumatological imagination'). In other words, although the reality of the Christological Foursquare Gospel is seen to be pneumatically mediated, the theological essence is still Christologically focused. The Foursquare Gospel also provides the 'hard core' for the Elim Pentecostal paradigm with the doctrinal statements functioning as 'auxiliary hypotheses'. So, what has been depicted in this chapter can be seen to propose a further articulation of what Oliverio's Pentecostal hermeneutical paradigm/research programme could consist of.

Third, Elim's rationality as *Pentecostal Biblical Pragmatism* underscores the need for (1) understanding Pentecostal epistemology in the context of its Evangelical and Pentecostal heritage (*Pentecostal*); (2) it highlights the centrality of the Bible, as articulated particularly in Smith's epistemology (*biblical*); and (3) it demonstrates the pragmatic nature of Pentecostal epistemology, a feature present in Yong's, Smith's and Oliverio's epistemologies (*pragmatism*). As a philosophical tradition, therefore, Elim is effectively a pragmatic tradition with a number of similarities to American Pragmatism.[133] In particular, it seems that the narrative nature of Elim and other (British) classical Pentecostals is closely connected to pragmatism to the extent that Pentecostals love to tell stories, because second-person accounts are the best way of communicating personal 'experiences' and the effects of those 'experiences'.

Fourth, I have outlined that as a living tradition the content and rationality of the Elim argument is inevitably socially embodied, with institutions and epistemic systems both reflecting and supporting the tradition. These social embodiments are more varied, complex and organized than suggested by Smith's focus just on a Pentecostal worship service, even if these dynamic gatherings are also important social embodiments as seen vis-à-vis the revivalistic meetings of Elim.

As a final note, in this chapter I have not evaluated or developed Elim's tradition specific *Pentecostal Biblical Pragmatism*, but I will do so in Part Three of the study. However, before this can be adequately done, I will need to narrate the Elim argument in light of its two major epistemological crises. To put it differently, this chapter has only provided the first scene (albeit a major scene) of the Elim narrative, and it is now time to narrate the next two major scenes.

---

132. Vondey, *Pentecostal Theology*, 5.

133. For the pragmatic nature of American classical Pentecostalism, see Randall Holm, 'Varieties of Pentecostal Experience: Pragmatism and the Doctrinal Development of Pentecostalism', *EJPT* (1996): no page numbers; Wacker, *Heaven Below*, 13; Koo Dong Yun, 'A Metaphysical Construct of Experience: Concerning the Problematic Usage of "Experience" within Pentecostal Horizons', in *The Role of Experience in Christian Life and Thought – Pentecostal Insights*, 368.

Chapter 5

THE ELIM ARGUMENT EXTENDED THROUGH TIME (I): THE RESIGNATION OF JEFFREYS AND ELIM'S FIRST EPISTEMOLOGICAL CRISIS

Chapter 4 outlined the birth of the Elim argument, with particular emphasis on the implied opponents, the content of the Elim argument, its tacit rationality and its social embodiment. In MacIntyrian terms this can be stated as the birth of the Elim tradition and the first stage of its tradition formation. However, after a tradition has been formed, MacIntyre sees traditions evolving and developing by going through two further stages.[1] As discussed in Chapter 2, at the second stage inadequacies and incoherencies are identified within the tradition, which can be fuelled by internal debates within, or external critique from outside, the community. This second stage can also be seen as an 'epistemological crisis' within the tradition, as it can cause the tradition to question not just its identity but also its existing beliefs, sources of knowledge and its practices regarding epistemic warrant.[2] The third stage provides a potential remedy for the epistemological crisis encountered during the second stage, resulting in reformulations and reinterpretations of the tradition.

For MacIntyre the degree to which the inadequacies can be resolved depends on the resources available within the community's tradition and on the community's inventiveness. Moreover, for the movement to continue after the reformulation, 'some core of shared belief, constitutive of allegiance to the tradition, has to survive',[3] because without some continuity the tradition bears no resemblance to its authoritative origins and thus has been transformed altogether into something else. As living traditions evolve and develop stages two and three are regularly revisited, and it is this continual process that makes a tradition effectively 'an argument extended through time'.

As has already been suggested in Chapter 4, by 1934 Elim had moved from its formational stage into a formalized tradition. The Elim historian, Maldwyn

---

1. MacIntyre, *Whose Justice?*, 354–5.
2. See MacIntyre, 'Epistemological Crises, Dramatic Narrative, and the Philosophy of Science', 3–23.
3. MacIntyre, *Whose Justice?*, 356.

Jones, points out that by 1934 Jeffreys had practically 'ceased his pioneering evangelistic crusades' and was now focusing on 're-visiting the larger churches that he had opened'.[4] In 1934 Elim also introduced the Deed Poll which cemented the movement's constitution and the young tradition's central tenets, as well as transferred its governance from Jeffreys and his group of overseers to the executive council approved by the ministerial conference. Thus, by 1934 it seems that as a tradition Elim had now 'come of age'.[5]

However, Jeffreys did not think that his work in Elim was done. On the contrary, in the 1930s he began his efforts to 'reform' the institutionalized movement which he had founded; an effort which eventually led to his own resignation from Elim and propelled the denomination into its first major epistemological crisis. The purported reasons for Jeffreys resignation, as well as the aftermath of his departure, are well documented by Noel Brooks (circa 1948),[6] Bryan Wilson (1961),[7] Desmond Cartwright (1986),[8] Albert Edsor (1989),[9] Malcolm Hathaway (1998),[10] Neil Hudson (1999),[11] Maldwyn Jones (2011)[12] and William Kay (2017).[13] My purpose in this chapter is not to revisit the various factors that led to the

---

4. Jones, 'An Assessment of the Leadership of E. J. Phillips', 61.

5. The year 1936 was officially commemorated as Elim's 'Coming of Age Year'; P. N. Corry and D. Vanstone, 'The Coming of Age Year', *EE* 17, no. 51–2 (25 December 1936): 816–17.

6. Brooks, *Fight for the Faith and Freedom*. This is a passionate defence of Jeffreys by one of his close associates.

7. Bryan R. Wilson, *Sects and Society: The Sociology of Three Religious Groups in Britain* (London: William Heinemann, 1961). This is the first academic work on Elim's schism, and it explores the issue in light of Max Weber's concept of 'routinization of charisma'.

8. Cartwright, *The Great Evangelists*. This is written by the former Elim historian and therefore broadly speaking, although not uncritically, reflects Elim's view on the matter.

9. Albert W. Edsor, *'Set Your House in Order': God's Call to George Jeffreys as the Founder of the Elim Pentecostal Movement* (Chichester: New Wine Press, 1989). This is a partisan defence of Jeffreys by his secretary and long serving ally.

10. Hathaway, 'The Elim Pentecostal Church', 1–39. This is written by an academic Elim minister and offers a balanced, albeit brief, account of the events.

11. D. Neil Hudson, 'A Schism and its Aftermath: an historical analysis of denomination discerption in the Elim Pentecostal Church, 1939–1940' (PhD diss., King's College, London, 1999). To date this is the most comprehensive academic account of the schism, and it is written by a critical insider of the Elim movement (i.e. an academically trained Elim minister).

12. Jones, 'An Assessment of the Leadership of E. J. Phillips'. This dissertation is written by the current Elim historian and offers a defence of Phillips.

13. Kay, *George Jeffreys*. This is the most recent academic work on the topic by a preeminent British Pentecostal historian/theologian. It focuses particularly on the British Israel issue and my argument in this chapter is most closely aligned with its overall conclusion.

schism in Elim, such as the potential personality clashes between E. J. Phillips and George Jeffreys, Phillips's and Jeffreys' respective illnesses, the tensions in the Irish churches, the claimed financial difficulties in Elim, the formation of the World Revival Crusade or even the major issue of church government.[14] My focus will be, however, on the issue of British Israelism (BI) in the context of Elim's eschatological beliefs. The exploration of the BI controversy in the 1930s is important not only in appreciating a main – if not *the* main – reason for Jeffreys' resignation but also in understanding how Elim developed its hard core doctrine of 'Jesus as coming King', and thus the BI debate helps illuminate the very nature of the Elim argument in terms of its content and rationality.

In discussing Elim's first epistemological crisis, with a particular emphasis on the BI controversy, I will (1) provide an overview of Elim's eschatological beliefs in the 1930s; (2) narrate the BI debates from 1932 to 1937, as well as suggest that Jeffreys' attempt to reform Elim's church governance in 1938 to 1940 was largely motivated by his desire to bring BI teaching into Elim; and (3) argue how the crisis resulting from Jeffreys' resignation and its resolution substantiates my argument regarding the content (Foursquare Gospel) and rationality (Pentecostal Biblical Pragmatism) of the Elim argument.

5.1 *The coming King: An overview of Elim's eschatology*

In Chapter 4 I have argued that the Foursquare Gospel of Jesus as Saviour, Healer, Baptiser in the Holy Spirit and coming King is the hard core of the Elim argument (see Section 4.2.4). I will now argue that the question of rightly interpreting the fourth of these foundational beliefs, namely, the eschatological doctrine of Jesus as coming King, was central in the Elim debates of the 1930s and a key factor leading to the eventual resignation of Jeffreys in 1939. Noel Brooks and Albert Edsor (close associates of Jeffreys) claimed that BI, which was Jeffreys' particular understanding of eschatology and fulfilment of biblical prophecy, had nothing to do with him leaving Elim but instead he was simply driven by a divine mandate for 'setting his house in order' and redeeming the local Elim churches from the tyranny of central government.[15] Such interpretation of the events, however, is neither supported by Elim's conference minutes or Jeffreys' letter correspondence with Elim's executive council in the 1930s, both of which demonstrate his constant attempt to bring BI into Elim. Moreover, such a reading also fails to appreciate the importance eschatology played in constituting the Elim tradition, particularly during a period when the movement's apocalyptic senses were heightened due

---

14. For a thorough analysis of these various reasons, see Hudson, 'A Schism and its Aftermath'.

15. Brooks, *Fight for the Faith and Freedom*, 74–7; Edsor, 'Set Your House in Order', 123–4. Brooks does acknowledge that BI highlighted to Jeffreys the inherent problems of Elim's centrally governed structure.

to the political uncertainties in Europe. To substantiate this argument, I will first discuss Elim's basic doctrine of Jesus as coming King and then explore the BI controversy.

5.1.1 Dispensational premillennialism

The doctrine of Jesus as coming King is expressed in the 1934 Deed Poll Fundamental Truths as: 'We believe in the personal and pre-millennial return of our Lord Jesus Christ to receive unto Himself the Church and afterwards to set up His Throne as King.'[16] Four aspects regarding this statement are worth highlighting.

First, the return of Christ is believed to be 'personal'. The Elim literature from the period commonly articulates why Christ's second coming should not be spiritualized. For example, the Elim minister Charles J. E. Kingston, at the outset of his book *The Coming of Christ and After*, seeks to demonstrate that Christ's return is personal and physical, and he argues against any interpretation that tries to equate it with regeneration, Pentecost or the soul of the Christian ascending to heaven after death.[17] This insistence on the literal and physical return of Christ is to a great extent due to Elim's Pentecostal reaction against the 'modernist teaching' on the spiritual and non-corporeal nature of the *parousia*, although Elim always maintained that its view regarding the matter was simply 'biblical'.

Second, this 'personal' and 'physical' return of Christ is understood to be premillennial with two distinct stages. In the first stage Christ 'receives[s] unto Himself the Church'. This stage is equated with the 'rapture' where Christians, both those who have already died and those who are still alive, are taken up from the earth to meet Christ in the clouds (the common proof-text used here was 1 Thess. 4.16-18). This is followed by the second stage where Christ 'will set up His Throne as King', which means that he will return to the earth with the church and begin his thousand year reign on earth (a literal understanding and chronological reading of Revelation 20 was generally assumed within Elim literature). The tribulation period is believed to take place between stages one and two, and the final judgment and the coming of the new heaven and the new earth is thought to succeed Christ's millennial reign.[18] Thus, Elim's eschatology of the period is effectively dispensational pre-tribulational premillennialism.

Third, linked to Elim's dispensational premillennialism, there is an assumption that 'things will get worse' before Christ returns. For example, W. G. Hathaway

---

16. Jeffreys, *Elim Foursquare Gospel Alliance*, 3.

17. Charles J. E. Kingston, *The Coming of Christ and After: Or What the Future Holds*. Revised and Enlarged Edition (London: Victory Press, 1939), 3–6; cf. Jeffreys, *The Miraculous Foursquare Gospel – Doctrinal*, 60; M. L. Lowe, 'The Fact of Christ's Second Coming', *EE* 20, no. 8 (24 February 1939): 113–14; F. L. French, 'The Blessed Hope', *EE* 20, no. 8 (24 February 1939): 120–1.

18. See Jeffreys, *The Miraculous Foursquare Gospel – Supernatural*, 71–3; W. G. Hathaway, 'That Glorious Hope', *EE* 20, no. 8 (24 February 1939): 115.

claims that as the return of Christ approaches, persecution of true Christians will increase and apostasy will be committed by many.[19] Kingston echoes this pessimistic outlook by arguing that optimism regarding world events is naïve as the current *'religious signs'* of 'false religions', 'pleasure loving' and 'superstition'; *'social signs'* of 'infidelity', 'crime' and 'immorality'; *'providential signs'* of 'famines', 'pestilences' and 'earthquakes'; and *'political signs'* of 'wars' and 'distress of nations' are all expected phenomena before the second coming.[20] This implies that Elim's eschatological imagination seems to be dominated by apocalyptic destructionism, and hence it is unsurprising that the movement emphasizes 'saving souls' rather than bringing social transformation. F. L. French's words in *Elim Evangel* are telling: 'To this day many in the high position in the professing Church see looming largely before them a "social gospel" of an improved and bettered world ... But God is not improving the world in this dispensation. He has judged and condemned it, and is gathering out of it a people for the Lord Jesus Christ, His Church.'[21] To put it simply, Elim's apocalyptic premillennialism assumes that the world is under judgment and therefore investing resources in trying to improve it in the current dispensation is at best futile and at worst going against the decrees of God.

Fourth, despite the dire apocalyptic understanding of world events, or perhaps exactly because of such dystopic view of the end times, the return of Christ is seen within Elim as the 'hope of the believer'.[22] In other words, the *parousia* is believed to complete the history of the world, and in contrast to the anticipated apocalyptic calamities, Christ's coming will initiate a harmonious existence between God, people and the whole of creation, which means that the new world will be free of death, war and injustice. It is in the light of this eschatological hope that Christians are encouraged to live holy lives and prepare the way for their coming King.[23]

5.1.2 Pentecostal Biblical Pragmatism and the three prophetic schools

Elim's eschatological vision reflects and is informed by its rationality of *Pentecostal Biblical Pragmatism*. That is, the general premillennial framework is inherited from Elim's (pre-) *Pentecostal* roots, particularly shaped by the dispensational premillennialism of John Nelson Darby which was popular in British Holiness and Evangelical circles at the turn of the century.[24] However, although the influence

---

19. W. G. Hathaway, 'A Peep into the Future', *EE* 16, no. 14 (5 April 1935): 222.
20. Kingston, *The Coming of Christ*, 15–49.
21. French, 'The Blessed Hope', 120.
22. Jeffreys, *The Miraculous Foursquare Gospel – Doctrinal*, 60.
23. See Jeffreys, *The Miraculous Foursquare Gospel – Doctrinal*, 60–3; Lowe, 'The Fact of Christ's Second Coming', 113–14; Hathaway, 'The Glorious Hope', 115–16; French, 'The Blessed Hope', 120–1; G. H. Clement, 'If Jesus Should Come To-night! What Then?' *EE* 20, no. 8 (24 February 1939): 126.
24. Sandeen, *The Roots of Fundamentalism*, 30–8; William K. Kay, *Pentecostalism: A Very Short Introduction* (Oxford: Oxford University Press, 2011), 12–13.

of the late-nineteenth-century radical Evangelical eschatology is significant, Elim was always quick to highlight that its views were *biblical*; that is, the Bible was maintained as the grounding document for its eschatological beliefs. M. L. Lowe represents Elim's perspective well when he writes that to rightly understand the nature of Christ's return one needs to simply '*take it to the Scriptures*'.[25] Correct exposition of the scriptures and its prophecies regarding the end times was then characterized by Elim's *pragmatism* with a focus on 'effects' and 'results'. To put it differently, Elim's eschatology was strongly characterized by an emphasis on biblical prophecies and an attempt to try to correlate them with real world events. Ernest C. W. Boulton, in an *Elim Evangel* editorial, went as far as to suggest that he could not think of a 'mightier or weightier argument' in the church's 'conflict with atheism, agnosticism and modern criticism, than that of fulfilled prophecy'.[26] This 'fulfilled prophecy' referred to the promises that were believed to have been fulfilled during the biblical era, as well as those that were now supposedly being fulfilled before the very eyes of Boulton and his contemporaries. The point was that the pragmatic effects of biblical prophecy were allegedly visible in the unfolding history of the world.

Elim's hard core doctrine of Jesus as Coming King understood in a premillennial framework was seen as a non-negotiable within the Elim tradition, not least as it seemed to be consonant with its rationality of Pentecostal Biblical Pragmatism. Nevertheless, within this agreed doctrinal framework, in the 1930s there were three interpretive schools of thought particularly with respect to understanding biblical prophecies. These were: (1) the Historicist School which saw biblical prophecies, particularly the Book of Revelation, being fulfilled during the different epochs of church history, with a view that the seven churches in Revelation 2–3 referred to the seven dispensations of the church; (2) the Futurist School which saw many biblical prophecies, and Revelation especially, as being fulfilled just before the return of Christ; (3) the BI School which saw Celto-Anglo-Saxon people as the lost tribes of Israel with the British Empire having an important role in fulfilling biblical prophecies.[27]

At the risk of repetition, it is worth underscoring that all three schools utilized Elim's rationality of biblical pragmatism in seeking to identify and point out the 'effects' of biblical prophecy on past, present and future world events. However, despite the shared rationality by these three schools within Elim, it was the debate

---

25. Lowe, 'The Fact of Christ's Second Coming', 113; cf. W. G. Hathaway, 'A Peep into the Future', 216.

26. Ernest C. W. Boulton, 'The Profit of Prophecy (Editorial)', *EE* 16, no. 14 (5 April 1935): 218.

27. W. G. Hathaway, 'A Peep into the Future', 217 and 222; Minutes of 'Elim Foursquare Gospel Alliance: Ministerial Conference 18th September to 22nd September 1933', Archives of the General Superintendent, EIC, Malvern, 8; Minutes of 'Elim Foursquare Gospel Alliance: Ministerial and General Conference. 21st October to 25th October, 1935', Archives of the General Superintendent, EIC, Malvern, 3–9.

between them, and particularly the rejection of BI by the majority of Elim ministers as a reasonable school of eschatological interpretation, that contributed to Elim's first 'epistemological crisis'.

5.2 The British Israel controversy

The origins of modern BI can be traced to John Wilson and his work *Our Israelitish Origin* (1840).[28] The BI teaching gained particular prominence towards the late nineteenth century probably due to the increasing interest in biblical prophecy, 'abounding racial theories' in Europe and the global dominance of the British Empire.[29] Indeed, at the beginning of the twentieth century BI had up to two million adherents,[30] and from 1919 onwards the British Israel World Federation functioned as the movement's leading society.[31] Some notable early Pentecostal pioneers, such as the American Charles Fox Parham and the British William Oliver Hutchinson, were followers of BI.[32] In Elim the three most vocal advocates of this doctrine were John Leech, George Jeffreys and James McWhirter.

There was no one official version of BI, and Jeffreys was in fact careful to distance himself from what he saw as the more extreme aspects of BI.[33] Nevertheless, the central feature of BI was the identification of the Celto-Anglo-Saxons as Israelites and Britain as Israel (or at least the Tribe of Ephraim).[34] To justify this 'identity' the following reasons were commonly offered by the advocates of BI.

The BI proponents believed that God promised Abraham that until the end of the age the people of Israel would survive and function as a nation. However, in light of the defeat and exile of Israel's Northern Kingdom (722 BCE) and Judah's Southern Kingdom (586 BCE), this promised continuity for Israel as a nation had not been realized in Palestine. Consequently, it was suggested by the supporters of

---

28. John Wilson, 'British Israelism: The Ideological Restraints on Sect Organisation', in *Patterns of Sectarianism*, ed. Bryan R. Wilson (London: Heinemann, 1967), 354 [Note: this is a different 'John Wilson' from the writer of *Our Israelith Origin*]; I. Hexham, 'British Israelism', in *Evangelical Dictionary of Theology*, ed. Walter A. Elwell (Grand Rapids, MI: Baker Books, 1995), 174. Although BI ideas are already present in John Sadler's *Rights of the Kingdom* (1649); see John Wilson, 'British Israelism', 349.

29. John Wilson, 'British Israelism', *The Sociological Review* 16 (March 1968): 41–2.

30. Hexham, 'British Israelism', 175.

31. Wilson, 'British Israelism' (1968), 43.

32. Faupel, *The Everlasting Gospel*, 167; Malcolm R. Hathaway, 'The Role of William Oliver Hutchinson and the Apostolic Faith Church in the Formation of British Pentecostal Churches', *JEPTA* 16, no. 1 (1996): 47.

33. George Jeffreys, letter to E. J. Phillips (28 January 1937), Elim Archives, Malvern.

34. See James McWhirter, *Britain and Palestine in Prophecy* (London: Methuen, 1937), chapter 4; cf. E. J. Phillips, letter to George Jeffreys (1 February 1937), Elim Archives, Malvern.

BI that this continuation of Israel as a nation needed to be actualized elsewhere for God to have fulfilled his promise to Abraham. Following from this assumption, it was then proposed that God had been faithful in fulfilling his promise in the Celto-Anglo-Saxon people who were in fact Israel.

Equating Britain as Israel was maintained by a historical narrative which claimed that after the destruction of Judah, Zedekiah's daughters escaped Egypt and took refuge in the 'isles of the sea' (Jer. 31.10), which was understood to be the British Isles. The descendants of Zedekiah's daughters were then believed to have become the royal house in Britain, meaning that 'the British royal family is directly linked to the house of David'.[35] The common Israelites followed the royal line to the British Isles gradually after wandering through Europe following their initial exile to Assyria in 722 BCE.[36] A key proof-text used here was 2 Sam. 7.10 which supposedly referred to God 'planting' Israel to a 'place' interpreted as Britain where they would 'dwell in their own place and be disturbed no more'.[37] Thus, Britain was seen as the modern-day Israel and the success of the British Empire, as well as other Celto-Anglo-Saxon nations (e.g. United States), was explained as God's divine favour on his chosen people.

A key assumption within BI was the distinction between 'Jews' and 'Israel'; that is, 'Jews' consisted of the tribes of Judah and Benjamin, whereas 'Israel' consisted of the remaining ten (or eleven) tribes. This distinction was important for BI because it allowed its adherents to argue that those who returned to Judah from 538 BCE onwards as recorded in Ezra-Nehemiah were primarily the 'Jews' rather than the ten tribes of 'Israel'.[38] The tribes of 'Israel', according to BI, did not return to Palestine but made their way to Britain. Furthermore, there was a common assumption that it had been the 'Jews' in Palestine during the first century rather than 'Israel' who had rejected Christ, and 'Israel' as the Celto-Anglo-Saxon peoples had on the whole accepted Christ. James McWhirter went as far as to suggest that this meant that the 'spiritual blessing' promised to Judah had now been transferred to 'Israel' (read: Britain), as apparently indicated by Jesus in Mt. 21.43.[39]

5.2.1 The first round of the British Israel controversy: Elim conferences 1932–34

Although Jeffreys seems to have adopted the BI position from around 1920 onwards – most likely due to the influence of John Leech – BI does not really feature within Elim literature until the early 1930s.[40] There seems to be no single

---

35. Hexham, 'British Israelism', 175.
36. McWhirter, *Britain and Palestine in Prophecy*, 30.
37. See 'Notes of the 1934 Elim Conference Debate on British Israelism', Archives of the General Superintendent, EIC, Malvern, 28.
38. Ibid., 48–57.
39. McWhirter, *Britain and Palestine in Prophecy*, 31.
40. Hathaway, 'The Elim Pentecostal Church', 22; cf. Cartwright, *The Great Evangelists*, 120. Although in 1925 Boulton already writes to Phillips raising his serious concerns about

reason why all of a sudden Jeffreys began to advocate strongly for BI. Nevertheless, it appears that for Elim as a movement the uncertain political climate of 1930s Europe brought eschatological questions increasingly to the forefront of its psyche. Moreover, by the 1930s the hard core of the Elim argument (read: Foursquare Gospel) and its Fundamental Truths had been firmly established, which means that there was a growing need to further develop the auxiliary hypotheses surrounding these core doctrines.

Whatever the reasons for the emergence of BI in Elim, it was seen as a significant doctrine by its advocates. Although in some correspondence Jeffreys refers to BI as a secondary doctrine and a 'minor question' in relation to Elim's Fundamental Truths,[41] his persistence, despite the strong opposition, in trying to make BI an acceptable prophetic interpretive school within Elim suggests that it had greater significance for Jeffreys than he publicly indicated. Indeed, James McWhirter – Jeffreys' close associate, member of his Revival Party and fellow supporter of BI – believed that

> The greatest spiritual awakening that has ever been will come with the realization of our identity with Israel. The psychological effect will be that the nation will begin to live up to it, and at that time the nation will be re-born. When our national privilege is understood it will beget in us a sacred sense of responsibility. The result will be transforming reaction from materialism to new spiritual life. That is Paul's argument to the Romans. 'Now if the fall of them (Israel) be the riches of the world, and the *loss* of them the riches of the Gentiles; how much more their fullness.' – Rom. Xi. 12 (R.V.).[42]

If Jeffreys shared these sentiments and believed that BI was the missing key in initiating 'the greatest spiritual awakening', it is no wonder why he passionately attempted to make Elim a BI movement.[43] Jeffreys' first attempt to bring BI into Elim came in 1932 at Elim's 'Northern Division Conference' at Glossop.[44] BI received a cold reception among the Elim ministers present, so Jeffreys decided to bring up the issue again in Elim's first ever national ministerial conference in 1933. The minutes of the 1933 conference note that the question of BI, Futurist and Historicist Interpretations of Prophecy were discussed under 'Supplementary Statement of Belief', and regarding BI the conference 'agreed that it should neither

---

BI infiltrating Elim; Ernest C. W. Boulton, letter to E. J. Phillips (30 November 1925), Elim Archives, Malvern; cf. Kingston, 'The Coming of Christ – and After', 255.

41. George Jeffreys, letter to J. I. MacDonald (9 May 1935), Elim Archives, Malvern; Jeffreys, letter to E. J. Phillips (28 January 1937).

42. McWhirter, *Britain and Palestine in Prophecy*, 80.

43. See also Hudson, 'A Schism and its Aftermath', 193; Kay, *George Jeffreys*, 264.

44. Minutes of the 'Northern Division Conference, 24th to 26th October, 1932', Archives of the General Superintendent, EIC, Malvern.

be preached nor attacked in our churches, and that it should be referred to in the Supplementary Statement of Belief'.[45]

The 1933 conference decision, however, did not weaken Jeffreys' resolve, and for the 1934 conference he requested that BI would be debated by the conference and almost two days was dedicated for this debate.[46] The 1934 conference debate proved to be a watershed moment for BI in Elim, albeit not for the reasons hoped for by Jeffreys. On the Tuesday morning of the conference, John Leech – a well-educated Crown prosecutor and an established debater[47] – 'spoke on the subject of British-Israelism, and his address was discussed for the remainder of the morning'.[48] The rest of Tuesday focused on other matters, and the debate continued on Wednesday with the whole day devoted for the topic. Leech started the morning by presenting the case for BI, after which 'he was questioned, and his address was discussed'.[49] This was followed by E. J. Phillips presenting his reasons against BI,[50] 'and he was questioned and his address discussed'.[51]

The content and nature of the conference BI debate is a practical demonstration of Elim's biblical pragmatism in action. Unfortunately, the official notes from the debate do not include Leech's opening speech.[52] Nevertheless, the questioning and criticism of Leech which have been preserved indicate what he probably covered in his initial presentation.[53] Based on these notes, William Kay reasonably suggests that Leech seemed to focus first in trying to provide evidence for the distinction between 'Jews' (Judah) and 'Israel' (the ten northern tribes), and the notion that Israel did not return to Palestine with Judah after the exile. Secondly, Leech attempted to show that the ten tribes of Israel made their way to Britain.[54]

To substantiate these two points, Leech appears to have argued primarily from the Bible and secondarily from history/ethnography. His biblical arguments explored 2 Sam. 7.10 which he saw as a reference to Israel being planted in Britain, and Isa. 41, 49.1 which he claimed spoke of the British Isles. At the risk of oversimplification, the logic of Leech's pragmatic biblical argument went along

---

45. Minutes of the Elim Conference (1933), 8.

46. Kay, *George Jeffreys*, 274.

47. Ibid., 266; cf. Cartwright, *The Great Evangelists*, 121; Hudson, 'A Schism and its Aftermath', 199.

48. Minutes of the 'Elim Foursquare Gospel Alliance: Ministerial and General Conference, 17th to 21st September 1934', Archives of the General Superintendent, EIC, Malvern, 2.

49. Ibid., 3.

50. Phillips stepped in last minute as Percy Corry, the dean of Elim Bible College, pulled out of the debate just before the event. Apparently Phillips 'stayed up all night to prepare'; Cartwright, *The Great Evangelists*, 121.

51. Minutes of the Elim Conference (1934), 3.

52. The first nineteen pages are missing from the 'Notes of the 1934 Elim Conference Debate'. The debate discussed below is primarily constructed from these notes.

53. Ibid., 20–47.

54. Kay, *George Jeffreys*, 275.

the following lines: (1) 2 Sam. 7.10 refers to God richly blessing his people by planting them to 'another place'; (2) the Isaiah passages indicate that this 'place' is the (British) Isles far away from Palestine; and (3) in light of God's perceived blessing of Britain and its current Empire, Britain must be the place referred to in these passages and the British people must be the lost tribes of Israel. He further supported his 'biblical' argument by historical/ethnographical claims that the British people are a pure nation, implying their ethnic purity as Israelites. In his own words, 'I can assure you that our people here are not a mixed people; they come from one stock, and all modern and learned ethnologists agree on that.'[55]

The conference members, however, were not convinced of Leech's arguments. They not only challenged his historical and ethnographical claims[56] but also particularly critiqued his biblical statements in two ways. First, they pointed out that his BI interpretations were not the natural reading of the texts. For example, W. G. Hathaway stated that 'the place' of 2 Sam. 7.10 probably simply refers to Palestine and actually in the text there is no reference to *'another place'*;[57] E. J. Phillips noted that in light of the context of 2 Sam. 7.10, the promise applies to all tribes of Israel, not just to Leech's proposed ten northern tribes, and so challenged the assumed distinction between 'Israel' and the 'Jews';[58] and Kingston remarked that Isaiah was actually written to Judah and not to the ten tribes of Israel, undermining Leech's idea that Isaiah somehow referred to the ten Northern tribes dwelling in the far away islands.[59] Moreover, Leech's interpretation of certain Hebrew words and verb tenses were questioned.[60] This interaction between Leech and his critics shows the centrality of the Bible within the debate, as well as the conference members' deep knowledge of the Bible and their ability to wrestle with hermeneutical questions. It also demonstrates that the Elim ministers did not accept beliefs blindly but evaluated doctrines in light of Scripture.

Second, as well as criticizing Leech's biblical exegesis, the conference also challenged the logic of Leech's argumentation. As already alluded to, Leech effectively utilized a pragmatic rationality to justify BI; that is, he maintained that the 'results' which for him was the superiority of Britain and its Empire demonstrated the truth of BI. However, both Phillips and Kingston objected to what they saw as inappropriate circularity and 'question begging' in Leech's argument.[61] Phillips and Kingston had a fair point, as in terms of propositional logic Leech seemed to suffer from the logical fallacy of 'affirming the consequent' (i.e. the 'converse error'). To spell this out, a pragmatic BI argument in a valid *modus ponens* format would probably have gone something along the lines of 'If Britain is Israel, then Britain experiences global dominance'. However, this need

55. 'Notes of the 1934 Elim Conference Debate', 21.
56. Ibid., 20–1.
57. Ibid., 21.
58. Ibid., 24.
59. Ibid., 36.
60. Ibid., 24–5, 28.
61. Ibid., 23, 36.

not imply the converse, namely, 'If Britain experiences global dominance, then Britain is Israel', since there could be various reasons why Britain could experience global dominance with no relation whatsoever to its identity as Israel. In fairness to Leech's logic, all pragmatic arguments are susceptible to this type of circularity. Therefore, as pointed out by Bruce Marshall, a pragmatic thesis can at best only falsify rather than verify a belief.[62] In other words, and in relation to Leech's BI argument, Britain's global dominance cannot verify the truth of BI, because there could be other reasons to explain this phenomenon. But, if Britain does not experience global dominance, then this lack of dominance may well falsify the BI doctrine (assuming, of course, that British dominance is a necessary sign for its identity as Israel). Consequently, the best that Leech's pragmatic argument could ever do by the very nature of being pragmatic was to suggest that BI was not false, but strictly speaking it could never prove the truth of BI.

This accusation of 'question begging', as well as the inability for Leech to *prove* his BI position, on their own would have probably not sufficiently undermined the BI position among the conference members, not least as the Elim tradition as whole embodied a pragmatic rationality not dissimilar to the one used by Leech. However, Leech's supposed 'question begging' combined with (1) the more natural and anti-BI readings of the biblical texts in question, (2) the more plausible eschatological schools of interpretation already within Elim (i.e. Futurist and Historicist), and (3) the possible falsifying evidence against BI provided by Phillips in his upcoming speech, ensured that BI doctrine remained unconvincing to the conference members.

Indeed, Phillips in his presentation was determined to provide this falsifying evidence against BI. Appreciating the centrality of the Bible within the Elim constituency, he maintained that 'in my arguments against [BI] I am going to confine myself entirely to the scriptures.'[63] Neil Hudson has suggested that Phillips's reasoning was primarily 'pragmatic' rather than 'theological'.[64] This inference, however, is not supported by the notes from the debate, where Phillips fundamentally produces biblical and theological arguments. In fact, Phillips produces eight distinct theological arguments. In the first argument, which is by far the most detailed, he states that the BI distinction between 'Jews' and 'Israel' cannot be maintained in light of Scripture. He systematically explores passages from 1 Chronicles, 2 Chronicles, Ezra, Nehemiah, Esther, Jeremiah, Ezekiel and Acts, with the following conclusion:

> I say [that] from these Scriptures we have overwhelming proof that the Jews and the Israelites are one people, and consequently it is useless to look for the 10 tribes outside the people today who are called Jews and generally known as Jews.

---

62. Bruce Marshall, *Trinity and Truth* (Cambridge: Cambridge University Press, 2000), 188.
63. 'Notes of the 1934 Elim Conference Debate', 48.
64. Hudson, 'A Schism and its Aftermath', 206.

There may be a few odd ones outside; I do not deny it; they have been scattered and left behind, but the Jews generally embrace the whole of Israel.[65]

His second argument notes that many of the promises to Israel, like 'growing in number', are actually conditional on Israel 'obeying the voice of the Lord and keeping His commandments'.[66] He does not think that any 'sanctified Christian' would suggest that Britain as a nation is obedient to God, and therefore many of the so-called blessings claimed by the advocates of BI to currently 'rest on' Britain (e.g. growing population) due to its identity as Israel cannot be right. To the contrary, argues Phillips, if Britain were Israel due to the nation's current disobedience to Christ they should actually be experiencing punishment (e.g. decline in population) rather than blessing (e.g. growth in population).[67]

The third and fourth arguments simply pointed out that unlike the Jews, Britain does not follow Israel's mandate of the Sabbath or circumcision.[68] The fifth proposed that, according to Jas 1.1 and Acts 26.6-7, the ten tribes were never lost in the first place (contra BI). The sixth claimed that Amos 9.8 suggests that God never intended just to restore the ten tribes of Israel;[69] the seventh argued that the Jews alone have remained as a distinct people group according to Num. 23.9, not the British;[70] and the final argument maintained that Britain cannot be Israel because it has 'borrowed millions of pounds' and has a significant national debt, and therefore does not fulfil the promise of Deut. 15.5 given to Israel.[71]

After making his speech, Phillips was questioned by the members of conference. Much of the questioning focuses on whether the 'bulk' of the ten tribes returned to Palestine with Judah, and whether the ten tribes had ever been reunited with Judah after the exile.[72] Leech also tried to explain how James, Peter and Paul in the NT could refer to the twelve tribes, but that did not mean that the bulk of the ten tribes were not lost.[73] The most vocal critics of Phillips's presentation seemed to be Leech (naturally), Robert Mercer and James McWhirter. Jeffreys functioned as the moderator of the debate, and although on the whole he chaired the debate objectively, on occasions his BI bias is apparent in his comments.[74]

---

65. 'Notes of the 1934 Elim Conference Debate', 62.
66. Ibid.
67. Ibid., 64.
68. Ibid., 64–5.
69. Ibid., 66.
70. Ibid., 68.
71. Ibid., 70.
72. Ibid., 71–117.
73. Ibid., 73–4.
74. Ibid., 113–14.

After the debate, it was discussed whether BI should be taught in Elim churches. According to the conference minutes,

> it was decided, evidently [and] unanimously that it [BI] should neither be preached nor attacked in any Elim Church under Direct Government, nor should any Minister under direct Government appear on any B.I. platform. As regards Elim Churches not under Direct Government the majority were apparently of the opinion that it should be permissible to preach it within certain limits provided that it would not harm in any way the rest of the work.[75]

A vote was also taken on the notion of BI 'identity'. Of the 131 eligible to vote, 17 accepted BI, 73 rejected it and 41 were neutral.[76] The conference decision to ban the teaching of BI in the main Elim churches and the vote with a majority of the conference rejecting BI indicates that Phillips was the clear winner of the debate, although based on the 1932 and 1933 conferences it seems that majority of Elim ministers were already predisposed against BI before the debate. Nevertheless, the biblical tour de force provided by Phillips seemed to provide a blow for BI within the Elim movement from which it would never recover. The potential appeal of Leech's faltering pragmatic logic and his questionable scriptural interpretations were dismantled by Phillips's systematic biblical arguments.

The debate underscores an important aspect of Elim's biblical pragmatism. That is, Elim's rationality is not just pragmatism. If its rationality would have simply been characterized by pragmatism, Leech may have been able to muster greater support for BI with his pragmatic arguments. However, he was not able to do so because Elim's rationality is *biblical* pragmatism. This means that a belief's 'effects' and 'results' on their own are not sufficient to convince an Elimite of its 'truth', if the belief does not also have sufficient grounding in Scripture. In other words, pragmatic effectiveness needs to be married with scriptural faithfulness within Elim's *biblical pragmatism*. Indeed, Leech was not criticized as such for his pragmatism by Phillips but for his poor biblical hermeneutics.[77] This suggests that within Elim's *biblical* pragmatism a text has certain interpretive limits and a text cannot be made to mean anything even if such an interpretation might have pragmatic potential. Some assumed hermeneutical principles need to guide the scope of possible interpretations. As discussed in Chapter 4, and as seen in this debate, these hermeneutical principles are informed by Elim's common sense 'Bible Reading Method'. That said, this does not mean that Elim's rationality is thus simply characterized by *biblicism*. Phillips's own rhetoric and biblical interpretation regarding the history of the Jewish people carried pragmatic elements, and as an experienced debater Leech most certainly would have not utilized pragmatic arguments if he believed them to carry no weight with his audience. In sum, Elim's tacit rationality in the 1934 conference debate was *biblical pragmatism*.

---

75. Minutes of the Elim Conference (1934), 3.
76. Ibid., 3–4.
77. See 'Notes of the 1934 Elim Conference Debate', 90.

5.2.2 The second round of the British Israel controversy: Elim conferences in 1935–39

Although in 1934 Leech was defeated by Phillips in the BI debate and the doctrine of BI was clearly rejected by the Elim conference, Jeffreys brought up BI once again in the 1935 Elim conference. Jeffreys' motivation for doing so seems to have been at least partly influenced by certain members of the conference being dissatisfied about not being able to preach BI within the centrally governed Elim churches. To that effect, the minutes of the 1935 conference note that Jeffreys 'suggested that there should be liberty to preach British-Israelism in Direct Government Churches and outlined the points of agreement in Futurist, Historicist, and British-Israel Schools'.[78] This was followed by a vote about these three main schools of prophetic interpretation. The question put to the conference was whether it accepted, rejected or was neutral with respect to these three schools. When it came to the 'Futurist Interpretation' of the 102 total votes, 68 accepted it, 11 rejected it and 23 were neutral; regarding the 'Historicists Interpretation' of the 103 total votes, 59 accepted it, 13 rejected it and 31 were neutral; and with respect to BI of the 107 votes, 22 accepted it, 45 rejected it and 40 were neutral.[79]

The voting results indicate that the 'Futurist Interpretation' regarding biblical prophecy was the most popular within Elim and the 'Historicist Interpretation' a close second. Both of these schools were also accepted by more people than the combined numbers of those who rejected or held neutral positions regarding them. This suggests that both positions were broadly accepted within Elim and the two interpretations were not necessarily seen as being mutually exclusive; that is, the numbers in favour of both suggest that indeed some accepted both interpretative frameworks.

BI, however, was not affirmed by the conference. In fact, more people rejected the position than affirmed it or expressed neutrality regarding it. This general acceptance of the Futurist and Historicist Interpretations and the rejection of BI is also reflected in the vote vis-à-vis which schools of prophecy should not be taught in Elim. Of the 84 who voted on this particular issue, five were against the Futurist School, seven against the Historicist School, and seventy-two against BI.[80] The numbers speak for themselves.

These votes were followed by further discussion and debate on the question of BI, until the following resolution was proposed by E. J. Phillips and carried by the conference:

> This Conference desires to place on record that while it has never imposed any definite ban on the teaching of British-Israel in any Elim Church, its Ministers

---

78. Minutes of the Elim Conference (1935), 3.
79. Ibid., 3.
80. Ibid., 4.

mutually agree that for the purpose of preserving unity it shall treat the teaching of British-Israel in the same way as is the custom with other matter on which there is an acute difference of opinion, viz: neither to propagate it nor attack it in any Direct Government Church. It further puts on record that for the same reason it considers it inadvisable for any Elim Minister under Direct Government to appear on any B.I. platform.[81]

So, yet again Jeffreys and his proposals in favour of BI were rejected by the conference. The defeat of BI at the 1934 conference could not be reversed by Jeffreys in 1935. In fact, the conference minutes read that after his defeat Jeffreys promised 'that he would never bring up the subject of B.I. again at the Conference'.[82]

Indeed, the question of BI seems not to have been discussed at the 1936 Elim Conference.[83] Nonetheless, Jeffreys had not yet given up on bringing BI into Elim. In 1937 from January to March there was an extended letter correspondence between Jeffreys and Phillips/Elim's executive council on the question of BI.[84] It was initiated by Phillips's concern that if Jeffreys was to launch his 'World Revival Crusade',[85] he would be leading an organization which 'would propagate doctrines which are considered unscriptural by the majority of Elim people',[86] and by these 'unscriptural' doctrines Phillips meant BI.[87] Jeffreys appears to have been offended by Phillips's allegation of him holding 'unscriptural' beliefs,[88] which is not surprising for a leader of movement that prides itself on being biblical.

Jeffreys then tried to justify the validity of his BI position and he pleads with Phillips that he should be 'given the same liberty in the pulpit and in the press, as is given to the other views on prophecy in Elim'.[89] He later also argues that if one was to follow 'strict neutrality' regarding BI, as suggested by the 1933, 1934 and 1935 conference decisions, then 'large proportion of Futurist Teaching would have to be cut out to maintain a neutral attitude. For example: There must be no

---

81. Ibid., 9.

82. Ibid.

83. Minutes of the 'Elim Foursquare Gospel Alliance: General and Ministerial Conference, 7th to 11th September 1936', archives of the General Superintendent, EIC, Malvern.

84. George Jeffreys, letter to E. J. Phillips (2 February 1937), Elim Archives, Malvern; George Jeffreys, letter to E. J. Phillips (19 February 1937), Elim Archives, Malvern; E. J. Phillips, letter to George Jeffreys (23 February 1937), Elim Archives, Malvern.

85. The World Revival Crusade was to be Jeffreys' new evangelistic organization with the aim of having a global and interdenominational audience.

86. E. J. Phillips, letter to George Jeffreys (25 January 1937), Elim Archives, Malvern.

87. E. J. Phillips, letter to George Jeffreys (26 January 1937), Elim Archives, Malvern.

88. George Jeffreys, letter to E. J. Phillips (26 January 1937), Elim Archives, Malvern; Jeffreys, letter to Phillips (28 January 1937).

89. Jeffreys, letter to Phillips (28 January 1937).

suggestion that the Jews constitute all Israel, or that the Jews have a special place in the Tribulation and the Millennium.'[90]

In Jeffreys' letters there is also an increasing undertone that if he will not have his way, he will resign from Elim.[91] The correspondence effectively finishes with Phillips frustratingly stating that Jeffreys seems to have given the executive only two options: (1) for Jeffreys to resign as the leader of the movement or (2) allow the teaching of BI in all Elim churches. Phillips thinks that both options would 'split the work'.[92] Phillips surmises that the executive is uncomfortable with both of these options, and thus the matter must be deferred to the Elim Conference.[93]

Phillips was not able to attend the September 1937 Elim Conference due to illness, caused predominantly by years of overworking and stress exacerbated by the BI controversy.[94] Nevertheless, before the conference he wrote a letter from his hospital bed to Boulton, Hathaway, Percy Corry, Kingston and Joseph Smith and advised them how to repudiate Jeffreys' attempts to make BI acceptable in Elim. Phillips also wrote a letter to Jeffreys where he pleaded with his old friend not to split Elim over BI. He states frankly that due to Jeffreys' insistence on making BI acceptable in Elim, there is a 'present crisis in the work' and the whole movement is now 'on the edge of a precipice'.[95]

The 1937 conference was made aware of the correspondence earlier in the year between Jeffreys and the executive council on the question of BI.[96] The minutes of the conference also note how, 'after much discussion, Principal suggested that possibly the only way to come to a satisfactory solution of the question of doctrine would be to cut out all three schools of thought, viz: Historicist, Futurist and National Historicists (British Israel)'.[97] This debate continued the following day and there seemed to be a genuine desire to keep the movement united. Samuel Gorman followed Jeffreys' thinking and 'suggested that if the subject of Prophecy was likely to cause any division in our Churches, he considered it would be best to drop the question of Prophecy altogether, and limit our preaching to the pure Evangelical message of the Gospel'.[98] This view, however, was challenged by Robert Mercer, who argued that if Gorman's proposal was adopted 'some feeling would

---

90. E. J. Phillips, 'Notes from a Meeting with Principal George Jeffreys' (17 February 1937), Elim Archives, Malvern; see also Jeffreys, letter to Phillips (19 February 1937).

91. Jeffreys' first clear articulation of stepping down as the leader of the movement is made in December 1936; George Jeffreys, letter to E. J. Phillips (12 December 1936), Elim Archives, Malvern.

92. Phillips, letter to Jeffreys (23 February 1937).

93. E. J. Phillips, letter to George Jeffreys (3 March 1937), Elim Archives, Malvern.

94. E. J. Phillips, letter to George Jeffreys (7 September 1937), Elim Archives, Malvern.

95. Phillips, letter to George Jeffreys (7 September 1937).

96. Minutes of the 'Elim Foursquare Gospel Alliance: Annual Ministerial and General Conferences, 13th September 1937', Archives of the General Superintendent, EIC, Malvern, 2–3.

97. Ibid., 3.

98. Ibid., 7.

remain that we were cutting out about one third of the Bible'. Consequently, argued Mercer, who seemed to be an advocate of BI, a more conducive way forward was to lift the conference ban of 1935 on BI.[99]

Despite the willingness of the conference to seek a compromise, not teaching biblical prophecy would have impinged on Elim trying to articulate one of its core doctrines (i.e. Jesus as coming King) and thus this option could not be accepted. However, at the same time, allowing for the teaching of BI in Elim would have meant that doctrines that were considered unscriptural and divisive by a majority of the movement's ministers could be taught within Elim, which made it an implausible option for the conference. In other words, the content and rationality of the Elim argument could not allow for either of these two options to be adopted. Thus, the following two resolutions were passed. First, it was

> RESOLVED that this Conference is of the opinion that there is sufficient common ground in the main schools of Prophecy to allow scope for teaching on this point without encroaching on debatable ground of Prophetical interpretation, and that where difficulties arise in a local Church over the teaching of debatable points of Prophecy, the Minister of such Church should be requested by the Council to keep to the common ground.[100]

This resolution acknowledged that the three schools of prophecy within Elim effectively still shared Elim's Fundamental Truth of dispensational premillennialism, it encouraged ministers to focus on this key doctrine, and steer away from the more debatable points. However, the second resolution reaffirmed the 1935 Conference ban on the teaching of BI in Elim's Direct Government Churches and advised against Elim ministers appearing on BI platforms. This clearly still identifies BI as the minority and opposed prophetic school in Elim. Both of the resolutions were passed with 59 in favour, 21 against and 6 abstaining.[101]

Therefore, in the 1937 conference Elim once again confirmed its rejection of BI and Jeffreys had now for the fifth time (1932, 1933, 1934, 1935 and 1937) tried to bring BI teaching into Elim in an Elim Conference, despite his promise at the 1935 conference that he would never do so again. The conference discussion and decision also point out how Elim could not do away with its core doctrine of Jesus as coming King, including the auxiliary hypothesis of biblical prophecy surrounding it, but in light of its rationality neither could it accept BI which it believed to be unscriptural and therefore irrational.

BI would not be discussed at the 1938 or the 1939 Elim Conference, despite there being a real threat of Jeffreys resigning from Elim. Nevertheless, a resolution was passed in the 1938 conference where all ministers and probationers needed to sign Elim's Fundamental Truths.[102] Moreover, it was agreed that 'doctrinal questions

---

99. Ibid.
100. Ibid., 8.
101. Ibid.
102. Minutes of the 'Elim Foursquare Gospel Alliance: Ministerial Conference Meeting, 12th September 1938', Archives of the General Superintendent, EIC, Malvern, 1.

[were] to be decided by the Conference with power in the hands of the Executive to deal with any matter between Annual Conference.'[103] The first resolution guaranteed that all Elim ministers would support the essential Elim argument and the second resolution ensured that no local Elim church could alter the doctrinal statements of the movement or its agreements about teaching certain doctrines (e.g. BI) without the conference's approval. The second resolution, namely, the notion that 'matters of doctrine be decided by the Ministerial Conference and not by the local church' was also reaffirmed at the 1939 Elim Conference.[104]

5.3 The 'epistemological crisis' and its resolution

By 1939 the threat of Jeffreys' resignation from Elim was imminent. As well as attempting to make Elim a BI movement, Jeffreys simultaneously sought to reform Elim's governance structures by giving greater autonomy to local churches. He personally maintained that there was no connection between the two issues, but many within Elim believed that Jeffreys' primary motivation to revise the movement's structure was to bring in BI. Based on Phillips's notes this was certainly his view, as well as the view of the elected members of the executive council.[105] Indeed, Phillips claimed that Jeffreys' personally told him in 1937 that he had introduced the Local Church Government scheme for the 'purpose of making an outlet for B.I'.[106] This would certainly explain Jeffreys' attempt to disband Elim's Direct Government Structure by introducing a new more inclusive body consisting of all ministers and lay representatives, as the ban on BI applied to Direct Government churches and BI was primarily opposed by its ministers. This interpretation is also made more plausible by the fact that in the conference debates the question of BI and church government were often closely discussed.[107] Furthermore, Jeffreys' aired 'dissatisfaction' with the Deed Poll of April 1934 does only seem to come after the Elim Conference in September 1934 when Leech lost the BI debate to Phillips and when the conference issued a ban on BI.

In fairness to Jeffreys, Elim's governance structures was not without its problems and some of Jeffreys' proposals would in fact be later adopted by Elim (see below). That said, it does appear that BI was a major (perhaps *the* major) contributing factor for Jeffreys' desire to reform Elim with a view of making BI acceptable in

---

103. Ibid., 5.

104. Minutes of the 'Elim Foursquare Gospel Alliance: Ministerial Conference November, 20th November to 1st December, 1939', Archives of the General Superintendent, EIC, Malvern, 5, 8.

105. E. J. Phillips, 'Typed Manuscript of 1939 Conference Speech on George Jeffreys' (21 November 1939), Elim Archives, Malvern, 2–3.

106. Ibid., 3.

107. Minutes of the Elim Conference (1935), 9–10; Minutes of the Elim Conference (1937), 7.

Elim. Jeffreys managed to initiate a number of institutional changes in Elim, but these reforms failed to make room for BI; hence, he resigned.[108]

Jeffreys handed his resignation from Elim on 1 December 1939. The Elim Conference expressed 'its deep and heartfelt gratitude to him' for his role within the movement and asked him to consider a new 'office as Moderator and spiritual leader of the Alliance, and remain Principal of the Elim Bible College'.[109] In May 1940 Jeffreys accepted this invitation from the conference to re-join Elim as the president and its spiritual leader, and the conference confirmed this with a vote.[110] However, the reconciliation between Jeffreys and Elim was short-lived as on 12 November 1940 Jeffreys resigned for the second and final time from the denomination he had founded. Jeffreys offered a number of reasons for his resignation, one of them being the inability for a local church to decide its own supplementary doctrines.[111] Elim's executive council responded with a pamphlet where they expressed their frustration that Jeffreys seemed only to be satisfied if the conference and the executive council would become 'Yes-men' and simply agree to all of his demands. They also pointed out that if Jeffreys' so-called biblical pattern for church government were followed through, among other things, ministers would be able to adopt 'their own peculiar doctrine or theories, as they may wish'.[112] This war of words, primarily in the form of pamphlets, continued for some time between the two sides.[113] Moreover, a handful of Elim ministers followed Jeffreys out of Elim and joined a competing movement that Jeffreys started: the Bible Pattern Church Fellowship.

Reflecting on Jeffreys' resignation from Elim, Neil Hudson states that 'there could be little disguising that the Movement was in the gravest danger of extinction'.[114] Or to put in MacIntyrian terms, the resignation of Jeffreys propelled Elim into its first 'epistemological crisis'. So, why did Jeffreys' resignation cause an epistemological crisis in Elim? Jeffreys' departure from Elim led to its epistemological crisis, because up until his resignation Jeffreys was the human embodiment of the Elim argument; that is, he was effectively the exemplification of the content (Foursquare Gospel) and rationality (Pentecostal Biblical

---

108. Kay shares this view; Kay, *George Jeffreys*, 348.

109. Minutes of the Elim Conference (1939), 7.

110. Minutes of the 'Elim Foursquare Gospel Alliance Conference, May 1940', Archives of the General Superintendent, EIC, Malvern, 4–5; see also No author, 'Unity in Elim: Mutual Recommendations', *EE* 21, no. 11 (15 March 1940): 173; No author, 'The Elim Conference of May, 1940', *EE* 21, no. 24 (10 June 1940): 379.

111. George Jeffreys, letter to the Executive Presbytery (12 November 1940), Elim Archives, Malvern.

112. The executive council of the Elim Foursquare Gospel Alliance, *Elim and George Jeffreys* (January 1941), 1–5.

113. Cartwright refers to '34 separate leaflets'; Cartwright, *The Great Evangelists*, 138. Many of these can be accessed at the Elim Archives.

114. Hudson, 'A Schism and its Aftermath', 312.

Pragmatism) of the Elim tradition. After all, Jeffreys had founded Elim, he had been its primary leader for twenty-five years, planted many of its churches and brought a number of Elim ministers and members to the Pentecostal experience through his campaigns. Thus, when Jeffreys left the essence of the Elim tradition was challenged. It would have been difficult for Elim's faithful adherents to avoid thinking that if they had been wrong about Jeffreys (read: the human embodiment of the Elim argument), perhaps they were also wrong about the viability of the Elim tradition as a whole?

As already discussed, according to MacIntyre, the degree to which an epistemological crisis can be overcome by a tradition depends on the resources available within the tradition, upon its inventiveness and their needs to be continuity within the tradition's past.[115] So how did Elim overcome this internal crisis and how was its tradition reformulated in the process?

5.3.1 Returning to the Bible, the Foursquare Gospel and evangelism

Elim's response to the crisis was effectively *ad fontes*; that is, Elim quickly reaffirmed the Bible as its grounding document. Shortly after the public announcement in *Elim Evangel* of Jeffreys' final resignation,[116] a series of articles appeared on 'Scriptural Principles of Church Government' written by senior Elim leaders with the aim of providing biblical justification for Elim's position on church governance.[117] The question of church governance was a contentious issue between Elim and Jeffreys and thus Elim needed to make sure that its argument was biblically grounded. Furthermore, when the *Elim Evangel* reported on the conference discussion on church property, another contentious issue between Elim and Jeffreys, the resolutions of the conference were apparently passed 'after careful and prayerful consideration, during which *Bibles were open* and *many scriptures quoted*' (my italics),[118] highlighting again the centrality of the Bible in providing epistemic warrant for the Elim tradition as it sought to overcome its crisis.

---

115. MacIntyre, *Whose Justice?*, 356.

116. E. J. Phillips, 'Editorial: Principal George Jeffreys', *EE* 22, no. 6 (10 February 1941): 90.

117. Charles J. Kingston, 'Scriptural Principles of Church Government – No. 1. Decisions on Doctrinal Matters', *EE* 22, no. 13 (31 March 1941): 203–5; J. T. Bradley, 'Scriptural Principles of Church Government – No. 2. The First Church Council', *EE* 22, no. 15 (14 April 1941): 227–8; Ernest C. W. Boulton, 'Scriptural Principles of Church Government – No. 3. The Call and Appointment of Ministers', *EE* 22, no. 16 (21 April 21 1941): 242–3; Joseph Smith, 'Scriptural Principles of Church Government – No. 4. Discipline in the Church', *EE* 22, no. 17 (28 April 1941): 267–9.

118. E. J. Phillips, 'An Epoch in the History of Elim: A Report of the Conference of September, 1941', *EE* 22, no. 38 (22 September 1941): 566.

However, Elim secondly also sought return to the main content of the movement's argument. The 1941 Elim Conference issued a 'Declaration', which was then published in *Elim Evangel* that

> the strife and contention that has lately arisen among us has not been engendered by the Spirit of God, but rather by the Adversary, in an endeavour to divert and distract our attention from the main purpose for which God Himself brought this work into being, namely the preaching of the *Gospel* of God to all men, the dissemination of the *Pentecostal doctrines* for the edifying of believers, the proclamation and practice of the highest standard of *Christian discipleship*, the teaching *of Divine Healing*, and the quickening among true believers of the Blessed Hope of the *Return of our Lord* and Saviour Jesus Christ. (my italics)[119]

What is clear here is the reiteration not only of the Foursquare Gospel (or Fivefold Gospel with the inclusion of 'highest standard of Christian discipleship') but also of the theological interpretation of Jeffreys' actions as orchestrated by the 'Adversary' in diverting Elim from its raison d'être. Thus, not only is the Foursquare Gospel reaffirmed as central to the tradition but the actions of Jeffreys are also condemned in light of the Full Gospel. In fact, the conference made a decision to disassociate itself completely from Jeffreys[120] because he was seen as distracting Elim from focusing on the essence of its argument.

This attempt to take Elim back to the Foursquare Gospel during its moment of crisis is also seen in Hathaway's fourteen *Elim Evangel* articles under the title 'This Pentecost' written predominantly after Jeffreys' first resignation.[121] Furthermore, reports from the 1944 Elim Conference indicate that in trying to come to terms with the departure of its leader, the movement returned to the Full Gospel, as the members of the conference were encouraged to 'think back again to those first principles of the early days' (W. G. Hathaway), to 'get back to Pentecost' (L. C. Quest), to restore the 'message of Pentecost' (G. L. W. Ladlow) and to not just emphasize the Pentecostal message but its 'practice' (S. Gorman).[122]

Although the doctrine of Jesus as coming King had been at the heart of the schism due to the BI controversy, this did not deter Elim from continuing to advocate its eschatological theories. The Futurist and Historicist interpretations of prophecy continued to capture the imaginations of Elim ministers, and during the war years Britain, Germany and Russia were boldly identified within the pages

---

119. Minutes of the 'Elim Conference Representative Session, September, 1941', Archives of the General Superintendent, EIC, Malvern, 6; No author, 'Declaration by the Elim Conference, 1941', *EE* 22, no. 38 (22 September 1941): 569.

120. Minutes of the Elim Conference (1941), 8.

121. The first and last articles were W. G. Hathaway, '"This Pentecost." I. The Pentecostal Revival', *EE* 21, no. 20 (13 May 1940): 305–6, and W. G. Hathaway, 'This Pentecost – No. 14: Are 'Tarrying Meetings' Necessary?' *EE* 21, no. 49 (16 December 1940): 770–1.

122. No author, 'A Touch from God at the Conference', *EE* 25, no. 23 (5 June 1944): 178–9, 182–3.

of Scripture.[123] That said, there is also some evidence that there was a movement away from making specific prophetic predictions, as well as a desire to stick to the bare minimum of Elim's dispensational premillennialism. For example, J. Dyke urged Elim not to merely speculate within its various prophetic schools, but for its members to examine their lives to see if they 'reflect the characteristics of a sincere Christian life, for the privilege of foreknowledge carries with it the responsibility for practical Christian living'.[124]

Third, as well as seeking to ground itself anew on Scripture and reaffirm the Foursquare Gospel, Elim sought to reclaim its evangelistic and revivalist mandate. Phillips firmly stated in an editorial titled 'Elim's Task – Evangelise!' that evangelism was 'the greatest task of the Elim Movement'.[125] In another article he noted that 'Elim was founded on aggressive Evangelism', highlighted by the names of 'Elim Evangelistic Band' and *Elim Evangel*.[126] Indeed, when in 1945 the Evangelistic Council was established, P. S. Brewster emerged as Elim's leading pioneer evangelist, and between 1944 and 1954 up to thirty-four new churches were established.[127]

However, it seems that evangelism was not only to be the prerogative and responsibility of a few individuals but a new-found emphasis was also placed on each member to engage in personal evangelism.[128] Samuel Gorman, Elim's Evangelistic Secretary, argued that Elim members and ministers should not leave evangelism 'to the recognised leading preachers and evangelists of to-day – get on with the job yourself, and God will bless you in the doing of it'.[129] This theme of personal evangelism is very visible in the *Elim Evangels* of the period and there was even a 'Special Personal Evangelism Number'.[130] Some of this change of emphasis from evangelistic campaigns to personal evangelism was certainly necessitated by the Second World War and the restrictions to hold major public gatherings.[131]

---

123. For example, Joseph Smith, 'Will this War End in Armageddon?' *EE* 21, no. 48 (9 December 1940): 765; Herbert E. Ward, 'Will the British Empire Fall?' *EE* 22, no. 8 (24 February 1941): 113–15; Frederick G. Cloke, 'Bible Study Course on the Book of Daniel – No. 6. European Government Antecedent to the Second Advent of Christ _ Chapter VIII', *EE* 22, no. 31 (4 August 1941): 477–9.

124. J. Dyke, 'A Personal Warning: A Devotional Address at the Annual Elim Conference at Clapham, London, in September, 1941', *EE* 22, no. 39 (29 September 1941): 574.

125. E. J. Phillips, 'Editorial: Elim's Task – Evangelise!', *EE* 22, no. 40 (6 October 1941): 592.

126. E. J. Phillips, 'The Need for Evangelism', *EE* 22, no. 42 (20 October 1941): 613.

127. Hudson, 'A Schism and Its Aftermath', 319–24.

128. See E. J. Phillips, 'Editorial: Personal Evangelism', *EE* 22, no. 45 (10 November 1941): 652; E. J. Phillips, 'Editorial: Evangelism', *EE* 22, no. 48 (1 December 1941): 688.

129. Samuel Gorman, 'Evangelism', *EE* 22, no. 26 (30 June 1941): 409.

130. *EE* 22, no. 33 (18 August 1941); cf. J. F. Hardman, 'A Plea for Personal Evangelism', *EE* 21, no. 47 (2 December 1940): 744–5, 749.

131. E. J. Phillips, 'Editorial: Pioneer Evangelism', *EE* 22, no. 9 (3 March 1941): 138.

Nevertheless, it appears that after Jeffreys' departure there was also a genuine desire by the senior leaders in Elim to see its argument being embodied and promulgated by all within Elim, not just by some.

5.3.2 Reforming the structure: Democratizing the embodiment of the Elim argument

So, it seems that Elim overcame its 'epistemological crisis' by restating the centrality of the Bible as its foundational document, reiterating its Pentecostal mandate of proclaiming the Foursquare Gospel and re-engaging in evangelism. However, aspects of the Elim tradition were also reformulated. Its founder, Jeffreys, who had been the face of the movement, was erased. Symbolically this 'erasing' of Jeffreys from Elim is evident in the pages of *Elim Evangel* where his picture still appears at the front page on 22 December 1940 as the movement's central figure, but then completely disappears from 5 January 1941 onwards.[132] Linked to this, there was also an attempt to downplay the significance of Jeffreys for Elim. In other words, the movement needed to self-identify itself as more than the figure and persona of Jeffreys.[133]

Although it needs to be acknowledged that Elim did have its new champions to replace Jeffreys (particularly Phillips, Hathaway, Boulton, Smith and the new evangelist Brewster), Elim also reformulated its structure so that the essence of the movement would no longer be embodied in one particular person (as had been the case with Jeffreys) or even in a small group of leaders (as was the case with the executive council), but rather in the conference that consisted of Elim's ministers and lay representatives of the local churches. Thus, Elim sought to move from an autocratic form of government to a democratic one, as it renewed its constitution.

Ironically, many of the constitutional changes towards the democratization in Elim had been initiated by Jeffreys. Moreover, the conference had already proven its ability to govern and make reasoned decisions from 1933 onwards, not least as it had consistently rejected the attempts of its leader to bring BI into Elim. Therefore, to make the conference, rather than the executive council, the governing body of Elim was reasonable and particularly important when the movement sought new ways of embodying its argument after Jeffreys' departure.

After Jeffreys' first resignation, the process for reform had already been actioned by the 1940 Conference with particular emphasis on making the conference – consisting of ministers and lay representatives – Elim's governing body and thus changing the Deed Poll. A draft of the new constitution was circulated to

---

132. See No author, 'The Elim Evangel and Foursquare Revivalist', *EE* 20, no. 51 (22 December 1939): 801; No author, 'The Elim Evangelist and Foursquare Revivalist', *EE* 21, no. 1 (5 January 1940): 10.

133. Cf. Hudson, 'A Schism and its Aftermath', 309–10.

ministers and churches on May 1941,[134] and discussed and agreed in principle at the September 1941 Elim Conference.[135] The new constitution came into effect on January 1942 when the Deed of Variation was issued,[136] and the 1942 Elim Conference was the first under the auspices of the new constitution.[137]

There were three main changes brought by Elim's new constitution through the Deed of Variation.[138] First, the conference consisting of ministers and lay representatives on an equal basis, rather than the executive council, became the governing body of the movement. This move continued the democratization of Elim's governance as the movement had initially been governed by Jeffreys, from 1934 onwards by the executive council (albeit with Jeffreys still possessing significant prerogatives), and now by the conference. With the inclusion of lay representatives Elim could boldly claim that 'the voice of the people will be heard on the central governing body of the Movement'.[139] Second, the local church structure was changed so that it was now 'controlled by the "Church Officers", who will consist of the deacons together with the elders (if any) and the minister'.[140] The deacons would be elected by the members of the church and the elders by the ministers and the district superintendent. This also signified a move from an autocratic model to a more democratic model of governance because for much of Elim's history the local church ministers had been in complete control of their congregations. Third, a new body of managing trustees was set up to oversee church buildings. This group would be elected by the conference and would consist of three ministers and three laymen. Furthermore, the new constitution would ensure that the local 'church cannot take it [the building] from the denomination nor can the denomination take it away from the church'.[141] Again this was a move of sharing power as up until 1934 Jeffreys had been the 'managing trustee', from 1934 this role had been carried by the executive council, and now it would be an elected body of ministers and laymen.

In sum, like Elim's revised evangelism strategy that focused on empowering all within Elim to evangelize, the constitutional changes vis-à-vis central

---

134. E. J. Phillips, letter to Ministers and Lay Representatives (16 May 1941), Elim Archives, Malvern.

135. Minutes of the Elim Conference (1941), 3.

136. Ernest J. Phillips, Joseph Smith, Ernest C. W. Boulton and W. G. Hathaway, *Elim Foursquare Gospel Alliance: Deed of Variation – of – Deed Poll by George Jeffreys Dated 10th April 1934* (London: Electric Law Press, 14 January 1942).

137. Minutes of the 'Elim Foursquare Gospel Alliance. Annual Conference 1942. Representative Session', Archives of the General Superintendent, EIC, Malvern; Selwyn Homer, 'The Elim Conference of 1942', *EE* 23, no. 40 (5 October 1942): 471.

138. No author, 'What is Elim's New Constitution?' *EE* 22, no. 24 (25 August 1941): 521, 523.

139. Ibid., 521.

140. Ibid.

141. Ibid., 523.

denominational governance, local church governance and management of buildings resulted in increasing democratization within Elim. The Elim argument would no longer be embodied by one person (i.e. Jeffreys) or even by a group of people (i.e. the executive council) but by Elim's members, lay representatives and ministers. This was the major reformulation of Elim resulting from its first 'epistemological crisis'.

5.4 Conclusion

In the above section I have narrated the first 'epistemological crisis' in Elim, which was caused by Jeffreys' resignation from the movement he had founded. I have argued that at the heart of the conflict between Jeffreys and the executive council was Elim's hard core doctrine of Jesus as coming King and Jeffreys' particular BI hypothesis regarding it. Thus, although I have acknowledged the various reasons that led to the schism in Elim (including the question of church governance), I have tried to demonstrate that the eschatological issue of BI was central. The general disagreement on the issues of BI between the two parties, and especially the 1934 BI Conference debate between Leech and Phillips, exemplifies the practical outworking of Elim's Pentecostal Biblical Pragmatism identified in Chapter 4 as Elim's tradition-specific rationality, and so also underscores that Elim's rationality is precisely biblical pragmatism with Pentecostal assumptions. That is, Elim's rationality is not mere *biblicism* nor mere *pragmatism*, but any pragmatic argument within Elim must also have some kind of prior justification based on a justified reading of a biblical text, and likewise a warranted interpretation of a biblical text must produce pragmatic results.

The resolution of Elim's epistemological crisis further underscores the essential content and method of the Elim argument. In other words, in the process of coming to terms with Jeffreys' departure Elim deliberately utilized its biblical reasoning, reclaimed its Pentecostal (i.e. Foursquare Gospel) heritage and sought to recapture is evangelistic zeal in promulgating the Elim argument. However, in the process Elim was also transformed structurally into a more democratic movement. To put it differently, the primary embodiment of the recalibrated Elim argument was now to be the Elim conference consisting of ministers and lay representatives of local churches, rather than being vested in one man (i.e. Jeffreys) or a selected group of leaders (i.e. the executive council). In MacIntyrian terms, Elim successfully moved from stage two (epistemological crisis) to stage three (resolution) and the Elim argument continued, albeit in a modified institutional embodiment.

In summation, my narration of the Elim argument through its first epistemological crisis has not only proposed fresh historical insights into understanding Jeffreys' resignation from Elim vis-à-vis Elim's wider eschatology, but more importantly, for my overall thesis, it has substantiated my claim that the *content* (read: hard core) of the Elim tradition is the Foursquare Gospel and the tacit *rationality* is Pentecostal Biblical Pragmatism.

Chapter 6

THE ELIM ARGUMENT EXTENDED THROUGH TIME (II): THE CHARISMATIC/RESTORATION MOVEMENTS AND ELIM'S SECOND EPISTEMOLOGICAL CRISIS

Up until the 1960s Elim and other classical Pentecostal denominations (e.g. Assemblies of God and the Apostolic Church) could claim uniqueness in British Christianity when it came to baptism in the Holy Spirit, spiritual gifts and divine healing. This, however, changed when the Charismatic movement emerged within mainline British churches from the 1960s onwards. Although many within Elim initially welcomed what they saw as the renewing work of the Spirit in the established churches,[1] the Charismatic Renewal, and particularly the Restoration movement which flowed from it,[2] collectively instigated Elim's second epistemological crisis.

In narrating Elim's second epistemological crisis, I will (1) briefly outline the birth of the Charismatic movement in Britain with particular emphasis on the 'Restoration Charismatics';[3] (2) discuss how the Restoration Charismatics challenged the Elim argument by seemingly providing an updated and improved version of it; and (3) analyse how Elim resolved its crisis by returning to the essential content and rationality of its argument and by also reformulating its structures and

---

1. John Lancaster, interview by author, Leeds, United Kingdom, 6 August 2015; Julian W. Ward, interview by author, Crewe, United Kingdom, 7 August 2017; K. John Cave, interview by author, Malvern, United Kingdom, 17 August 2017; John C. Smyth, interview by author, Plymouth, United Kingdom, 15 September 2017.

2. I will use the terms Restoration movement, Restoration Charismatics, House Churches, British New Church movement, etc. more or less interchangeably.

3. 'Renewal Charismatics' can be seen as those who believed that the purpose of the charismatic revival was to 'renew' existing churches and thus they remained within the established churches, whereas 'Restoration Charismatics' were those who believed that the charismatic revival could not be fully realized within existing church structures and thus they formed new churches; William K. Kay, *Apostolic Networks in Britain: New Ways of Being Church* (Paternoster: Milton Keynes, 2007), 21; Nigel Scotland, 'From the "Not Yet" to the "Now and the Not Yet:" Charismatic Kingdom Theology 1960–2010', *JPT* 20, no. 2 (2011): 274.

re-interpreting one of its hard core doctrines. In exploring these three themes, my aim is again to provide an exemplification of the Elim argument and, therefore, substantiate and develop my overall argument regarding the content, rationality and embodiment of the Elim tradition.

Like in Chapters 4 and 5, the primary sources used in this chapter are Elim publications, reports, constitutional documents and doctrinal statements. However, to supplement the limited written material on Elim's history during this period, I have conducted five semi-structured interviews for the purpose of 'oral history'. As stated by John Creswell, 'oral history consists of gathering personal reflections of events and their causes and effects from one individual or several individuals.'[4] Thus, these five recorded interviews are treated as individual sources which provide description and interpretation of Elim in the late 1970s and early 1980s. I do not claim that they provide a comprehensive account of how Elim ministers and members experienced Elim's second epistemological crisis; that is, I have not engaged in 'phenomenological' or 'grounded theory' empirical research.[5] That said, the five Elim ministers interviewed – namely, John Lancaster,[6] Maldwyn Jones,[7] Julian Ward,[8] John Cave[9] and John Smyth[10] – all had influential roles within Elim during the period and, therefore, their first-person accounts provide valuable individual insights into this phase of Elim's history.

6.1 The Charismatic movement: The 'Renewal Charismatics' and the 'Restoration Charismatics'

A key event in the emergence of the Charismatic movement in Britain occurred in 1962 when the Anglican minister Michael Harper was 'baptized in the Holy Spirit'. Following from this spiritual experience, Harper went on to establish

---

4. John W. Creswell, *Qualitative Inquiry and Research Design: Choosing Among Five Approaches*, 3rd edn (London: Sage, 2013), 73. For further discussion on 'oral history', see Alan Bryman, *Social Research Methods*, 4th edn (Oxford: Oxford University Press, 2012), 488–91; Donald A. Ritchie, *Doing Oral History*, 3rd edn (Oxford: Oxford University Press, 2015).

5. Creswell, *Qualitative Inquiry*, 76–81, 83; Ritchie, *Doing Oral History*, 123.

6. Lancaster was a member of Elim's Executive Council from early 1960s until mid-1980s. He also contributed to the 1981 Southport Conference; Lancaster, interview by author.

7. Jones is the official Elim historian and he contributed to the 1981 Southport Conference; Maldwyn Jones, interview by author, Malvern, United Kingdom, 25 July 2016.

8. Ward was the Director of Studies at Elim Bible College (now Regents Theological College) and he contributed to the 1981 Southport Conference; Ward, interview by author.

9. Cave was the host of the 1981 Southport Conference; Cave, interview by author.

10. Smyth was the field superintendent, member of the executive council and keynote speaker at the 1981 Southport Conference. Latterly he was also the principal of Regents Theological College; Smyth, interview by author.

the Fountain Trust in 1964, an ecumenical organization with the purpose of bringing Charismatic Renewal to British churches. Over the 1960s and 1970s the Fountain Trust was relatively successful in encouraging the established churches to embrace charismatic spirituality and theology.[11] It did this by holding a number of conferences, publishing its *Renewal* magazine and bringing together Christian leaders and theologians from various church traditions.

While reflecting on this period, the Elim veteran John Lancaster points out the challenge the Charismatic movement posed for Elim, as there now was a fresh movement within the historic churches which appeared to be 'outdoing' Elim in being Pentecostal. Lancaster notes that the situation was exacerbated by the fact that by the early 1960s Elim had become increasingly Evangelical at the expense of its Pentecostal ethos.[12] These two aspects, the arrival of the Charismatic movement and Elim's increasing Evangelicalization, surmises Lancaster, forced Elim to ask questions about its identity as a movement or, in MacIntyrian terms, revisit the exact nature of its current argument.[13]

Nevertheless, in the end it was not the Charismatic Renewal per se, but the Restoration movement which flowed from the Charismatic movement that led Elim to its second major epistemological crisis. Unlike the 'Renewal Charismatics' within the Charismatic movement who emphasized the revitalization of existing denominations, the 'Restorationist Charismatics' not only argued for the need to establish new churches freed from the structures of existing denominations but also encouraged existing Christians to leave their denominations to join what they saw as a 'fresh' move of God.[14]

The main theological architect of the 'Restoration Charismatics' was Arthur Wallis.[15] Wallis had an Open Brethren background and thus had been nurtured in an environment emphasizing the primacy of local congregations and the

---

11. David Hilborn, 'Charismatic Renewal in Britain: Roots, Influences and Later Developments', *Evangelical Alliance: Better Together*, accessed 20 June 2015, http://www.eauk.org/church/resources/theological-articles/charismatic-renewal-in-britain.cfm; Peter Hocken, *Streams of Renewal: The Origins and Early Development of the Charismatic Movement in Great Britain*. Revised Edition (Carlisle: Paternoster Press, 1997), 115–22.

12. By Pentecostal, Lancaster means focus on baptism in the Holy Spirit and spiritual gifts; Lancaster, interview by author. Elim also joined the Evangelical Alliance in 1964, which fits well with Lancaster's historical analysis of Elim.

13. Lancaster, interview by author.

14. See David Watson, 'Stay In or Come Out? New Life From Inside', *Renewal* 52 (August/September 1974): 10–13; Arthur Wallis, 'Stay In or Come Out? The Church in the House', *Renewal* 52 (August/September 1974): 14–16.

15. Andrew Walker identifies Wallis as the 'theological architect' of Restorationism together with David Lillie; Andrew Walker, *Restoring the Kingdom: The Radical Christianity of the House Church Movement*. Fully Revised and Expanded Edition (Guildford: Eagle, 1998), 21.

ineffectiveness of denominations.[16] In 1951 he was 'baptized in the Holy Spirit', but rather than joining a Pentecostal denomination he began advocating for a revival which would break down denominational walls and unite the universal church ready for the second coming of Christ.[17] From the early 1970s onwards he began to increasingly work towards the achievement of this restorationist goal, and in 1972 he invited five men (Bryn Jones, Peter Lyne, David Mansell, Graham Perrins and Hugh Thompson) to his home to discuss eschatology.[18] This gathering proved to be momentous by bringing together key leaders with a shared vision for the charismatically restored church and can, in effect, be seen as the birth of the British Restoration movement. The six men formed covenant relationships with each other and after John Noble joined their ranks they became known as the 'magnificent seven' (John Noble joined the group after Bryn Jones prophesied that 'seven shall be your number, and thrice you shall meet').[19]

The so-called 'magnificent seven' met at least three times and then decided to broaden the leadership by inviting seven others (Gerald Coates, Barney Coombs, John MacLaughlin, Campbell McAlpine, Ian McCullogh, Maurice Smith and George Tartleton) into their number and so making the 'magnificent seven' into the 'fabulous fourteen'.[20] However, as early as 1974 onwards the 'fabulous fourteen' began to show signs of having two factions, with John Noble leading in the south and Bryn Jones in the north.[21] This was not just a geographical divide but there appears to have been personality differences and stylistic preferences between the northern and southern 'brothers'. Moreover, the northern leaders were becoming worried that their southern colleagues were falling into antinomianism.[22] Indeed in 1976 Wallis, part of the northern group, wrote a letter to the southern brothers (probably with the approval of Bryn Jones) questioning their motives, raising concerns about their approach to 'law and grace', and even suggesting that they were being deceived by demonic forces.[23] This letter seriously severed the relationships between the two groups and eventually led to a split between them.

Andrew Walker has famously called the northern group, albeit it included the likes of Terry Virgo from the South East of England, as Restoration 1 (R1) and the southern grouping as Restoration 2 (R2).[24] It is worth noting that from

---

16. Ibid., 52. Walker is of the view that the roots of Restorationism can be identified in the Brethren movement, the Catholic Apostolic Church and classical Pentecostalism; ibid., 51–3.

17. See Arthur Wallis, *In the Day of Thy Power* (London: Christian Literature Crusade, 1967 [1956]).

18. Walker, *Restoring the Kingdom*, 75; Kay, *Apostolic Networks*, 24.

19. Walker, *Restoring the Kingdom*, 76.

20. Ibid.; Kay, *Apostolic Networks*, 24.

21. Walker, *Restoring the Kingdom*, 81–2. Kay, *Apostolic Networks*, 25.

22. Walker, *Restoring the Kingdom*, 88–92, 103–8.

23. Kay, *Apostolic Networks*, 25.

24. Walker, *Restoring the Kingdom*, 38–42.

the beginning differences already existed between the leaders of the Restoration movement. Nevertheless, after the split they became clearly expressed and embodied in the two factions. The differences between R1 and R2 are succinctly summarized by William Kay: 'R1 was the more exclusive, organised, authoritarian and radical of the two groups, and R2, centred largely in London, was more flexible, more expressive and more willing to work in conjunction with other Christian groups and agencies.'[25] Interestingly, it was R1 as the more radical wing of 'Restoration Charismatics' which seemed to pose the greater threat to Elim. Indeed, R1 appeared to directly challenge the Elim argument by providing a theologically improved expression of Pentecostalism.

6.2 The Restoration Charismatic movement: Ecclesiologically and eschatologically updated Elim argument

The theological similarities between the 'Restorationist Charismatic' (particularly R1) and Elim are noteworthy. Like Elim, the Restorationists saw the Bible as the grounding document for beliefs and practices and their outworking of biblical exposition was effectively pragmatic.[26] Their theology was also mainly Christocentric with an emphasis on conversion and believers baptism (read: Jesus as Saviour). Baptism in the Holy Spirit was also seen along Pentecostal lines as a subsequent experience to conversion, and spiritual gifts were believed to be for the contemporary church (read: Jesus as Baptiser in the Holy Spirit and Jesus as Healer). Moreover, their theology was characterized by adventism (read: Jesus as coming King).[27]

However, despite these significant theological similarities, there were also important differences, particularly when it came to (1) ecclesiology and (2) eschatology. In terms of *ecclesiology*, Arthur Wallis consistently argued that there is only one church which consists of people who have had a true revelation of Christ and have confessed him as their Lord.[28] Wallis further maintained that this universal church is expressed in local congregations which he identified as a 'company of committed believers who could act together.'[29] In the words of Bryn Jones, 'the [local] church is the representative community of the cosmic kingdom [or universal church] in a given locality.'[30] The implication of having only one universal church expressed simply in local congregations was that there was no

---

25. Kay, *Apostolic Networks*, 20.
26. Walker, *Restoring the Kingdom*, 134.
27. Ibid., 134–5.
28. Wallis, 'Stay In or Come Out?', 14.
29. Ibid.
30. Bryn Jones, 'What is the Church?', *Leadership Today – A Supplement to Restoration Magazine*, 3 (no date), accessed 26 August 2017, http://storage.cloversites.com/shakedesign/documents/Leadership%20Today%20Supplement%203.pdf.

place for denominations. As Wallis put it: 'our only loyalty is to Christ, and then to the local church where He wants us to be ... But *denominational* loyalty (as distinct from loyalty to a local church that may happen to be denominational) only weakens the unity of the body as a whole.'[31]

This universal church of Christ embodied in the local church (not institutions or denominations) was understood to be a charismatic community which should manifest the four/five offices ('gifts') of Eph. 4.11, as well as the 'spiritual gifts' of 1 Cor. 12.4-7, 11.[32] These charismatic congregations were believed to be living organisms which would freely worship together and function naturally under the governance of leadership teams consisting of apostle(s), prophets, evangelists and pastor teachers. The 'glue' that would hold the members of a congregation together, unite the various local congregations and allow the leaders to lead at local and national level was not to be a constitution or a doctrinal statement, but 'covenant' relationships between the various members of the congregation and their leaders.[33]

The Restorationist ecclesiological vision challenged Elim on three fronts. First, it questioned Elim's denominationalism. This anti-denominational stance would have found at least some resonance within Elim, if for no other reason that Elim itself had developed into a denomination by default rather than by design (see Chapter 4), and its founder George Jeffreys had himself boldly proclaimed in Royal Albert Hall that 'thank God we are living in days when, as far as spiritual people are concerned, denominational walls are falling flat before the trumpet call to stand uncompromisingly for the whole Bible, and nothing but the Bible.'[34]

Second, the biblical emphasis on (local) church governance managed by an apostolic team in line with Eph. 4.11 and united by deep relational connections, would have made Elim question its local church leadership structure. In fact, already in 1972 Elim's 'Doctrine of the Church Committee' had concluded that the movement's leadership structures were too clerical and that its concept of deacons in local churches was unbiblical.[35] Third, the freedom and charismatic enthusiasm flowing from the Restorationist ecclesiology provided new vibrancy compared to the seemingly old-fashioned subculture of Elim and its diminishing Pentecostal fervour (see Lancaster's comments above).[36]

---

31. Wallis, 'Stay In or Come Out?', 16.
32. Jones, 'What is the Church?'; Walker, *Restoring the Kingdom*, 173.
33. Jones, 'What is the Church?'. For the central role of the so-called apostles see Walker, *Restoring the Kingdom*, 151.
34. Jeffreys, *The Miraculous Foursquare Gospel – Supernatural*, 2.
35. No author, 'First Interim Report of the Doctrine of the Church Committee' (1972), Elim Archives, Malvern, 5.
36. Maldwyn Jones also notes that by the arrival of the Restoration movement there was increasingly a 'dryness' in Elim regarding the 'gifts of the Spirit'; Jones, interview by author.

However, it was not *just* the ecclesiology of the Restoration movement that challenged Elim, but its *eschatology* also seemed to provide 'greater hope'. In other words, the Restorationist Charismatics provided a more optimistic eschatological imagination regarding the future. As discussed above, Elim's eschatology was essentially dispensational premillennialism that expected 'things to get worse' before Christ would return (see Section 5.1.1). In contrast, the Restorationist eschatology was post-millennial or amillennial.[37] As pointed out by William Kay, the basic difference was that 'restorationism exchanged stoic pessimism for charismatic optimism'.[38] This positive eschatology is well captured by Andrew Walker when he writes that

> The 'end-time', which Restorationists believe is now, will be characterized not so much by world chaos and 'wars and rumours of wars', but by an outpouring of God's Spirit, culminating in the establishment of the Kingdom that is ready and fit for the return of the King.[39]

The appeal of this 'charismatic optimism' for Elim was not only in the Charismatic Restorationists providing biblical arguments for their perspective, but also because the optimism fitted better with the 'popular mood of the 1970s and 1980s'.[40] That is, for the experientially and pragmatically minded Elim members and ministers, postmillennialism seemed a good way forward, not least when after sixty years the assumed imminent apocalyptic destruction of the world had not yet taken place despite the Elim tradition going through the First World War, the Second World War and three decades of the Cold War.

In conclusion, the Restoration Charismatic movement in many ways appeared to be providing an updated version of the Elim tradition. On one hand, it shared to a great extent Elim's rationality of biblical pragmatism and theological emphasis on aspects of the Foursquare Gospel, which would have made Elim members and ministers feel at home in the Restoration movement. On the other hand, in light of this shared rationality, it also provided ecclesiological and eschatological modifications which could be seen as improvements to the existing Elim tradition. These improvements on first appearance were justified in light of the Bible, and pragmatically seemed to have strong warrant as the Restorationists were growing as a movement and manifesting charismatic 'signs' in their activities, while Elim appeared to have lost much of its Pentecostal focus and was not presently

---

37. See Walker, *Restoring the Kingdom*, 141; Scotland, 'From the "Not Yet" to the "Now and Not Yet"', 277; Andrew Ewen Robertson, 'The Distinctive Missiology of the New Churches, an Analysis and Evaluation' (PhD diss., University of Wales, 2014), 8.
38. Kay, *Apostolic Networks*, 29.
39. Walker, *Restoring the Kingdom*, 40. Cf. Wallis, *In the Day of Thy Power*, 35–42.
40. Hathaway, 'The Elim Pentecostal Church', 29.

experiencing significant growth.⁴¹ In other words, prima facie the Restoration movement provided an updated Elim argument and so presented itself as a more progressive tradition.

6.3 The 'epistemological crisis' and its resolution

The Restoration movement not only was presenting itself as a 'restored' and 'renewed' expression of the Elim argument but also invited Elim churches and ministers to join its ranks in building what is saw as the restored church. For example, the Dales Bible Week organized by Bryn Jones was in the words of Walker a 'successful recruitment office for R1' with respect to 'Baptist, Elim and Assemblies of God churches'.⁴² Kay also points out how the first edition of Bryn Jones's *Restoration* magazine was 'sent out free of charge to various people including ministers of Elim Pentecostal churches',⁴³ and John Cave remembers leaders of R1 directly asking Elim ministers to join them (although he was not personally approached).⁴⁴ Indeed, by the early 1980s Elim had lost some of its ministers and congregations to the Restoration movement,⁴⁵ and Elim's national leaders feared that if nothing was done a schism within Elim was imminent.⁴⁶

It was the Southport Conference of 1981 that launched the process of instigating new reforms within Elim, with the aim of overcoming the potential crisis.⁴⁷ This two-and-a-half-day conference gathered 200 Elim ministers and allowed the movement to discuss the current state of Elim in groups and subgroups.⁴⁸

---

41. Ward is of the view that in the 1970s Elim was becoming stagnant; Ward, interview by author. This view is corroborated by Philip Walker who refers to years 1961–80 as one of Elim's 'least productive as far as the planting of new churches is concerned'; Phillip L. Walker, 'Church Growth Report', *1993 Elim Conference Reports*, Elim Archives, Malvern, 70.

42. Walker, *Restoring the Kingdom*, 115. Ironically, the Dales Bible Week developed from the Capel Bible Week held at the grounds of the Elim Bible College, albeit Elim was not really involved in organizing the Capel Bible Week; Walker, *Restoring the Kingdom*, 84–85. Philip Hidderley, conversation with author, Malvern, 30 August 2017.

43. Kay, *Apostolic Networks*, 22.

44. Cave, interview by author.

45. Maldwyn Jones believes that by 1980 Elim had lost six congregations; Jones, interview by author, 2016; cf. John C. Smyth, 'Southport Conference: Keynote Address', in *Southport Papers: Discussion Document* (1981), Archives of the General Superintendent, EIC, Malvern, 4.

46. Maldwyn Jones reckons that without the Southport Conferences Elim would have lost at least 100 churches to the Restoration movement; Jones, interview by author.

47. Hathaway, 'The Elim Pentecostal Church', 30.

48. One of the strengths of the Southport Conference was that it allowed a multiplicity of voices to be heard; that is, as well as there being keynote sessions from John Smyth,

John Smyth set the context for the conference in his opening keynote speech by articulating how the 'House Church Movement' (i.e. Restoration movement) was posing a challenge for Elim and he advised Elim to reform.[49] The agenda for the discussion groups was clearly influenced by the Restorationist themes and were: (1) 'Ministry and Leadership' with respect to its 'purpose' (Section A), role 'in the local church' (Section B) and 'in the Church as a whole' (Section C); (2) 'Law and Grace' (Section D); (3) 'Church Membership' (Sections E and F); (4) 'Worship' (Section G); and (5) 'The Basis of Fellowship' (Section H) with other Christians.[50] John Lancaster refers to this period as a 'vital part' in Elim's history. He states that it was during this time that the movement yet again subjected itself to close self-analysis by asking what Elim was really about, what it believed, and how it practised those beliefs.[51] So, how did Elim conduct its self-analysis and seek to resolve its second major epistemological crisis?

6.3.1 Returning to Pentecostal Biblical Pragmatism and the Foursquare Gospel

Interestingly but not surprisingly, this self-evaluation was primarily conducted through a biblical lens. For example, when Ron Jones, Elim's General Secretary at the time, called for the Southport Conference he made it clear that in exploring the issues Elim must have 'the Bible as our text book'.[52] This biblical focus is further reflected in the 1981 Southport Papers, as much of the analyses of the issues focuses on exposition of key biblical concepts and passages. Moreover, Elim's biblicism is also evident in the ensuring discussion when the report of the steering committee on church leadership at local and national levels presented its findings to the Elim Conference in 1982 on what it called the '*irreducible minimum of Scriptural guidance*' (my italics) regarding the topics in question.[53] Therefore, as with the crisis of 1939–40, Elim again sought to ground its argument on the Bible.

However, these biblical principles were intended to be applied through the 'leading of the Holy Spirit'. Ron Jones noted that as Elim evaluated its present condition and future direction, 'there should be a constant freshness and awareness of the moving of the Holy Spirit.'[54] This view was shared by Jones's successor as

---

Eldin Corsie and Wesley Gilpin, thirty-two speakers gave papers and group discussion was effectively facilitated; see Tom W. Walker, 'Introduction', in *Southport Papers* (1981), Elim Archives, Malvern, 1.

49. Smyth, 'Southport Conference: Keynote Address', 3–13.

50. The Southport Papers (1981).

51. John Lancaster, 'Elim 100', accessed 26 June 2015, http://www.elim.org.uk/Groups/243516/ELIM_100.aspx.

52. W. R. Jones, 'Secretary General's Report', in Elim Pentecostal Church: Annual Conference 1981. Conference Agendas and Reports, 6.

53. Tom W. Walker, ed., 'Report from the Steering Committee appointed by the Executive Council', 31 April 1982, Elim Archives, Malvern, 1.

54. W. R. Jones, 'Secretary General's Report' (1981), 8.

general secretary, Tom Walker, when he wrote that 'as we continue to search the Word and *seek the mind of the Holy Spirit*, God will surely lead us on' (my italics).[55]

Now, neither Jones nor Walker define what being 'Spirit led' looks like. Nevertheless, it is not hard to argue that in practice it is analogous with *Pentecostal pragmatism*, which I have argued in Chapter 4 consists of *experientialism* and *experimentalism*. The *experiential* aspect expects the Spirit to lead individuals, local gatherings and Elim as a movement through an inner witness, (supernatural) wisdom, prophecies, tongues, words of knowledge or something similar. And the *experimental* aspect then subjects the charismatic experience to pragmatic criteria of 'effects' and 'results' that ought to have been produced by a genuine leading of the Spirit; that is, the 'prophet' and the 'leading of the Spirit' is judged by its 'fruits'.

This rationality of *experiential experimentalism* (read: Pentecostal pragmatism) can be shown to be at work in Tom Walker's thinking when he writes that the 'Steering Committee [for the Southport Conference 1981] were obviously led by the Holy Spirit in the plans and format produced.'[56] So, what made Walker think that the committee were led by the Spirit? Well, in his own words: 'That the Groups and Sub-Groups [at Southport] where the right approach *manifested itself in one of two resolutions passed by the final Plenary Session*' (my italics).[57] In other words, for Walker the committee must have been led by the Spirit because the 'results' of the conference, despite the present challenges, produced desired 'fruit'.

To give another example of Elim's Pentecostal pragmatism at work during this phase, before the second and final Southport Conference in 1984, an Elim minister called Johnny Barr apparently had a spiritual 'revelation' from 'the Lord' where Elim was called to repent regarding its 'morality, party spirit and money' or else 'the Lord' would 'remove their candlestick from its place'.[58] Barr shared this prophecy at the second Southport Conference in 1984,[59] and as a result 'scheduled business was dispensed with as the implications of the message were assimilated and responded to'.[60] Reflecting thirty years later, John Glass, who was present at the meeting and later became Elim's general superintendent, notes that 'it is my belief that it is because of those actions [i.e. Barr's prophecy and the following repentance within Elim] that the Lord has allowed us, thirty years later, to be able to acquire the level of prime properties that we own today'.[61] Thus, again the same pragmatic rationality seems to be at work, namely, spiritual experience (i.e.

---

55. Tom W. Walker, 'Introduction', in Elim Pentecostal Church – Annual Conference 1982 – Conference Minutes, Elim Archives, Malvern, 1.

56. Walker, 'Introduction', in *Southport Papers* (1981), 1.

57. Ibid.

58. John Glass, 'Southport Conference 1984', in *Defining Moments*, 104.

59. Altogether there were two Southport Conferences (1981 and 1984), and between these conferences there were naturally the annual Elim Conferences.

60. Glass, 'Southport Conference 1984', 104.

61. Ibid., 105.

prophecy) is justified by its effects (i.e. repentance by Elim ministers and future financial integrity of Elim).

However, as well as falling back on its rationality of Pentecostal Biblical Pragmatism, Elim also sought to return to the essence of its argument. Wesley Gilpin – an Elim statesman and principal of the Elim Bible College from 1958 to 1980 – gave the final speech at the 1981 Southport Conference.[62] In his speech he referred to the events surrounding the Southport Conference as the second 'significant crisis' within Elim (implying that the resignation of Jeffreys had been the first). He continued by pointing out that during both of these crises the raison d'etre of Elim and its 'confessed purpose for the future' was under scrutiny. He then went on to reflect on Elim's destiny by claiming that 'we are challenged to take the lead, with vision and inspiration, before our own people, in the vanguard of the cause of the *Full Gospel* and, indeed, as a significant and potent force in the Evangelical world' (my italics).[63]

Two years later, as the movement had made important steps to recovering from its crisis, Tom Walker highlighted to Elim's ministers and churches how Gilpin's wish had in effect been fulfilled as the movement was now back 'in the vanguard of the cause of the Full Gospel' (although he does not actually mention Gilpin). Writing to the 1983 Elim Conference, Walker states that 'the ministry of the Word throughout was of high quality and clearly indicated our determination always to stand *foursquare on the Word of God*' (my italics).[64] He then remarked: 'The many *saved, healed* or *filled with the Holy Spirit*, the large number receiving their call to commitment, renewal or ministry, the tremendous spirit of worship – all these and more made it a splendid Conference.'[65]

Thus, it seems that in overcoming its moment of crisis, Elim had again returned to the essence of its argument, that is, the Foursquare Gospel, at least if the rhetoric is anything to go by. It was also this reaffirmation of Foursquare Gospel as the raison d'etre of Elim that helped it fend off the anti-denominationalism of the Restorationists, because Elim could maintain that as a denomination it had a special argument to make to the wider church and the world.[66]

6.3.2 Structural and theological reformulations

However, Elim also changed in and through the process of overcoming its epistemological crisis. These reformulations of the Elim tradition were primarily to do with (1) *ecclesiology* and (2) *eschatology*.

---

62. G. Wesley Gilpin, 'Wholehearted Affirmation', in *Southport Papers* (1981), Elim Archives, Malvern.
63. Ibid.
64. Tom W. Walker, 'In His Name to All Nations', Elim Pentecostal Church – Annual Conference 1983 – Minutes of the Representative Session, Elim Archives, Malvern, 1.
65. Ibid., 2.
66. See Gilpin, 'Wholehearted Affirmation'.

6.3.2.1 Structural changes With respect to Elim's *ecclesiology*, or church governance structures, there were two important modifications. First, Elim devolved increasing powers to the local churches so that they were able to agree their own leadership structures, albeit with certain biblical and constitutional caveats. Before Southport 1981, Elim's local church governance was constitutionally restricted to simply adopting a diaconate church session that left no real room for elders.[67] This was considered to be not only ineffective but more worryingly also unbiblical.[68] Consequently, the Elim Conference amended its constitution by stipulating that the church session would now consist of pastor(s), elders and deacons and provide 'oversight' for the local church. Local congregations were also given freedom to appoint elders and deacons in a manner of their choosing, although the method of appointing elders and deacons needed to be approved by Elim's Head Quarters.[69] This constitutional change had been clearly influenced by the Restoration teaching on Eph. 4.11 and the importance it gave to elders in a local church. Hence, in a sense Elim simply adopted the Restorationist local church structure, although the justification for Elim's change was always made on biblical grounds, as well as on the pragmatic hope that perhaps 'greater spiritual renewal would ensue' as a result of this more biblical model of governance.[70] The local churches also now had greater autonomy, which in turn gave them greater freedom to adopt Restoration style of worship and an ability to more effectively manage their church members.[71]

The second modification regarding Elim's church structure came with regionalization in 1985.[72] The Restoration movement had a huge emphasis on (covenant) relationships, including relationships between 'elders' and 'apostolic leaders'. This was seen as lacking within Elim and, as a result, many ministers felt isolated despite the districts that had been introduced during the 1940s.[73] Thus, the idea of introducing regions and regional leaders was to help ministers connect better with each other and also for them to have a personal pastor in the regional leader. The process of regionalization was rolled out gradually and,

---

67. Hathaway, 'The Elim Pentecostal Church', 30; Jones, interview by author, 2016.

68. The unbiblical nature of Elim's concept of deacons governing the local church was of great concern in Southport; Southport Papers 1981, A1, B1, B13.

69. Elim Pentecostal Church: Annual Conference 1983. Conference Agenda and Report, Elim Archives, Malvern, 2–3; cf. Malcolm Hathaway, 'The Elim Pentecostal Church', 30.

70. Malcolm Hathaway, 'The Elim Pentecostal Church', 30.

71. Worship and church membership where two other major themes discussed at Southport; Southport Papers 1981, Sections E, F and G.

72. John C. Smyth, 'Formation of Regions', in Elim Pentecostal Church: Annual Conference 1985. Conference Agendas and Reports, Elim Archives, Malvern, 75–7; Minutes of the 'Elim Pentecostal Church: Annual Conference 1985. Representative Session', Archives of the General Superintendent, EIC, Malvern, 8–9.

73. See Southport Papers (1981), B13.

according to the Elim Conference Minutes, provided welcome improvements,[74] although Malcolm Hathaway has suggested that in the end the 'result was a rather bureaucratic structure which inhibited the original objective.'[75] Either way, the aspiration at least was to make Elim more relationally connected and devolve power from the centre to the regions.

In sum, both of the ecclesiological changes (i.e. local church governance and regionalization) demonstrated Elim's flexibility to reform its structures, if there were good biblical and pragmatic reasons for doing so. Moreover, they both show increasing devolution of power within Elim from the Headquarters/Conference to the local churches and regions.

6.3.2.2 Eschatological changes The change in Elim's *eschatology* is the second major modification following from its second epistemological crisis. As has been noted above, the Restoration movement was characterized by a more optimistic post-millennial and/or amillennial eschatology in comparison to Elim's apocalyptic premillennialism. This, however, changed in 1993 when the Elim Conference adopted a revised Statement of Fundamental Truths and deleted premillennialism as one of its Fundamental Truths.[76] Apparently the removal of premillennialism was 'decided upon on the grounds that the Fundamental truth is that He [Jesus] will return and not the context of that coming in relation to a fixed period of time'.[77] What is interesting about the revision is that the previous precision regarding the doctrine of the second coming was removed. Therefore, although the hard core doctrine of Jesus as coming King was upheld by the conference, the interpretation of this doctrine (or auxiliary hypothesis) of premillennialism was removed. Moreover, the nature of Christ's return was left vague with simply affirming that He will return to 'reign in power and glory' in a 'personal', 'physical' and 'visible' manner.[78] This does raise the question whether Elim, by removing premillennialism and expressing general vagueness about its eschatology, was starting to show signs of becoming, in the words of Lakatos, a 'degenerative scientific research programme' regarding one of its hard core doctrines.

It has been suggested that the removal of premillennialism was not directly connected to Elim's epistemological crisis of the late 1970s and early 1980s as

---

74. T. Gordon Hills, 'Regionalisation Report', in Elim Pentecostal Church: Annual Conference 1987. Conference Agendas and Reports, Elim Archives, Malvern, 64–5.

75. Malcolm Hathaway, 'The Elim Pentecostal Church', 31.

76. Minutes of the 'Elim Pentecostal Church: Annual Conference 1993. Representative Session', Archives of the General Superintendent, EIC, Malvern, Item No. 19 and 27.

77. John C. Smyth, 'Fundamental Committee Report', in 1993 Elim Conference Reports, Archives of the General Superintendent, EIC, Malvern, 63.

78. Elim Pentecostal Church: Annual Conference 1993. Conference Agenda and Reports, Elim Archives, Malvern, 91; cf. *The Constitution of the Elim Pentecostal Church (Elim Foursquare Gospel Alliance)*. 2016 Edition. The Elim Pentecostal Church, Malvern, United Kingdom, 2.

such.[79] However, if there were no connection between the two, it would seem like an amazing coincidence of history for Elim to change its eschatological views to allow Elim ministers to subscribe to postmillennialism and amillennialism after a direct challenge from the Restoration movement on this very issue few years previously. The fact that this change happened only twelve years after the first Southport Conference is not surprising, as it is not uncommon for *official* doctrines to be changed after and in response to the *actual* doctrines having changed in practice some time before. Thus, it is proposed that Elim changed its interpretation of Jesus as coming King as part of its reformulations in overcoming its second epistemological crisis. This is also further evidence to suggest that it is not the Fundamental Truths (e.g. premillennialism) that is the hard core of the Elim tradition, but the hard core is the Foursquare Gospel (e.g. Jesus as coming King) implicit in the Fundamental Truths. That said, as has already been suggested, this particular modification in the Fundamental Truths does raise questions whether something in the hard core of Elim was also altered.

6.4 Conclusion

In this chapter I have tried to establish that it was the Charismatic movement, and the Restoration Charismatics particularly, that caused Elim's second epistemological crisis. By the late 1970s Elim had lost some of its Pentecostal zeal and as a movement was not really growing. This made it vulnerable to the emergence of the Restoration movement which not only shared Elim's basic Pentecostal rationality and theology but also offered novel views on ecclesiology and eschatology. In other words, Restorationism seemed to provide an improved and updated version of the apparently stagnant Elim argument. Elim, however, responded to this challenge by reaffirming its rationality of Pentecostal Biblical Pragmatism and theology of the Foursquare Gospel. It also reformulated its ecclesiological structures, and was ready to reinterpret one of its hard core doctrines of Jesus as coming King by removing its insistence on premillennialism. Therefore, in MacIntyrian terms, Elim successfully moved from stage two (epistemological crisis) to stage three (resolution) by remaining true to its core beliefs and rationality while demonstrating creativity and flexibility in recalibrating aspects of the Elim tradition.

In providing a historical narration of Elim's two epistemological crises here and in Chapter 5, I believe I have substantiated my claim that the *content* of the Elim *argument* is indeed the Foursquare Gospel and its *rationality* is Pentecostal Biblical Pragmatism. However, the historical analysis provided seems to also suggest that the *implied opponents* of the Elim argument have broadened; that is, the 'opponent' instigating the first crisis came from inside the movement, whereas the second

---

79. For example, Ward did not see an explicit connection between the two; Ward, interview by author.

'opponent' came from like-minded Charismatic Christians. The change in the implied opponents, as well as the changing context of the argument, has meant that Elim has had to revise and reformulate aspects of its argument to maintain itself as a progressive tradition. This reformulation has particularly been demonstrated in the changing *embodiment* of the Elim argument. In other words, through these crises Elim has significantly changed its institutional structures. The trajectory of the change in the embodiment of the Elim argument has been from *the few to the many*; that is, the initial Elim argument can be seen to be primarily embodied in one man (i.e. George Jeffreys), in 1934 this moved to few key leaders (i.e. the executive council), in 1942 it progressed to Elim ministers and representatives of congregations (i.e. the Elim Conference), before increasingly shifting to leadership teams and members of local churches (i.e. approved church sessions). To put it in political language, there has been an increasing democratization and devolving of power in Elim. Interestingly, this change in Elim is also reflective of the developments in Western democracies. Nevertheless, this change in the way the Elim argument has been embodied has not been done at the expense of the argument's content or its rationality, if anything it seems to have been informed by them, particularly by Elim's biblical pragmatism.

Chapters 5 and 6 have also raised some interesting questions about Elim's rationality and the hard core doctrines of its argument. Regarding Elim's rationality, the BI debate of 1934 highlighted how Elim's rationality is not *merely* biblicism or pragmatism but *biblical pragmatism*. This means, among other things, that the pragmatic beliefs of Elim must 'naturally' arise from the biblical text, which in turn begs the question: What is a 'natural' reading of a text? This hermeneutical matter needs to be addressed to help clarify Elim's biblical pragmatism, and it is something that I will seek to do in Chapter 8.

In terms of Elim's *hard core doctrines*, the deleting of premillennialism as a Fundamental Truth should not be quickly passed by, not least when during the movement's first epistemological crisis premillennialism was a central tenet of Elim's eschatology. To put it differently, has Elim effectively changed one of its hard core doctrines, namely, Jesus as coming King, by moving from a premillennial position to a general eschatological position? Or at least in generalizing its eschatology is Elim showing signs of becoming in Lakatosian terms a 'degenerative' tradition by no longer being able to predict 'novel facts'? I will return to this question in the conclusion of the book.

Part Three

(RE)CONSTRUCTING PENTECOSTAL BIBLICAL PRAGMATISM

I began the book with a search for a Pentecostal rationality, epistemology and theological hermeneutics that would stem from and/or be compatible with Pentecostal spirituality, beliefs and practices. In doing so I evaluated the Pentecostal rationalities of Amos Yong, James K. A. Smith and L. William Oliverio Jr. (Chapter 1). After engaging with the valuable contributions of Yong, Smith and Oliverio, I concluded that despite the various strengths of their proposals, their rationalities and epistemologies seem to suffer from being ahistorical and non-narrative and thus are in danger of not necessarily being Pentecostal, or at least not representing any particular Pentecostal/charismatic tradition. Following from this concern, I suggested that Alasdair MacIntyre's concepts of 'tradition' and 'tradition-dependent rationality' provides a useful way forward for articulating a more historical, narrative and tradition-specific Pentecostal rationality (Chapter 2).

Utilizing MacIntyre's philosophical insights in constructing a tradition-specific Pentecostal rationality, however, cannot be done apart from historically exemplifying an existing Pentecostal tradition or, in MacIntyrian terms, articulating a Pentecostal 'argument extended through time'. Consequently, Chapters 3 to 6 of the volume have tried to narrate along MacIntyrian lines the Elim Pentecostal tradition as an example of a classical Pentecostal tradition, with particular emphasis on the context and roots of Elim (Chapter 3); the early opponents, content, rationality and embodiment of the Elim argument (Chapter 4); and Elim's two major epistemological crises (Chapters 5–6). The underlying argument from this narration has been that Elim's tacit Pentecostal rationality is best described as *Pentecostal Biblical Pragmatism* and the theological hard core constituting this rationality is the *Foursquare Gospel*. Moreover, I have tried to demonstrate that Elim has shown flexibility regarding the 'embodiment' of the argument by revising its constitution and institutional structures in order to more effectively live out the Full Gospel. This narration has enabled me not only to provide a historical, narrative and tradition-specific Pentecostal rationality but, in doing so, to also present the first intellectual history of Elim.

The purpose of the last section is to focus explicitly on Elim's tradition-dependent rationality with the aim of developing it along theological and philosophical lines. Consequently, the last section is significantly narrower in its focus compared to the previous section. In other words, whereas in Part Two I have focused on the wider intellectual and religious context of the Elim argument (Chapter 3), before narrating it with respect to its implied opponents, content, rationality and embodiment (Chapters 4–6), my focus will now be explicitly on Elim's rationality of Pentecostal Biblical Pragmatism. This is not because I do not consider it important to explore these other facets of the Elim argument (in fact, I will make brief comments about them in the conclusion of the book), but simply because I am not able to do all of this with sufficient detail within a single work. Furthermore, I believe that the broader historical narration of Part Two has provided the needed theological and philosophical resources to (re)construct a truly tradition-constituted Pentecostal rationality.

Therefore, Part Three will exclusively discuss Elim's *Pentecostal Biblical Pragmatism* by first exploring the *Pentecostal* aspect with particular emphasis on Elim's concept of truth (Chapter 7). This I believe is a necessary precursor for a working theological rationality. After this I will bring Elim's *biblicism* under closer scrutiny with the aim of proposing an appropriate biblical hermeneutic for Elim in light of its doctrine of Scripture (Chapter 8). As has become clear in Chapters 3 to 6, throughout Elim's existence the Bible has remained the grounding document for its beliefs and practices, and thus the question of biblical hermeneutics cannot really be ignored when developing Elim's rationality. Finally, I will focus on Elim's *pragmatism* which is the underlying ethos of the movement's rationality. I will do so by suggesting a pragmatic theory of epistemic justification with an emphasis on both 'experientialism' and 'experimentalism'.

In doing the above, I do not claim to provide the official Elim views on Pentecostal truth, biblical hermeneutics or pragmatic justification. However, I do believe that my proposals are compatible with, and flow out of, the Elim tradition. Moreover, they are suggestive (if nothing else) of what a theological/philosophical articulation of Elim's explicit rationality and epistemology should look like, and therefore will hopefully serve as a constructive contribution in the search for a Pentecostal rationality and epistemology.

Chapter 7

PENTECOSTAL TRUTH: PENTECOSTAL THEOLOGICAL REALISM

In Chapter 3, I have argued that the basic theological and intellectual assumptions of Elim's rationality have been inherited from its Pentecostal and Evangelical forefathers. In other words, the underlying 'spirituality' (Land), 'social imaginary' (Taylor) and/or 'worldview' (Smith) of Elim has been significantly informed by late-nineteenth- and early-twentieth-century British Evangelicalism (particularly the Holiness movement and the Welsh Revival),[1] as well as by the early British Pentecostalism exemplified in Boddy's Sunderland Conventions (1908–14) and *Confidence* magazine. It is important to stress, not least in light of the Pentecostal scholarship that tries to distance Pentecostalism from Evangelicalism,[2] that for Elim the question has never been whether the movement is Pentecostal *or* Evangelical; Elim has, after all, always been Pentecostal *and* Evangelical. As I have pointed out, the early Elim pioneers came predominantly from Evangelical backgrounds (Chapter 3) and saw their movement as being Evangelical (Chapter 4). Elim was also keen to join the Evangelical Alliance in 1964 (Chapter 6), and throughout its history has shared key doctrines with British Evangelicals (Chapters 4 and 6). Nevertheless, as well as being Evangelical, Elim has also identified itself (primarily) as a Pentecostal movement with certain distinctive and specific emphases implying that Elim has also gone beyond mainline Evangelicalism, although this 'going beyond' has not been perceived as going against Evangelicalism.

Elim's *Evangelical* Pentecostalism has naturally shared a number of basic theological beliefs with Evangelicalism vis-à-vis the nature of God, creation, humanity, sin, redemption and final consummation, although Elim's Evangelical *Pentecostalism* has also interpreted some of these doctrines in a distinct way. For example, the doctrine of God has increasingly been perceived through Christological and pneumatological lenses, redemption has been viewed 'holistically' with an emphasis on both the salvation of the soul and the healing

---

1. See Land, *Pentecostal Spirituality*; Taylor, *Modern Social Imaginaries*; Smith, *Thinking in Tongues*.
2. See Castelo, *Pentecostalism as a Christian Mystical Tradition*, 83–125. For further discussion on whether Pentecostals are Evangelicals, see Terry L. Cross, 'The Rich Feast of Theology: Can Pentecostals Bring the Main Course or Only the Relish?', *JPT* 8, no. 16 (2000): 33–4; McGee, '"More Than Evangelical"'.

of the body, and the final consummation has been understood as an immanent eschatological event.

These Evangelical and Pentecostal theological convictions have been seminal not just in constituting Elim's rationality of *biblical pragmatism* but also in shaping Elim's tacit assumptions about the nature of *truth*. However, despite the importance of 'truth' in formulating a working rationality,[3] thus far I have paid little attention to Elim's concept of truth. Consequently, this chapter's discussion on the *Pentecostal* aspect of Elim's rationality will focus explicitly on Elim's concept of truth. In exploring this, my aim is not to argue for the truth of Elim's theory of truth vis-à-vis its theological and philosophical competitors, but to provide a working definition of truth that is 'truthful' to the Elim tradition and thus sufficient in grounding Elim's rational enquiry according to its own Pentecostal standards.

7.1 Pentecostal theological realism

Truth matters for Elim. The importance of the concept of truth for Elim was highlighted in a 2013 Elim Conference debate on changing the name of the 'Fundamental Truths' to 'Core Beliefs'.[4] Much of the rhetoric defending the phrase 'Fundamental Truths' appealed to Elim standing on theological 'truth(s)', which the majority of the conference seemed to understand as referring to universal and objective reality, rather than on 'mere beliefs' which were taken as relative and subjective opinions. After the debate, the conference voted in favour of maintaining the language of 'Fundamental Truths' because it concluded that 'truth' as an idea was too important to be jettisoned, even if the term 'Fundamental' was seen by many as unhelpful in the contemporary religious climate of militant religious *Fundamentalism*.[5]

Nevertheless, despite the purported importance of truth for Elim, the nature of truth has received little discussion within the movement (although see Section 4.3.2). Consequently, I will now try to suggest a theological concept of

---

3. It seems that even if 'truth' is not the primary epistemic goal, it certainly is a central goal of epistemic enquiry, and therefore a working definition of 'truth' is important for any epistemology and/or rationality; see Jonathan Kvanvig, 'Truth Is not the Primary Epistemic Goal', in *Contemporary Debates in Epistemology*, ed. Matthias Steup and Ernest Sosa (Oxford: Blackwell Publishing, 2011), 285–96; Marian David, 'Truth as the Primary Epistemic Goal: A Working Hypothesis', in *Contemporary Debates in Epistemology*, 296–312.

4. Elim Pentecostal Church: Annual Conference, 2013. Conference Agenda and Reports, Elim Archives, Malvern, 15. The author was present at the conference.

5. Indeed, the phrase 'Fundamental Truths' was changed to 'Foundational Truths' in 2015/2016; Elim Pentecostal Church: Annual Conference, 2015. Conference Agenda and Reports, Elim Archives, Malvern, 23; Elim Pentecostal Church: Annual Conference, 2016. Conference Agenda and Reports, Elim Archives, Malvern, 24. The author was present at both conferences.

truth that emerges from the Elim tradition and is coherent with it. My basic assumption is that a theory of truth that is both informed by and compatible with the Elim tradition needs to be grounded in Elim's Pentecostal beliefs, it needs to be biblically based, realist in nature and eschatological in its disposition. In light of this, I will argue that truth for Elim ought to be characterized as *Pentecostal theological realism*. This theological realism can be seen to maintain and share three common theses of realism, namely,

1. Reality exists independently of the human mind (Thesis 1);
2. A sufficient relationship between truth and 'beliefs' can be established; that is, true beliefs are those that 'correspond', in one way or another, with reality (Thesis 2);
3. 'Beliefs' and 'propositions' about God and the world are either true or false (i.e. principle of bivalence) (Thesis 3).[6]

It is worth clarifying that I will not discuss the various options for 'truth-bearers' but will simply assume that 'beliefs' and 'propositions' are sufficient bearers of truth,[7] and my focus is primarily on theological truth, even if there are obvious overlaps with 'truth' generally speaking. I will begin by trying to theologically ground Thesis 1, before more explicitly focusing on Thesis 2 and 3. I will seek to justify the three theses from a biblically based 'Elim' theology with particular emphasis on the doctrines of God, creation, humanity, sin, revelation and eschatology.

7.2 God as ultimate reality

In line with other Christian and Evangelical traditions, the basic assumption in Elim appears to be that God is the 'ultimate truth'.[8] The theological justification for believing this is based on the concept of God ontologically being *the* 'ultimate

---

6. These three aspects constitute William P. Alston's 'alethic realism'; William P. Alston, 'Realism and the Christian Faith', *IJPR* 38, no. 1 (December 1995): 39. For further categorization of the realist/anti-realist debate; see Michael Glanzberg, 'Truth', in *The Stanford Encyclopedia of Philosophy* (Winter 2016 Edition), ed. Edward N. Zalta, accessed 20 October 2017, https://plato.stanford.edu/archives/win2016/entries/truth/; Christopher J. Insole, 'Realism and Anti-Realism', in *The Oxford Handbook of The Epistemology of Theology*, 274–89.

7. For further discussion see William P. Alston, *A Realist Conception of Truth* (Ithaca, NY: Cornell University Press, 1996), 9–22; Glanzberg 'Truth'.

8. See Hicks, *Evangelicals and Truth*, 179; Marshall, *Trinity and Truth*, 2; Mark A. McIntosh, *Discernment and Truth: The Spirituality and Theology of Knowledge* (New York, NY: The Crossroad Publishing Company, 2004), 4.

reality' as *the creator and ground of being* (see Gen. 1.1; Jn 1.3). God as creator is conceived as the only necessarily existing being, implying that everything else that exists is contingent on His existence. As the unique creator, God is perceived as the source of all things and hence all of creation is dependent on God for its existence. This leads to an asymmetrical relationship between God and creation; that is, the created order is dependent on God for its existence, but God is not dependent on creation for His existence. In the language of realism, this means that the transcendent God as the ultimate reality exists independently of the creation's perceiving of Him. Or to put it differently, ultimate reality (read: God) exists independently of the human mind (Thesis 1).

In a theistic worldview affirming *theological realism* with respect to Thesis 1 is generally uncontroversial. Even James K. A. Smith – who is no supporter of 'realism as correspondence' – acknowledges 'the reality and *in*dependence of the transcendent God on whom creation depends for its existence'.[9] However, even if Thesis 1 one is believed and God is seen as the 'ultimate reality', this need not mean that humans can have access to this 'reality' to the extent of enabling them to have sufficiently corresponding 'beliefs' about it (Thesis 2) or of allowing them to articulate truthful statements about this reality, at least not in the realist sense (Thesis 3). Indeed, John Hick has argued that there is the 'Real' (i.e. 'ultimate reality'), but the human experience of the Real is always informed by specific religious contexts and cultural-linguistic frameworks to the extent that the 'truth' of one's beliefs and propositions of the Real are found significantly wanting. To use Hick's own example, it is impossible to discern whether the Real is in fact personal or non-personal; the best one can do is to speculate that the Real is 'good or gracious, namely as the necessary condition of our highest good'.[10] In other words, there is, or at least could be, real theological truth(s) out there, but human beliefs and statements cannot accurately correspond with them.[11]

The denial of Thesis 2 and 3, despite accepting Thesis 1, however, does not seem to be justified in light of Elim's broader Evangelical/Pentecostal theology with respect to the doctrines of creation, *imago dei* (despite human 'sin') and special revelation in Christ through the Holy Spirit. In fact, these doctrines provide good theological reasons for Elim to embrace the two remaining realist theses, namely, the possibility of human beliefs to sufficiently correspond with reality and for humans, therefore, to be able to make sufficient truths claims about God and his relationship with the world.

---

9. Smith, *Who's Afraid of Relativism?*, 106.

10. John Hick, *Dialogues in the Philosophy of Religion* (Basingstoke: Palgrave Macmillan, 2001), 16; cf. John Hick, *An Interpretation of Religion: Human Responses to the Transcendent*, 2nd edn (Basingstoke: Palgrave Macmillan, 2004).

11. Smith seems to be leaning towards this position; Smith, *Who's Afraid of Relativism?*, 107.

7.3 The possibility for beliefs and talk about reality

Although Elim does not have a developed theology of creation and/or humanity,[12] the movement appears to share the basic principles of other Evangelical and Pentecostal traditions. For example, Julian Ward notes in an official Elim publication that 'all human beings were and are created in the image and likeness of God and intended to be the summit of God's creative acts (Gen. 1.26-28; Ps. 139.13, 14). We have been created as rational, moral and spiritual beings, with distinctive personalities endowed with intellects, emotions, creativity and the capacity to love and communicate.'[13]

Regarding human ability to have 'true' beliefs and make 'truthful' propositions about God, even if not explicitly stated here, this seems to be assumed in Ward's statement of humans being 'created in the image and likeness of God' as 'rational' beings with intellects and communicative abilities. Indeed Peter Hicks surmises that the basic Evangelical doctrine of *imago dei* implies, among other things, that humans can relate to God and have sufficiently realist knowledge of Him. Moreover, stemming from humanity's 'God like' status there are reasons to assume that humans are also able to experience the world and interact with other people with sufficient accuracy.[14] Thus, the Evangelical and Pentecostal concept of *imago dei* seems to provide a prima facie theological grounding for humans to be able to have true beliefs that correspond with the reality about God (Thesis 2), and also be able to state and communicate these beliefs in a manner that reflects reality (Thesis 3).

That said, the concept of *imago dei* also appears to cause some limitations for the human ability to grasp truth. For a start, humans are made as *embodied* beings in the *image* of God, and as such embodied creatures and mere images of 'God' (rather than 'gods'), humans are not able to have 'God's point of view' on truth but are limited by their very humanness (see Gen. 3.5-6). Consequently, both Amos Yong and James K. A. Smith rightly emphasize the partial and perspectival nature of human comprehension of truth.[15]

These natural human limitations to know the truth are further exacerbated by the doctrine of 'sin'. To quote Ward again: 'Sin darkens our understanding and corrupts the image of God in us and makes us self-centred ... Sin has the unfortunate consequence of turning people away from the truth.'[16] These sentiments expressed

---

12. Although see George Canty, *In My Father's House: Pentecostal Expositions of the Major Christian Truths* (London: Marshall, Morgan & Scott, 1969), 11–20; cf. Veli-Matti Kärkkäinen, *A Constructive Christian Theology for the Pluralistic World, Volume 3: Creation and Humanity* (Grand Rapids, MI: Eerdmans, 2015).

13. Julian Ward, 'Humanity and Sin', in *The Message: Elim's Core Beliefs*, ed. Keith Warrington (Malvern: Elim Training, n/d), 43.

14. Hicks, *Evangelicals and Truth*, 152–4.

15. Yong, *Spirit-Word-Community*, 176, 180, 182; Smith, *The Fall of Interpretation*, 10.

16. Ward, 'Humanity and Sin', 44–5.

by Ward are not without support from NT theology. For example, Paul speaks of the hardening of human hearts due to sin as resulting in people being 'darkened in their understanding' (Eph. 4.18),[17] as well as the 'ungodliness and unrighteousness' of people leading to the 'suppressing of truth' (Rom. 1.18).[18] In John's Gospel the effects of human sin vis-à-vis knowing the truth are equally stark, as the world is portrayed to be in 'epistemic darkness' when it comes to knowing the 'truth' about God (Jn 8.12, 12.46).[19] Therefore, from a biblical perspective at least, Alvin Plantinga is justified in stating that 'the most serious noetic effects of sin have to do with our knowledge of God'.[20]

Following from the epistemic limitations based on humans being both embodied and 'fallen', two alethiological implications can be drawn.[21] First, as well as being able to have true beliefs and to make true statements about God, humans are equally 'able' to have false beliefs and to make false statements about God. This does not undermine 'realism' (Thesis 2 or 3) as such, but it does point towards the significant likelihood of humans having false beliefs about God. In light of this, any theory of truth that takes the biblical concept of *imago dei* and human sin seriously should probably embrace some kind of fallibilism in its epistemology.

Second, and following closely from the first implication, the doctrines of creation and sin suggest that simplistic or naïve correspondence theories of truth should be avoided. To put it differently, human beliefs and articulations of reality will always be characterized by their partiality and perspectivism because humans are limited in their access to absolute truth by the very fact of being created. To be created means to have perspectival and contextual knowledge, as there is 'no view from nowhere' or 'God's point of view' for humanity. As contextual beings, humans are therefore inevitably also shaped by their (limited) experiences, history, culture and linguistic abilities, and there is no obvious way of transcending these limitations. When these natural limitations are coupled with those arising from

---

17. I am assuming Pauline authorship of Ephesians.

18. For further analysis of Pauline theological epistemology, see Richard B. Gaffin, 'Some Epistemological Reflections on 1 Cor. 2:6–16', *WTJ* 57, no. 1 (1995): 103–24; Ian W. Scott, *Implicit Epistemology in the Letters of Paul: Story, Experience and the Spirit* (Tübingen: Mohr-Siebeck, 2006); Mary Healy, 'Knowledge and Mystery: A Study of Pauline Epistemology', in *The Bible and Epistemology: Biblical Soundings on the Knowledge of God*, ed. Mary Healy and Robin Parry (Milton Keynes: Paternoster, 2007), 134–58; Simo Frestadius, 'The Spirit and Wisdom in 1 Corinthians 2:1-13', *JBPR* 3 (Fall 2011): 52–70.

19. See Cornelis Bennema, *The Power of Saving Wisdom: An Investigation of Spirit and Wisdom in Relation to the Soteriology of the Fourth Gospel* (Eugene, OR: Wipf and Stock, 2007); Cornelis Bennema, 'Christ, the Spirit, and the Knowledge of God: A Study in Johannine Epistemology', in *The Bible and Epistemology*, 107–33.

20. Plantinga, *Warranted Christian Belief*, 214.

21. Strictly speaking the limitations from creation are part of the 'goodness' of creation (Gen. 1.31) and therefore arguably something that humans should not try to transcend, whereas the limitations from the 'fall' are distortions to be corrected in redemption.

human sinfulness, human ability to have beliefs that really correspond with reality is further weakened. Consequently, a Pentecostal correspondence theory of truth should probably follow a version expressed by Amos Yong in which correspondence is seen as 'correlation', rather than 'congruence', meaning that true propositions need not be identical with their referents but should, nevertheless, resemble them sufficiently. Therefore, a theologically responsible 'Elim correspondence theory of truth' should acknowledge the perspectival and mediated nature of all human knowing, and thus some form of 'critical realism' is probably in order.[22]

This does re-raise the issue that are the alethiological limitations stemming from human (fallen) nature too great to be able to sustain any meaningful theory of realism (apart from Thesis 1)? And thus should Elim's realism simply accept Smith's concept of '"realism" without correspondence'?[23] Surrendering Thesis 2 and 3, however, would be moving away from what seems to be implicitly assumed within the Elim tradition. Of course, having these tacit realist assumptions does not necessarily mean that one should not significantly revise or even reject them, particularly if there are good theological reasons for doing so. Nonetheless, it seems that theologically rejecting Thesis 2 and 3 would in Elim's case be a premature step. That is, once Elim's Pentecostal theology of special revelation is added into the theological mix of doctrines, with particular emphasis on the revelation of Christ mediated through the Spirit, there seems to be no reason for Elim to abandon Thesis 2 and 3.

Like other Evangelicals and Pentecostals, Elim believes that God has and continues to make Himself known through *general* and *special revelation*. The first refers to God *generally* revealing himself 'in the things that have been made' (Rom. 1.20; cf. Ps. 19.1-6), and the latter, of God *specially* revealing himself through specific actions, interactions and communicative events. These special revealing acts in a biblical framework are fundamentally culminated in the person and ministry of Jesus Christ (Col. 1.15-19; Heb. 1.3). In fact, it is the special revelation found in Christ and illuminated by the Spirit that should be essential in Elim's theory of truth, not least as the movement is Christologically focused on the pneumatically experienced Foursquare Gospel. To try sketch out the repercussion of the pneumatically mediated special revelation in Christ for Thesis 2 and 3, I will briefly interact with Johannine theology as a biblical example of what this might mean for Elim's theory of truth.

In the Gospel John, Christ is presented not only as the one who 'bears witness to the truth' (Jn 18.37), but also as 'the truth' (Jn 14.6).[24] That is, He is portrayed as the perfect revealer of God because He is in fact the divine *Logos* (Jn 1.1) who was and is incarnated in human 'flesh' (Jn 1.14). While being the embodied point of contact between humanity and 'ultimate reality', Christ maintains His

---

22. Yong, *Spirit-Word-Community*, 167–8, 185.

23. Smith, *Who's Afraid of Relativism?*, 101.

24. See Andrew T. Lincoln, *Truth on Trial: The Lawsuit Motif in the Fourth Gospel* (Peabody, MA: Hendrickson, 2000).

full humanity with all its corollary limitations (Jn 4.6, 19.28) but simultaneously remains one with God (Jn 10:30). Consequently, ultimate reality is brought to the epistemic domain of humanity as to 'perceive' Jesus is to perceive God (Jn 14.9). This means that the revelation of God in Christ enables one to experience 'ultimate reality' by experiencing the person of Christ, despite the experiencer's limitations resulting from their (fallen) human nature. Therefore, it is not hard to argue theologically that the revelation of God in Christ enables one to form, in a manageable way, beliefs about God which correspond sufficiently with His 'ultimate reality' (Thesis 2).

Moreover, according to John, the possibility of coming face-to-face with the revelation of God in Christ is not just available to those who physically encountered Jesus of Nazareth in first-century Palestine, but is a genuine possibility for others through the work of the Holy Spirit. In other words, the 'Paraclete' and 'Spirit of Truth' will 'teach' and 'remind' Christians about the 'truth' that is embodied in Christ (Jn 14.26, 16.12-15); and when it comes to other humans, the Spirit will also bear 'witness' to the 'truth' (Jn 15.26) and 'convict' them in accordance with the truth (Jn 16.7-11). A major vehicle for the Spirit to continue this revelatory work seems to be through the witness of the written Gospel(s) (Jn 20.31). In sum, for John the revelatory ministry of Jesus continues to have efficacy through the agency of the Spirit and thus the possibility of forming appropriately corresponding beliefs about God remains a theological possibility even after the ascension of Christ.

Interestingly in the Gospel of John, those who encounter Christ are expected to be able not only to form sufficiently accurate beliefs about Him and God (Thesis 2) but also to articulate true or false statements about God through human language (Thesis 3). For example, in the Gospel there are those who are depicted as making 'true' statements about God; that is, statements that correspond with the reality of God revealed in Christ. This includes figures such as John the Baptist (Jn 1.29, 34), the blind man who was healed (Jn 9.38), Thomas (Jn 20.28) and most importantly for the Gospel the 'beloved disciple' (Jn 21.24). However, there are also those who are depicted as making false claims that do not correspond with the reality revealed by Christ, most notably 'the Jews' (Jn 8.48) and the Pharisees (Jn 9.24). Thus, the Johannine record seems to suggest that statements about God can be either true or false, indicating that a biblically informed Pentecostal theology can comfortably embrace the principle of bivalence regarding theological truth (Thesis 3).

Now without a doubt the revelatory role of Christ and the Spirit from a Pentecostal and Elim perspective merits further discussion and development. Nevertheless, the rudimentary sketch provided based primarily on Johannine theology is at least suggestive for why Elim – a movement which boasts of being biblically, as well as Christologically and pneumatologically, focused – has theological grounds for maintaining its theological realism not just regarding Thesis 1 but also regarding Thesis 2 and 3. To put it differently, the doctrine of special revelation with particular emphasis on Christ and the Spirit seems to counter the elements of anti-realism potentially inherent within (fallen) humanity. In fact, such is the 'truthfulness' of the revelation in Christ mediated by the Spirit for humans to embrace, that for John those who encounter 'the truth' in Christ but fail to form sufficiently corresponding beliefs stand judged before 'ultimate truth' (Jn 3.17-21; 9.39-41; 12.48-49).

7.4 (Under-)realized realism

So far the discussion on Elim's concept of truth has focused on *Pentecostal theological realism* with a proposal that theological true beliefs should be understood as beliefs that appropriately correspond with the reality of God. Such theological realism has been argued for in light of Pentecostal doctrines of God, creation, *imago dei*, sin and revelation of God in Christ as illuminated by the Spirit. However, Pentecostal realism thus conceived lacks a crucial element within Pentecostal theology, namely, eschatology. Indeed, Pentecostal eschatology is necessary to 'complete' the concept of *Pentecostal theological realism*.

As has been suggested, the notion of God as 'ultimate reality' is based to a great extent on the idea of God as the *creator* and *ground of being*. However, despite God grounding the existence of His creation, eschatologically speaking the 'ultimate reality' of God has not yet been fully 'realized' on earth. As Paul puts it, in the end God will be 'all in all' (1 Cor. 15.28), suggesting that currently creation is not experiencing the fullness of God. A similar idea is depicted in the Book of Revelation where the final consummation of the created order is characterized by God saturating the (new) world with his presence and reality (Rev. 21.1-8), which again implies that as things stand the 'reality' of God is under-realized. Indeed, Paul seems to draw a direct epistemological conclusion regarding one's limited access to truth in the current dispensation when compared to the age to come. In his words: 'For now we see in a mirror dimly, but then face to face. Now I know in part; then I shall know fully' (1 Cor. 13.12; cf. Isa. 11.9).

This kind of eschatological vision has two important repercussions for an Elim concept of truth and realism. First, as already implied, the fact that God is not yet 'all in all' within His creation means that in the current dispensation any human access to God as 'ultimate reality' is in fact incomplete, which suggests that eschatologically sensitive Pentecostal realism should be *mitigated realism*. To put it more strongly, the realist Thesis 2 and 3 are weakened not only by the limits of human (fallen) nature but also by the not yet fully realized reality of God in the present age.[25]

Second, as well as God being the *creator* and *ground of being*, according to NT eschatology, He also seems to be the *completer* and *goal of being*. For a Pentecostal realist concept of truth this means that one should focus on not only 'what is' but also what 'will be'. In other words, truth can be seen to be the *telos* of enquiry in a double sense: (1) it is the *goal* of enquiry in terms directing one towards the full

---

25. Indeed, according to the biblical eschatological vision there seems to be a direct correlation between 'sin' and 'under-realized presence of God', as well as 'absence of sin' and 'fully realized presence of God' (see Isa. 59.1-2; 1 Jn 3.2; Rev. 21.1-8).

realization of ultimate reality in creation and (2) it is the *end* of enquiry at the moment of this full realization. In sum, 'truth' is eschatological.[26]

7.5 Conclusion

In this short chapter I have tried to sketch an Elim concept of truth that stems from the implicit assumptions within the Elim tradition, as well as being explicitly informed by biblical and Pentecostal theology regarding God, creation, *imago dei*, sin, revelation and eschatology. In doing so, it seems that despite the various theological obstacles for a realist theory of truth, there are adequate reasons for Elim to continue with its assumed theory of truth as *Pentecostal realism* consisting of the three realist theses. However, in light of the epistemological limitations caused by human (fallen) nature and eschatology, Elim's theological realism should be strongly characterized by fallibilism regarding its beliefs (Thesis 2) and propositions (Thesis 3). Moreover, when it comes to the correspondent aspect of its theory of truth (Thesis 2), correspondence should be seen as 'correlation' rather than 'congruence' (see Amos Yong). Finally, 'truth' should be seen not just as that which corresponds with reality but also as the *telos* of enquiry.

This 'Elim' theory of truth has important similarities with the theory of truth offered by Alasdair MacIntyre (see Section 2.2.1). That is, MacIntyre's theory of truth has two major characteristics: (1) It adopts a Thomistic correspondence theory of truth as *adaequatio intellectus ad rem*, which means that MacIntyre holds to a version of correspondence but rejects any theories of 'truth as correspondence-to-fact';[27] (2) For MacIntyre truth is 'the *telos* of rational enquiry'.[28] This similarity is noteworthy as it suggests that utilizing a MacIntyrian methodology for constructing the Elim tradition and rationality (Chapters 3–6) is not forcing Elim into an alien framework, at least when it comes to the concept of truth.

Elim's *Pentecostal theological realism* outlined in this section also serves as the ontological backdrop for understanding the *biblicist* and *pragmatist* elements of Elim's rationality. Indeed, I will now focus on each of these elements in the following two chapters of the book.

---

26. See Hick, *Dialogues in the Philosophy of Religion*, 5; Yong, 'The Demise of Foundationalism', 580; Oliverio Jr., *Theological Hermeneutics in the Classical Pentecostal Tradition*, 342.

27. MacIntyre, 'Truth as a Good: A Reflection on *Fides et Ratio*', 200, 203.

28. MacIntyre, 'Moral Relativism', 68–9.

Chapter 8

BIBLICAL HERMENEUTICS: COMMUNITY DISCERNMENT OF MEANING IN A DIALECTICAL BIBLE

From its inception Elim has seen the Bible as the grounding document for its beliefs and practices. As discussed in Chapter 4, the Bible's primacy as a theological source of knowledge for Elim is based on the concept that God is the foundation of all truth (see also Chapter 7), and He has revealed the truth about Himself and the world in the Bible by inspiring its very words. Since the (Protestant) Bible as a whole is considered to be verbally inspired by God, and since God is believed to be perfect, it naturally follows for Elim that the Bible is seen as an infallible document. Indeed, the centrality of the Bible has been underscored when Elim navigated through its two epistemological crises (Chapters 5 and 6), as during both of these crises Elim was adamant about the need to recalibrate its tradition in light of the Scriptures. Therefore, it is no surprise that Elim's latest Foundational Truths affirm the Bible's authority, inspiration, infallibility and inerrancy. The current statement reads: 'We believe the Bible, as originally given, to be without error, the fully inspired and infallible Word of God and the supreme and final authority in all matters of faith and conduct.'[1]

So, why does Elim believe that the Bible is 'the fully inspired and infallible Word of God' and thus the supreme epistemic authority regarding Christian beliefs and practices? In Chapter 4, I noted that the primary reasons offered by Elim have been pragmatic. In other words, Elim has historically offered *arguments from transformed lives*, emphasizing the ability of the Bible to produce 'results' in the lives of individuals and communities, and *arguments from the uniqueness of the Bible*, highlighting (among other things) the uniqueness and force of the Bible's divine message.[2] These two pragmatic arguments have then supposedly given

---

1. Minutes of the 'Elim Pentecostal Church: Annual Conference 1993. Representative Session', Archives of the General Superintendent, EIC, Malvern, Item No. 27. For an official interpretation of the article on the Bible, see Geoff Richardson, 'The Bible', in *The Message*, 11–18.

2. Elim's pragmatic arguments are masterfully demonstrated by the Elim Minister/Evangelist George Canty when he writes: 'If it were possible to know that the Bible is the authentic Word of God, outside of personal experience, it would be no more use than

credence for Elim to accept the *argument from the Bible's own testimony*, which is claimed to support the concept of divine inspiration and infallibility of the whole Bible, not just parts of it (e.g. 2 Tim. 3.16; 2 Pet. 1.21).

I will further explore and develop Elim's pragmatic theory of justification (see Chapter 9). However, before doing so, what surfaced in the narration of Elim's first epistemological crisis (see particularly the BI debate in Chapter 5) was that despite Elim's pragmatic approach to the Bible, the biblical text is believed to have certain interpretive limitations and thus cannot be made to mean anything in Elim, even if such a reading may possess pragmatic potential. In other words, for Elim certain hermeneutical principles need to guide the scope of what the biblical text *can* and *cannot mean*. Elim's 'hermeneutical principles' will therefore be the focus of this chapter since it seems to be meaningless to simply state that Elim's rationality is characterized by biblicism without reflecting on how the Bible *has* and *should be* interpreted within this Pentecostal movement.

8.1 Historical reflections on Elim's Pentecostal hermeneutics

It seems that a community's concept of the Bible, as well as their purpose for reading it, will inevitably influence their hermeneutical approach.[3] For Elim, the Bible has been primarily conceived as the 'Word of God', rather than *just* ancient literature or history, and as such it has been believed to be 'the final authority in all matters of faith and conduct'.[4] This characterization implies that for Elim the Bible is and consists of the very 'words God has spoken to man',[5] and therefore the purpose of engaging with it is to inform 'faith' (read: theology) and to transform 'conduct' (read: practice). So, if this identifies for Elim *what* the Bible is and *why* it should be interacted with, the question then becomes: *How* should it be read?

8.1.1 The 'Bible Reading Method'

Elim's early hermeneutical method can be identified in the words of Kenneth J. Archer as 'the Bible Reading Method' (see Section 4.3.2). Although Archer is

---

knowing Mars is made of red sandstone. Such knowledge will not help us live or go places. ... Let the passage[s] prove itself as inspired'; Canty, *In My Father's House*, 66–7. Interestingly, the more recent articulation on the authority of the Bible by Geoff Richardson does not really identify reasons why one should believe in a divinely inspired Bible; Richardson, 'The Bible', 11–18.

3. See Nicholas Wolterstorff, *Divine Discourse: Philosophical Reflection on the Claim that God Speaks* (Cambridge: Cambridge University Press, 1995), 17; Craig S. Keener, *Spirit Hermeneutics: Reading Scripture in Light of Pentecost* (Grand Rapids, MI: Eerdmans, 2016), 139.

4. Elim Conference Minutes (1993), Item No. 27.

5. G. W. Gilpin, 'The Inspiration of the Bible', in *Pentecostal Doctrine*, ed. P. S. Brewster (No city: P. S. Brewster, 1976), 127–36.

referring to the early classical Pentecostal hermeneutics in the United States, his description, nevertheless, accurately reflects Elim's early hermeneutics:

> The 'Bible Reading Method' was a modified form of the proof-text system. It involved looking up a specific word in an English Bible concordance, compiling an exhaustive list of its occurrences, and deducing a biblical truth based on the reading of the texts … the focal point and primary concern of the Bible Reading Method was to synthesize concerning the data into a doctrinal statement and thereby produce a biblical understanding concerning the topic or theme under investigation. … The Pentecostal reading scheme was thoroughly popularistic, thus a 'pre-critical', canonical and text centered synchronic approach from a revivalistic-restorational biblicist perspective.[6]

As pointed out by French Arrington this hermeneutical approach was to a great extent based on the assumption of divine 'inspiration as dictation'.[7] To put it differently, it was believed that since the words of the Bible were directly dictated by God, the Bible could effectively be viewed as one book (not sixty-six books) and therefore could also be interpreted at face value without focusing on the socio-historical contexts of its various writings. For example, Elim's J. Robinson surmised that 'by *verbal inspiration* we mean that not only was the general sense of the message inspired, but that the writers were actually guided as to their various modes of expression and choice of words'.[8]

The concept of direct dictation, however, is no longer maintained within Elim, or in most other classical Pentecostal traditions. In Elim's latest official explanatory document regarding the doctrine of the Bible, Geoff Richardson explicitly writes that 'we do not believe that God *dictated* the words of the Bible to those who wrote it, since that would deny the writers any significant role in the process'.[9]

---

6. Archer, *A Pentecostal Hermeneutic*, 74–5. However, it should also be pointed out that the goal of Pentecostal/Elim biblical interpretation was not merely doctrinal data but also personal transformation. Indeed, the devotional reading was arguably the most common approach to reading the Bible within early Pentecostalism and Elim. For helpful analysis of early Pentecostal hermeneutics, see Veli-Matti Kärkkäinen, 'Pentecostal Hermeneutics in the Making: On the Way from Fundamentalism to Postmodernism', *JEPTA* 18, no. 1 (1998): 77–80.

7. French Arrington, 'Hermeneutics: Historical Perspectives on Pentecostal and Charismatic', in *Dictionary of Pentecostal and Charismatic Movements*, ed. M. Burgess and G. B. McGee (Grand Rapids, MI: Zondervan, 1988), 380.

8. Robinson, 'Why I Believe in Verbal Inspiration', 413. Similar view is expressed by F. E. Marsh, 'The Holy Spirit and the Bible', *EE* 13, no. 45 (4 November 1932): 705. More room is given to the authors' distinct styles by Parker, 'To What Extent *is the* Bible Inspired?', 27; Bradley et al., *Elim Lay Preachers' Handbook*, 6.

9. Richardson, 'The Bible', 11; cf. Gilpin, 'The Inspiration of the Bible', 130; Warrington, *Pentecostal Theology*, 182.

8.1.2 'Evangelical-Pentecostal Hermeneutic'

The change from direct dictation to increasingly acknowledging the role of the human authors in the writing process has also resulted in Elim changing its hermeneutical approach. Like other classical Pentecostal denominations, Elim has moved towards what L. William Oliverio Jr. calls the 'Evangelical-Pentecostal Hermeneutic'.[10] This method of interpretation is primarily historical-grammatical with a focus on both the internal and external contexts of the text. In this approach the human author's intent is commonly identified as fundamental in discerning the meaning of the text. Gordon Fee has been an influential champion of this interpretive method among Pentecostals.[11] For example, Fee's jointly authored book with Douglas Stuart, *How to Read the Bible for All Its Worth*, has been the main textbook on hermeneutics within Elim's national training centre (Regents Theological College) in the twenty-first century.[12]

In *How to Read the Bible for All Its Worth*, Fee and Stuart make a distinction between what the text meant in its original context (*then and there*) and what it means in the reader's context (*here and now*). They call the first task 'exegesis' and the second task 'hermeneutics'.[13] This distinction is more or less identical with E. D. Hirsch's concepts of 'meaning' and 'significance'.[14] For Fee and Stuart an appropriate interpretation of a text must always start with 'exegesis' (Hirsch's 'meaning') which explores the 'historical context', 'literary context' and 'questions of content' regarding 'the meaning of words, the grammatical relationships in sentences, and the choice of the original text where the manuscripts ... differ from one another'.[15] The second task of 'hermeneutics' (Hirsch's 'significance') apparently can then only arise from the '*original intent of the biblical text*'.[16] Fee and Stuart go as far as to argue that a '*text cannot mean what it never meant*', and the role of the Spirit seems to be to simply help the reader to discern first this 'original intent' and to then secondly apply it to their own situation.[17]

---

10. Oliverio Jr, *Theological Hermeneutics in the Classical Pentecostal Tradition*, 16; cf. Kärkkäinen, 'Pentecostal Hermeneutics in the Making', 80–3; Archer, *A Pentecostal Hermeneutic*, 131–7.

11. See Gordon D. Fee, *Listening to the Spirit in the Text* (Grand Rapids, MI: Eerdmans, 2000), 7–8.

12. See Gordon D. Fee and Douglas Stuart, *How to Read the Bible for All It's Worth*, 3rd edn (Grand Rapids, MI: Zondervan, 2003).

13. Ibid., 23.

14. E. D. Hirsch Jr., *Validity in Interpretation* (New Haven, CT: Yale University Press, 1967).

15. Fee and Stuart, *How to Read*, 26–8.

16. Ibid., 29.

17. Ibid., 30.

Although Fee and Stuart helpfully acknowledge that the Bible is simultaneously a human and divine text,[18] in practice their hermeneutics seems to have shifted the focus from the divine author to the human author. So, if the early Pentecostal hermeneutic underplayed the role of the human author in interpretation, Fee's 'Evangelical-Pentecostal hermeneutic' appears to underplay the role of the divine author in the interpretive process. In other words, by assuming that the biblical text can only mean what the human author meant when they wrote it to their first audience, the text's possible domain of meaning(s) is limited to the intentions of the human author. This kind of *hermeneutical humanism* seems to have two inherent problems for the Elim tradition.

First, it does not accurately reflect Elim's theology of the Bible being an inspired 'living and acting' Word of God (Heb. 4.12). That is, the excessive emphasis on the human author at the expense of its divine author is in danger of effectively demythologizing the text. To put it simply, the Bible within Elim is maintained as 'the fully inspired' and 'the supreme and final authority in all matters of faith and conduct', which strongly suggests that the Bible should probably be seen as ontologically different from other writings, and thus the hermeneutical method utilized for interpreting it should reflect this ontological difference. However, Fee's and Stuart's claim that '*a text cannot mean what it never could have meant to its* [human] *author or his or her readers*' [emphasis in original] does not seem to fully appreciate the divine nature of the Bible.[19]

Secondly, the 'Evangelical-Pentecostal hermeneutic' is at odds with the hermeneutical approach of the NT writers. To give just one example, Fee and Stuart note that in 1 Cor. 10.4 the Apostle Paul interprets Exod. 17.1-7 and Num. 20.1-13 in a way that could have not been meant by its human author(s) or first readers when Paul identifies the 'rock' as Christ.[20] However, rather than acknowledging that under certain circumstances such a *sensus plenior* (fuller meaning) interpretive approach could be acceptable for contemporary readers due to the text's divine nature, Fee and Stuart write that Paul was unique in his ability to interpret the text in this way because he was 'inspired' by the Spirit, but 'what Paul did we are not authorized to do'.[21] In other words, for Fee and Stuart the *sensus plenior* 'is a function of inspiration, not illumination'.[22] Although one can see the practical wisdom of deterring Christians, and particularly Pentecostals, from overly subjective readings

---

18. Ibid., 21.

19. Ibid., 74. Fee's hermeneutics also underplays the dynamism of a Pentecostal reading of the text where it is assumed that the Spirit who inspired the text is also present illuminating the text to the Pentecostal believer in the reading process. Consequently, in light of Pentecostal spirituality it is difficult maintain this clinical and chronological distinction between 'exegesis' and 'hermeneutics'; see Archer, *A Pentecostal Hermeneutic*, 142.

20. Fee and Stuart, *How to Read*, 202.

21. Ibid.

22. Ibid., 202–3.

of the text, it seems surprising that the divine author's ability to communicate to the contemporary believer through the text in a manner apparently communicated to Paul is seen as a hermeneutical impossibility. For a Pentecostal movement like Elim that seeks to restore the fullness of NT Christianity, this kind of *hermeneutical cessationism* appears unwarranted. This also seems to contradict Elim's Foundational Truth of allowing the Bible to be the authority 'in matters of faith and conduct'; that is, why should the example of the Apostles and the Early Church as recorded in Scripture not function as a guide for 'conducting' Pentecostal hermeneutics?[23] Indeed, Craig Keener has recently argued that Scripture itself should be allowed to model hermeneutical approaches for Pentecostals.[24]

8.2 A proposal for Elim's Pentecostal hermeneutics

In light of this seeming *hermeneutical humanism* and *hermeneutical cessationism* of the 'Evangelical-Pentecostal hermeneutic', a different hermeneutical approach needs to be articulated that is more attuned with both (1) the hermeneutics of the New Testament and (2) the concept of the Bible reflecting both its human and divine authors. To this end, I will first propose that John Christopher Thomas's hermeneutical method based on Acts 15 is a useful overarching biblical hermeneutical model for Elim to utilize. Secondly, I will suggest how a biblical text as 'divine discourse' through 'human discourse' can 'mean' more than its human author meant without either violating the human author or assuming that the text can mean anything.

8.2.1 Experiential- and community-based hermeneutic

John Christopher Thomas's 1994 article 'Women, Pentecostals and the Bible: An Experiment in Pentecostal Hermeneutics', in the words of Jacqueline Grey, 'has been one of the most influential writings on Pentecostal Hermeneutics'.[25] In his

---

23. Fee and Stuart would probably respond by noting that the Scripture does not explicitly encourage Christians to adopt this hermeneutical approach; ibid., 202. See also Fee's distinction between what is 'normal' and 'normative'.

24. Keener, *Spirit Hermeneutics*, 1.

25. John Christopher Thomas, 'Women, Pentecostals and the Bible: An Experiment in Pentecostal Hermeneutics', *JPT* 2, no. 5 (1994): 41–56; Jacqueline Grey, 'When the Spirit Trumps Tradition: A Pentecostal Reading of Isaiah 56:1-8', in *Constructive Pneumatological Hermeneutics in Pentecostal Christianity*, ed. Kenneth J. Archer and L. William Oliverio Jr (New York, NY: Palgrave MacMillan, 2016), 143; For Thomas's more recent hermeneutical articulation, see John Christopher Thomas, '"What is the Spirit Saying to the Church" – The Testimony of a Pentecostal in New Testament Studies', in *Spirit and Scripture: Exploring a Pneumatic Hermeneutic*, ed. Kevin L. Spawn and Archie T. Wright (London: Bloomsbury, 2013), 115–29.

article Thomas explores the possibility of utilizing the Jerusalem Council of Acts 15.1-29 as a hermeneutical paradigm for Pentecostals.

To give some textual context for Thomas's hermeneutical ruminations, in Acts 15 the council of 'apostles and elders' gathers to consider whether the newly converted Gentiles need to be circumcised (i.e. become Jews) to be part of the Christian Church (Acts 15.1-6). After serious discussion, the council decides that the Gentiles who have converted to Christianity need not become Jews but must abstain from food associated with 'idol worship' and refrain from any acts of 'sexual immorality' (Acts 15.29). The decision was a watershed moment in the history of the early church as recorded in Acts, because it meant that Gentile Christians were now officially accepted into the household of God without having to embrace Judaism (cf. Acts 10).[26]

In reflecting on the council's deliberations, Thomas draws three hermeneutical conclusions. First, he emphasizes the role of the *'community'* (in this case the council of apostles and elders) in making sense of both the church's experience (e.g. conversion and Spirit baptism of the Gentiles) and the interpretation of Scripture (e.g. Amos 9.11, 12). Second, the *'experience'* of the Spirit is seen as an important precursor in how Scriptures are interpreted; that is, Peter refers to his experience of seeing the Gentiles receive the Holy Spirit (Acts 15.7-11), and Barnabas and Paul describe the 'signs and wonders God had done through them among the Gentiles' (Acts 15.12). Third, the *Scriptures* are referred to as confirming the community's interpreted experience of the Spirit (Acts 15.15-19).[27] In sum, Thomas argues that for discerning the voice of God one needs to have an interpretive *community* that reflects both on pneumatic *experiences* and *scriptural* witness.

The strength of using Acts 15 as a paradigm for Elim's biblical hermeneutics is not just that it provides a biblical model for hermeneutics, and thus allows the Bible itself to be an epistemic authority in how it should be interpreted, but that it also reflects closely Elim's own *rationality* and *historical practice*. Regarding Elim's *rationality*, the Acts 15 methodology acknowledges the role of the 'community (read: living tradition), 'experience' (read: pragmatism) and 'Scriptures' (read: the Bible). So, it corresponds closely with Elim's rationality of Pentecostal Biblical Pragmatism. In terms of Elim's *historical practice*, the Acts 15 hermeneutical model resembles Elim's approach in resolving both of its epistemological crises. When it came to the first crisis, the Elim Conference consisting of ministers (elders) and members of executive council (apostles?) was central in rejecting BI, as well as helping Elim to come to terms with the experience of Jeffreys' leaving (see Chapter 5). Moreover, both the British Israel controversy and the explanation for

---

26. F. F. Bruce refers to Acts 15.1-29 as 'epoch-making'; F. F. Bruce, *The Book of Acts* (Grand Rapids, MI: Eerdmans, 1975), 298; cf. Joseph A. Fitzmyer, *The Acts of the Apostles*. The Anchor Bible. Vol. 31 (New York, NY: Doubleday, 1998), 543–5; Darrell L. Bock, *Acts*. Baker Exegetical Commentary on the New Testament (Grand Rapids, MI: Baker Academic, 2007), 507–8.

27. Thomas, 'Women, Pentecostals and the Bible', 54–6.

Jeffreys' departure were interpreted in the light of Scripture. During Elim's second epistemological crisis, the conference again played a crucial role, particularly at the Southport Conference of 1981, in recalibrating the Elim tradition vis-à-vis its experience of the Restoration movement and by reflecting on Scripture.

In fact, although there are obviously also differences between the Jerusalem Council of Acts 15 and the Elim Conferences during the two epistemological crises,[28] the similarities regarding the epistemic practice of discernment are striking. Therefore, my first proposal for Elim's future hermeneutics in an attempt to move *beyond* (note: not *against*) 'Evangelical-Pentecostal hermeneutic' is for Elim to increasingly embrace the model represented in Acts 15, as it provides a biblical precedence for its hermeneutics and also naturally fits with Elim's rationality and historical practice.

8.2.2 Discerning divine meaning(s) in 'dialectical relations'

However, adopting the Acts 15 hermeneutical model with particular focus on community, pneumatic experience and the Bible has still not explicitly answered the question what the biblical texts *can* and *cannot* 'mean'. Thus, I will now offer brief hermeneutical discussion on how Elim should construct 'meaning' from the Bible which is simultaneously divine and human word(s). I will suggest that *pace* Fee and Stuart the text can mean more than its human author meant, but this need not result in undermining the text's 'humanity' or in allowing the text to simply mean anything. However, this can only be done by appreciating the text's dialectical relation(s) stemming from its divinity and humanity.

8.2.2.1 The text's 'dialectical relation(s)' Merold Westphal points out that the notion of the Bible being simultaneously divine and human creates a 'dialectical relation' not dissimilar to the Christological concept of Christ's two natures.[29] Westphal notes that

> the Docetists and Ebionites fell into heresy by trying to ease the tension by emphasizing one pole to the effective elimination of the other. We have a similar dialectic in Scripture itself. It is both human and divine, and the church has often pendulumed between affirming the divine at the expense of the human and then the human at the expense of the divine.[30]

Indeed, the pendulum swing identified by Westphal is perceivable in Elim's historical approach to Scripture; that is, Elim initially emphasized the divine at the expense

---

28. For example, the Jerusalem Council seemed to represent the universal church of its day and was dealing with a major shift in salvation history with the inclusion of Gentiles.

29. Merold Westphal, 'Spirit and Prejudice: The Dialectic of Interpretation', in *Constructive Pneumatological Hermeneutics in Pentecostal Christianity*, 17.

30. Ibid.

of the human, and then seems to have emphasized the human at the expense of the divine. If the Christological comparison has any merit for understanding the nature of Scripture – and I think it does due to Christ being identified as *the* 'Word of God' and the pinnacle of divine revelation (Jn 1.1; 14.9; Heb. 1.3)[31] – it would seem that a sufficient concept of Scripture should also adopt a Chalcedonian-type definition which tries to navigate between Nestorianism which divides the two natures of Christ within one person and Monophysitism which emphasizes the two natures being indivisible within one person.[32] However, in walking this tightrope between Nestorianism and Monophysitism, Elim's concept of Scripture being 'the inspired word of God' seems to naturally lean more towards Cyril of Alexandria's Monophysitism with the human and divine natures being indivisible within the text; rather than the divine aspect being somehow layered on top of the human element after the text has been written,[33] or the human authors simply functioning as mechanical typewriters in divine hands. In fact, it could even be suggested that Elim's historical overemphasis on *either* the human *or* divine aspects of Scripture has resembled the Nestorian 'heresy'.

This kind of indivisible relationship between the human and the divine in Scripture also has implications for how the text should be interpreted and what it 'can(not) mean'. In other words, if one is to truly appreciate the dialectical relation in the text it is meaningless to talk about what the text 'means' without focusing on both aspects. This also means that a strong dichotomy between the human element (e.g. what it meant for the human author) and divine element (e.g. what it means for the divine author) in the interpretive process should be guarded against. I appreciate that this is easier said than done. Nevertheless, I will propose two *interpretive dialectical relations* that might provide some guidance for Elim's Pentecostal hermeneutics à la Chalcedon.

---

31. The *Elim Lay Preachers' Handbook* also makes the comparison between the incarnation and the inspiration of Scripture; Bradley et al., *Elim Lay Preachers' Handbook*, 6.

32. The 451 Chalcedonian definition reads that Christ is 'to be acknowledged in two natures, inconfusedly, unchangeably, indivisibly, inseparably; the distinction of natures being by no means taken away by the union, but rather the property of each nature being preserved, and concurring in *one Person* and one Subsistence, not parted or divided into two persons'; quoted in Wayne Grudem, *Bible Doctrine: Essential Teachings of the Christian Faith* (Leicester: IVP, 1999), 244. For a historical analysis of Chalcedon see Diarmaid MacCulloch, *A History of Christianity* (London: Penguin Books, 2010), 222–8.

33. In light of the incarnation analogy it appears that Nicholas Wolterstorff's theory of Scripture being the Word of God through 'appropriation' seems to imply a more of a Nestorian approach, namely the human and divine nature of Scripture are distinct to the point of (almost) possessing two separate 'natures' (i.e. human and divine). In fact, the idea of 'appropriation' could even be seen as a version of Adoptionism where the human text is adopted to become the divine text. This not only has implications for how Wolterstorff perceives Scripture as the Word of God, but also how he interprets it as such; see Wolterstorff, *Divine Discourse*, 222.

8.2.2.2 Historical and dynamic sense The first dialectical relation is between the text's *historical sense* and the *dynamic sense*.[34] Craig Keener states that 'the incarnation would show us that history and historical particularity matter'.[35] In other words, if the incarnation is anything to go by then *historical sense* of the biblical text would appear to be central for appropriately understanding it. Keener identifies three basic interpretive principles for doing due diligence to the text's historicity:

- 'Read a passage in light of its immediate context';
- 'Read a passage for its function as part of the larger book to which it belongs';
- 'Read a passage in light of the cultural context that its language, assumptions and often allusions take for granted.'[36]

It seems that in taking the 'human nature' of the text seriously, these are reasonable steps to *begin* discerning the 'meaning' of the text. However, while having one ear tuned to the *historical sense* that is grounded in the text's humanity, the other ear should be concurrently tuned to the *dynamic sense* grounded in the text's divinity. That is, as well as appreciating the human historical discourse present in the text, the Pentecostal hermeneut should simultaneously appreciate the divine discourse directed at the present reader. To put it in Pentecostal parlance: what is the Spirit saying to the present reader through the text which is written by the human author? This implies that the reader should not just have a historical appreciation of the text, but a prayerful and pneumatically oriented disposition towards it.

I acknowledge that the similarities between my so-called *historical sense* and *dynamic sense* are similar to Fee's and Stuart's concepts of 'exegesis' and 'hermeneutics'. However, I also believe that there are two important differences. First, my concept of *historical sense* places *greater* emphasis on the need for the hermeneut to approach the historical sense of the text, as well as the dynamic sense, in a 'spiritually' sensitive way.[37] The reason being, that if the text is truly divine and human then it would appear that one cannot fully appreciate even its historical meaning without some revelatory insight and/or reliance on divine illumination. This is a potentially controversial claim, because it implies that the 'natural' person cannot have the same insight of the biblical historical text as the 'spiritual' person. However, if the Bible is genuinely believed to be divine revelation, then Paul's argument that divine revelation can only truly be comprehended by those to whom the Spirit reveals it and who approach the text with spiritual sensitivity

---

34. My notion of 'historical sense' is very similar to Craig Keener's 'designed sense' which he defines as 'the sense projected by the ideal author or at least the ancient cultural sense'; Keener, *Spirit Hermeneutics*, 99.

35. Ibid.

36. Ibid., 117.

37. Although in fairness to Fee and Stuart this is not completely absent from their concept of 'exegesis'.

should probably also apply to the Bible (1 Cor. 2.1-16).[38] Thus, if Elim allows the biblical concept of revelation to inform its view about the Bible as divine revelation then this view should not be considered unreasonable.[39]

The second difference is that I claim that the *dynamic sense* of the text can mean to the reader what the human authors did not intend it to mean. With respect to seeing the biblical text as divine discourse, Wolterstorff helpfully identifies the difference between what *was* God saying historically to the Scripture's first audience, and 'what *is* God saying to us today by way of confronting us with this passage of Scripture?'[40] Wolterstorff expands this idea by pointing out that in fact 'a single illocutionary act may have more than one addressee' and 'one may address one's remark to a number of people'.[41] Furthermore, he maintains that this one remark can mean different things to different people. The example used by Wolterstorff is of a mother remarking at dinner that there are only two days to Christmas. For the children this might mean that 'don't lose hope' as Christmas is now just 'around the corner', whereas for the husband it might mean 'hurry up' and 'get the Christmas shopping done'.[42] Westphal further clarifies Wolterstorff's example by distinguishing between the mother knowing that the father 'will overhear the conversation from the one in which he does so without her knowing'.[43] In the first instance 'she intends both speech acts', whereas in the second she only intends 'the speech act of comfort to the children'.[44] Westphal surmises that when it comes to Scripture, God can be seen to be in the first position of knowing the multiple audiences who will hear the 'speech act' communicated through the text, whereas the human author is in the second position of not knowing the multiple audiences hearing the 'speech act'.[45] Therefore, it appears that the *dynamic sense* of the text can 'mean' to the readers what was never intended by the human author (*pace* Fee and Stuart), although not what was unintended by the divine author and articulated by the human author.

In sum, the first dialectical relation suggests that the 'meaning' of the text is grounded in its human *historical sense*. However, this historical sense can only be truly understood not just through historical interpretive methods but through

---

38. See Frestadius, 'The Spirit and Wisdom in 1 Corinthians 2:1-13', 52–70.

39. Indeed, Elim's P. S. Brewster wrote: 'In so many ways the Bible is a closed book and cannot be fully understood through human or by the carnal mind. ... The only key to attainment in knowledge of the Scripture is the power of the Holy Spirt; it is certainly not through general academic training, important as this can be. The student who is not in right relationship with God and man cannot hope to make progress in the study of the Word of God'; P. S. Brewster, 'The Seven-Fold Work of the Holy Spirit', in *Pentecostal Doctrine*, 10.

40. Wolterstorff, *Divine Discourse*, 216.

41. Ibid., 55.

42. Ibid.

43. Westphal, 'Spirit and Prejudice', 26.

44. Ibid.

45. Ibid.

spiritual discernment. Moreover, it only becomes 'meaningful' when the reader or community of readers also 'hear' the divine *dynamic sense* in the text. To put it simply, the historical sense without the dynamic sense is *senseless*, and the dynamic sense without the historical sense is *non-sense*.

8.2.2.3 Canonical plurality and unity If the first dialectical relation focused more on the human and divine 'sense' or 'meaning' of individual biblical texts, the second dialectical tension emanates from the human and divine natures intermingling in the biblical canon. Elim, like most Pentecostal movements, believe that the (Protestant) canon with its sixty-six books in its entirety is the Word of God. As seen in Elim's early hermeneutic this is why the Bible was generally read as one book without necessarily distinguishing between the different human authors or their contexts, because the Bible was fundamentally seen to have been written by one author, namely, God. However, as Elim's hermeneutical approach developed, the humanity and diversity of the canon was increasingly acknowledged. Indeed, the second dialectical relation that should inform Elim's hermeneutics should appreciate this tension of *canonical unity* that emanates from the Bible's divine author and its *canonical plurality* which is founded in its humanity.

This suggests that Elim should read the Bible both as one book with a unified message and as many books with particular messages. To explain this tension, Robert Wall and John Christopher Thomas have both helpfully conceptualized the canon through the metaphor of a (gospel) 'choir'.[46] In other words, the biblical canon can be viewed as a choir of many human members who sing a song in harmony under the inspiration and direction of its divine conductor. This, however, does not mean that all members of the choir are singing the same notes, at the same time, or even the same songs.[47] Nevertheless, they are all in the same choir and performing within the same set of songs, all of which have been arranged by the divine conductor. So, the 'canon' as a human 'choir' under the divine conductor explains both the 'plurality' and 'unity' found in the Bible.

The canonical plurality and unity has two important implications. First, it provides grounds for distinct theological emphases within different Christian theological traditions and denominations.[48] Secondly, and more importantly for hermeneutics, it provides certain freedom for the Spirit-led community to discern

---

46. Robert W. Wall, 'Reading New Testament in Canonical Context', in *Hearing the New Testament: Strategies for Interpretation*, ed. Joel B. Green (Grand Rapids, MI: Eerdmans, 1995), 381; Thomas, 'What is the Spirit Saying to the Church', 128.

47. Richard Swinburne refers to the Bible as 'a symphony written and conducted by a genius, but played by an orchestra of wilful amateurs'; Richard Swinburne, *Revelation: From Metaphor to Analogy*, 2nd edn (Oxford: Oxford University Press, 2007), 278.

48. Ernst Käsemann noted that the NT canon did not 'ground the unity of the church' but 'the diversity of denominations'; Thomas Söding, *Eisenheit der Heiligen Schrift? Zur Theologie des biblischen Kanons* (Freiburg: Herder, 2005), 69. I am indebted to Martin Clay for directing me to this source.

which biblical text might be of particular importance in a given context. For example, Jacqueline Grey makes the valid point that the Jerusalem Council of Acts 15 chose Amos 9.11-12 but they could have easily chosen another Old Testament text that would have provided a different perspective on what should be demanded of the Gentile Christians.[49]

This does raise the question of 'discernment'; that is, how does one discern which texts should or should not be applied to a particular context? In line with the Acts 15 model, the discernment process should be done by a believing and Spirit-filled community (or council of elders and apostles), as well as in the light of pneumatic experiences of the Spirit. Furthermore, with respect to Elim's rationality of biblical *pragmatism*, discerning the specific divine voice in the canon should be influenced not only by 'experientialism' but also by 'experimentalism'. It is the living, moving, acting and experimenting Pentecostal community 'in dialogue with the bi-partite biblical canon' that truly allows the Word of God to shape its faith and conduct.[50]

8.3 Conclusion

In this chapter I have explored the biblicist aspect of Elim's rationality. Throughout its existence Elim has insisted that its beliefs need to be grounded on the Bible because the Bible is believed to be the 'word of God' and so the authority in matters of faith and conduct. This assumption is logically consistent with Elim's concept of *Pentecostal theological realism* where God is seen as ultimate truth (read: reality) and as the agent who has communicated and continues to communicate the truth about Himself and the world through the human authors in the biblical text.

However, to talk about the Bible's authority within Elim cannot be done apart from discussing biblical hermeneutics. Consequently, I have outlined Elim's historical approach to biblical hermeneutics by suggesting that while the early hermeneutic was characterized by a simplistic 'Bible Reading Method' (see Archer) that emphasized the divine author often at the expense of the human author, the latter 'Evangelical-Pentecostal Hermeneutic' (see Oliverio) has been in danger of focusing on the human author at the expense of the divine author.

In light of these one-dimensional approaches, my suggestion for Elim's future biblical hermeneutics has been twofold. First, I have proposed that Elim should explicitly adopt the Acts 15 model that allows the Elim community informed by its pneumatic experience to discern the meaning of the biblical text(s) for its faith and

---

49. Grey, 'When the Spirit Trumps Tradition', 152.

50. Martin Clay, 'From "Unity" to "Dialogue" in the *Theology of the New Testament*: A Methodological and Hermeneutical Proposal' (PhD diss., University of Bangor, 2012), 329. Clark Pinnock identifies 'fruitfulness' as an important criterion for a Pentecostal/charismatic biblical interpretation; Clark H. Pinnock, 'The Work of the Spirit in the Interpretation of Holy Scripture from the Perspective of a Charismatic Biblical Theologian', in *Pentecostal Hermeneutics: A Reader*, ed. Lee Roy Martin (Leiden: Brill, 2013), 244.

conduct (see Thomas). Indeed, it seems that this model has already been implicitly practised by Elim during its two epistemological crises.

Second, I have argued that Elim should fully appreciate the dialectical relation in the text emanating from its divine *and* human nature, as well as its canonical unity *and* diversity. The divine and human nature of the text implies that its meaning is grounded in the historical sense of the human authors but nevertheless only becomes meaningful when the divine sense is incorporated. This is an important development from Fee's distinction between 'exegesis' (Hirsch's 'meaning') and 'hermeneutics' (Hirsch's 'significance'), even if at first appearance it may seem little more than a subtle difference. That is, the historical human sense of the biblical text without the dynamic divine sense is *senseless*, and the divine dynamic sense without the historical human sense is *non-sense*.

Coupled with the dialectical relation arising from the divine and human nature of the text, I have also noted that the canonical unity and diversity of the Bible provides its own further hermeneutical tension. In other words, Elim should maintain that the Bible has a unified overarching *message* but simultaneously acknowledge that it also has particular *messages*. This means that, although all of Scripture is inspired by God, some passages may be 'more inspired' than others for certain situations. This is not a licence for modern-day Marcionism where less palatable parts of the Bible can simply be eliminated, but it is a call for Elim's careful communal discernment in the Spirit of particular texts in the context of the underlying canonical message.

An important aspect for discerning the right biblical interpretation for the community is the pragmatism inherent within Elim's rationality. Moreover, it is this pragmatism that provides epistemic justification for Elim's belief regarding the authority of the Bible. Hence, in Chapter 9 I will explicitly develop Elim's pragmatism.

Chapter 9

PRAGMATIC JUSTIFICATION: EXPERIENTIAL AWARENESS AND PRAGMATIC SIGNS OF THE FOURSQUARE GOSPEL

In the third part of the book I have thus far argued that Elim's rationality of *Pentecostal Biblical Pragmatism* should be underlined by a *Pentecostal* realist correspondence theory of truth (Chapter 7), and I have noted that the *Bible* as a primary source of theological knowledge for Elim should be interpreted by a community of believers who appreciate simultaneously the Bible's divine and human nature (Chapter 8). Informed by these two chapters, the final chapter focuses on the *pragmatic* side of Elim's rationality, with particular emphasis on epistemic justification. In other words, I have sketched Elim's Pentecostal concept of truth and proposed that the Bible should be the primary source of theological knowledge for the movement, so the question now becomes: How will Elim know whether its biblical beliefs are in fact 'true' or have justification/warrant?

In Chapter 4, I stated that Elim's early pragmatism was characterized by *experientialism* and *experimentalism*; that is, human (spiritual) experiences are central in forming and justifying Elim's Pentecostal beliefs, and these beliefs are further corroborated and tested in light of experimental practices. I also discussed how Elim's experiential experimentalism shares significant similarities with the American Pragmatism of Charles Sander Peirce and William James, and how this rationality was not just present during the birth of Elim but also visible during its two major epistemological crises (see Chapters 5 and 6).

My aim is now to further develop Elim's pragmatic concepts of *experientialism* and *experimentalism*, and I will do so in dialogue with the philosopher William P. Alston. In doing this I will (1) outline Alston's 'Theory of Appearing'; (2) propose how phenomenologically many Pentecostal experiences can be seen as either direct or indirect awareness of God; (3) suggest that despite some differences, the analogy between sense and mystical perception is adequate; and (4) argue how Elim's explicit *pragmatic experimentalism* helps to overcome the main challenge directed at Alston's theory, namely, the objection from religious pluralism. In the discussion below the terms 'religious experience', 'spiritual experience' and 'mystical experience' are used synonymously.¹

9.1 Pentecostal experience and Alston's 'Theory of Appearing'

George Jeffreys aptly summarized Elim's experientialism and the role of experience in justifying theological beliefs when he claimed: *'He that hath an experience is not at the mercy of him that hath an argument.'*² This emphasis on 'experience' is not unique to Elim as a Pentecostal movement. Indeed, it has become somewhat of a truism within Pentecostal theology to point out the centrality of 'experience' for Pentecostals.³ However, despite the maturing theological and philosophical discussion on the concept of 'Pentecostal experience', Pentecostal interaction with the work of the Christian philosopher William P. Alston on the topic has been minimal.⁴ For example, key Pentecostal contributors on the topic, such as James K. A. Smith, L. William Oliverio Jr., Peter D. Neumann and Daniel Castelo do not refer to Alston in their major works

---

1. It is not uncommon for philosophers of religion to distinguish between spiritual, religious and mystical experiences; see Gellman, 'Mysticism and Religious Experience', 138–41; Wesley J. Wildman, *Religious and Spiritual Experiences* (New York, NY: Cambridge University Press, 2014), 77–82.

2. Jeffreys, *Healing Rays*, 56.

3. See Mathew S. Clark and Henry I. Lederle, *What is Distinctive about Pentecostal Theology?* (Koedoespoort: UNISA, 1989), 17, 40; Donald Gelpi, 'The Theological Challenge of Charismatic Spirituality', *Pneuma* 14, no. 2 (Fall 1992): 188; Cox, *Fire From Heaven*, 14; Joel Shuman, 'Towards a Cultural-Linguistic Account of the Pentecostal Doctrine of the Baptism of the Holy Spirit', *Pneuma* 19, no. 2 (Fall 1997): 211; Peter Althouse, 'Toward a Theological Understanding of The Pentecostal Appeal to Experience', *JES* 38, no. 4 (Fall 2001): 399; Lewis, 'Towards a Pentecostal Epistemology', 95; Veli-Matti Kärkkäinen, *Toward a Pneumatological Theology*, ed. Amos Yong (Lanham, MD: University Press of America, 2002), 6; Macchia, 'Christian Experience and Authority in the World'; Tony Richie, 'Awe-Full Encounters: A Pentecostal Conversation with C. S. Lewis Concerning Spiritual Experience', *JPT* 14, no. 1 (2005): 100; Warrington, 'Experience: The *sine qua non* of Pentecostalism', in *The Role of Experience in Christian Life and Thought - Pentecostal Insights*, 335; Terry L. Cross, 'The Divine-Human Encounter: Towards a Pentecostal Theology of Experience', *Pneuma* 31, no. 1 (2009): 6; Neumann, *Pentecostal Experience*, 5; Eriksen, 'The Epistemology of Imagination and Religious Experience', 48.

4. See William P. Alston, 'Christian Experience and Christian Belief', in *Faith and Rationality: Reason and Belief in God*, ed. Alvin Plantinga and Nicholas Wolterstorff (Notre Dame, IN: University of Notre Dame, 2009), 103–34; Alston, *Perceiving God*. William P. Alston, 'Religious Experience Justifies Religious Belief', in *Contemporary Debates in Philosophy of Religion*, ed. Michael L. Peterson and Raymond J. VanArragon (Oxford: Blackwell Publishing, 2004), 135–45.

on experience/epistemology,[5] and Amos Yong does so only twice in his influential *Spirit-Word-Community* but not explicitly in relation to religious experience.[6] This is a surprising omission, not least as Alston's work on the topic of religious experience epistemically justifying Christian belief(s) is commonly considered as the most articulate to date.[7] Moreover, Alston is a realist regarding the nature of truth and his 'Theory of Appearing' follows a common-sense approach to rationality. Both of these elements are shared by Elim (see Chapters 4 and 7), and therefore Alston seems to be a natural philosophical source for articulating a Pentecostal experiential epistemology. In light of this, I will seek to develop Elim's pragmatic epistemology in relation to Alston's important work. This will not only help to construct a more robust theological epistemology for Elim but also bring the primary Christian philosopher on religious experience into dialogue with the 'experiential' Pentecostal movement.

9.1.1 Alston's 'Theory of Appearing'

In his magnum opus on religious experience, *Perceiving God* (1991), Alston's central argument is that in the same way as objects seem to directly 'appear' to individuals through sense experience, God can 'appear' to individuals undergoing religious experiences and that this kind of 'putative direct awareness of God can provide justification for certain kinds of beliefs about God'.[8] To ground his 'parity thesis' between 'sense perception' and 'mystical perception', Alston utilizes what he calls the Theory of Appearing to explain both types of 'perception'.[9] According to Alston's Theory of Appearing,

> for S to perceive X is just for X to be the entity that is appearing to S as so-and-so; and on externalist theories, to perceive X, in undergoing experience, E, is for X to figure in certain way in the causal chain leading up to E, and/or for E to lead to beliefs, or tendencies to beliefs, about X.[10]

---

5. See the indexes of Smith, *Thinking in Tongues*; Oliverio Jr., *Theological Hermeneutics in the Classical Pentecostal Tradition*; Neumann, *Pentecostal Experience*; Castelo, *Pentecostalism as a Christian Mystical Tradition*.

6. Yong, *Spirit-Word-Community*, 97, 167.

7. Matthew C. Bagger, *Religious Experience, Justification, and History* (Cambridge: Cambridge University Press, 1999), 8; Wildman, *Religious and Spiritual Experiences*, 157; Thomas D. Senor, 'The Experiential Grounding of Religious Belief', in *The Oxford Handbook of the Epistemology of Theology*, 64.

8. Alston, *Perceiving God*, 9.

9. Alston is aware how articulating an account of sense perception 'is a notoriously controversial topic'; ibid; see also William P. Alston, *The Reliability of Sense Perception* (Ithaca, NY: Cornell University Press, 1993).

10. Alston, *Perceiving God*, 58. Alston's account is very similar to Richard Swinburne's 'Principle of Credulity'; Richard Swinburne, *The Existence of God*, 2nd edn (Oxford: Oxford University Press, 2004), 303. Alston acknowledges the similarity; Alston, 'Religious Experience', 138.

As seen from this definition, Alston's Theory of Appearing is effectively a form of 'direct realism' as it assumes that experience can provide 'direct awareness of an object that is presented to consciousness, usually an external physical object'.[11] However, although Alston adopts a direct realist position – a position which has been unfashionable after the so-called linguistic turn in philosophy – he does not do so uncritically. Rather, he acknowledges (1) it is possible that an object may appear to the subject when there actually is no real object (e.g. hallucination),[12] and (2) 'that a person's conceptual scheme and beliefs can affect the way in which an object presents itself to him'.[13] Nevertheless, Alston still insists that in normal circumstances if an object appears to a person, the person is prima facie justified in believing that a real object has, in fact, appeared; and that even if the appearing experience is influenced by the subject's background beliefs, this does not mean that the belief formed from the experience simply mimics information previously known by the subject about the object that has been experienced.[14]

So, why does Alston adopt his Theory of Appearing and its concomitant direct realism? It seems that Alston's primary reason for accepting the Theory of Appearing is that for him 'it is the only alternative to complete scepticism about experience'.[15] Indeed, Alston has convincingly argued that it is very difficult (if not impossible) to establish the reliability of sense perception without some kind of 'epistemic circularity', namely, the assumption that sense perception is in fact reliable.[16] However, for Alston such epistemic circularity should not result in scepticism regarding sense perception, because he believes that the doxastic practices that rely on the senses for formulating beliefs about the external world have proved effective in understanding and making sense of the world, which for Alston suggests that it is reasonable to adopt the Theory of Appearing or a similar kind of theory with respect to sense perception.[17] If such an epistemic disposition is adopted vis-à-vis doxastic practices on sense perception, Alston argues that a

---

11. Alston, *Perceiving God*, 55.
12. Ibid., 56.
13. Ibid., 38.
14. Ibid., 38–9. Wildman argues that Alston fails to acknowledge the true implications of these two qualifications and thus offers his own 'ecological-semiotic theory of dynamic engagement' as a way forward; Wildman, *Religious and Spiritual Experiences*, 162–6. However, as I will argue below, in light of Elim's Pentecostal metaphysics and concept of truth, there are no obvious reasons to reject Alston's Theory of Appearing, even if Wildman has a point in that Alston's theory would probably benefit from a greater appreciation of the interpretive and semiotic nature of all experiences.
15. Alston, 'Religious Experience', 138.
16. Alston, *Perceiving God*, 102–45; Alston, *The Reliability of Sense Perception*.
17. Alston is utilizing here a type of a pragmatic logic; that is, judging a practice on its 'fruits'. See Alston, *Perceiving God*, 149.

similar approach should be employed for doxastic practices on mystical perception due to the similarities between sense and mystical perception.[18]

However, although Alston maintains the basic reliability of both sense and mystical perception, he is careful to clarify that beliefs formed by these experiences are only prima facie justified or have 'initial credibility', since they can be challenged by belief 'overriders'.[19] In other words, he is not advocating for a naïve fideistic position where religious experiences are simply immune from all criticism. On the contrary, Alston believes that there can be two kinds of overriders: 'rebutters' and 'underminers'. 'Rebutters' refers to things that render the appearing of an object improbable and 'underminers' to factors that question the efficacy of the belief-forming process in its current circumstances.[20] To illustrate the difference, Alston uses an example of seeing an elephant in his garden: 'My belief that there is an elephant there would be justified unless there are strong reasons for thinking that there is no elephant in the area (rebutter) or that my vision is not working properly (underminer).'[21]

Therefore, Alston's Theory of Appearing is in many ways aligned with the so-called Jamesian Epistemic Justification, as opposed to Cliffordian Epistemic Justification. That is, he adopts the more latitudinarian epistemic approach where 'one is justified in engaging in a practice provided one does not have sufficient reasons for regarding it as unreliable' (James), rather than the more sceptical perspective where 'one is obliged to refrain from engaging in a practice unless one has adequate reasons for supposing it to be reliable' (Clifford).[22] To put it simply, beliefs stemming from one's experience are 'innocent until proven guilty', rather than 'guilty until proven innocent', but nonetheless they can be proven guilty.

9.1.2 Pentecostal experience

Alston's direct realism and Theory of Appearing seems to have a natural affinity with Elim's implicit epistemological convictions, not least due to Elim's theological realism and the Scottish Common Sense Realism influences on Elim's rationality.[23] However, based on Elim's concept of truth and theological assumptions (Chapter 7), Elim should probably also qualify Alston's Theory of Appearing in two ways. First, as has already been pointed out in Chapter 7, following from Elim's Pentecostal

---

18. Critics of this approach commonly try to demonstrate the difference between sense and mystical perception; Evan Fales, 'Do Mystics See God?', in *Contemporary Debates in Philosophy of Religion*, 146; Philipse, *God in the Age of Science?*, 321–4.
19. Alston, 'Religious Experience', 138.
20. Alston, *Perceiving God*, 191.
21. Alston, 'Religious Experience', 138.
22. Alston, 'Christian Experience', 116.
23. Alston himself follows the basic intuition of the Scottish Common Sense Realism philosophical tradition. In his own words: 'we will follow the lead of Thomas Reid in taking all our established doxastic practices to be acceptable as such, as innocent until proven guilty'; Alston, *Perceiving God*, 153.

doctrines of *imago dei*, sin and eschatology, Elim's theological correspondence theory of truth should be seen as 'correlation' rather than 'congruence' (see Amos Yong). This means that Alston's 'direct realism' should really be seen as '*critical direct realism*', with a greater emphasis on the perspectival and semiotic nature of human engagement with God and the world.[24] Second, any Reidian reliabilist or Jamesian 'innocent until proven guilty' type epistemological assumptions should be accompanied with a strong dose of fallibilism, as for Elim humans are fallen beings living in the not yet fully realized eschaton and thus limited in their ability to experience and perceive God. So, epistemologically speaking one might be 'innocent until proven guilty' but only by a small margin. Furthermore, in some cases due to human sin the balance of probability regarding epistemic 'guilt' might actually be against the experiencer. Nevertheless, due to the revelation found in Christ and the epistemic agency of the Spirit, for Elim a genuine experience of God – or in Alston's terms of God 'appearing' to the experiencer – should be seen as a real theological possibility. That is, Elim and other Pentecostals will insist that despite human limitations, it is possible to experience and thus become 'aware' of the real God in Christ through the Spirit, which is altogether a different experience to simply reflecting on the inner workings of one's human and sinful cultural-linguistic framework.[25] How this Pentecostal experience can be conceived as a real 'awareness of God' will be explored next.

9.2 Pentecostal experience as direct and indirect awareness of God

Alston acknowledges that religious experience can be defined in a 'wide sense' which refers to any experiences connected 'with one's religious life, including a sense of guilt or release, joys, longings, a sense of gratitude, etc.,'[26] or in a more 'narrow sense' with an emphasis on experience of God or what Alston calls '*perception* of God.'[27] Focusing on this narrower sense, Alston refers to six 'paradigm cases' of religious experience from which he highlights three key characteristics.[28]

9.2.1 Experiential awareness

First, in the phenomenological accounts of religious experience referred to by Alston, people 'report an *experiential* awareness of God.'[29] This causes Alston to conclude that the religious experiences in question cannot be easily reduced to 'subjective feelings or sensations to which is superadded an *explanation* according

---

24. Cf. Wildman, *Religious and Spiritual Experiences*, 164.
25. Lewis, 'Towards a Pentecostal Epistemology', 100; Macchia, 'Christian Experience and Authority in the World'.
26. Alston, 'Religious Experience', 135–6.
27. Ibid., 136.
28. Alston, *Perceiving God*, 12–14.
29. Ibid., 14.

to which they are due to God, the Holy Spirit, or some other agent recognized by the theology of the subject's tradition'.[30] To the contrary, there seems to be a genuine mystical perception of something not dissimilar from sense perception.

Now without a doubt many religious experiences of Elim Pentecostals fall within Alston's 'wide sense' and hence are effectively more common human experiences 'to which is superadded an *explanation*' in line with a Pentecostal worldview. However, there also appear to be religious experiences within Elim that 'report an *experiential* awareness of God' that is different from God simply becoming an 'explanation' of a broader human experience. For example, experiences of conversion, baptism in the Holy Spirit and the manifestation of spiritual gifts often reflect (even if not always) this more direct 'experiential' awareness of God.[31]

9.2.2 Direct and indirect awareness

Following from the first characteristic, Alston points out that secondly 'the awareness is *direct*'.[32] In other words, the awareness of God is '*directly presented* or *immediately present* to the subject'.[33] Alston helpfully explores different levels and categories of immediacy vis-à-vis one's experience.[34] Nevertheless, his central point is that in 'direct awareness' or 'direct perception' one does not perceive something by inferring it from something else, but rather the object perceived directly presents itself to the perceiver without an *explicit* intermediate. Alston acknowledges that there are probably a number of *implicit* intermediaries between the object and one's direct awareness of it (e.g. different parts of the brain/mind processing the experience), but the experiencer does not 'perceive any of this' and thus the experience can still be understood as direct.[35]

Indeed, the concept of non-mediated and direct awareness of God is part of Elim's spirituality. In fact, it is not hard to argue that a key reason why the early Elim pioneers argued against 'ritualism' was because it was seen as an obstacle and an unnecessary system of mediation between the believer and their direct experience of God in Christ through the Spirit (see Section 4.1.3). To put it differently, Elim saw the sacramentalism of Roman Catholicism and Anglo-Catholicism as superfluous

---

30. Ibid., 16.
31. See George Jeffreys, *Pentecostal Rays: The Baptism and Gifts of the Holy Spirit* (London: Henry E. Walter LTD, 1954 [1933]); P. S. Brewster, *The Spreading Flame of Pentecost* (London: Elim Publishing House, 1970); George Canty, *The Practice of Pentecost: Recognising, Receiving and using the Gifts of the Spirit* (Basingstoke: Marshall Pickering, 1987); Colin Dye, *Living in the Presence: The Holy Spirit's Agenda for You* (Eastbourne: Kingsway Publications, 1996).
32. Alston, *Perceiving God*, 14.
33. Ibid., 21.
34. For example, he identifies (1) 'absolute immediacy', (2) 'mediated immediacy' and (3) 'mediate perception'; ibid.
35. Ibid.

and misleading, because God could be experienced directly. The former Elim minister Mathew Clark summarizes the immediate Pentecostal experientialism well when he writes that 'to be Pentecostal is to have experienced the power of God in Jesus ... Precisely because it is Christ who is encountered, Pentecostals feel they are free from the dangers of subjectivism.'[36]

This 'direct' encounter of God/Christ that is different from humans simply reflecting on their subjective sense of God in a spiritual experience is also emphasized in Elim's concept of the spiritual gifts, with the insistence on the gifts being supernatural and objective manifestations of God.[37] For example, referring to 'words of wisdom' and 'words of knowledge' (1 Cor. 12.8), the Elim pioneer W. G. Hathaway writes that through these gifts 'we get an understanding of the Divine mind. In them we get a manifestation which appeals to our intellect, our understanding. The word of wisdom and the world of knowledge give us an understanding of His wisdom and mind.'[38] Hathaway's description speaks of direct revelation of God being imparted to the believer through a religious experience; that is, the experiencer is purportedly given direct access to 'the Divine mind' which will help them form religious beliefs accordingly.

This concept of '*direct perception*' of God helps to conceptualize important aspects of Elim's experientialism. Moreover, it provides philosophical grounding for why these types of experiences can potentially offer experiential warrant for Elim's theological beliefs. Just like direct sense perception provides prima facie justification for beliefs about the natural world, in the same way direct mystical perception can provide prima facie justification about the spiritual world. Nevertheless, it seems that although some of Elim's Pentecostal experiences can be understood as '*direct perception*' of God, a number of such experiences are better conceived as '*indirect perception*' of God.

So, what is meant by 'indirect perception' of God? As well as highlighting various reports of people having directly perceived God, Alston also identifies that others witness to 'experiencing God in the beauties of nature, of hearing God's voice in the Bible or in sermons or in the dictates of conscience.'[39] Interestingly, Alston notes that historically he has been sceptical that such 'indirect *mystical* perception' occurs, but rather has believed that these kinds of experiences are better seen as examples of 'indirect perceptual recognition', which for Alston is 'taking something to manifest, indicate, or be the effect of, the divine presence or activity.'[40] In other words, he has thought that 'indirect perceptual recognition'

---

36. Clark and Lederle, *What is Distinctive?*, 43–5. However, at time of writing Clark was a member of the Apostolic Faith Mission of South Africa.

37. W. G. Hathaway, *Spiritual Gifts in the Church* (London: Elim Publishing, 1933), 12–13; W. R. Jones, 'The Nine Gifts of the Holy Spirit', in *Pentecostal Doctrine*, ed. P. S. Brewster (No city: P. S. Brewster, 1976), 47; Canty, *The Practice of Pentecost*, 97.

38. Hathaway, *Spiritual Gifts in the Church*, 15.

39. Alston, *Perceiving God*, 25.

40. Ibid., 28.

is not analogous to *perception* since the appearing is not immediate but inferred from something else that is perceived. However, in *Perceiving God* Alston rejects this conclusion by surmising that if he assumes that God can be directly presented to 'one's awareness, *why shouldn't something that is phenomenologically just like that happen by way of one's direct awareness of something in creation?*'[41] In sum, Alston cannot think of any reason why God could not be 'indirectly perceived', not just 'indirectly recognised' through mediums such as the heavens above, the moral law within, the reading and preaching of the Bible, music and so on.[42]

Alston's notion of 'indirect perception' is helpful in describing the experience of many Pentecostals, including those within Elim. That is, although 'direct perception' of God appears to characterize some Pentecostal experiences, many of the so-called divine encounters seem to be more aligned with 'indirect perception'. For example, Elim's Keith Warrington notes how the Pentecostal practices of prayer, worship and preaching in a congregational context are meant to function as platforms for divine encounters.[43] Daniel Albrecht states along similar lines that through Pentecostal liturgy, comprising music, proclamation and communal practice of spiritual gifts, the aim of the worshipping community is 'to construct a sphere in which together a congregation most likely will *encounter* their God'.[44] Moreover, Frank Macchia has argued that even the Pentecostal idea of 'tongues as a sign' should be understood in a sacramental manner where God's presence and action is mediated through this gift (in)directly.[45] These examples demonstrate that experiences of God are very much at the heart of Pentecostalism, but they also point out that these God encounters are often experienced through another medium, such as Bible reading, corporate prayer, musical worship and speaking in tongues. Indeed, Peter D. Neumann in his detailed discussion on 'Pentecostal experience' concludes that 'a maturing Pentecostal theology ... needs to acknowledge the ways in which experience of God is mediated, while simultaneously upholding the belief in the immediacy (or directness) of encounter with God'.[46]

---

41. Ibid.

42. Robert Audi refers to this type of religious experience as 'theistic perception' with a 'naturalistic *base*, as opposed to the case of *pure* mystical experience in which theistic perception is taken to be as it were free-standing'; Robert Audi, *Rationality and Religious Commitment* (Oxford: Oxford University Press, 2011), 114.

43. Warrington, *Pentecostal Theology*, 202–3, 214–15, 219.

44. Daniel Albrecht, *Rites in the Spirit: A Ritual Approach to Pentecostal/Charismatic Spirituality* (Sheffield: Sheffield Academic Press, 1999), 149; cf. Jean-Daniel Plüss, 'Religious Experience in Worship: A Pentecostal Perspective', *PS* 2, no. 1 (2003): no page numbers.

45. Frank Macchia, 'Tongues as a Sign: Towards a Sacramental Understanding of Pentecostal Experience', *Pneuma* 15, no. 1 (Spring 1993): 68; cf. Mark Cartledge, 'Interpreting Charismatic Experience: Hypnosis, Altered States of Consciousness and the Holy Spirit?' *JPT* 6, no. 13 (1998): 132.

46. Neumann, *Pentecostal Experience*, 161.

The idea of 'indirect perception' seems to provide the philosophical concept for appreciating this kind of 'mediated immediacy', where, on the one hand, what is experienced of God is mediated through something else but, on the other hand, through this mediation a genuine *perception of God* can take place that is different from 'indirect perceptual recognition', where one makes a conscious inference about God from a physical object that has been perceived. This, of course, does not mean that Pentecostals do not also have 'indirect perceptual recognitions' of God, but it does mean that much of Pentecostal and Elim experientialism is purportedly 'indirect perception' of God and so seems to have similarities to sense perception.

9.2.3 Awareness of God

Thirdly and finally, Alston does not only see the paradigmatic cases of religious experience consisting of some kind of '(in)direct awareness' of a greater power, but this 'awareness is reported *of God*'.[47] Alston categorizes the perceptions of God as being either (1) 'what God is experienced as *being*' or (2) 'what God is experienced as *doing*'.[48] Regarding God's *being*, it seems that Elim's experience of God is fundamentally Christological even if there is a strong pneumatological element. In the words of Mathew Clark: 'It is Christ who lies at the heart of the Pentecostal experience, although the power by which he is known is that of the Spirit.'[49] And when it comes to God's *doing*, this seems to include divine activities such as convicting sin, providing guidance, offering reassurance, empowering for witness, bringing new revelation and healing supernaturally.[50]

9.2.4 Summary

To summarize the most salient points with respect to Elim's Pentecostal experience of God in light of Alston's philosophical categories: Elim's *religious experientialism* can be seen to consist of three types of divine encounters – (1) *general experiences of God in the world* which are effectively common human experiences, but as they are experienced and interpreted through a Pentecostal lens, they carry spiritual significance for the experiencer (this has not been developed above); (2) *indirect perceptions of God* which can be seen as genuine awareness of God but this awareness is mediated through something else (e.g. nature, Bible, tongues and musical worship); and (3) *direct perceptions of God* which are characterized by God being perceived directly without any obvious mediation. All three types of experiences arguably provide some experiential justification for Elim's theological beliefs and for the experiential viability of the Elim argument. However, it is

---

47. Alston, *Perceiving God*, 14.
48. Ibid., 43.
49. Clark and Lederle, *What is Distinctive?*, 44; cf. Warrington, 'Experience', 338.
50. See Brewster, 'The Seven-Fold Work of the Holy Spirit', 9–24; Jones, 'The Nine Gifts of the Holy Spirit', 48; Dye, *Living in the Presence*, 83, 85–6.

categories two and three that seem to provide 'fresh' theological data, as well as greater epistemic justification by their virtue of being more analogous to sense perception. Indeed, the third type of experience is most similar to sense perception and therefore probably the most reliable source of theological knowledge and prima facie justification for Elim's Pentecostal beliefs.

9.3 (Dis)analogy between sense and mystical perception

I have suggested that Alston's Theory of Appearing and the various categories of religious experience are useful in conceptualizing Elim's Pentecostal experientialism. However, as has been noted above, Alston's theory assumes there to be sufficient parity between sense and mystical perception, but there seem to be some obvious differences between the two types of experience. In fact, at least five common objections regarding the analogy between sense and mystical perception can be identified:[51]

1. Sense perception is universal, whereas religious perception is not.
2. Sense perception is constant, whereas religious perceptions come and go.
3. Sense perception perceives actual objects, whereas religious perception usually perceives God in something else.
4. Sense perception provides detailed information, whereas religious perceptions are vague.
5. Sense perception deals with physical objects, whereas religious perceptions supposedly perceive a God who is nonphysical and spiritual.

Space does not permit a detailed discussion of each objection, but I will offer brief comments on each. The fact that religious perception is not universal (Objection 1) or constant (Objection 2) is not surprising within Elim's theological framework. After all, it is believed that sin mars human ability to perceive God and the current eschatological dispensation means that God's presence in the world is not yet fully realized. However, the fact that the perception of God is neither universal nor constant does not make it dissimilar to certain types of sense perception. For example, Robert Audi notes that 'in complicated matters such as aesthetic perception in music and painting ... what is directly heard or seen nevertheless cannot be seen or heard

---

51. See Caroline Frank Davis, *The Evidential Force of Religious Experience* (Oxford: Clarendon Press, 1989), 76; Nancey Murphy, *Anglo-American Postmodernity: Philosophical Perspective on Science, Religion, and Ethics* (Boulder, CO: Westview Press, 1997), 156; Alston, 'Religious Experience', 139; Fales, 'Do Mystics See God?', 145–58; Gellman, 'Mysticism and Religious Experience', 155–7; Audi, *Rationality and Religious Commitment*, 117–25; Philipse, *God in the Age of Science?*, 322–3; Jeff Astley, 'Beyond Science and Nature? Reflections on Scientific Reductionism and Mental and Religious Experience', *JSRE* 1, no. 1 (2015): 41.

without both practice and sensitivity.'[52] Alston echoes this when he writes: 'Why suppose that what happens only rarely cannot have cognitive value? We wouldn't dream of applying this principle to scientific or philosophical insight. That comes only rarely and to few people, but it is not denigrated for that reason.'[53]

Moreover, within a Pentecostal movement like Elim, the central assumption is that, although the perception of God may not be universal or constant at all times, it is nevertheless available for all those who genuinely seek it. In the words of Hathaway, 'Pentecost may still become the *personal experience* of every believing child of God.'[54] The possibility for genuine seekers of God to experience divine reality is an important Pentecostal emphasis and it implies that in theory it is possible to cross-check many of the perceptions of God, because these perceptions are not restricted to few mystical experts but the Spirit of God is believed to have been poured out on 'all [believing] flesh' (Acts 2.17).[55]

Objection three is true to some extent, particularly in relation to *general experiences of God* and *indirect perceptions of God*. However, the objection cannot be applied to *direct perceptions of God*. Furthermore, even in physical perceiving we often perceive realities through something else. For example, I can perceive my three-year-old son being happy (a supposedly physical state in his brain/mind) through perceiving the smile on his face, and hence perceive something (i.e. cognitive/mental state of happiness) in perceiving something else (i.e. smile). Therefore, it appears that even in some instances of physical perceiving we perceive things through other physical mediators, and so spiritual (indirect) perceiving is not necessarily so different from certain forms of physical (indirect) perception.

The idea of experiencing God through created things is also a natural expectation within a Pentecostal worldview. As argued above, Elim, along with most other Pentecostals, maintains that God is the creator and ground of being and that creation is thus contingent on God's existence and providential presence. Indeed, as part of this doctrinal framework Pentecostals are known to view the world as being 'enchanted', where God, as well as other spiritual beings, can be experienced in the things that have been made.[56] This might not be full panentheism, but neither is it far from it.

In terms of objection four, it does seem to be the case that sense perception typically provides greater detail than mystical perception. That said, many of the

---

52. Audi, *Rationality and Religious Commitment*, 122.
53. Alston, 'Religious Experience', 140.
54. Hathaway, *Spiritual Gifts in the Church*, 3.
55. This does mean that arguments about the hiddenness of God by the likes of John Schellenberg are particularly challenging for Pentecostals; J. L. Schellenberg, *Divine Hiddenness and Human Reason* (Ithaca, NY: Cornell University Press, 2006). For a Christian response, see Paul K. Moser, *The Elusive God: Reorienting Religious Epistemology* (Cambridge: Cambridge University Press, 2008); Paul K. Moser, *The Evidence for God: Religious Knowledge Reexamined* (Cambridge: Cambridge University Press, 2010).
56. See Yong, *Spirit-Word-Community*, 43; Smith, *Thinking in Tongues*, 39–43.

purported Pentecostal experiences of prophecy, words of knowledge, and words of wisdom do also claim to provide fairly detailed information.[57] Nevertheless, even if many Pentecostal experiences do not provide equivalent detail to sense perception, 'we cannot sensibly hold that less information is no information at all'.[58]

Objection five rightly notes the (dis)analogy between sense and religious perception. After all, the Christian God is understood to be a spiritual being (see Jn 4.24) and it is also not wholly clear what human faculty perceives God in the religious experience. Nevertheless, the whole point of an analogy is to show similarity between the two entities not equivalence between them, and in light of the discussion above, it seems that there is sufficient similarity between God and physical objects appearing to the perceiver to indicate that the two types of experiencing are 'similar in an *appropriate respect*, not merely in any arbitrary respect'.[59] To put it differently, the analogy seems to hold with respect to how the 'objects' appear to the perceiver, even if 'what' appears are very different entities (i.e. spiritual and/or physical realities).[60] Therefore, it seems that the analogy between sense and religious perception cannot be easily dismissed.

9.4 Pragmatic justification

Even if there is sufficient parity between sense and mystical perception, which I believe there is, at best the (in)direct appearing of God through religious experiences only provides prima facie epistemic justification. That is, beliefs based on or informed by religious experiences only have warrant in the absence of what Alston calls belief 'overriders' (see above).[61] For Elim, there seem to be three main challenges or 'overriders' for such beliefs. First, in light of Elim's doctrine of (fallen) humanity (see Chapter 7), the human ability to form accurate theological beliefs is significantly limited and always fallible. Such human perspectivism and sinfulness can be categorized in Alston's terms as a potential belief 'underminer', as these doctrines undermine the cognitive ability of humans to form appropriate

---

57. For example, when discussing the Pentecostal understanding of the words of wisdom and knowledge, Lancaster refers to the biblical examples of Acts 5.3 and 9.11, which provide very detailed information; John Lancaster, *The Spirit-Filled Church: A Complete Handbook for the Charismatic Church* (Chichester: Sovereign World, 1987), 82.

58. Alston, 'Religious Experience', 140.

59. Yujin Nagasawa, *The Existence of God: A Philosophical Introduction* (London: Routledge, 2011), 78. Nagasawa makes this point in relation to teleological argument(s) for the existence of God.

60. For further discussion on the objection from God's 'non-dimensionality', see Jerome Gellman, *Mystical Experience of God: A Philosophical Inquiry* (Aldershot: Ashgate, 2001), 39–52.

61. Plantinga's belief 'defeaters' are very similar to Alston's 'overriders'; Plantinga, *Warranted Christian Belief*, 359–66.

beliefs based on their experience of God. Second, as has been argued in Chapters 3 and 4, British Pentecostalism and Elim were birthed in the context of increasing religious pluralism. The fact of competing religious traditions arguing that their religious beliefs are also experientially justified can be seen as a belief 'rebutter' by providing contradictory evidence to Elim's own experiential claims.[62] Third, following from the previous point, one predominant type of competing (non-) religious tradition has been exclusive naturalism, which has sought to explain all religious experiences naturalistically, and thus attempts to be a belief 'underminer' in explaining away the involvement of any super/supranatural agency.[63]

Elim's implicit *experimentalism* seems to provide the necessary further justification in light of the potential 'overriders', at least in theory, to supplement Elim's experiential beliefs. This is the explicitly pragmatic rather than just empirical, characteristic of Elim's rationality. In other words, if Elim's empirical experientialism looks at 'what produced the belief', Elim's pragmatic experimentalism looks at 'what the belief produces'. The emphasis of the latter is on the 'effects' and 'results' produced by the belief, which has been identified as the basic tenet of Peirce's and James's philosophical pragmatism (see Section 4.3.3). Interestingly, Alston is aware of the challenges provided by certain 'overriders' for experientially based Christian beliefs, particularly religious pluralism, and has argued for the need of some kind of further pragmatic justification.[64] But, as pointed out by Wesley J. Wildman, Alston's pragmatism remains 'underdeveloped',[65] and therefore Elim's pragmatism may provide a way forward.

So, my aim is now to articulate Elim's doxastic practice of pragmatism as a proposal to help Elim's experiential beliefs move from initial to more established justification. I will do so by first focusing on the internal criteria used by Elim to discern 'true' religious experiences. Although this internal criteria has a strong pragmatic emphasis, it also uses biblical and doctrinal criteria to 'judge' religious experiences and thus it can be seen as a combination of coherentism and pragmatism. Second, I will evaluate the more explicit and evidentialist pragmatism of Elim, and finally, I will argue that Elim should maintain the logic of its evidentialist pragmatism but recalibrate it with an increased emphasis on the Pentecostal concept of 'outward *signs* following'.

---

62. Religious pluralism is commonly identified as the main challenge for Alston's theory; Hick, *Dialogues in the Philosophy of Religion*, 27; Baker, *Tayloring Reformed Epistemology*, 49–50; Wildman, *Religious and Spiritual Experiences*, 164–5; Senor, 'The Experiential Grounding of Religious Belief', 76–7.

63. For example, like Nietzsche, Herman Philipse categorizes Paul's religious experience on the road to Damascus as an 'epileptic attack'; Philipse, *God in the Age of Science?*, 331; cf. Davies, *The Evidential Force of Religious Experience*, 3; Fales, 'Do Mystics See God?', 154–5.

64. Alston, *Perceiving God*, 304; William P. Alston, 'The Epistemological Challenge of Religious Pluralism: Responses and Discussion', in *Dialogues in the Philosophy of Religion*, 46–8.

65. Wildman, *Religious and Spiritual Experiences*, 160.

9.4.1 Coherentist pragmatism

Throughout its history Elim has adhered to the NT mandate to 'test the spirits' (1 Jn 4.1; cf. 1 Cor. 14.29; 1 Thess. 5.21), not least due to the fallible and fallen ability of humans to perceive the things of God. Elim's internal criteria for distinguishing the authentic from the inauthentic can be seen to consist of three components.

First, genuine religious experiences of God within Elim need to be *consistent with the Bible*. In the words of the Elim minister D. J. Ayling: 'The power of God must come to us by a Scriptural experience. The Bible is the only safe ground for any spiritual experience. Any claim to experiences that cannot be validated by an appeal to the Word of God must be suspect.'[66] In other words, within Elim any spiritual encounters that are incompatible with what is clearly stated in the Bible are questionable at best. The general logic being that if God is the divine author of Scripture, then he would not contradict Himself in revealing something which opposes His previous revelation. However, in light of the Scripture's *dynamic sense* and *canonical plurality* (see Section 8.2), the hermeneutical community needs to carefully evaluate all seemingly contradictory experiences of the Spirit, because Scripture cannot be viewed as a simplistic manual for rejecting human religious experiences since the reality of God is increasingly being made manifest at the dawn of the coming King. That said, the *historical sense* and the *canonical unity* do provide some historical grounding in enabling Scripture to be the plumb line to judge Elim's contemporary spiritual encounters.

Second, Elim's religious experiences need to be *doctrinally sound*. It is no accident that from 1916 onwards Elim has had official statements of faith. These doctrinal statements seem to stem from three primary sources. First, as has been pointed out in Chapter 4 (Section 4.2) Elim's doctrinal statements were to a great extent borrowed consciously or unconsciously from existing Evangelical statements of faith. Second, these doctrines seem to have reflected the collective experience of the Elim Pentecostal community. As such, the Evangelical doctrines were supplemented with doctrines reflecting the Pentecostal experience. Therefore, the doctrines are to some extent the articulated storehouse of past experiences of the Pentecostal community. Third, Elim leaders throughout its history have argued that, despite the influence of Evangelical theology and personal encounters with God, their doctrines are fundamentally biblical.[67]

However, more so than with the Bible, Elim's doctrinal statements function as guidelines of what should be expected of religious experiences. In other words, they do not have the final say on whether an experience is or is not of God. Indeed, as has been pointed out, Elim's Fundamental and Foundational Truths changed in 1922, 1928/1934 and 1993 and, as I have argued, these changes seem to have been instigated by experiences (or lack of experiences), as well as changes in biblical interpretation.

---

66. D. J. Ayling, 'A Baptism of Power', in *Pentecostal Doctrine*, 237.
67. Jeffreys, *The Miraculous Foursquare Gospel – Doctrinal*, 1; Jeffreys, *The Miraculous Foursquare Gospel – Supernatural*, 2.

Third, Elim has always insisted that religious experiences are *known by their fruits*.[68] The expressions of the fruit have included a purported super/supranatural enabling to fulfil the Great Commission through witnessing to the world and building up the church. For example, Colin Dye writes that 'the Spirit enabled men and women to speak with a power and authority that they did not naturally possess'.[69] And Ron Jones argues in line with 1 Corinthians 14 that the purpose of Spirit(ual) manifestations are 'for the edifying (building up) of the Church'.[70] These more dynamic expressions of the 'fruit' have also been supplemented with the expected moral qualities that have been expected to accompany a true encounter with God. John Lancaster captures this well when he writes that 'Christianity must prove its authenticity by the moral results it produces in its disciples. Christ himself laid this down as the acid test of all teaching, 'Ye, shall know them by their fruits (Matthew 7:16)'.[71]

In sum, to help Elim mitigate the potential 'overriders' for religious encounters resulting from 'fallen humanness', the movement has used the Bible, doctrine and the 'fruit' of the experience as benchmarks for 'testing the spirits'. Thus, *pragmatic coherentism* has been and can be utilized for evaluating religious experiences. It is the pragmatic side that might also help Elim to respond to the two other main 'overriders', namely, religious pluralism and naturalism.

9.4.2 Evidentialist pragmatism

Just like religious experiences can be defined in a 'wide' and 'narrow sense' (see above), the same categorization can be used with respect to religious experimentalism. I will focus primarily on the narrow sense of experimentalism, but before doing so I will touch briefly on the wide sense experimentalism, as it is not without its pragmatic significance.

9.4.2.1 Wide experimentalism It is difficult to strictly delineate between 'experientialism' and 'experimentalism' in the wide sense. That said, religious 'experientialism' broadly conceived can be seen to refer to general human experiences that are *interpreted* through a religious framework. The ability of a religious worldview (e.g. Elim's Pentecostalism) to interpret lived experience is important, because if it fails to make sense of everyday experiences, it quickly

---

68. Clark and Lederle note that Pentecostal experience insists 'observable results'; Clark and Lederle, *What Is Distinctive?*, 55.

69. Dye, *Living in the Presence*, 83; Ayling, 'A Baptism of Power', 238.

70. Jones, 'The Nine Gifts of the Holy Spirit', 48.

71. John Lancaster, 'The Nine-Fold Fruit of the Spirit', in *Pentecostal Doctrine*, 64; Siegfried S. Schatzmann, 'The Gifts of the Spirit: Pentecostal Interpretation of Pauline Pneumatology', in *Pentecostal Perspectives*, ed. Keith Warrington (Carlisle: Paternoster, 1998), 88.

becomes suspect for its experientially minded followers.[72] Broad religious 'experimentalism', on the other hand, can be seen as the *effects* produced by the religious belief for general human experience. These effects can be also characterized as the 'fruits' referred to above by Dye, Jones and Lancaster. For example, increased boldness to stand for one's beliefs, building others up in love, compassion for the poor, transformed family life, improved work ethic and freedom from addictive behaviour are some of the effects that Pentecostals commonly identify as resulting from their experience of God. Again, like with general religious experiences, these varied effects may not verify the truth of a religious tradition, but the inability of a religion to produce such effects quickly begin to call it into question. This concept of general experientialism is similar to William James's religious pragmatism when he writes: 'If theological ideas prove to have value for concrete life, they will be true, for pragmatism, in the sense of being good for so much. For how much more they are true, will depend entirely on their relations to other truths that also have to be acknowledged.'[73]

Without delving into James's concept of 'truth',[74] his basic point seems to be that the justification of religion is to a great extent determined by its 'value for concrete life' in comparison with the value provided by other factors and frameworks one is aware of. Indeed, in the final pages of *Perceiving God*, Alston echoes a similar sentiment when he surmises that 'the final test of the Christian scheme comes from trying it out in one's life ... and seeing whether it leads to the new life of the Spirit'.[75] Therefore, it is not hard to argue that religious experimentalism in the wide sense seems to have epistemic merit not only in helping to make Elim's Pentecostalism a 'live option' but also in giving pragmatic justification to live one's life in line with the Full Gospel.

9.4.2.2 Narrow experimentalism This 'wide sense' experimentalism or pragmatism found within Elim, however, is not Elim's only type of pragmatism. As has been argued in Chapter 4 (see Section 4.3.3), Elim's early pragmatism appears to have had significant similarities to C. S. Peirce's more scientific and

---

72. This is particularly the case if there is an alternative religious or non-religious tradition that can make better sense of human experience. For example, Charles Taylor refers to alternative philosophies/religions in trying to provide the 'best account' in making sense of human experience; Charles Taylor, *Sources of the Self: The Making of Modern Identity* (Cambridge, MA: Harvard University Press, 1989), 58; cf. Oliverio, *Theological Hermeneutics*, 339. Thus, the ability of religious tradition to interpret general experiences may not be able to verify the truth of the religious tradition in question, but its failure to interpret general experiences may begin to falsify it.

73. James, *Pragmatism and Other Writings*, 36.

74. For helpful corrective essay on common (mis)interpretations of James's concept of truth, see Hilary Putnam, 'James's Theory of Truth', in *Pragmatism as a Way of Life: The Lasting Legacy of William James and John Dewey*, ed. David MacArthur (Cambridge, MA: The Belknap Press of Harvard University Press, 2017), 167–87.

75. Alston, *Perceiving God*, 304.

narrow experimentalism. For example, it seems that Elim's doctrines regarding divine healing and tongues as initial evidence for baptism in the Holy Spirit were both revised on the basis of this pragmatic logic. That is, (1) hypotheses regarding the nature of divine healing and Spirit baptism were articulated based on spiritual experience and reading of the Scriptures; (2) these hypotheses were lived out and 'tested' in practice; and (3) the hypotheses were then revised based on the results of the 'tested' experience. In sum, historically Elim's rationality seems to have been one of *evidentialist pragmatism*.

Despite this historical precedence, Daniel Castelo has recently argued that Pentecostal epistemology should move away from this type of 'evidentialist logic' because, for him, this is a 'modern thought-paradigm' and thus antithetical to Pentecostal spirituality.[76] Castelo expands that (American) classical Pentecostalism has uncritically taken on board this logic from Charles Fox Parham who insisted that tongues were the 'Bible *evidence*' of Spirit baptism. Castelo writes that 'doing so has put this branch of Pentecostalism at odds with other Pentecostal constituencies across the globe, one for whom initial-evidence logic is *not* compelling or mandated'.[77] Indeed, Castelo concludes that the 'initial-evidence logic' should *not* be retained within Pentecostal epistemology, but instead Pentecostalism should be seen as a mystical tradition of the church catholic.[78]

Although Castelo rightly warns against the obsession that some Pentecostals may have had regarding the doctrine of 'initial *evidence*', he seems to too quickly jettison a central aspect of the Anglo-American Pentecostal rationality. In other words, what he believes to be a borrowed 'evidential logic' from Evangelicalism actually appears to be a lynchpin of the Pentecostal rationality, at least as far as Elim is concerned. In effect, Castelo's rejection of the 'initial-evidence logic' seems to be problematic for three reasons with respect to Anglo-American Pentecostalism.[79]

First, as I have argued in Chapter 3 (see Section 3.1.3), British classical Pentecostalism – and the same could probably be said of American classical Pentecostalism – is itself a modern religious movement. Despite the rhetoric of some early Pentecostal pioneers, which suggested that early Pentecostals simply returned to a pre-modern and first-century Christianity of the apostles, historically speaking Anglo-American Pentecostalism emerged within modernity and thus only really makes sense as a modern movement. This does not mean that Pentecostals were not critical of positivist aspects of early-twentieth-century modernity, but it does mean that their own spiritual alternative was itself also a child of modernity. To put it simply, classical Pentecostalism was not anti-modern per se, but it was *modernity plus*; namely, modernity enchanted with the super/

---

76. Castelo, *Pentecostalism as a Christian Mystical Tradition*, 131–2.
77. Ibid., 139.
78. Ibid., 158.
79. Castelo acknowledges that the Pentecostalism he knows the best are 'the Mexican, Latino, and Latin American varieties', but in his work he primarily explores 'the Anglo-American forms'; ibid., xvii.

supranatural reality of God. Therefore, the modernistic evidentialist rationality of Anglo-American Pentecostalism should not be seen as peripheral but central to Pentecostal epistemology.

Second, it is a mistake to assume that those classical Pentecostal movements that rejected tongues as initial evidence also rejected the concept of 'external evidence' for baptism in the Holy Spirit. For example, Elim abandoned the doctrine of 'tongues as initial evidence', but still insisted that a genuine baptism of the Holy Spirit is accompanied by external signs. At the birth of the Elim argument 'divine healings' were presented as the main 'sign' to justify that the Spirit of God was at work within the movement (see Section 4.3.3), and throughout its history other 'signs' have also been emphasized. So, the 'initial-evidence logic' was very much maintained, even if 'tongues' as the first sign was not adopted. In fact, ironically for Elim, the pragmatic Evidentialism seems to have been the reason why *tongues* as initial evidence was itself rejected; that is, the *evidence* suggested that some were baptized in the Spirit without necessarily speaking in tongues.[80]

Third, by rejecting the evidentialist pragmatic logic Castelo removes an important epistemological resource that helps Elim and other Pentecostal movements to respond to potential belief 'overriders'. Without evidentialist experimentalism Elim and other forms of Pentecostal experientialism are left particularly vulnerable against the objection from religious pluralism. Thus, it is not only historically but also philosophically problematic to do away with this evidentialist logic of Pentecostalism.

Having said all of that, Elim's evidential experimentalism has historically been characterized by elements of triumphalism which is unwarranted in light of Elim's wider Pentecostal theology. In other words, at the heart of Elim's Foursquare Gospel is the *person* of Christ, and if the personhood of Christ is taken seriously within the Full Gospel structure, then it would be misleading to try to demonstrate its truth in the same way as one were to demonstrate the truth of a non-personal scientific theory within the natural realm. Moreover, the eschatological (*under-*)*realized realism* of Elim (see Section 7.4) implies that although aspects of the reality of Christ's truth can be experienced and grasped in the present dispensation, this reality is not yet fully realized and, therefore, any pragmatic verification will inevitably be partial in the present age.

Consequently, within this Christological and eschatological framework it is not surprising that Elim has had to qualify, for example, its statements regarding divine healing from the initial boldness of healing being guaranteed in the atonement (1916/1922)[81] to applying it for only those who 'walk in obedience' (1928/1934),[82]

---

80. This same logic was used by other European Pentecostal pioneers such as Gerrit R. Polman and Jonathan Paul in rejecting tongues as *the* sign of Spirit baptism; Boddy, ed., 'The Place of Tongues in the Pentecostal Movement', 177, 182.

81. Jeffreys, *Elim Christ Church*, 5; Jeffreys, *The Constitution of the Elim Pentecostal Alliance*, 6.

82. Jeffreys, *Constitution of the Foursquare Gospel Churches of the British Isles*, 6; Jeffreys, *Elim Foursquare Gospel Alliance*, 3.

before replacing this with the more humble assertion that the church is 'to fulfil a ministry of healing and deliverance to the spiritual and physical needs of mankind' (1993).[83] To put it differently, it is unsurprising that the evidence regarding divine healing did not support Elim's earlier triumphalism which assumed that the person of Christ was somehow under divine obligation to heal everyone ('who walked in obedience') in the current age, and hence Elim's doctrine of healing needed to be modified accordingly.

Nevertheless, despite not seeing the 'results' and 'effects' anticipated in some of the earlier doctrinal statements, Elim has still maintained the pragmatic logic and the assumption that external evidence does support the truth of the Foursquare Gospel. Hence, in the remainder of this section I will propose that Elim's *pragmatic experimentalism* should be developed from 'hard' (naïve?) *pragmatic Evidentialism* to a more nuanced *signs-based pragmatism*.

9.4.3 Signs-based pragmatism

My articulation of Elim's *signs-based pragmatism* follows the common epistemic principle of allowing the order of things (ontology) to determine how things are known (epistemology).[84] As I have argued throughout this book, the assumed 'order of things' (i.e. the hard core) of the Elim argument is the Christological Foursquare Gospel, and this presupposed 'ontology' can be seen to have two important characteristics for further developing Elim's pragmatic epistemology: (1) at the centre of what one seeks to know is a personal God revealed in Christ Jesus; (2) this revealed God in Christ is not a passive God of deism but an active reality who purportedly manifests Himself pneumatically in the world as Saviour, Healer, Baptiser in the Holy Spirit and soon coming King. So with respect to these two theological facets, my aim is now to spell out their implications for Elim's pragmatism of signs.

9.4.3.1 'I-Thou' knowledge
The first aspect of Elim's Christological Foursquare Gospel is that what is supposedly known and/or sought to be known is a divine *person* (i.e. God revealed in Christ through the Spirit). If the divine person of Christ is central to the Elim movement, which I believe it is, then in Martin Buber's terminology one should avoid the category mistake of confusing 'I-Thou' knowledge with 'I-It' knowledge.[85] The difference being that 'I-Thou' knowledge is characterized by relationality and mutual involvement, whereas 'I-It' knowledge is impersonal with the subject seeking control over the object of enquiry. The 'I-Thou' is commonly exemplified in (meaningful) human relationships, whereas

---

83. Elim Pentecostal Church: Annual Conference 1993. Conference Agenda and Reports, Elim Archives, Malvern, 62.

84. See Aristotle, *Nicomachean Ethics*; Moser, *The Evidence for God*, 37.

85. Martin Buber, *I and Thou*. Translated by Ronald Gregor Smith (London: Bloomsbury Academic, 2017).

the 'I-It' is often reflected in human dealings with nature (e.g. natural sciences).[86] It seems that, like in mutual human relationships, the Christ of the Full Gospel needs to be known primarily in the 'I-Thou' dynamic, at least if the personal nature of the divine Christ is to be taken seriously and the category mistake of treating Christ as a mere object is to be avoided.[87]

For Elim's pragmatic epistemology the 'I-Thou' dynamic has three implications. First, knowing Christ in a personal relationship means that one can only truly know Him if Christ reveals Himself (see Lk. 10.21-22; Jn 2.24). Indeed, this is the case with all genuine personal relationships; that is, the knowledge of another person requires that the person sought to be known makes themselves known. In light of this, knowledge of Christ can never be simply a matter of human achievement or effort, and therefore the pragmatic 'effects' and 'results' of the Foursquare Gospel cannot be guaranteed to the seeker by simply following particular methodological steps, unless one is willing to compromise the divine sovereignty and freedom of Christ.[88]

Second, personal knowledge of Christ does *also* entail human 'effort' or, perhaps better stated, human involvement, faith and trust. As with personal knowledge between two humans, the divine human relational knowing requires not only Christ revealing himself but also the human individual likewise investing something of themselves within the epistemological quest. In biblical language this personal investment is commonly referred to as 'faith' (*pistis*), without which 'it is impossible to please Him [God]' (Heb. 11.6). A full discussion on a Pentecostal concept of 'faith' is beyond our focus, but following general Protestant theology it can be stated that 'faith' is not *merely* propositional knowledge (*notitia*) or public confession (*assensus*) but fundamentally consists of 'trust' (*fiducia*).[89] Trust, however, by its very nature carries with it an element of risk. For example, in an intimate human relationship there has to be an element of trust between the two parties for the relationship to develop, and whenever someone places trust in another person they take a risk since there is a real possibility that the trust will be misplaced or indeed will be misused by the other. Nevertheless, the risk is the price humans pay for being able to have a genuine relationship, and it is not hard

---

86. Ibid., Part 1.

87. Paul Moser makes a similar point about the Christian God of love; Moser, *The Elusive God*, 72.

88. Buber makes a similar distinction by contrasting 'magic' with 'praying' to a personal God; Buber, *I and Thou*, 58; cf. C. S. Lewis, 'The Efficacy of Prayer', in *Fern-Seed and Elephants and Other Essay on Christianity by C. S. Lewis*, ed. Walter Hooper (Glasgow: Collins, 1975), 96–103.

89. See Karl Barth, *Dogmatics in Outline* (London: SCM, 1949), chapters 2–4; Grudem, *Bible Doctrine*, 307–9; Swinburne, *Faith and Reason*, 142. It is also misleading to assume that chronologically *notitia* necessarily comes before *fiducia*. In fact, Barth discusses 'Faith as Trust' (chapter 2) before exploring 'Faith as Knowledge' (chapter 3) and 'Faith as Confession' (chapter 4).

to argue that this risk is also necessary in the human-divine relationship.[90] Thus, the possibility of *spectator pragmatic Evidentialism*, where the person in search of Christ tries to remain detached from the personal implications of coming in contact with Christ's Full Gospel, is questionable at best.[91] This seems to be particularly the case when the purpose of the 'I-You' relationship is brought to the forefront.

Third, and following from the second point, the purpose of the 'I-You' relationship in a Christological framework seems to be love, namely, God demonstrating his love towards humanity in the life, death and resurrection of Christ with the aim of (some) humans responding in love and obedience (see Jn 3.16; 14.23; Rom. 5.8; 2 Cor. 5.19-20).[92] This means that the purpose of theological knowledge is not knowledge as such, but in the words of Paul Moser, 'for humans to enter into fellowship with God via human repentance and obedience'.[93] In other words, for Pentecostals as for many other Christians the knowledge of God is to be transformative in nature, and without such transformation the knowledge itself becomes meaningless and possibly even dangerous (see 1 Cor. 8.1; Jas 2.19). This suggests that unless the theological epistemologist is rightly disposed towards the Christ of the Full Gospel, it is more than likely that Christ may not be revealed to the seeker because the fundamental purpose of the Full Gospel is not to increase one's theological knowledge but to call one to participate in its transforming reality.

To summarize, the 'I-Thou' aspect of the Christological Foursquare Gospel means that the pragmatic verification of Elim's argument may not have universal appeal, but may only have significance for those who have 'eyes to see' and 'ears to hear' (see Mk 8.18). This conclusion is further substantiated by Elim's under-realized eschatology, where the complete effects of Christ and the Full Gospel are not yet fully realized and thus any fully fledged scientifically based empirical pragmatism could at best only point to aspects of the Foursquare Gospel truth.

9.4.3.2 Full Gospel signs Having said all of that, the above should not lead to a complete *deconstruction* of Elim's Pentecostal evidentialist pragmatism but rather for its *reconstruction*. In other words, although the *Christological* 'I-Thou' aspect of the Elim argument mitigates the simplistic pragmatic Evidentialism, Elim's *Foursquare* conviction that Christ is the active Saviour, Healer, Baptiser in the Holy Spirit and soon coming King calls for maintaining some form of pragmatic

---

90. Although it should be noted that in the classical Pentecostal tradition God in Christ is considered to be perfectly trustworthy, even if His ways are considered to be different from those of humans (Isa. 55.8-9).

91. I have adapted my concept of 'spectator pragmatic Evidentialism' from Moser's notion of 'spectator evidence'; Moser, *The Elusive God*, 53.

92. My aim is not to get into the discussion about divine election. Within Elim there are representatives of both Arminian and Calvinist positions.

93. Moser, *The Elusive God*, 53. Cf. Abraham, *Crossing the Threshold of Divine Revelation*, 188.

justification. That is, the Elim tradition has assumed throughout its history that the activity of Christ has real effects and results in the world, and that Christ's presence in the power of the Spirit is indeed accompanied 'with signs following'.[94] Therefore, what is needed is not a complete rejection of Elim's evidentialist pragmatism but a more nuanced religious pragmatism, namely, *signs-based pragmatism*.

Phillip H. Wiebe, following the philosopher Stephen Braude, proposes that with respect to experimentalism we should distinguish between (1) 'experimental evidence' of the (natural) sciences, (2) 'semi-experimental evidence', which includes 'accounts of lived experience' and 'consists of claims that cannot be readily obtained at will, but are sufficiently numerous to be worthy of being included in serious theorizing', and (3) 'anecdotal evidence', which 'consists of claims – often one-off claims – that are insufficiently numerous to be rendered plausible, and consequently may not be included in theorizing about the world'.[95] When it comes to Elim's signs-based pragmatism, in light of the personal 'I-Thou' aspect of the Foursquare Gospel, it would be theologically and philosophically inappropriate to assume that 'experimental evidence' of the natural sciences could be mustered to justify the truth of the Elim argument. However, in relation to the claim that the activity of Christ is accompanied 'with signs following', it would also be inconsistent with the Elim argument to maintain that only 'anecdotal evidence' is available to justify the truth of the Foursquare Gospel. Consequently, there seem to be good reasons to adopt the middle position of 'semi-experimental evidence'.

Wiebe expands by explaining that the semi-experimental approach treats religious beliefs as 'theoretical entities', and thus although the entity itself may be strictly speaking nonphysical (e.g. God), the effects of the entity can still be empirically investigated and analysed.[96] Indeed, Elim's Pentecostal pragmatic logic seems to be naturally aligned with this kind of an approach. For example, as discussed in Chapter 4 (see Section 4.3.3), the Elim pioneers tried to justify the truth of the Foursquare Gospel by documenting purported healings as empirical evidence,[97] and by doing so were trailblazers for those who have used biomedical and social scientific methods to analyse Pentecostal/Charismatic phenomena, even if they lacked the methodological robustness of their successors.[98]

---

94. Elim 1993 Conference Reports, 61.

95. Phillip H. Wiebe, 'Religious Experience, Cognitive Science, and the Future of Religion', in *The Oxford Handbook of Religion and Science*, ed. Philip Clayton (Oxford: Oxford University Press, 2009), 513–14.

96. Ibid., 19.

97. Boulton, *George Jeffreys* (1928); Darragh, *In Defence of His Word*.

98. For example, David C. Lewis, 'Signs and Wonders in Sheffield: A Social Anthropologist's Analysis of Words of Knowledge, Manifestations of the Spirit, and the Effectiveness of Divine Healing' (Appendix D), in *Power Healing*, ed. John Wimber with Kevin Springer (London: Hodder and Stoughton, 1986), 252–73; Kathryn Kuhlman, *I Believe in Miracles: Streams of Healing from the Heart of a Woman of Faith*. Revised and Updated (North Brunswick, NJ: Bridge-Logos Publishers, 1992); Benny Hinn, *Lord I Need*

However, even when the results of Elim's Foursquare Gospel can be supposedly empirically and pragmatically observed and evaluated, Candy Gunther Brown points out that even the more objective medical records regarding healing, for example, are not self-explanatory but 'require human interpretation'.[99] Consequently, Amos Yong with good reason concludes that empirical evidence for the 'eschatological transformation of all things as signs of the kingdom … are empirically discernible as divine action only in faith'.[100] Nevertheless, the effects of the Full Gospel should still provide 'pragmatic signs' even if they require 'the eyes of faith'.

As 'pragmatic signs' the Full Gospel phenomena should, in the words of Blaise Pascal, provide 'enough light for those who desire only to see, and enough darkness for those of contrary disposition'.[101] That is, there should be sufficient accessibility for genuine seekers to perceive the evidence for the truth of the Foursquare Gospel, since the purpose of the 'I-Thou' knowing of Christ appears to be for humans to enter a loving and transformative relationship with Christ. However, since the purpose of believing in Christ is not to simply have more spectator knowledge about God but to be in a loving relationship with the Triune God revealed in Christ Jesus, it seems appropriate for this evidence not to be overwhelming so that those who do not want to have such a personal relationship with Christ are not forced or coerced into it, as well as for Christ to maintain His divine freedom in both revealing and hiding Himself. C. Stephen Evans has referred to these two aspects of Pascal's dictum as the 'Wide Accessibility Principle' and the 'Easy Resistibility Principle' of Christian signs.[102]

Indeed, the 'revealing' and 'hidden' nature of 'pragmatic signs' seems to be in line with the NT concept of revelation. For example, in the *incarnation*, some witnessed in Christ the fullness of God (Jn 1.14, 18), while others perceived Christ to be simply a deluded human being (Jn 7.5); on the *cross*, the centurion acknowledged Jesus as the Son of God (Mk 15.39), while others mocked what they believed to be a failed religious and political leader (Mk 15.29-31); and at the *resurrection* the disciples saw the risen Christ (1 Cor. 15.3-8), while the Jewish leaders sceptically claimed that Christ's body had been stolen by the disciple (Mt. 28.11-15). This same motif of simultaneously 'revealing' and 'hiding' is also

---

a Miracle (Milton Keynes: Word Publishing, 1993); Margaret Poloma, *Main Street Mystics: The Toronto Blessing and Reviving Pentecostalism* (Walnut Creek, CA: Altamira Press, 2003); Candy Gunther Brown, *Testing Prayer: Science and Healing* (Cambridge, MA: Harvard University Press, 2012).

99. Brown, *Testing Prayer*, 153.

100. Yong, *The Spirit of Creation*, 100.

101. Blaise Pascal, *Pensées*. Translated by A. J. Krailsheimer (London: Penguin Books, 1995), 50 (XI).

102. C. Stephen Evans, *Natural Signs and Knowledge of God: A New Look at Theistic Arguments* (Oxford: Oxford University Press, 2012), ixx. Although Evans refers to signs in nature, these two principles can be applied to experimental and pragmatic signs.

present in Jesus' use of parables (Mk 4.1-12, 33-34), and in Jesus' refusal to give an explicit sign to the Pharisees on demand, despite performing many signs during His ministry (Lk. 11.29-32).

9.4.3.3 Summary In sum, my proposal of Elim's *signs-based pragmatism* which stems from the Christological Foursquare Gospel is a recalibration of Elim's Pentecostal evidentialist pragmatism. In other words, it maintains an empirical and pragmatic element by embracing a 'semi-experimental' approach to Pentecostal 'signs', but does so by simultaneously appreciating the 'I-Thou' dynamic inherent within the Full Gospel. This means that the 'signs' are not self-explanatory but need to be 'spiritually discerned' (1 Cor. 2.14). That said, the purported signs cannot simply be interpreted to mean anything, because there is still real empirical content that guides the interpretation. Indeed, the history of Elim suggests that some interpretations can be empirically falsified (e.g. the concept that all who walk in obedience to Christ can enjoy perfect health in the current dispensation).

This *signs-based pragmatism* provides further justification for Elim's experiential beliefs and helps to rebut some of the belief 'overriders' stemming from religious pluralism and naturalistic explanations. In all fairness, this pragmatism of signs does not provide the 'experimental evidence' of the natural sciences and, therefore, anyone expecting this level of epistemic warrant will be disappointed. However, as has been argued above, theologically speaking assuming the methodology of the natural sciences to apply to the truth of the Christological Foursquare Gospel would be inappropriate with respect to the 'I-Thou' nature of the knowledge inherent within this theoretical framework, not to mention the current not yet fully realized eschatological dispensation. Nevertheless, the 'semi-experimental evidence' regarding the Full Gospel signs should provide sufficient grounds for both an adherent of the Elim movement and a genuine would-be-adherent, to embrace the truth of the Foursquare Gospel. Thus, in this sense it would provide reasons to respond to objections from other religions and naturalistic explanations, or at least this evidence should enable Elim to compare the pragmatic 'effects' and explanatory power of the Foursquare Gospel vis-à-vis its alternatives.

9.5 Conclusion

In this chapter I have developed the inherent *experientialism* and *experimentalism* in the Elim tradition with particular emphasis on epistemic justification. In dialogue with William P. Alston, I have proposed that Elim's *experientialism* can be seen to consist of (1) *general experiences of God in the world* which are effectively common human experiences that are experienced and interpreted through a Pentecostal lens, (2) *indirect experiences of God* which can be seen as genuine awareness of God but this awareness is mediated through something else (e.g. nature, Bible, tongues and musical worship), and (3) *direct experiences of God* that are characterized by God being perceived directly without any obvious mediation. All of these religious experiences – but particularly the indirect experiences and even more so the direct experiences of God (see the analogy above with sense perception) – can provide prima facie warrant for the truth of the Foursquare Gospel.

However, due to potential belief 'overriders' for these experiential beliefs (e.g. religious pluralism), the epistemic warrant provided by these experiences are at best only provisional. Consequently, I have suggested that Elim's *experimentalism* (read: pragmatism) provides the necessary assistance to strengthen Elim's epistemological position. As with experientialism, Elim's experimentalism can be understood in a 'wide' (Jamesian) sense, which focuses more on the existential and practical effects caused by living in accordance with the Full Gospel, and in a 'narrow' (Peircean) sense with a more evidential, empirical and observational logic. I have primarily focused on this latter 'narrow' sense and in doing so have defended the evidentialist logic of Elim's Pentecostalism as central to any classical Pentecostal rationality (*pace* Castelo). That said, I have also argued that the evidentialist logic needs to be recalibrated in light of a more theologically informed Pentecostal pragmatism of 'signs'. Such pragmatism should take seriously the 'I-Thou' dynamic in the Christological Foursquare Gospel, but also appreciate the pragmatic effects expected within the Full Gospel remit.[103] Hence, with Phillip H. Wiebe, I have stated that the evidence expected within this theoretical framework is 'semi-experimental evidence'. It provides 'enough light for those who desire only to see, and enough darkness for those of contrary disposition'.[104] Or in the words of the Psalmist it is a call to 'taste and see that the Lord is good' (Ps. 34.8). That is, real pragmatic and even empirical effects are to be expected, not through 'testing' as spectators but through 'tasting' as participants.

Now, what has been provided in this chapter is suggestive rather than comprehensive. Moreover, I have not tried to argue that there is epistemic warrant for the Elim position, only that, according to Elim's own tradition-specific rationality, this is the kind of warrant one should expect. That said, the Pentecostal pragmatism articulated in this chapter not only is a contribution to the intellectual self-understanding of the Elim movement but also makes a contribution to Pentecostal theology and philosophical/theological pragmatism. It also offers the first detailed Pentecostal interaction with Alston.

---

103. I have not explored *if* and *how* a super/supranatural being can interact with the natural world; see Alvin Plantinga. *Where the Conflict Really Lies: Science, Religion, and Naturalism* (Oxford: Oxford University Press, 2011), chapters 3–4; Yong, *The Spirit of Creation*, chapters 3–4.

104. Pascal, *Pensées*, 50 (XI).

CONCLUSION

In conclusion, I will first provide a summary of the book, with particular emphasis on its contributions to the disciplines of Pentecostal, philosophical and historical theology. Second, I will identify suggestions for future research.

Summary and contributions

In the introduction I identified 'the problem' as the need for Pentecostal theological methodology to be informed by a Pentecostal rationality, or at least a rationality that is compatible with Pentecostalism(s). In an attempt to contribute towards resolving this problem – I am under no illusion that a single work could actually *solve* the problem – I began the discussion in Part One by analysing significant academic articulations of Pentecostal rationalities by Amos Yong, James K. A. Smith and L. William Oliverio Jr. (Chapter 1). Although I noted the various strengths of these epistemological constructions, I also highlighted the seeming *ahistoricism* in the methodologies of Yong and Smith and in the practice of Oliverio. The implication of this ahistoricism is that it is questionable as to what extent their epistemologies are in fact 'Pentecostal', or at least that they do not reflect any particular Pentecostal tradition. As a way forward, I outlined Alasdair MacIntyre's concept of 'tradition-constituted' rationality as a method of developing a historical, narrative and tradition-specific Pentecostal rationality (Chapter 2).

Part Two of the book moved on to provide such a historically informed tradition-specific rationality. In doing so, I used Elim as an exemplar of a classical Pentecostal tradition and a Foursquare movement. I began by providing the 'prologues' to the Elim tradition by focusing especially on the philosophical and theological context, as well as the Holiness, revival and British Pentecostal roots of Elim (Chapter 3). My central claims were that the Elim movement, and British Pentecostalism as a whole, needs to be increasingly understood as a modern movement; and that the British Pentecostal logic developed Keswick *Romanticism* and the Welsh Revival *communal experientialism* into full-blown Pentecostal *Evidentialism*. In Chapter 4, I then narrated the birth of the Elim tradition and explored how the emerging movement argued *against* theological Liberalism, fundamentalist cessationism and high church ritualism; it argued *for* the Foursquare Gospel; it argued *by* using the rationality of Pentecostal Biblical Pragmatism; and it argued *within* the social embodiment of revivalistic meetings, denominational alliance and publishing/ training institutions. I continued my historical exploration by narrating Elim's two major 'epistemological crises' to date; that is, the resignation of Jeffreys (Chapter 5) and the arrival of the Charismatic/Restoration movements (Chapter 6). These two chapters substantiated my claim that the hard core content of the Elim argument is the Foursquare Gospel and its tacit rationality is Pentecostal Biblical Pragmatism. They also identified that although Elim has always structurally had a centrally governed leaning, it has also demonstrated great flexibility on how the Elim argument is socially and institutionally embodied.

Part Three built on the historical, theological and philosophical foundations of Part Two by taking Elim's implicit rationality of Pentecostal Biblical Pragmatism and developing it in line with the narrated Elim tradition. Chapter 7 did so by focusing on the underlying *Pentecostal* assumptions regarding the nature of truth, and then argued for a *Pentecostal theological realism* as an ontological foundation for Elim's rationality. I effectively rejected Smith's (possible) anti-realism as theologically unnecessary, and aligned Elim's rationality more closely with Yong's and Oliverio's critical/hermeneutical realism (not to mention MacIntyre's critical realism). Chapter 8 then focused on the *biblical* aspect of Elim's rationality and proposed a revised biblical hermeneutic in keeping with Elim's Pentecostal doctrine of the Bible. I believe that my proposal for an experiential and community-based biblical hermeneutic, which seeks to discern divine meaning(s) in 'dialectical relations', is a contribution not only to Elim's biblical hermeneutics but also to the ongoing scholarly debate on Pentecostal hermeneutics. The final chapter of the book (Chapter 9) developed the *pragmatic* epistemic justification within Elim's rationality. I did so by bringing Elim's Pentecostal 'experientialism' into dialogue with William P. Alston and proposed the possibility of Elim having prima facie justification for its theological beliefs based on its purported experiences of God revealed in Christ through the Spirit. Moreover, I went on to reconstruct Elim's pragmatic logic by focusing on Elim's historical doxastic practices of coherentist and evidentialist pragmatism. However, although I argued that such pragmatic logic should not be abandoned (*pace* Daniel Castelo), I sought to recalibrate it as *semi-experimentalism* (see Phillip H. Wiebe); that is, I argued for *signs-based pragmatism* that appreciates both the personal nature and effects-oriented Christological Foursquare Gospel.

In doing the above, I believe the book has made three major contributions to knowledge. First, it has provided a MacIntyrian tradition-specific *Pentecostal* rationality and thus offered a new methodological approach in the search for a Pentecostal epistemology. Second, it has presented the first substantial intellectual history of Elim and therefore has contributed to not only Elim's self-understanding but also to Pentecostal history of ideas. Third, in arguing that Elim's rationality is *Pentecostal Biblical Pragmatism*, as well as developing a theory of truth, biblical hermeneutics and epistemic justification in line with this rationality, the book has made its own contribution to Pentecostal philosophical theology.

So returning to the initial problem of the study – having a Pentecostal theological methodology based on a Pentecostal rationality – I would like to make two further observations. First, it seems that methodologically it is insufficient for Pentecostal philosophical theologians to talk about Pentecostal rationality without firmly rooting it in the history and practice of Pentecostal communities.[1] Ludwig Wittgenstein's 'don't think, but look!' is apposite advice for Pentecostal philosophical theologians,[2] and MacIntyre's insights employed in this work may provide some of the necessary tools for analysing other Pentecostal traditions and rationalities.

Second, based on the historical 'looking' at a particular Pentecostal tradition (i.e. Elim) and early British Pentecostalism, it appears that the underlying logic of classical Pentecostalism is indeed Pentecostally informed and biblically focused religious *pragmatism*. Therefore, despite criticizing the ahistorical elements of Yong's, Smith's and Oliverio's Pentecostal rationalities, as well as questioning to what extent they are in fact Pentecostal, the *pragmatist* elements within all of their epistemologies follows a deep and justified Pentecostal intuition. In sum, if Elim and early British Pentecostalism is anything to go by, Pentecostalism is indeed a *biblically* and *pragmatically* focused movement, and this should be reflected in the *how* and *what* of its future theologizing. This means that Pentecostal theology is a pragmatic enterprise, which means not only 'living the Full Gospel' but also justifying this life pragmatically.[3]

Further tasks

In terms of future tasks, I think there are particularly three aspects that would merit further exploration regarding Elim's 'Pentecostal argument'. The first relates to the reasonableness of the contemporary Elim tradition as a 'progressive argument' according to its own standards; the second to Elim's strength as a tradition vis-à-vis its main religious and non-religious competitors; and the third to the effectiveness of Elim's current structures and institutions in embodying its argument effectively. I will articulate these three issues as questions.

1. Is the Elim Pentecostal tradition a coherent argument according to its own rationality?

In Chapters 4, 5 and 6 I have tried to demonstrate how the Foursquare Gospel of Jesus as Saviour, Healer, Baptiser in the Holy Spirit and coming King should

---

1. I appreciate that my focus has primarily been historical rather than exploring contemporary practice. In fact, I will suggest under 'Further tasks' that such empirical research into the current rationality of Elim ministers and members would be a welcomed addition to the book.

2. Wittgenstein, *Philosophical Investigations*, 36.

3. I propose that Pentecostal theology should be primarily characterized by 'pragmatism' rather than 'play', although I appreciate some of the overlap between the terms; Vondey, *Pentecostal Theology*, 12–14.

be viewed in Lakatosian terms as the *hard core* of the Elim argument. In other words, if Elim is seen as a type of a '[semi-]Scientific Research Programme', then the Foursquare Gospel provides its essential doctrinal core, and its Foundational Truths are the *auxiliary hypotheses* which interpret the Foursquare Gospel and function as the protective belt against *modus tollens* arguments directed at the hard core.

Furthermore, in line with MacIntyre's concept of 'tradition-specific rationality' I have tried to show (see particularly Chapter 4) how Elim's rationality of *Pentecostal Biblical Pragmatism* stems from the movement's essential core of the Foursquare Gospel with its auxiliary hypotheses. However, in accordance with MacIntyre, I have also argued that Elim's Pentecostal Biblical Pragmatism has not just been 'tradition-constituted' but has also been 'tradition-constitutive'. That is, as well as being shaped by the Elim tradition, Elim's rationality has also shaped its tradition from its inception (Chapter 4) to the present day through its two epistemological crises (Chapters 5 and 6). Consequently, the relationship between tradition and rationality has been interdependent and mutually informing.

In light of these two claims – (1) the *Foursquare Gospel* is Elim's hard core, and (2) the Foursquare Gospel with its auxiliary hypotheses has both constituted and been constituted by Elim's rationality of *Pentecostal Biblical Pragmatism* – the question arises to what extent is Elim today coherent as an argument vis-à-vis its own hard core and rationality? To give two examples: first, is the current doctrine of Jesus as Healer pragmatically evidenced within Elim to provide the necessary 'semi-experimental evidence' to justify this as a hard core doctrine? Secondly, is the current doctrinal articulation and expectation of Jesus as coming King so vague that pragmatically it makes no difference to the Elim movement? If the answer to the first question is that there is no sufficient semi-experimental evidence to warrant Jesus as Healer, and/or if the current doctrinal articulation of Jesus as coming King makes no practical difference to Elim members and ministers, then it could be argued that the Elim tradition has become incoherent according to its own rationality and that its hard core has lost its potency.

These questions need further investigation for Elim to remain a coherent and progressive Pentecostal tradition according to its own standards. Therefore, further empirical research into the current state of Elim, as well as subsequent theological analysis, is essential. Regarding the 'semi-experimental evidence' relating to Jesus as Healer, the empirically and theologically informed methodology of Candy Gunther Brown could be utilized in studying healing within Elim.[4] Brown's theologically sensitive empirical approach would fit well with Elim's pragmatic rationality – that is, if Jesus is the Healer as Elim believes, then, according to Elim's own rationality, the effects of this belief should be observable in a semi-experimental manner. With respect to the eschatological beliefs of Elim members

---

4. Brown, *Testing Prayer*.

and ministers, contemporary quantitative and qualitative studies similar to those that have been carried out by William K. Kay and Mark J. Cartledge among British Pentecostals could be undertaken.[5] This quantitative/qualitative research would demonstrate whether Elim still embodies the fourth pillar of its hard core. If Elim ministers and members no longer see Jesus as coming King as a central doctrine, then in MacIntyrian terms, it could be argued that the Elim tradition has been transformed effectively into another tradition by losing this core belief.

2. Is the Elim tradition intellectually more progressive than its main 'competing' religious and non-religious traditions?

According to MacIntyre, traditions are justified or defeated not only in relation to their own rationality and core content but also in dialogue with the main 'competing' traditions. This means that for Elim to be a fully rational and warranted tradition in its current expression, its main contemporary religious and non-religious competitors should be identified and then brought into dialogue with Elim. To do so in a comprehensive manner would be a significant piece of work, since this would imply not only updating my narration of Elim with contemporary empirical data (see above) but also providing a historical narration of Elim's main competitors along MacIntyrian lines. Nevertheless, this might become a philosophical necessity, if Elim seeks broader dialectical justification for its argument in the public sphere. In a British (non-)religious context this would probably mean bringing Elim into dialogue with 'live options' such as secular humanism, Buddhism, Islam, Roman Catholicism, 'Liberal' Christianity and other forms of Charismatic Christianity (e.g. Charismatic Anglicanism).

3. Is the current embodiment of Elim fit for purpose vis-à-vis the movement's core beliefs and rationality?

In Chapter 4, I identified the initial embodiment of the Elim argument, and in Chapters 5 and 6, I noted how Elim has been relatively flexible regarding its structures if it has had good reasons for revising them in accordance with its rationality. In light of this, further research could be done in evaluating Elim's existing structures vis-à-vis the *Foursquare Gospel* and *Pentecostal Biblical Pragmatism*. In other words, are the current Elim institutions, constitution, governance structures and ecclesiological frameworks best suited for embodying the Elim argument in the context of the twenty-first century? The Elim movement under its current general superintendent is effectively exploring these questions,[6]

---

5. William K. Kay, *Pentecostals in Britain* (Carlisle: Paternoster Press, 2000); Cartledge, *Testimony in the Spirit: Rescripting Ordinary Theology*.

6. Chris Cartwright, '20/20 Vision: The Challenge to Step into more Focused Outreach, Mission and Expansion', January 2017, accessed February 21, 2018, https://www.elim.org.uk/Articles/510713/Respond_to_the.aspx.

but this assessment would be further enhanced through academic study into Elim's social epistemic systems.[7]

That said, these three further tasks should not be seen as undermining my thesis in this book; to the contrary, they flow out of my argument that Elim's essential core is the Foursquare Gospel and its rationality is Pentecostal Biblical Pragmatism. In other words, the possibility of doing the further tasks relies on the central arguments of this work. Therefore, despite the tasks that lie ahead, the work for now is done.

---

7. See Goldman, 'A Guide to Social Epistemology', 18–20.

APPENDIX 1: ELIM'S CHRONOLOGY[1]

1915	The Elim Evangelistic Band is formed by George Jeffreys and six others in January in Monaghan, Ireland. The first Elim church, Elim Christ Church, is established in August in Belfast with Jeffreys as its pastor.
1916	Elim's first doctrinal statement, *Elim Christ Church: What We Believe*, is produced by George Jeffreys in January 1916.
1918	The Elim Pentecostal Alliance is formed in June 1918, consisting of the Elim Evangelistic Band, local churches and Elim missions. This effectively makes Elim a denomination.
1919	The first *Elim Evangel* is published in December 1919 and becomes the official organ for promulgating the movement's Pentecostal message.
1921	Elim expands from Ireland to mainland Britain and establishes churches in Wales and England. George Jeffreys begins to travel increasingly in Britain holding evangelistic campaigns.
1922	Elim produces the *Constitution of the Elim Pentecostal Alliance* which includes a 'Statement of Fundamental Truths', and moves its administration from Belfast to Clapham, London.
1924	The Elim Publishing House and Elim Crusaders (Elim's youth movement) are established.
1925	The Elim Bible College (now Regents Theological College) begins to train people for ministry.
1926	Elim holds its first Easter Convention at Royal Albert Hall, an event which becomes a highlight in the movement's calendar for years.
1927	The Elim Church Incorporated is formed with a view of allowing local churches to be part of Elim without being Direct Government churches.
1929	Elim changes its name from Elim Pentecostal Alliance to Elim Foursquare Gospel Alliance.
1934	The Deed Poll cements Elim's constitution and doctrinal statement and makes the executive council the governing body of the movement.
1939	George Jeffreys resigns from Elim for the first time in December 1939.

---

1. The sources used for the chronology include the Elim Archives; Archives of the General Superintendent; Cartwright, *The Great Evangelists*; Hathaway, 'The Elim Pentecostal Church', 1–39; Cartwright, *Defining Moments*; No author, 'Historic Timeline of Elim,' accessed 16 March 2018, https://www.elim.org.uk/Articles/410266/Historic_Timeline.aspx.

1940	After having been reinstated as Elim's spiritual leader, George Jeffreys resigns from Elim for the second and final time in November 1940.
1942	The Deed Poll is altered through the Deed of Variation to make the Elim Conference, consisting of ministers and lay representatives, the governing body of the movement.
1944–1945	An Evangelistic committee is formed, and P. S. Brewster emerges as Elim's 'national' evangelist.
1961	Elim holds a special Prayer Conference in Birmingham in light of the changing attitudes towards morality and religion in Britain.
1964	Elim joins the Evangelical Alliance.
1965	The Elim Bible College moves to Capel, Surrey.
1968	The Elim Headquarters moves to Cheltenham, Gloucestershire.
1970–1976	The Doctrine of the Church Committee is set up by the executive council, following a conference decision in 1970, to evaluate Elim's ecclesiology.
1978	On 13 June Elim missionaries (including five children) are murdered in Vumba, Zimbabwe.
1981	The first Southport Conference is held in response to the rise of the Restoration movement in Britain.
1984	The second Southport Conference is held with a view of recalibrating Elim.
1987	The Elim Bible College moves to Nantwich, Cheshire.
1989	*Elim Evangel* is rebranded as *Direction Magazine*.
1993–1994	Revisions to Elim's Fundamental Truths are approved by the Elim Conference.
2000s	A number of Elim departments are rebranded and relaunched.
2009	The Elim Headquarters and Regents Theological College (formerly Elim Bible College) move to Malvern, Worcestershire.

APPENDIX 2: FRONT PAGE OF *ELIM EVANGEL* 6, NO. 1 (JANUARY 1925)

APPENDIX 3: BACK PAGE OF *ELIM EVANGEL* 6, NO. 1 (JANUARY 1925)

WHAT WE BELIEVE

SAVIOUR

COMING KING

1. We believe that the Bible is the inspired Word of God, and that none may add or take away therefrom, except at their peril.
2. We believe that the Godhead eternally exists in three persons, Father, Son, and Holy Ghost, and that these three are one God.
3. We believe that all have sinned and come short of the glory of God.
4. We believe that through the death and risen power of Christ all who believe are saved from the penalty and power of sin.
5. We believe that the present latter day outpouring of the Holy Ghost, which is the promise of God to all believers, is accompanied by speaking in other tongues as the Spirit gives utterance.
6. We believe that God is restoring all the gifts of the Holy Ghost to the Church, which is a living organism, a living body composed of all true believers.
7. We believe that God has given some apostles, and some prophets, and some evangelists, and some pastors and teachers, for the perfecting of the saints, for the work of the ministry, for the edifying of the body of Christ.
8. We believe that deliverance from sickness is provided for in the Atonement, and is the privilege of all who believe.
9. We believe in the personal and pre-millenial return of our Lord Jesus Christ to receive unto Himself the Church.
10. We believe in the eternal conscious bliss of all true believers in Christ, and also in the eternal conscious punishment of all Christ rejectors.

HEALER

BAPTISER

Foursquare on the Word of God

INDEX

affections 9, 12, 17, 20–8, 31, 89
Alston, William P. 4, 108, 189–202, 205, 213–14, 216
American Pragmatism 20, 110–11, 120, 189, *see also* James, William; Peirce, Charles Sanders
amillennial 153, 159–60, *see also* eschatology
anti-realism 8, 31, 37, 172, 216
Aquinas, Thomas 50–1, 53
Archer, Kenneth J. 59, 76, 89, 107, 119, 176–7, 187
Aristotle 2, 49, 51–3, 57
auxiliary hypotheses 37, 40, 42, 56, 92, 101–3, 119–20, 129, 138, 159, 218
Azusa Street 32, 39, 42, 85–6

Bacon, Francis 34, 66–7, 90, 95
Barratt, Thomas Ball 81, 85–7, 98–9, 104
Bebbington, David 66, 77
Bible Reading Method 107, 134, 176–7, 187
biblical hermeneutics 59, 107, 134, 164, 175–88, 216
biblicism 104, 118, 134, 146, 155, 161, 164, 176, *see also* biblical hermeneutics
Boddy, Alexander 77, 79, 81, 85–90, 165
Boulton, Ernest C. W. 77, 81, 97, 104, 109, 116, 126, 137, 144
Brewster, P. S. 143–4
British Israel 122–40, 142, 144, 146, 161, 176, 181
Brooks, Noel 82, 122–3
Brown, Candy Gunther 212, 218
Buber, Martin 208–9

Cartledge, Mark J. 58, 87, 219
Cartwright, Desmond 96, 122
Castelo, Daniel 190, 206–7, 214, 216
Cave, John K. 148, 154
cessationism 93, 95–7, 103, 180, 215

Charismatic movement 62, 110, 147–54, 160–1, 216, 219, *see also* Renewal Charismatics; Restoration Charismatics
Clifford, W. K. 68, 89, 193
Coleridge, Samuel Taylor 69, 80, 89
coming King, *see* eschatology; Foursquare Gospel
commensurability 40, 55
common sense (realism) 33–4, 66–7, 70, 74, 90, 112, 134, 193
correlationism 7, 13–4, 18, 20
creation 10–11, 17–18, 31, 39–40, 42, 74, 125, 165, 167–70, 173–4, 197, 200
critical realism 15–16, 38, 53, 171, 216
cultural-linguistic 12–13, 16–17, 30, 36, 42, 56, 168, 194, *see also* Lindbeck, George

Darwin, Charles 66–7, 70, 94
Dayton, Donald W. 63, 85
defeaters, *see* overriders
dialectical justification 45, 52, 54–7, 219
direct realism 192–4
doxastic practices 192–3, 202, 216
Dye, Colin 204–5

ecclesiology 19, 84, 114–19, 144–6 151–3, 157–60, 216, 219–20
Edsor, Albert 122–3
Elim Bible College, *see* Regents Theological College
Elim Evangelistic Band 97, 101, 115–19, 143
embodiment 4, 22, 24, 48, 61, 92, 114–20, 140–1, 144–6, 148, 161, 163–4, 216, 219–20
empiricism 11, 17, 24, 39, 41, 65–9, 74, 107–12, 115, 202, 210–14, 218–9,
Enlightenment 32, 46–7, 50, 65–6, 69–70, 74

enthusiasm   109–10, 152, *see also* experientialism
epistemological crisis, defined   50–2
eschatology   19, 78, 87, 99–102, 123–7, 138, 142, 146, 150–1, 153, 157, 159–61, 167, 173–4, 194, 203, 208, 210, 217–19
Evangelical   2, 12, 17, 34, 57, 66, 68–9, 71–8, 80, 82, 90, 96–8, 102–5, 107, 120, 125–6, 137, 149, 157, 165–9, 171, 178–80, 182, 187, 203, 206
Evangelical-Pentecostal hermeneutic   34–5, 41, 178–80, 182, 187
Evidentialism   68, 89–91, 108–10, 202, 204–8, 210–11, 213–16
experientialism   4, 5, 11, 13, 17, 19, 29–31, 39, 70, 80, 82, 85–6, 89–91, 95–6, 107–11, 113, 115, 153, 156, 164, 180–2, 187, 189–91, 194, 196, 198–9, 201–8, 213–16, *see also* Empiricism; mystical perception
experimentalism   4, 90, 108–13, 156, 164, 187, 189, 202, 204–8, 211–14, 216, 218, *see also* Pragmatism

Fall, *see* sin
fallibilism   12, 16, 41, 54, 170, 174, 194, 201, 203
Fee, Gordon   34, 178–80, 182, 184–5, 188
fideism   3, 17, 45, 56
Fivefold Gospel   5, 33, 87–8, 90, 142, *see also* Foursquare Gospel; Full Gospel
formal rationality   46–7, 55
foundationalism   12, 17, 41
foundational pneumatology   10–11, 13–18
Fourfold Gospel, *see* Foursquare Gospel
Foursquare Gospel   3, 4–5, 62, 78, 87–8, 90, 97–103, 104, 109, 113, 115, 117, 119, 120, 123, 129, 140–4, 146, 153, 155–7, 160, 163, 171, 207–20, *see also* Full Gospel
Full Gospel   4, 75, 95–9, 102–3, 109, 114, 116–19, 142, 157, 163, 205, 207, 209–10, 212–14, 217
Fundamental/Foundational Truths   99–104, 117, 124, 129, 138, 159–61, 166, 175, 180, 203, 218, *see also* truth

fundamentalism   20, 89, 93–5, 106, 119, 166

Gee, Donald   78, 81, 87, 108

habits   12, 15, 19–20, 24, 27
hard core   37, 40, 42, 56, 62, 78, 92, 101–3, 119–20, 123, 126, 129, 146, 148, 159–61, 163, 208, 216, 218–19
Hathaway, Malcolm   80, 118, 122, 159
Hathaway, W. G.   124, 131, 137, 142, 144, 196, 200
Healer, *see* Foursquare Gospel; healing
healing   23, 78–9, 83, 85, 87–8, 96, 98–102, 108–14, 123, 142, 147, 151, 157, 165, 172, 198, 206–8, 210–2, 217–18
heart, *see* affections
hermeneutical realism   8–9, 32, 35–9, 41–3, 216
Hick, John   168
Holiness movement(s)   64, 76–81, 84–5, 87–8, 90–1, 94, 96, 125, 165, 215
Hollenweger, Walter J.   58, 63
House Church Movement, *see* Restoration Charismatics
Hudson, Neil   81, 92, 114, 122, 132, 140
Huxley, T. H.   67–8

Idealism   69–70, 74
image of God   66, 168–70, 173–4, 194
initial evidence   90, 99–101, 108, 112, 206–7

James, William   110–13, 189, 193–4, 202, 205, 214
Jeffreys, George   62, 75, 77, 81–2, 84, 87, 92–146, 152, 157, 161, 181–2, 190, 216
Jones, Bryn   150–2, 154
Jones, Maldwyn   121–2, 148
Jones, Ron   155–6, 204–5

Kay, William K.   122, 130, 151, 153–4, 219
Keener, Craig S.   180, 184
Keswick   77–84, 89–92, 108, 215, *see also* Holiness movement(s)
Kingston, Charles J.   124–5, 131, 137
Kuhn, Thomas   36–44, 56

Index

Lakatos, Imre 36–44, 56, 102, 159, 161, 218
Lancaster, John 148–9, 152, 155, 204–5
Land, Steven J. 28, 165
Leech, John 127–35, 139, 146
Lindbeck, George A. 13–14, 29, 56
liturgy 20, 24–5, 197
Locke, John 109–10

MacIntyre, Alasdair 3–5, 8, 44–59, 61, 91, 101, 113, 121, 141, 163, 174, 215–19
McLeod, Hugh 64, 73
McWhirter, James 127–9, 133
metanarrative 24–5, 30, *see also* narrative
metaphysics, *see* ontology
Middlemiss, David 110
Mill, John Stuart 67–70, 74, 90
modernity 2, 33–4, 46, 57, 64–70, 74–6, 82, 91, 93, 109, 112, 126, 206, 215
Moore, G. E. 70, 74
Murphy, Nancey 36–9, 42–4, 56, 89, 101
mystical perception 189–201, 213–14, *see also* experientialism

narrative 4, 7–9, 15, 20–35, 45, 49, 51–2, 56–8, 61, 72, 120, 128, 163, 215
Neumann, Peter D. 190, 197
Nietzsche, Friedrich 50–1

Oliverio Jr., L. William 3, 5, 7–9, 18, 31–45, 56–9, 61–2, 89, 119–20, 163, 178, 187, 190, 215–17
ontology 2, 10–11, 26, 31, 49, 51, 192 n. 14, 208
overriders 193, 201–2, 204, 207, 213–14

Parham, Charles Fox 33, 85–6, 127, 206
Pascal, Blaise 212
Peirce, Charles Sanders 11, 15–16, 23, 111–12, 189, 202, 205, 214
Pentecostal, defined 1 n.1
Phillips, E. J. 77, 87, 101, 117, 123, 130–7, 139, 143–6
Plantinga, Alvin 108, 170
pluralism 64, 72–4, 84, 189, 202, 204, 207, 213–14
pneumatological imagination 9–20, 120
pneumatology 10–20, 33, 35, 39, 42, 58, 75, 78–9, 83, 85–8, 90–1, 95–6, 98–103, 108–9, 112–14, 120, 123, 142, 147–57, 168, 171–3, 178–9, 181, 184–8, 194–5, 198, 200, 203–11, 216–17
positivism 37, 68–70, 74
postliberal 7, 13–14, 18, 20, 27, 29–31, 44, 56
postmillennialism 79, 153, 159–60, *see also* eschatology
postmodern 2, 21–2, 57
pragmatism 3–5, 14–5, 17, 20, 26–7, 33, 52, 62, 70, 90, 103–13, 118–20, 123, 125–6, 130, 134, 140–1, 146, 153, 155–7, 160–1, 163–4, 166, 181, 187–220
premillennial 79, 98–100, 124–6, 138, 143, 153, 159–61, *see also* eschatology

Regents Theological College 6, 97, 117–19, 140, 157, 178
Reid, Thomas 66–7, 194
relativism 17, 41, 45–6, 50, 52, 56–7
religious experience, *see* experientialism; mystical perception
religious perception, *see* mystical perception
Renewal Charismatics 147–9, *see also* Charismatic movement
Restoration Charismatics 62, 147–60, 182, 216
Restoration movement, *see* Restoration Charismatics
revelation 19, 31, 36, 39, 109, 151, 156, 167–8, 171–4, 183–5, 194, 196, 198, 203, 212
ritualism 74–5, 93, 96–7, 103, 195, 215
Roberts, Evan 81–4
Romanticism 69–70, 74, 79–80, 82, 89–91, 108, 215
Russell, Bertrand 70, 74

Schiller, F. C. S. 70, 112
Scientific Research Programmes 36–43, 56–7, 159, 218
secularization 64–72, 74, 76, 84
semiotic 12–13, 15–17, 35–6, 194
Seymour, William Joseph 33, 85
signs 13, 16, 84, 88–91, 98, 101–2, 108–9, 112–14, 125, 132, 138, 150, 153, 181, 189, 197, 202, 207–14, 216
Simpson, Albert Benjamin 86, 101

sin   74, 78, 93, 99, 165, 167–70, 173–4, 194, 198–9
Smith, James K. A.   3, 5, 7–9, 18, 20–32, 35, 38–9, 42, 44–5, 57–8, 61–2, 119–20, 163, 165, 168–9, 171, 190, 215–7
Smith, Joseph   137, 144
Smyth, John C.   155
social embodiment, *see* embodiment
Spirit *see* pneumatology
substantive rationality   46–8

Taylor, Charles   22, 28, 36, 38–44, 72, 74, 165
telos   48–9, 53–4, 173–4
theological realism   165–74, 187, 193, 216
Theory of Appearing   189–94, 199
Thomas, John Christopher   180–1, 186, 188
Thomism, *see* Aquinas, Thomas
Tracy, David   13–14
tradition, defined   48–52
tradition-specific/tradition-dependent/tradition-constituted rationality, defined   46–52
Trinity   10, 98–100

truth   4, 13, 15, 19, 35, 41, 45–7, 50, 52–7, 66, 71, 79, 97–8, 101, 104–5, 107, 109, 111, 115, 119, 131–2, 134, 138, 159, 161, 164–75, 177, 180, 187, 189, 191, 193–4, 205, 207–8, 210–14, 216

Vondey, Wolfgang   4–5, 120, 217 n.3

Walker, Andrew   81, 114, 150, 153–4
Walker, Tom W.   156–7
Wallis, Arthur   149–52
Ward, Julian W.   148, 169–70
Warrington, Keith   17, 197
Welsh Revival   64, 76, 80–5, 89–92, 108, 114, 116, 165, 215
Wesley, John   71–2
Wittgenstein, Ludwig   52, 217
Wolterstorff, Nicholas   39, 185
Word of God   10, 39, 42, 93, 95, 104–7, 118, 157, 175–6, 179, 183, 185–7, 203
worldview   22, 25, 36, 74, 76, 105, 165, 168, 195, 200, 204

Yong, Amos   3, 5, 7–20, 22–4, 27, 31–2, 35, 39, 41–2, 44–5, 57–8, 61–2, 119–20, 163, 169, 171, 174, 191, 194, 212, 215–17

www.ingramcontent.com/pod-product-compliance
Lightning Source LLC
Chambersburg PA
CBHW052036300426
44117CB00012B/1840